Praise for THE WHITE ROCK

"A gem of a book, an intelligent, balanced and indeed original look at the empire of the Incas . . . transcends the travel-writing genre . . . an excellent introduction to the Incas and what is known about them."
—*Los Angeles Times*

"The sort of book that inspires the armchair traveler with a desire to follow in its author's footsteps . . . Everywhere Thomson goes, he finds good tales to tell . . . Engrossing." —*The New York Times Book Review*

"A lively account . . . Thomson has a great ability to find both local color and a human heart in characters who, to other eyes, might be merely ridiculous or dull . . . I'll look forward to all his future stories if they're even half as well told, as vivid and funny and human, as this one." —*The Washington Post Book World*

"In *The White Rock*, the whole continent becomes a plot with suspense and a cast of outrageous characters . . . This is Bruce Chatwin with *cojones*." —*Independent*

"The long-awaited, definitive travel book on Peru."
—JOHN HEMMING, author of *Conquest of the Incas*

"Thomson proves terrific at weaving snippets of history into his travels, sketching not only the defiant Incas and relentless *conquistadores* but also the wacky cast of archaeological buccaneers and New Agers that would eventually follow." —*Outside*

"Excellent . . . a thoroughly engaging tour of a giant, magnificent landscape. . . . This book is an intoxicating and compelling mix of information and adventure." —*National Geographic Adventure*

"Thomson has done a masterful job . . . .the exploration of Vilcabamba comes alive." —*Archeology*

"Belying his casual, kid-with-a-backpack approach, Thomson reveals a sophisticated grasp of Andean history, a canny understanding of the complex encounter between Indian and Spaniard, and a firm grasp of the interaction between human society and the Peruvian mountains."
—*The Christian Science Monitor*

"A delightfully personal, skeptical, and ebullient journey, with just the right degree of humor necessary for hard travel to distant places."
—*Kirkus Reviews*

"So entertaining and appealing is Thomson's story of his exploration of the Inca empire that readers will wish they could take off and follow in his footsteps . . . he is as good a companion as a traveler could hope for."
—*Publishers Weekly*

"Part travelog, part history lesson . . . Thomson is an impressive adventurer and an equally skilled writer."
—*Library Journal*

"Fascinating . . . besides telling readers of his own discoveries, he gives us a concise history of the Incan empire from its founding to its destruction. Further, he places his book in the long and magical string of literature of Inca exploration . . . *The White Rock* has a moral depth and intellectual integrity most similar work lacks . . . a tremendously valuable and entertaining book."
—*The Providence Journal* (Rhode Island)

"Superb . . . Thomson has an extraordinary knack for finding fascinating characters straight out of central casting."
—*The Plain Dealer* (Cleveland)

"Engaging . . . a pleasing mix of discovery, colorful personalities, history, and archeology."
—*Longitude*

"An intrepid tale . . . fascinating, and intelligently told." —*Sunday Times*

"Thomson's account of his travels through the Inca heartlands weaves geographical, spiritual, personal, and historical strands to an effect as rich and varied as a Peruvian shawl."
—*Daily Telegraph*

"Offers telling insights into the Inca culture and vividly recreates their extraordinary civilization . . . a comprehensive, clear-sighted account of the Inca legacy."
—*Global Adventure*

"The mixture of historian, traveler, filmmaker makes *The White Rock* come alive on the page as few other books about South America have done."
—*Sunday Independent*

THE WHITE ROCK

An Exploration of the Inca Heartland

HUGH THOMSON

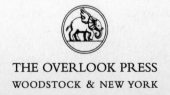

THE OVERLOOK PRESS
WOODSTOCK & NEW YORK

First published in paperback in the United States in 2004 by
The Overlook Press, Peter Mayer Publishers, Inc.
Woodstock & New York

WOODSTOCK:
One Overlook Drive
Woodstock, NY 12498
www.overlookpress.com
[for individual orders, bulk and special sales, contact our Woodstock office]

NEW YORK:
141 Wooster Street
New York, NY 10012

Library of Congress Cataloging-in-Publication Data

Thomson, Hugh.
The white rock : an exploration of the Inca heartland / Hugh Thomson.
p. cm.
Originally published: London : Weidenfeld & Nicolson, 2001.
Includes bibliographical references and index.
1. Thomson, Hugh—Journeys—Peru—Cuzco (Province) 2. Incas—Peru—
Cuzco (Province)—History. 3. Inca architecture—Peru—Cuzco (Province)
4. Incas—Peru—Cuzco (Province)—Antiquities. 5. Cuzco (Peru: Province)—
Antiquities. 6. Vilcabamba Mountains (Peru)—Discovery and exploration.
7. Vilcabamba Mountains (Peru)—Antiquities. I. Title
F3429.T28 2003   985'.37019—dc21   2002034606

Printed in the United States of America
ISBN 1-58567-503-2
FIRST EDITION
1 3 5 7 9 8 6 4 2

CONTENTS

ILLUSTRATIONS

Unless otherwise indicated all photographs are by Hugh Thomson (© Hugh Thomson 2001).

Martín Chambi: *Juicio Oral, Corte Superior* (Judgement in the High Court, Cuzco), 1928. (Courtesy of Julia Chambi)

Martín Chambi: *Early dawn at the Plaza de Armas*, 1925. (Courtesy of Julia Chambi)

Martín Chambi: *Cuzco after the earthquake in 1950*. (Courtesy of Julia Chambi)

The carved steps of the Throne of the Inca on Rodadero hill above Cuzco.

The Coricancha, or Sun Temple, in Cuzco after its post-earthquake restoration.

Martín Chambi: Carved *huacas* at Sahuite. (Courtesy of Julia Chambi)

Martín Chambi: Machu Picchu in 1925. (Courtesy of Julia Chambi)

The Funerary Rock at Machu Picchu.

The so-called 'Incahuatana' (hitching-place of the Inca) above the main site at Ollantaytambo.

The carved stone of Qenko above Cuzco.

Between pages 236 and 237
View of Olinda, Brazil by Frans Post, 1662. (© Rijksmuseum, Amsterdam)

Pizarro Seizing the Inca of Peru by Sir John Everett Millais, 1846. (© V&A Picture Library, London)

Bolivians picnicking near the start of the Takesi trail.

The Takesi trail in Bolivia, descending towards the Yungas lowlands.

Lake Titicaca.

Ollantaytambo: the monoliths of the eastern wall of the Sun Temple at dawn.

Gary Ziegler.

Camp near Inca Wasi at dawn, with Pumasillo massif beyond.

Inca Wasi in the mist.

Chuquipalta, the White Rock.

Chuquipalta, the White Rock: the northern side, with projecting bosses.

Just below the pass of Ccolpo Cosa.

Rónal with horse.

Gene Savoy. (Courtesy of Gene Savoy)

The ruins of Old Vilcabamba at Espíritu Pampa.

Endpapers: Copy of Raimondi's 1891 Mapa del Peru, with annotations by travellers. (© Royal Geographical Society)

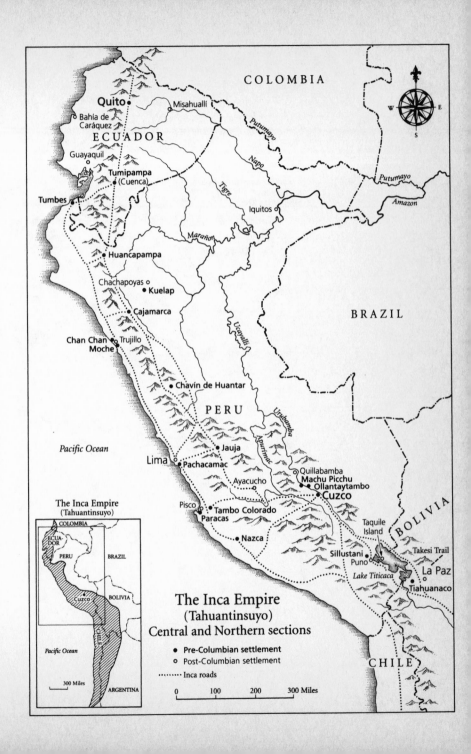

COLOMBIA

Putumayo

Quito

Misahuallí

Bahía de
Caráquez

ECUADOR

Napo

Guayaquil

Tigre

Tumipampa
(Cuenca)

Putumayo

Amazon

Tumbes

Iquitos

Marañón

Huancapampa

Chachapoyas
Kuelap

Cajamarca

BRAZIL

Chan Chan
Moche
Trujillo

Ucayali

Chavín de Huantar

PERU

Pacific Ocean

Urubamba

Jauja

Lima
Pachacamac

Apurímac

Ayacucho

Quillabamba
Machu Picchu
Ollantaytambo
Cuzco

Pisco
Paracas
Tambo Colorado

Nazca

Taquile
Island

BOLIVIA

Takesi Trail

Sillustani

Puno

Lake Titicaca

La Paz

Tiahuanaco

The Inca Empire
(Tahuantinsuyo)

COLOMBIA

**ECUA-
DOR**

PERU

BRAZIL

Cuzco

BOLIVIA

CHILE

Pacific Ocean

ARGENTINA

300 Miles

The Inca Empire
(Tahuantinsuyo)
Central and Northern sections

● Pre-Columbian settlement
○ Post-Columbian settlement
······ Inca roads

0   100   200   300 Miles

CHILE

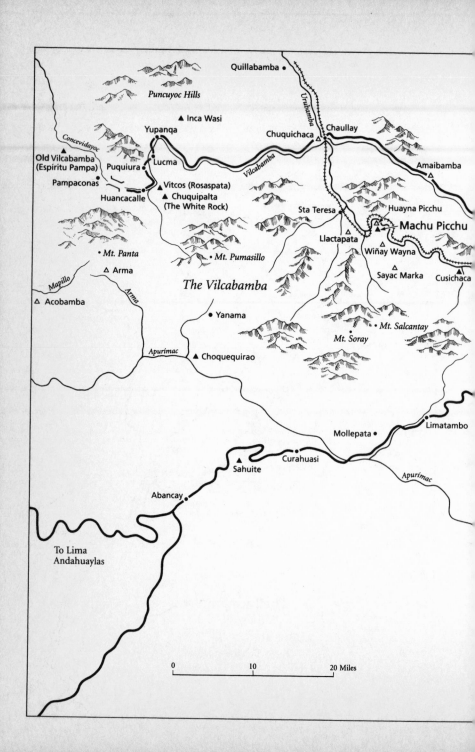

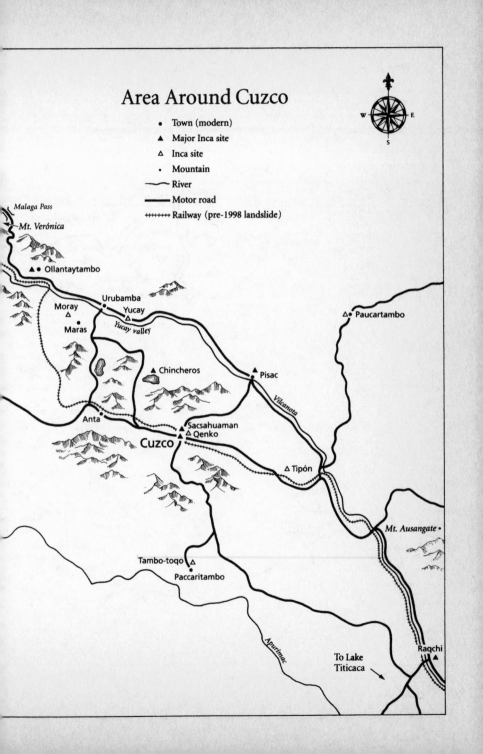

Area Around Cuzco

- Town (modern)
- ▲ Major Inca site
- △ Inca site
- · Mountain
- River
- Motor road
- ++++++ Railway (pre-1998 landslide)

Malaga Pass

Mt. Verónica

▲● Ollantaytambo

Moray
△

Maras

Urubamba

Yucay
△

Yucay valley

▲ Chincheros

Anta

● Pisac

Vilcanota

△● Paucartambo

▲ Sacsahuaman
△ Qenko

Cuzco

△ Tipón

Mt. Ausangate ·

Tambo-toqo ● △

Paccaritambo

Apurímac

To Lake
Titicaca

Raqchi ▲

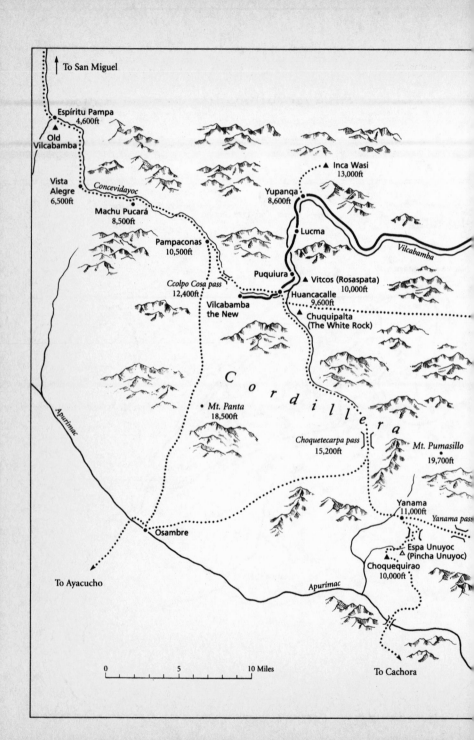

To San Miguel

Espíritu Pampa
4,600ft

Old
Vilcabamba

Vista
Alegre
6,500ft

Concevidayoc

Machu Pucará
8,500ft

Pampaconas
10,500ft

Ccolpo Cosa pass
12,400ft

Vilcabamba
the New

Inca Wasi
13,000ft

Yupanqa
8,600ft

Lucma

Vilcabamba

Puquiura

Vitcos (Rosaspata)
10,000ft

Huancacalle
9,600ft

Chuquipalta
(The White Rock)

Apurímac

Mt. Panta
18,500ft

C o r d i l l e r a

Choquetecarpa pass
15,200ft

Mt. Pumasillo
19,700ft

Yanama
11,000ft

Yanama pass

Osambre

Espa Unuyoc
(Pincha Unuyoc)

Choquequirao
10,000ft

To Ayacucho

Apurímac

To Cachora

0   5   10 Miles

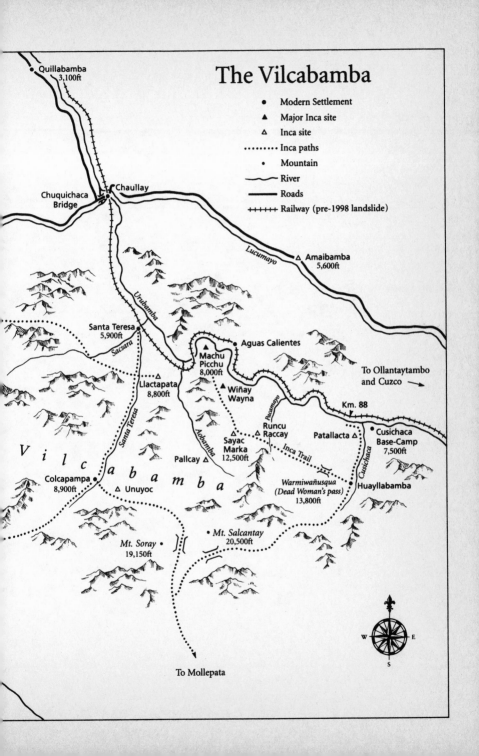

INTRODUCTION

PERU NOW OCCUPIES THE SAME PLACE in the popular imagination as Tibet used to have in the latter days of Empire, before the communist invasion made it more a place of pity than of mystery – a Shangri-La where the imagination is licensed to allow all manner of utopias and adventure.

In 1982, I returned from the Andes to find *Raiders of the Lost Ark* playing in British cinemas. The opening sequence, in which Harrison Ford rolled down a series of booby-trapped tunnels in order to seize a solid-gold idol was a *tour de force*. It managed in just ten minutes to pack in every conceivable myth about South American exploration: the silhouetted Indians padding through the shafts of light thrown by the jungle canopy; the lone explorer, let down by treacherous assistants but determined to find the temple, come what may; the battered map almost disintegrating in the sunlight. Best (and, perversely, most true to life) was the moment when Indiana Jones loses the idol to his arch rival, René Belloq, the suave but of course treacherous French archaeologist, simply because he hasn't taken the time to learn the local language: 'If only you had learnt Hovitos,' sneers Belloq (who has), as Jones flees the oncoming Indians with their arrows and poisonous blow-pipes.

Seen at full volume in a West End cinema when I was fresh from Peru, it was terrific, even if far removed from the less glamorous reality I had been experiencing. *Raiders* was a replay of many a matinée movie cliché, like the old deodorant ad in which the hero or heroine, sprayed with a symbolic 'v' on their back, hacks up to the top of an ancient temple and still emerges with the sprayed area immaculate.

Since then, the computer game *Tomb Raiders* has provided endless cybernetic variants of the same story. Players can live out Indiana Jones type adventures of discovery as they advance into pseudo-Incaic labyrinths. What's more, their leader Lara Croft has the considerable advantage of being more nubile and less bossy than your average sweaty, real-life explorer.

As a powerful mythopoeic base on which to build fantasies of confrontation with an alien culture, the Inca world has few rivals. But just as the lure of the Inca myth has increased, so any actual understanding of the Incas themselves has become obscured, let alone of the nature of exploration in the Andes.

The White Rock is an attempt to present a clear-sighted view of that Inca culture, drawing on my journeys throughout the Inca heartland near Cuzco and across the vast empire they created. Along the way I travelled to some of the most remote Inca sites and talked to leading archaeologists and explorers working in the area.

As I did so, I became more and more aware of the discrepancy between popular preconceptions about the Incas and the actual evidence on the ground. Deciphering that evidence is complicated by the fact that the Incas left no written history and almost all that we know about them comes from the often biased accounts of Spanish conquistadors and from the suppositions of archaeologists. Inca studies, compared to Egyptology or our knowledge of the Classical World, are still in their infancy.

The very familiarity of Machu Picchu causes problems and can lead us to forget how little we still know about the people who built the place. Few visitors to Peru travel beyond it.

I have taken Chuquipalta – 'The White Rock' of the title, deep in the Vilcabamba – as being emblematic of that hidden and lost Inca world which is rarely visited and which I have tried to explore.

*

This book has taken twenty years to write and over that time I have incurred many debts to many people for assistance.

The resulting canvas of twenty years does at least provide a useful sense of the time needed for archaeological discoveries to unfold. All the events recounted happened as described, but I have slightly changed their order so as to give the book more narrative and geographical cohesion. When writing about a site visited in the early 1980s where research has since corrected the then prevailing view, I have updated my account to include that new evidence, as not to do so would seem wilfully perverse.

There are different possible spellings of the various Inca sites, from Cuzco (Cusco or Qosco) to Choquequirao (Choqek'iraw) and indeed Inca itself (Inka), and I have tried to adopt those that are most familiar. The term Inca also gives rise to potential confusion in that it can mean both the generic race and the ruler of that race (the Inca). I have tried to avoid this by occasionally referring to him as Emperor, which while unconventional is descriptively true, although with the qualification that the Inca Empire was a more loose-knit affair than some of its European counterparts.

Any book on this area of Peru is written in the shadow of the great volumes of Inca history by William Prescott in the nineteenth century and John Hemming in the twentieth. I would also particularly like to thank John Hemming for his advice given both at the time of my first expedition in 1982 and more recently.

A brief chronology of events during the Inca Empire and Conquest is attached at the end, together with one for the history of exploration in the area and a glossary. Where a translation from the Spanish original is not listed in the bibliography, the translation used is my own. Rather than constantly interrupt the reader with footnotes, the 'Notes and References' section at the back of the book indicates sources and specialist points of information.

Most of the original books of Hiram Bingham are long out of print and many of the explorers' stories live on only in an oral tradition, passed from one old South American hand to another. I have therefore been dependent on those explorers and archaeologists who have spent so much time in this area and who at different times have been generous with their discussion and help: Nicholas Asheshov, David Drew, Peter Frost, Paolo Greer, Adriana von Hagen, Ann Kendall, Vincent Lee, Perci Paz, Gene Savoy, Elva Torres, Barry Walker and my *compadre* Gary Ziegler. Adriana von Hagen and David Drew also gave invaluable help with sections of the text.

Unlike mountaineering and the climbing of summits, there is no 'registered log' for the discovery of Inca sites and, while I have tried to attribute each successive discovery in the area to the correct team, there may be some unpublished explorers of whom I am unaware. I apologise to anyone who may have been inadvertently omitted as a result. In the words of Vincent Lee: 'I don't know who you are. I wish I did.'

I would like to thank those companions who shared journeys with me: Jonathan Baird, Rónal Cobos, Willie Delgado, Vaughan Fleming, Aurelio Huaman, Harvey Lilley, Judy Moore, Presentación and Roderick Simpson, with particular thanks to Adrian Gallop for, among many other contributions, killing the snake.

In Peru I was given hospitality and support by many, including Filip Boyen, Julia and Teo Allain Chambi, the many members of the Cobos family in Huancacalle, Deborah MacLaughlan and Fernando de la Rosa. Ken Duncan, Lucía Mercon and Alejandra Peralta generously provided me with accommodation in Cuzco while I was studying the archives and Wendy Weeks, Adela and all those at the Ollantaytambo Albergue have made me feel a member of their own family since 1982.

I would also like to thank the librarians of the Museo del Inka and the

Archivo de Bartolomé de las Casas in Cuzco and of the Royal Geographical Society in London.

In the United States, Elizabeth Deane, Susan Emanuel, Amy Finger, Joan Harrell, Uscha Pohl and David Saah gave me long-distance support. I am also grateful to the staff of the South American Explorers Club.

In Britain, Ann Barton, John Elliott, William Heath, Jan Klimkowski, Andy Martin, Angus O'Neill, Bayard Roberts, Chris and Jane Somerville, Joan Solomon, Peter Spry-Leverton, Benedict Taylor and Sara Taylor all gave help and useful advice, while my agent Georgina Capel and the editorial team of Richard Milner, Martin Redfern and Rebecca Wilson at Weidenfeld and Nicolson guided the book through to publication.

Helen Phillips provided immaculate line drawings from my photographs of sites to illustrate the chapter-headings. The maps, drawn by John Gilkes, are based on my travels through the area and also incorporate elements from previous maps of Gasparini & Margolies, John Hemming, Michael Moseley, Peter Frost, Gary Ziegler and many others, to all of whom grateful acknowledgement is made.

Finally I would like to dedicate this book to Sally, Daisy, Owen, Elliot, David, Patience and all of my extended family for their support both now and over twenty years of wanderings.

Hugh Thomson
February 2001

Those snow-capped peaks in an unknown and unexplored part of Peru fascinated me greatly. They tempted me to go and see what lay beyond. In the ever famous words of Rudyard Kipling there was 'Something hidden! Go find it! Go and look beyond the ranges – Something lost behind the ranges. Lost and waiting for you. Go!'

Hiram Bingham, 1909

The native in front of us stopped suddenly and pointed out the *ruinas*. With horror we all came to our senses. He was pointing at some scattered stones on the side of the mountain. We were frozen in our tracks with shock. Had we come all this way and made all this effort to be shown a few stones imbedded in a rock?

Julian Tennant, 'Quest for Paititi' expedition, 1953

Look for roads. Then follow them.

Gene Savoy (discoverer of Old Vilcabamba,
the 'last city of the Incas', in 1964)
giving advice to explorers

Exploration is not so much a covering of surface distance as a study in depth: a fleeting episode, a fragment of landscape and a remark overheard may provide the only means of understanding and interpreting areas which would otherwise remain barren of meaning.

Claude Lévi-Strauss, *Tristes Tropiques*, 1955

In this new world of the Indies, as they knew nothing of letters, we are in a state of blindness concerning many things.

Pedro Cieza de León, 1553

PART 1

A NEW WORLD

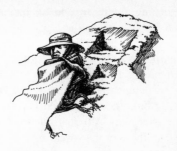

THE ONLY SOUND is the inchoate cry of the *arrieros* moving through the high ridges to either side of me as we fan across the slope, losing sight of each other for long minutes in the body of the mountain. Occasionally there is the dull, distant thud of a machete blade hitting a stone in passing.

I can see the bright orange flash of Aurelio's down jacket as he hacks at the branches that form impenetrable thickets over the boulders and wet bog. Grey Spanish moss covers trees that seem almost dead, save for a spurt of green at the base, or a twisted offshoot.

The high altitude and the long climb make me feel I'm beginning to hyperventilate. I enter a dense thicket and now around me are different shades of bleached green – cyan mosses, deep-green leaves, the ash-green of mountain lupins, violet-tinted bromeliads – all brushing past in waves, with washes of light in the gaps against the sky.

Below the contour line of what is an insignificant, unnamed ridge of peaks, in a range where a mountain the size of Mont Blanc could pass unnoticed, we converge together. The trees give way to shrub as we ascend above 15,000 feet.

Over the ridge itself and covering it, there is a soft, green-red grass that the sun burnishes with an intense translucence. And there they are, a necklace of small burial chambers, *chullpas*, spread out evenly in a curve across the top, just as we have hoped and expected, unseen for hundreds of years, each one with its window gazing blankly at the Apurímac thousands of feet below and across and beyond to the distant hills of the north-western Vilcabamba.

Inside each tomb, with a shock that always draws me deeper and deeper in, there is nothing.

*

Chance conversations are dangerous things.

In the summer of 1982 I was working for a West London pub landlord with an unsavoury reputation. In his previous incarnations, Albert had been through several encounters with the law, and usually lost. When he first arrived to take over the pub, the local residents had gone so far as to sign a petition against him. I was working there because it was one of the few jobs in London where I could earn cash-in-hand and supplement the dole while working out what to do in life. I was twenty-one.

Albert ran a tough house. He was not above hitting bar-staff if they didn't live up to his high standards of immorality. Drinks were regularly sold short – particularly Pimms, which could be served ready-mixed and was one of the few jobs of work Albert insisted on doing himself. A big man, he would appear in the mornings wearing nothing but a voluminous pair of purple underpants, as he re-counted the takings from the previous night and swore at us before we opened.

The pub sold a lot of Pimms: it was in the sleazy shadow of Fulham where the criminals liked to pretend to be flash and the Sloanes pretended to be low-life. They combined well and the evenings were riots of exchanged gambling information, Pimms, pool and vodka doubles.

But the mornings were quieter and I had a few regulars who slid in to begin their day's work at half past eleven when we opened. George was one of these and the begetter of the chance conversation.

A conversation which I started while drying the glasses behind the bar: 'I met a man who told me a good story.' This got George's concentration. Stories were currency. 'There's a ruin in the South American jungle that's got lost again. An Inca fortress.'

George was sober enough to spot the discrepancy. 'How can a ruin get lost *again* – either it's been found or it hasn't been.'

'Not this one. The jungle came back so fast it covered up the ruin after they discovered it – and now no one can find their way back.'

George reflected. 'Well, I'm glad in a way,' he laughed. 'I mean, where would we fucking be if we'd found everything there was to find in life?' George appreciated a good failure.

'In fact I was thinking of trying to find it myself.' This was loose talk, a way of keeping the conversation going, a joke.

But George took me seriously. 'That's one of the first ideas I've heard from you with any sense to it. Given a choice between wasting your time serving old farts like me and getting lost in the South American jungle, I'd have thought the jungle was a far more constructive alternative.'

George was not the most reliable source of worldly advice. He was an alcoholic who used our pub as a starting point so that later in the day, when he hit the Colony in Soho, he would already be at full stretch and ready to cross swords with Francis Bacon, Tom Baker and the other names he enjoyed dropping into our pre-match conversations. But perhaps precisely because he lacked any real interest in my fate, it meant more from him than anybody else, and what had previously just been a febrile possibility started to harden into something I could conceivably make happen.

I had first heard the story from an extremely reliable source – indeed, in the betting parlance of the pub, it was a cert. John Hemming was a distinguished South American explorer who had gone down the Amazon and up the Andes in some style. I had met him through a chance family connection and he had told me the story of a lost (or more properly mislaid) ruin, which was waiting to be re-found in the Peruvian Andes, close to Machu Picchu.

Not only was it a glamorous idea, it was, unlike most of those told in the pub, a true story. Hemming was a celebrated explorer, but he also wore a suit in his capacity as Director of the Royal Geographical Society and had impeccable academic respectability.

For months, washing glasses or watching the world slide by from the top of a London bus on the way to and from the pub, I merely toyed with the thought of the ruin in much the same way as I had toyed with how to spend a pools win or make a fortune. But that morning's conversation with George stayed with me, through the endless days of arrogant customers and low pay, and it began to seem very attractive. If the ruin had been found once, it could be found again. I had nothing to lose.

So I went.

*

There is another way of telling the story. Hearing of a ruin that could be found was of course the stimulus, the motor, that drove me to Peru for the first time, but the reflexes were already in place. I would never have gone if it had not been something I already wanted to do.

I remembered an image I'd seen some years before. It was the perfect beginning to a film and an introduction to the *conquistadores*. In long shot, a group of men appeared at the top of an impossibly tall mountain and started to descend, almost as if tumbling down the slope, in total silence. It was a strangely nursery image: they were like puppets falling from a shelf. The film was *Aguirre: The Wrath of God*, Werner Herzog's wild and extreme production of 1972, and I'd seen it at a college film society on a scratchy 16mm release print. The image, however distressed by the old projector and screen, was a powerful one that had stayed with me.

Playing the role of the renegade Lope de Aguirre, Klaus Kinski went on to lead his men on a futile and obsessive search into the Amazon. *Aguirre* was one of the great 'let's get lost' tales. But it differed from many art-house movies in that while the narrative was wayward, the sense of an overbearing present was not. At the time when the term was no longer even fashionable, it was an existential film in the starkest sense: what it was like to be drifting down a river, delirious, with no direction home.

The eastern edges of Peru, where the Andes sloped down to the Amazon and where *Aguirre* had been filmed, were clearly still a testing ground: in a world which was otherwise largely mapped and pinned to the wall, here was a blank. The NASA satellite maps still marked much of it as 'unsurveyed: no field checks possible', the modern equivalent of *'terra incognita'*. It seemed a good place to go when you were twenty-one. I had already lived for a while in Mexico and been drawn by the wayward, accidental rhythms of Latin American life. I spoke fluent Spanish and had read Borges, Cortázar, García Márquez and any other writer from the continent I could get my hands on. I only realised when it came, but this was an opportunity waiting to happen.

*

I went back to see John Hemming and find out more about the Inca ruin, which was called Llactapata. John lived in a quiet, residential Kensington square. He led me down the dark hall of his house and then into a study lined with books about South America, with shafts of light coming down from high windows. In a curious way, that moment of entering his study with him felt like the first step in the process of discovery.

John was a tall, reserved man of about forty-five, and it helped to know of his passion both for Inca history and of his sustained support for the natives of Amazonia before you met him, as those who did not sometimes mistook his reserve for indifference. As Director of the Royal Geographical Society he also radiated a certain *gravitas*. He was married, with very small children, and their voices echoed down from above as we talked.

Before going to see him again, I had diligently found out as much as I could about his past work. I knew he had travelled widely in Amazonia and had made 'first contact' with many tribes, an experience that could still emulate that of the early conquistadors in terms of shock and ethical dilemmas. In the course of these expeditions, he or his friends had suffered bouts of malaria, been bitten by piranhas (which he dismissed with breath-taking assurance as 'over-rated'), by snakes and by stingrays, often the most dangerous hazard of the rivers.

His most celebrated expedition had been in 1961 to some unexplored territory near the Cachimbo area of Brazil, and he now told me the story. It had been a three-man group, led by John's friend Richard Mason and with the slightly unexpected bohemian figure of Kit Lambert, later to be The Who's manager, making up the party. They were working under the umbrella of the Villas Boas brothers, famous for having opened up new areas of Brazil and for protecting the Indian tribes they had thus found (John suggested that if I took a group out to Peru, we should similarly try to hook up with some archaeologists working in the area, so they could help us with advice and logistics).

The three young friends were out to enjoy themselves, in so far as charting new territory in the Amazon allowed. They started by flying down an unexplored river, the Iriri, and crash-landing in the dense forest close to its source. Then they followed the river downstream, naming any new geographical features they came across after their girlfriends (Theodore Roosevelt, when he led an American expedition to the Amazon in 1913, had named a river after his son Kermit: I liked to think of there being a Río Kermit deep in Amazonia). One striking detail John mentioned was that, despite the heat, in the time the three friends worked there they grew pale from never seeing the sun – indeed, they had to hack down the trees above them just to get directional readings off the stars.

After months of happily descending the Iriri, the expedition took a tragic turn. The leader of the group, Richard Mason, was ambushed and killed while walking on his own down a trail they had cut through what was thought to be uninhabited jungle. John Hemming and Kit Lambert found his body carefully laid out on the path, surrounded by arrows and clubs. A bag of sugar was spilled nearby, untouched – as was a lighter. Nothing had been taken. He was still in his twenties and a close friend of John's.

It seemed that a previously uncontacted tribe had strayed into the territory on a hunting expedition, come across the newly made path and waited in ambush. Mason was the first person to walk along it.

I found it difficult to reconcile this sobering story with the mild family man who had met me at the door, in a house full of prams. As John told me of the days that followed – the dreamlike returning to camp along the path that had seemed so familiar, the arrangements to have the corpse embalmed and shipped out to a cemetery – the voices above us in the nursery were raised in some infant squabble and the floor reverberated with the sound of an adult moving around to restore order. I didn't know what to say. 'So there you are,' said John, and gave me a cup of tea.

After his experiences in Amazonia, he had spent a considerable time in Peru and had written *The Conquest of the Incas*, a twentieth-century update of William Prescott's classic 1847 account of the Conquest. This had drawn on many original sources that had only come to light since Prescott's time. Looking at the rows of academic source books on John's walls, I felt conspicuously aware of my own ignorance.

'I expect you'll want to see an account of the Fejos expedition,' said John. I had never heard of the Fejos expedition. He produced a pamphlet with some pride. As I was soon to learn, one of the biggest problems with South American exploration was the inaccessibility of information about discoveries which had already been made. The key articles were either in obscure magazines, or had been self-published by the explorers themselves and as such were extremely difficult to obtain.

Paul Fejos had led a big American expedition to the Peruvian Andes in 1940. Although the report naturally concentrated on the team's successes, it also indicated that they had tried but failed to relocate the 'mislaid' site of Llactapata, once it was clear that it had got lost after its initial discovery some thirty years before. Fejos had upwards of 200 men to help him, but had still been unable to locate it – although he had found another major site at Wiñay Wayna, near Machu Picchu. I noticed with curiosity that although they had such a large group, none were archaeologists, an anomaly common to many exploring expeditions which I would only later come to understand.

Given that the Fejos team had so many people – and I would be travelling with, at best, a mere handful – it seemed as if the odds might be against us. 'Not at all,' said John breezily. 'It's a matter of luck.'

What he did impress upon me was that exploring was a serious business, which demanded discipline and real inquiry if anything was to be achieved. Anyone could blunder around in a jungle, or for that matter go missing. But the discovery of a site meant more than letting off a few fire-crackers – it involved the far more difficult task of trying to understand precisely what it was that you had found.

*

It was strange how, once I'd decided on a totally illogical course of action, life became clearer and more focused. The complications of living in London without any money fell away. I was able to send a suitably rude letter to the DHSS when they cross-questioned me on the vexed issue of my housing benefit. Equally I could walk away from the various emotional entanglements I found myself in.

The concept of a 'team' was at first daunting. Three seemed a good number, just like the Hemming expedition. There was a clear choice when it came to choosing companions. Either I could find people who had all the right expedition qualifications – first-aid courses, army backgrounds, degrees in archaeology or anthropology – or I could choose people who I knew could tell a joke if we did get lost in the jungle. Instinctively I chose the latter.

Roddy and J.B. had many sterling qualities, but none that would have automatically qualified them for the job. They were good friends and drinking buddies (one startling memory of college days was a competition to see who could drink the most glasses of burning tequila). Apart from speaking Spanish and a love of mountains, I had no qualifications myself. In short, we were typical explorers, fired up more by enthusiasm than experience and would probably not have attempted the adventure if we had been older and wiser.

I discovered a talent for organisation previously unsuspected by me or indeed anybody else. The local library had a list of trusts who seemed only too eager to give money away to expeditions or deserving charities, in which category we righteously felt we now belonged (by affiliating through our old university, we found we could actually become a charity ourselves in some strange tax-efficient way).

The money trickled in. There were several long-shots that worked: I cheekily wrote to the writer Hammond Innes asking for help – a cheque came back in reply. He liked the idea of us wandering off into the jungle with only a bad map to guide us.

Better still, one of Albert's dodgier contacts left a message at the bar for him about a horse which, for various reasons, had been 'insured' to come in. It was and so did I, helped by a starting float from the cash-bar. I bought everyone (including Albert) a magnanimous final drink and left.

Impressed by the spurious note-paper we'd printed ('a multi-disciplinary team will attempt to locate the ruin of Llactapata ...'), various companies donated food to take, which we promptly sold to traders in the North End Road Market. Somehow it all came together.

On a perfect June day, we drove through the green fields of Oxfordshire on our way to the airport. In a short-sighted way, I had never noticed how spectacularly green England was. We had shiny new packs, but I at least felt like an impostor. Up until then it had been a game that everyone had let us keep playing. Now we had to deliver.

*

I have been to Lima many times since that first arrival and have always experienced the same emotions. Something about the flatness of the city and its position on the edge of the desert by the sea makes it one of the most surreal of South American cities. Rather than the extraordinary, ferocious energy of Mexico City or Buenos Aires, it has a dreamy de Chirico quietude and suppression.

We first saw it in the half-light of what was technically dusk but felt to our bodies like well after midnight. In winter the light is anyway continually grey and flat in Lima, a light the inhabitants onomatopoeically call *la grua*. As the airport lay outside the city, we drove past endless shanty houses to get to the centre, watching it all through the smoke-screened windows of the cab: dogs barking, kids shuffling, silhouetted against the headlights, slums arranged with the regularity of suburbia.

Our hotel was a cheap one on the main road. The rooms had deep-red lampshades and bad flamenco music was playing too loudly in the corridors. The porter established where we were from. 'Ah yes,' he nodded knowledgeably, 'England ... the home of Freddie Mercury ...' He held out his hand for a tip. Roddy shook it.

Next morning the porter was horrified to discover that we would be spending several months around the old Inca capital, Cuzco, high up in the Andes and far inland from Lima. '*Pero, ¿que van a hacer allá?* what on earth are you going to do up there?' Like most Limeños, he regarded the mountains as essentially backward. Lima had been founded by Francisco Pizarro and his *conquistadores* in the sixteenth century, who had called it *La Ciudad de los Reyes*, 'The City of Kings'. The new capital's coastal position was far more convenient than Cuzco for the Viceroys and merchants, who saw Peru primarily as an export opportunity. A polarisation between coast and mountains had begun then and continued to the present day.

Heading up into those mountains, we were following in the footsteps of one of the world's most glamorous explorers. In a famous tale, often told by himself, Hiram Bingham had come down to Peru in 1911 as a young man, not long after a road had been opened from Cuzco towards the Amazon. The way he told the story, Bingham had wandered almost by chance up this new route and had been directed by a local Indian to take a look at the top of a nearby hill. The resulting discovery was Machu Picchu, an Inca city sprawled across a remote ridge in a picturesque setting, conveniently postcard-sized and indubitably one of the seven wonders of the modern world. It had made Bingham a celebrity throughout his lifetime.

He went on, in typically all-American fashion, to become an Ivy League professor, then an Air Force hero and finally a Senator. It was surprising that Hollywood had never made a film about him.

Although in a sense they had. The archetypal image of the South American explorer is presented in those first few minutes of *Raiders of the*

Lost Ark: Harrison Ford escaping from a temple with the gold idol in his hand, swinging through the air on a liana and avoiding poison arrows with a flick of his rawhide whip and an astutely angled jungle hat. In his writings, Bingham had done much to popularise that image.

Yet while the lost cities of South America have always had a powerful hold on the popular imagination, the true history of exploration there is both less exotic and more interesting. Bingham and others who followed him, such as Gene Savoy, were complex characters, viewed with considerable misgivings by the staid archaeologists who depended on them to find their ruins in the first place.

No one has ever needed any qualifications to be a South American explorer other than an instinct for stubbornness and survival. The ruins that the Incas and other pre-Columbian civilisations left behind are scattered over thousands of miles of still largely uncharted territory, particularly in the hinterland of the Andes where the mountains slope down towards the Amazon. As such they are hardly sign-posted.

Bingham himself was candid about his own lack of qualifications: 'Archaeology lies outside my field and I know very little about the Incas, except the fascinating story told by Prescott in his famous *Conquest of Peru*,' he told a presumably surprised Prefect of the Peruvian Department that he intended to explore.

Yet to his great credit, Bingham did not rest on his laurels after discovering Machu Picchu: he pushed on into the wild country beyond and made several further discoveries in a surprisingly short space of time, over one glorious summer season. So excited did he become with these discoveries, as he hurtled from ruin to ruin, that with one of the more important second-division ones, Llactapata, a fortress site overlooking the valley approaches to Machu Picchu from the west, he forgot to take proper map references or bearings.

The first archaeologists and explorers to follow in his footsteps concentrated on Machu Picchu. By the time anyone tried to retrace his steps to Llactapata, the site had been swallowed up again by the jungle. Various expeditions (like the Fejos one) had tried and failed over the following seventy years to re-find it. All that was left was Bingham's seductive account of the ruin, which he presumed to have been built by one of the Inca Emperor's captains, 'on a strategic spot'. This was what we had come to find.

*

In the plane from Lima, I remember looking down at the foothills of the

Andes as they rose out of the desert and thinking how brown they looked, how scorched, like flayed animal skins left out to dry. The early morning sun cut across the tops of the hills, leaving savagely indented valleys in the dark below. In one of the broadest of these valleys, with snow-covered peaks around it, lay Cuzco.

The three of us arrived in the old Inca capital looking like ghosts. On the plane the airline's sick-bags had been incongruously printed with the slogan '*Nacimos para volar*', 'We were born to fly'. We could not but disagree. The combination of Lima smog, jetlag, too much to drink on the way over and the shock of the altitude had left us the worse for wear. It took a few days in a more comfortable hotel than we could afford before we felt well enough to venture out into the town.

For Cuzco, while large, still felt like a town. The amphitheatre of hills that the Incas had chosen for their capital was naturally containing, and no amount of colonial development could ever have expanded it into a city. Nor probably would the Spanish have wanted to do so. At an oxygen-pumping 11,000 feet, it was neither agreeable to live in nor commercially interesting. During much of the previous 300 years it had been ignored, a provincial town on the margins of Peru.

Our first and most vivid impression was at the market. Roddy showed an immediate enthusiasm for the fruit and insisted we buy one of everything. We tried it all, ripping into the flesh with our brand-new pocket-knives. There was *granadilla*, a passion-fruit of a spawn-like vitality that seemed to flop into the mouth in one congealed mass. The market-women produced a species which tasted like bread-fruit, called *lúcuma*, and curious, small, striped, orange-and-green fruit which were the size of peaches yet had the flavour of melon. For further experimentation, we could blend up a mix in an old Kenwood mixer, with a raw egg for real kick. Roddy and I had doubles.

His enthusiasm and animation in trying the fruit surprised me. Back home he had always affected a laconic indifference to everything, perhaps because, being a South African in England, he thought he should. Here in Peru, the indifference started to fall away.

We walked up to Sacsahuaman, the great Inca ruin above Cuzco. Roddy's father was an architect and as we admired the Inca stonework, he revealed a detailed knowledge of building terms that was unexpected and later extremely useful.

In architectural terms, Sacsahuaman was phenomenal. Despite having been almost levelled by the Spanish in the centuries since the Conquest, enough survived to show why the first *conquistadores* were both impressed and terrified by it. The great walls that guarded its flanks in three imposing lines of defence would have made any attacker hesitate.

A Peruvian was posing for a photograph in front of one of the largest stones. He held out his arms sideways. The circle he made with his body would have fitted twelve times into the stone he was standing against. And this was quarried stone, cut and transplanted here, then fitted magnificently into a wall of similar stones. Some of the blocks weighed as much as 120 tons.

It was easy to see why the Spanish supposed the buildings to have been the work of gods or giants, in an inversion of the usual narrative in which it is the natives who think that the invaders are divine. Like Stonehenge (to which Sacsahuaman has many parallels), it seemed difficult to imagine the labour involved in moving the stones, let alone fitting them so accurately.

I found Sacsahuaman daunting, not just because of its military might. The enormous stones were indeed fitted together with extraordinary precision, without mortar, as was the custom for ceremonial or important buildings. But there was something infinitely unknowable about the place, perhaps because the scale made it unassimilable to any reference of mine. It was not like the impossibly picturesque Machu Picchu, restored and set in a nest of mountains.

These destroyed remains spread out over a large hill above Cuzco, a long line of grey stone walls crossing the landscape. The nearest I could get in concept, if not in scale, was the experience I'd had walking to the old forts of Iron Age England, like Cadbury Camp near Bristol: an empty site, which seemed to give little away. Looking at the bare slabs of rock, I thought how relatively small our knowledge of the Incas was compared to some of the other great ancient civilisations of the world – the Egyptians, the Greeks, or Meso-American cultures such as the Aztecs and the Maya.

Every schoolchild knows the basic outlines of the Conquest: how Pizarro and his brothers invaded Peru in 1532 with a handful of men, took Atahualpa (the *Sapa Inca* or Emperor) hostage and in one bold and brutal stroke literally held the Empire to ransom, forcing his followers to fill a room with gold for his release, then killing him anyway. Thereafter the usual litany of disease, exploitation and lust for minerals followed and drove the course of Spanish domination. (No one could say that the brutal Spanish treatment of the natives was particularly racist – they were quite capable of killing just as many Europeans in cold blood. During the reign of Charles V alone, about 50,000–100,000 Protestant 'heretics' were executed, burnt or buried alive by the Spanish in the Netherlands – and this in the country that the Spanish Emperor had himself originally come from.)

Of the Incas prior to the invasion much less seemed to be known: the usual comment was that they were stupendous masons, as evidenced here, and had built up their empire over a relatively brief expansionist period of a hundred or so years, despite never having discovered the wheel or a system of writing. The implication was always that they had simply crumbled in the face of Old World technology and aggression.

However, Sacsahuaman was enough to disconcert some of these easy, broad-brush generalisations. For it was the site of one of the last great moments of the Incas when, three years after the Spanish invasion and the death of Atahualpa, and with the conquistadors thinking they had destroyed the Empire completely, it fought back.

Before leaving England, I had read an eyewitness description of the battle of Sacsahuaman and the first years of the Spanish Conquest by someone ideally placed to give such an account: Pedro Pizarro. Pedro was a young cousin of the four Pizarro brothers who played such pivotal parts in the Conquest, and he had come out to Peru as Francisco Pizarro's page. He was only seventeen.

For some reason his account was completely out of print (perhaps because it lacked the more measured and scholarly tones of the later Spanish commentators who followed him, which was precisely why I liked it), but I had managed to find an old folio edition of his memoirs at the Royal Geographical Society, its leaves still uncut. The memoirs give a vivid account of what it was like to be seventeen and almost overwhelmed by what would have been astounding adventures for a mature man twice his age. The conquistadors were advancing into the heart of an unknown empire, a party of less than 200 men against an Empire of millions which stretched, in Pedro's words, 'for a thousand leagues'.

His memoirs recount his experiences of those tumultuous days. Although written some thirty-five years later, when in conquistador terms he was an old man (he proudly points out how few of his contemporaries were still alive), the memoirs read as freshly as if they were diaries. His impressions of those extraordinary times come tumbling out in a rush. At one point, after a particularly idiosyncratic aside, he excuses himself by saying, 'I am inserting some of these things just as they come to my memory, in order not to forget them.'

The moment I most relished was his conversation with Atahualpa after the doomed Emperor had been captured by Francisco Pizarro. As Pizarro's page, Pedro spent a considerable amount of time in Atahualpa's company. During the months after his capture, the Inca tried to keep up the pretence that he could still preside over the affairs of his empire, as if being held by the Spanish were merely a temporary inconvenience. Like Pedro, Atahualpa was still virtually a teenager, but he had the fully developed appetite for power of a natural autocrat, and even in captivity enjoyed all the trappings of a rock star of the most demanding sort (Jim Morrison would have been a good role model).

One day Pedro was sitting with him when Atahualpa dropped a bit of food on his clothing. The Inca immediately got up and changed, coming back in a much finer dark brown *manta*. When Pedro felt the cloth, and realised that even by Quechuan high standards it was an exceptionally rich cloak, 'smoother than silk', he asked Atahualpa what it was made from. 'The finest hair of vampire bats,' replied the Inca haughtily. Pedro asked how it had been possible to catch enough bats to make an entire cloak. 'Those dogs of Tumbez and Puerto Viejo [Inca settlements in the north], what else have they to do there but to capture such animals so as to make clothes for me?' Even in defeat, Atahualpa always had plenty of attitude and as an Emperor he had been supremely arrogant. When the Spanish first arrived, he had sent them an insulting present of ducks gutted and filled with straw. This, went the inference, was what he could do to the conquistadors whenever he wanted.

Pedro became fascinated by Atahualpa's wardrobe. He discovered that all his clothes were only worn once. Then they were guarded in special chests by his retainers, to prevent others from ever touching them, and burnt at an annual ceremony. Appalled by this profligacy, the young Pizarro noted that this applied even to those garments that the Inca had handled but then rejected, indeed 'to everything which he had ever touched'.

He was mortified by the manner of the Inca's death a few months later, a shoddy affair even by the low standards of the Spanish treatment of the Indians and one which all concerned seemed to have become ashamed of. Francisco Pizarro and some of the other Spanish leaders were worried by rumours that an Inca rebellion was imminent. Their response was to condemn Atahualpa to be executed, thinking that he would be the focus of any revolt and that while he lived they would always be unsafe. He was originally to have been burnt at the stake, but on learning that if he converted to Christianity his body would not then be cremated (and so could be mummified by the Indians for future worship), the Emperor allowed himself to be baptised. It did him little good. On 26 July 1533 he was executed by strangulation in the square of Cajamarca, where he had first been captured. After garrotting him, the Spanish were careful to burn his body anyway.

In his memoirs, Pedro tried to blame this brutal murder on mis-communication, saying that a native translator had fallen for one of Atahualpa's wives and so deliberately made the Inca's words sound trea-sonable, but he is truthful enough to admit that the Spanish acted dis-honourably and that the Inca should never have been killed. As many argued at the time, he could at the very least have been sent into exile, either to Panama or Spain. According to William Prescott, the half-blind lawyer from Boston whose nineteenth-century history of the Conquest was the first to attempt impartiality, 'the treatment of Atahualpa was one of the darkest chapters in Spanish Colonial History'.

After Atahualpa's death, the Spanish marched on Cuzco and soon controlled Tahuantinsuyo, as the Inca Empire was known. They decided to install a puppet emperor on the throne, a brother of Atahualpa's called Manco, but this proved to be a mistake. After a few years of obedience, he revolted, calling troops up from all over Tahuantinsuyo for one last blowing up of the fire from the dying embers.

Pedro described the conquistadors' dismay at suddenly seeing the strength of Manco's forces camped around Cuzco: 'So numerous were the [Indian] troops who came here that they covered the fields, and by day it looked as if a black cloth had been spread over the ground for half a league.' Many of the Pizarros' comrades had gone to Chile on an expedition, while others were in the newly founded city of Lima. The remaining Spanish were taken by surprise and trapped in the streets of the town, while the Incas gathered outside the walls and in the fortress above at Sacsahuaman.

Strictly speaking, it would be wrong to describe it as a fortress, even though this is how it must have appeared to the Spanish. Like so many Inca sites, it had multiple functions – as a shrine, as a storehouse and as another residence for the Inca. But it was as a fortress that it most impressed me, and certainly for Pedro Pizarro and the other conquistadors, trapped in Cuzco below, it must have presented a daunting prospect.

The military position was astonishing. A sheer rock-face dropped away in front of it, while behind, on the higher approaches, a series of buttressed walls prevented any direct attack on the gates: attackers had to come at the wall from an angle, thus exposing their own flanks. Beyond this first, massive line of defence were two further terraces protecting the centre of the site. In this centre were three great towers, two rectangular, one circular, which dominated the city below.

It seems clear, given the defences of Sacsahuaman, that Cuzco itself was only lightly fortified. So with Manco's revolt, the Spanish found themselves in an unenviable position, besieged by an enemy who had now got the measure of their superior weapons and were in a superb fortress above them, while they were surrounded on all sides.

The Incas came remarkably close to finishing the Spanish off, setting fire to the roofs of Cuzco and keeping up a punishing siege. There were fewer than 200 conquistadors, and of these, as Pedro candidly admits, only the cavalrymen really mattered, as the Spanish on foot were no match for the agile Indians ('the Indians hold them [the infantrymen] in slight account').

It was the European horses which were the Spaniards' only hope if they were to hold at bay over 100,000 Inca soldiers. On open ground, an armoured Spanish horseman with steel weapons against a native infantryman was like a tank against an archer. But in the cramped streets of Cuzco, the horses were no longer so agile or effective. The Indians built palisades to contain them, and used slings to hurl burning cloth at the buildings the Spanish were sheltering in. Hernando Pizarro, leading the defenders, soon realised they were in an impossible position.

He felt there was no choice but to ride up and try to take Sacsahuaman itself, before Manco could assemble even more native troops for the siege. However much one might dislike the motives or morals of the conquistadors, this was a bold and brave move, given how few of them there were and the overwhelming superiority of the Incas.

Standing on the site, the neatness of the geometry made visualising the conflict very easy, even though the site was now so destroyed. On one side was the main hill above Cuzco, with its giant fortified walls zig-zagging along the bottom. This was where the Incas would have massed, knowing that they were fighting for the survival of their culture, as well as for their lives.

Facing this main hill was a smaller one, unfortified but with various carvings in the rock, now known as the Rodadero after the long, rutted rock-slides that the local kids used as a playground. The Spanish wheeled round to this hill from Cuzco, having cleverly feinted to the Incas that they were trying to escape to the coast. The two armies faced each other hill to hill, with no more than a hundred metres between them. Then the Spanish charged.

It was hard not to feel some *schadenfreude* that one of the Pizarro brothers, Juan, had met his death here, after riding at the head of the charge across the small dip that divided the two hills. He had previously hurt his jaw and so was not wearing a helmet. With echoes of David and Goliath, a shot fired by a sling during the fierce fighting within the castle walls caught him on this one exposed area. He was the first of the Pizarro brothers to perish in the Conquest they had initiated. Although Pedro reports that he valiantly kept on fighting, he died of his wounds within a fortnight.

Pedro Pizarro's account of the scenes that followed – knights scaling up ladders and leaping through turret windows – clearly tried to re-live the romances on which the conquistadors had been weaned back home in Trujillo. Pedro, like his companions, had been brought up on the comic-book heroics of the *Amadis de Gaul* saga, a Spanish B-movie equivalent to the Arthurian legends in which single knights would defeat thousands of Saracens and infidels, vault draw-bridges or rescue damsels and justify any action as being for God and Country.

Peru must have been like a virtual-reality game for the conquistadors who had read this stuff as kids, in that while they arrived with weapons of steel designed to kill (and horses from which to do so), the indigenous peoples ranged against them on the ground had wooden clubs and bronze axes. Pizarro and his 'knights' (many of whom were in reality rough-edged chancers from small-town Spain) could now emulate their romantic heroes by taking on an enemy of thousands – and winning.

The *Amadis de Gaul* was first published in 1508. A runaway success, it went into numerous editions and prompted a wave of lesser imitations (including one by its own author, Montalvo, who in a pot-boiling sequel about Amadis's son, *Sergas de Esplandán*, postulated a 'land of the Amazons' and a mythical country of plenty called 'California', myths that were both to be potent spurs to Spanish exploration).

During the first half of the sixteenth century, as the conquistadors were spreading through South America, the appeal of these romances seems to have dominated the Spanish psyche (even the Emperor, Charles V, collected them avidly) and fresh books were quickly shipped out to Peru. The heady nature of these chivalric epics was more than equalled by the fabulous reports of the treasures being discovered in the New World and of the men who found them. Cortés used the literary language of the romances to describe his conquest of Mexico in letters to Charles V. Only with the next century and Cervantes' savage parody in *Don Quijote* did the genre of the chivalric epic finally begin to wane, just as disillusionment set in with what Spain had actually achieved in the New World.

So Pedro Pizarro deliberately built up an account of a particular Inca nobleman, an *orejón*, who led the resistance to the Spanish from one of the high towers:

> And we arrived at the last level [of Sacsahuaman], which had as its captain an *orejón* so valiant that the same might be written of him as has been written of some Romans. This *orejón* bore a shield upon his arms and a sword in his hand, a cudgel in his shield-hand and a helmet upon his head ... This *orejón* marched like a lion from one end to another of the highest level of all, preventing the Spanish who wished to mount with ladders from doing so and killing the Indians who surrendered.

Despite Pedro's high-flown attempt to confer chivalric status on the *orejón* with his assumed coat of arms, the end of the battle for Sacsahuaman was far from romantic. The Spanish took the fortifications (as much by depriving the defenders of their water-supply as by fighting them) and killed all prisoners taken. 'The *orejón*, perceiving that they had conquered him and had taken his stronghold at two or three points, threw down his arms, covered his head and face with his *manta* and threw himself down from the level to a spot more than one hundred *estados* below, where he was shattered.'

Over the following years, the main towers of Sacsahuaman were razed, leaving only the outer surrounding walls standing like toothless gums above the city. But there was no question even then of the Incas submitting quietly to Spanish rule.

The remnants of two of the old towers had been uncovered in the twentieth century – one, a great circular structure, the other rectangular. Both looked oddly tranquil in the grass. Even from their razed bases, one could still see down to the city below, much of which had kept the original street-plan left by the Incas. The occasional church spire raised its head above the Spanish red tiles which had been laid over the Inca walls. From the great central square, roads radiated out to the four quarters of what, by the time the Spanish arrived, was a vast empire called Tahuantinsuyo, spanning the Andean spine of the continent from Colombia to Chile. In the distance, past the airport, the giant snow-capped mountain of Ausangate marked the way to the Eastern Quarter.

When the fortress was taken, many of the other defenders followed the *orejón* in leaping to their deaths from the walls. Manco's son, Titu Cusi, one of the few chroniclers to give an Inca perspective on the Conquest, recorded later that 'as the walls are high, and as all those who first fell died, a few of those that followed survived, because of the great number of corpses for them to fall on'.

In the year we arrived, heavy rain had washed away at the foundations of some of the outer walls and caused a partial collapse: eleven bodies had been found, apparently of Inca warriors who, it was presumed, had died in the siege.

Yet although Sacsahuaman should have been a tragic place, there was a surprisingly festive air. The day we were there was a holiday and the fields below were full of picnickers unwrapping white muslin parcels full of enticing food: a salad of quails, *choclo y queso* (corn and cheese) and *lomo saltado*, an elaborate stew of beef and vegetables. *Chicha* was being passed around, the maize drink traditionally made with saliva to ferment it. There was a sense that even though the Spanish might have imposed their own rule for 300 years after the Inca defeat, some Quechuan spirit had refused to be eradicated and had survived to see the conquerors finally ejected in the Wars of Independence.

Even the towering Christ figure which had been erected, Rio de Janeiro style, on a nearby hill was less supremacist than might at first appear – it was a gift from Palestinian Christians who had taken refuge in Peru after the partition of their country.

Children were sliding down the long grooved stones of Rodadero Hill, near to the so-called 'Inca Throne', an immaculately carved set of shallow steps that, despite the wearing of centuries of kids' feet, still had a military precision to them. The legend that from there the Inca could have reviewed his own troops in the dip between the fort and the hill seemed entirely credible. Certainly it was a fine place to see the visitors to the stones put in their proper scale.

I photographed a woman leaning against another carved Inca stone, which had some steps cut into the rock. The woman stared impassively at me with the same opaqueness as the stone and Sacsahuaman itself. The Quechua character is not always an open, accessible one: it can be *cerrado*, 'closed', as the Castilian conquerors would have said, probably admiringly.

I wandered some way behind the fortress and came across something which strangely excited me – lying a little way off the road, unmarked and with just a few boys sitting on it watching their goats, was a large boulder, with steps carved into it at unusual angles. Most of the boulder had been left unsculpted, as if the steps and platforms were designed to point up the strength and beauty of the natural stone. Although I did not yet know it, this was my first experience of a *huaca*, an Inca carved rock, and a foretaste of the great White Rock, Chuquipalta, which lay in the heart of the Vilcabamba.

*

Next morning, on a grey dawn, we left for the first stage of the expedition proper, nervous and unsure of ourselves. The previous night we had laid out our kit on the floor and tried to re-pack with some semblance of order. As we looked at the tent, the food and the large box of Wrigleys Chewing Gum the company had graciously donated to us, I felt as if our bluff was going to be called. How could we, a motley crew of friends, have any pretence at venturing into this world of which we knew so little?

J.B. was looking after all the supplies – indeed, he had been billed as 'Quartermaster' on our laughably grandiose fund-raising brochures, as well as 'Medical Officer'. Now he was reassuringly bluff about our prospects. He was an incurable optimist anyway. While not speaking any Spanish, he felt certain that if he spoke slowly and deliberately in French any Peruvian would be able to understand him. Irritatingly, this sometimes worked. Meanwhile Roddy managed to combine in his large form a boundless enthusiasm with an equal capacity to mock, like a cross between Tigger and Terry Thomas.

We stumbled to the station with our heavy packs in the half-light.

The train we were taking was full of tourists, as it was also the train to Machu Picchu and, as such, one of the most canonised routes on the so-called 'gringo trail' that ran down the continent. The tourists and hikers eyed other passengers warily. Travellers in South America did not much like to acknowledge one another – they had, after all, come here to be independent, to be different – and there was that inevitable declension: 'I'm a traveller, you're a tourist, he's an American tourist,' which meant that most were keeping very much to themselves. As the majority couldn't speak Spanish, let alone Quechua, the language of the Andean Indians, there was little conversation with Peruvians that went beyond buying trinkets and glaring at anyone who went dangerously near a rucksack.

Paranoia about robberies was running high and not just because of the usual worries about petty thieves in the station. The first whispers of the roar that in later years was to become the Sendero Luminoso had begun, with fanciful stories of back-packers being kidnapped.

The whole area we were travelling into – and would spend months exploring – was perfect for guerrilla activity. Indeed, it was precisely for this reason that the last of the Incas had made their way up here after the final rout at Sacsahuaman. Manco and his successors managed to hold out against the Spanish from a series of natural mountain redoubts for another remarkable thirty-five years. It was in this area that some of their most deliberately inaccessible ruins could still be found.

The red-and-orange train (the carriages had 'PULLMAN' neatly stencilled on the sides) jolted across the grey landscape. It was bitterly cold: the plateau above Cuzco, the Pampa de Anta, lies at over 12,000 windswept feet. A window had broken further down the carriage and the doors kept banging open.

But as we swung into the valley of the Vilcanota – now often described as *el Valle Sagrado*, 'the Sacred Valley', because of the Incas' attachment to it – the morning sun came through. At Ollantaytambo we bought *choclo y queso*, corn on the cob with a hunk of cheese, and the valley started plunging down into lower, less austere, climes. The railway followed the line of the river exactly and so we could see it turn from a lazy river crossing the high plain into a charged mountain torrent that seemed almost to keep up with the train itself. Even the river's name changed – from the Vilcanota to the Urubamba – as if it were now a different geographical entity. The banks were lined with willows and shocks of yellow *retama*, the Andean broom. In places the glassy white of the turbulent water was relieved by deep rock-pools of a still green.

We got off seemingly in the middle of nowhere, by a kilometre stone on the track, and watched the train peal away down the valley with a curious chiming noise as it went over the points, like a bird calling.

It was only as we trudged along the railway track that I realised how much my pack weighed. I'd never had to walk any real distance with it. My packing technique in England had been to throw in anything I could remotely need, from an electric razor to a bottle of celebratory brandy, to be consumed if we actually found anything. I was also carrying part of the tent and some cooking supplies. Now it all weighed a ton.

By the time we got to the arroyo-pulley across the Urubamba river, I was already exhausted. Roddy and J.B. were sweating like pigs. We tried to blame it on the sun.

The pulley that confronted us was a sort of sling arrangement with which you had to haul yourself by hand over the Urubamba, a distance of some fifty feet. On the other side we could see a reception party of various archaeologists from our destination, the Cusichaca camp, so we were determined not to make fools of ourselves on the crossing. There was an excitement anyway in pulling oneself across a river roaring for your blood, even if this was a relatively small one. Nearly every explorer to the area had written about such tenuous river-crossings, and the Spanish had frequently been prevented from finally pinning down the Inca guerrillas by destroyed bridges or their own inability to cross canyons.

We made it across without disgrace, but must have looked a pretty unpromising bunch on arrival. J.B. was wearing a pair of baggy khaki shorts that might have been worn by a scoutmaster in the 1950s and I had bought a hat at Cuzco market which, while functional, for some reason made both Roddy and J.B. laugh every time they saw me in it.

Ann Kendall, who was running the archaeological camp, seemed distinctly unimpressed when we arrived. Leaders of archaeological expeditions have always had slightly fearsome reputations. Men like Schliemann and Sir Mortimer Wheeler had egos the size of the empires they were trying to resurrect. Trying to set up what is almost a military operation in the outback of what are often indifferent or hostile regimes calls for a certain forcefulness.

Ann had an equally powerful presence, but in a much subtler way. She spoke in a soft voice and seldom. But it was unwise to cross her and she had firm views. When I had first written to her to introduce myself, she began her reply by saying that while it was optional to spell her profession as either 'archaeologist' or 'archeologist', she preferred people always to do so with the second 'a'. I have done so ever since.

She showed us around the site. Cusichaca was by the confluence of two rivers, an important divide, where the river Cusichaca came down from the snowfields around Mount Salcantay and met the Urubamba. The merged rivers then carried on down the valley towards Machu Picchu, along with the railway. The so-called 'Inca Trail', beloved of tour agencies, began here and then twisted around over various high passes to come at Machu Picchu from behind.

The Cusichaca valley was rich in early settlements and it was clear why Ann had chosen it for a long-term archaeological project that had already been running for several years. She showed us around. I tried hard to ask the right questions, but was handicapped by Roddy's tendency to make *sotto voce* remarks in a booming voice that could have been heard at the top of Mount Salcantay. He had decided that Ann Kendall should be called 'Mintcake' and kept referring to her as such in loud asides, to our intense embarrassment. Any attempt to shut him up would be met with a blank expression of curiosity and surprise.

One of the archaeologists with us tripped over a stone. 'Archaeologists are always so clumsy,' said Ann. 'Is that why you leave so many ruins everywhere?' asked Roddy. It was time for lunch.

The base-camp was a large one which over the years had already evolved a considerable level of comfort. Presiding over day-to-day operations was Davina Copley, who was about our age and came across initially as a brisk, head-girl sort. She showed us our tents and how the place worked. There was a pump-shower, a large mess-tent and an engaging American cook called Jack. 'Oh really,' said Roddy, trying to make conversation in a polite, Duke-of-Edinburgh sort of way, 'and who does the washing up?' It was precisely the opening Davina had been waiting for. 'You do.'

We soon found that there was a certain tension in the camp between those who were digging – the true archaeologists – and those, like us, who were more interested in exploration. This was almost a historical necessity. Archaeologists have traditionally regarded explorers as blundering, self-serving adventurers, 'cowboys' who are likely to disrupt all the evidence at the scene of a site. Meanwhile explorers think of archaeologists as tunnel-visioned academics who rarely get around to publishing their research and leave boxes of pottery shards gathering dust in sheds. Moreover, claim the explorers, when archaeologists do write anything, it is in such migraine-inducing prose that even Machu Picchu sounds dull – 'Stage IV Project Development, anyone?' The accusations of each side are deeply irritating to the other, not least because there is a certain element of truth to them.

Hiram Bingham had undoubtedly given the archaeologists grounds for complaint. John Rowe, the patriarch of Peruvian archaeological studies, once pointedly remarked that Bingham would not have gone so wrong 'if the expedition had had anyone with archaeological training on its staff'. Despite the incredible success of Bingham's exploration, his later excavations at Machu Picchu were generally acknowledged to have been over-enthusiastic and cack-handed. Worse, he had acted with the over-confidence of an age of certainty and excavated so totally that there was little for later archaeologists to find using more developed techniques (the modern, more modest convention is always to leave something behind for the next generation to work on). This problem had been compounded by the authorities' desire to restore Machu Picchu for the tourists with a zealousness that had done little for archaeological preservation. As a result – and to my considerable surprise – it seemed there had been hardly any further excavation at the best-known Inca monument of all since Bingham's day.

There was a further reason for this. The site of Machu Picchu was apparently unoccupied before the Incas. They themselves inhabited it for less than a hundred years, leaving a very shallow historical layer to dig. However, the Cusichaca area had been lived in for a much longer period and so the archaeologists could use their beloved tools of stratigraphy to some effect. While Bingham had begun to excavate here as well, he had moved on before doing too much damage, presumably bored by the unglamorous nature of the site.

For a modern archaeologist, Patallacta was worthy of study precisely because of its unremarkable nature. One of the Cusichaca team described it to me as an Inca New Town, put up in a hurry with pedestrian architecture, 'slightly middle-class dormitory housing, built as a satellite to Machu Picchu and probably used to supply it with both food and workers'. Above the hundred or so buildings of the town was a fort, Huillca Raccay, which Ann and her team had been excavating and which had a commanding position over both valleys. Still further above in the valley was Leoniyuc, a place from the more shadowy pre-Inca period.

We headed up the hill behind the camp to have a look at these higher sites and to gingerly test out our mountain legs. Ann had just begun what was later to become an important feature of her work – collaborating with the local community to restore some of the disused ancient canals that had once irrigated the valley. We came to one called Quishuarpata, a canal that ran as straight as a die across and then down the mountain slope, stone-lined and purposeful. It was apparently in use before the Inca occupation and had been adapted by them as part of their successful attempt to extract as much cultivated land as possible from the Andes. We had already seen a set of impossibly designed terraces slicing up the mountain face at Q'ente in the valley below, opposite the Cusichaca camp – and we were to see many more in the months ahead.

The Incas were able to squeeze a terrace out of land that most Europeans would have thought unsuitable even for a goat, and then maintain it through the *mita* system of compulsory community labour. Bingham had some hyperbolic descriptions of this: 'We marvelled at the exquisite pains with which the ancient folk had rescued incredibly narrow strips of arable land from the tumbling rapids. How could they have ever managed to build a retaining wall of heavy stones along the very edge of the dangerous river, which it is death to try to cross?'

Unfortunately the disruption caused by the Spanish invasion had been so great that an estimated three-quarters of the agricultural land once used by the Incas now lay abandoned – a quite astonishing statistic of waste. At Cusichaca, land that had once supported up to 5000 people now barely supported fifteen families. It was to counteract this that Ann had begun her scheme, neatly combining archaeological reconstruction with the needs of the community: the locals restored the canals, working to her plans, and so increased their available land, while Ann got a reconstructed Inca irrigation system.

There were still many canals in disrepair left to restore, but Ann had already recovered about thirty acres of land. It was an admirable idea which she hoped could then be adopted in other areas of the Andes where the collapse of agricultural communities since the agrarian reforms of the 1960s was a continuing worry.

Ann had seen this collapse at first hand. She had first gone to Peru in 1968 as a young mother, signing up as a columnist with the *Daily Mail*, which commissioned her to send back reports on 'life in the remote Andes'. All would have been well had not the *Daily Express* got wind of Ann's assignment for its rival and decided to run a spoiler campaign of its own. It despatched Nicholas Asheshov, a young reporter (and, as it happens, part-time explorer) based in Peru, to write up a quite different version of events, painting Ann (and the *Mail*) as wilfully irresponsible for taking her very small child 'up the Amazon'. Ann had been shaken by this tabloid attack, but had persevered with her work in Peru, winning considerable respect from the political authorities (who had now awarded her the Peruvian Order of Merit) and from the communities with whom she worked. She had assembled an impressive team of collaborators from Britain to establish the Cusichaca Trust, which ran her project.

Most of the diggers were volunteers for the summer season, either students or part of the touring group of young archaeologists who seemed to move from site to site around the Americas. The talk in the mess-tent was all of other sites people had worked at and extreme journeys to isolated communities. Being there was like having a crash course in pre-Columbian studies.

On that first day we climbed high enough to see the whole site laid out below us in relief: the residential area of Patallacta hugging the contours of the mountain; the fort looming over it, reminding the workers of their Inca domination; the canals running high up the hills, the only straight lines on the tumbling slopes – and beyond, the mountain ranges, with remote Inca ruins hidden in their folds.

It was the Inca world in miniature and it was to be the base for all our future exploration.

protected from Cuzco by the gigantic barrier of Salcantay, isolated from Vitcos by deep valleys and inhospitable, high windswept bleak regions called *punas*, they seem to have been unknown to the Spanish Conquerors and unsuspected by the historians … it appears to have been a *terra incognita*.

We came to Sayac Marka ('the inaccessible town') overlooking the Aobamba valley. While a very different structure to Runcu Raccay, it shared a certain spirit which I was beginning to recognise as characteristic of Inca architecture. Sayac Marka had the same curving wall in a semi-oblong extending out from the valley which I had first seen at the Huillca Raccay fort back at Cusichaca.

The great architectural achievement of the Incas was their ability to shape a building into the wildest and most inaccessible environment. The appeal to the traveller was partly because of this inaccessibility, the remoteness from any normal ideas of comfortable and practical living. The stairways were the feature which immediately attracted me, because of the sense of building around a landscape rather than on it, in a peculiarly delicate way, as if celebrating the natural contours of the rock. While Petra was built into the stone, the Inca buildings projected from it. One explorer had quoted Frank Lloyd Wright to describe them: 'It is the nature of an organic building to grow from its site, come out of the ground into the light.'

The most characteristic emblem of Inca architecture was the trapezoidal shape of the doors and niches, sloping inwards as they rose. This seems to have been a genuine Inca innovation that was not present in the buildings of their predecessors and so must have been an instantly recognisable symbol of the new Imperial presence as they built across the Andes. Aesthetically it achieved something of the power of a pyramid – rooting the building in the ground and the granite from which it had come – and it also fulfilled a valuable technical function. The Inca civilisation had not discovered the arch, so doors which sloped inwards allowed for a much shorter lintel.

What was also noticeable, though, was the very deliberate siting of Sayac Marka, as if to draw attention to the difficulty with which it was placed against the mountain. There was a far simpler location nearby, a relatively flat area, where it could easily have been built instead. But the Incas had chosen to build here, where the only advantage was a spectacularly better view.

This was where we left the Inca Trail, and headed up into the Aobamba valley. Hiram Bingham had described this as 'extremely difficult of access, its jungles dense; it was one of the obstacles that kept the Spaniards from discovering Machu Picchu'.

INCA ROADS

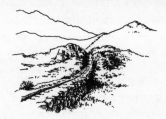

FOR US, THE MOST IMPORTANT PERSON in the camp was David Drew, with whom we would be mounting our expeditions. He had already done some exploration in previous seasons and so had acquired a patina of experience. He looked the part – tall, with a black beard and jungle fatigues. It took a certain nerve and style to be able to wear a machete permanently strapped to your waist when on the trail. David could carry it off and yet somehow seem self-deprecating at the same time.

He had knocked around too. A part-time antiques dealer on the Portobello Road, he had also just completed a postgraduate degree on the pre-Columbian cultures and so had managed to cross the usual swaying rope-bridge between the explorers and the archaeologists.

David suggested that we should do an exploratory trip before starting to look for Llactapata, our 'mislaid ruin'. As it happened, the well-known Inca Trail began from Cusichaca. This was a five-day hike leading up to Machu Picchu by an old Inca road that Bingham had discovered, regularly sold by package-holiday teams as part of their South American Experience. We could begin along it before striking off south-west into less charted territory, in the elusive search for more Inca pathways which, it was thought, must criss-cross the region.

J.B. knew all about the Inca Trail. 'There are regular staging posts, aren't there?' he said helpfully. We had seen the back-packers setting off on the path up the valley, some of them looking decidedly out of condition. Even though many had porters to carry their gear, and we would be carrying our own, we knew we could at least keep up with them, if not with David.

'Well, there are,' said David, 'but the hikers take two days to do the first stretch. We're all fit. I'm sure we can manage it in just the one. It will give us more time on the other side for actual exploration. It will get us all up to speed.'

We received this intelligence in silence. Next morning J.B. had contracted an overnight attack of laryngitis and was unable to come. 'It's only a reconnaissance anyway, isn't it?' he said, eyeing up the sun-spots closest to camp. Roddy and I looked at him morosely. Even David seemed to be having second thoughts about the austerity of our plan. 'I wish I was still in bed,' he remarked as we set off on the at first gentle climb up the Huayllabamba valley.

Our guide was called Presentación, in a satisfyingly Asterix and Obelix way. He, like us, was impressed by the amount of chocolates and sweets contained in our Army 'compo' packs: Cadbury's milk chocolate, Callard and Bowser barley-sugar, Rollos, squashed-fly biscuits and, in the surely unlikely event that our blood-sugar was still low, glucose tablets. 'So that's why your hair is so blond and curly,' Presentación told Roddy. It was a joke that amused him enormously and which he was to repeat often over the next few days.

In the early morning, and in the woods, the walk up seemed beatific, even with the weight of our packs (Roddy and I were now carrying J.B.'s share of the tent and cooking gear, a fact we would use against him to our advantage in later negotiations).

But as we turned up towards the high mountains around the village of Huayllabamba, the packs started to bite. We had already passed what was often a camp-site for the tour-groups. There was another one in a meadow higher up. Finally, after many long hours of walking, we came to an admirably flat meadow called Llullupampaca, with a fine forest below it and what the brochures would describe as 'views'. Roddy and I looked at it longingly. 'How far to go?' we asked David, in voices that suggested we had surely come far enough. 'Oh, it's not too bad. Once we cross this pass, we descend into a valley and then go up towards the next. We'll camp near a ruin called Runcu Raccay.'

'Jesus,' muttered Roddy under his breath.

At the next stop, Roddy managed to trade some of our Callard and Bowser for a supply of coca leaves from Presentación. We followed his amused directions and masticated each leaf slowly, then tucked it into our cheeks before adding another to the cud. A pinch of bicarbonate of soda helped break down the leaves. Any expectation that the experience would be as remotely pleasurable as the name suggested was soon dashed. Rather it was a numbing feeling to the jaw and a sensation like being force-fed boiled cabbage while under dental anaesthetic, with a green slime constantly trying to escape from the side of one's mouth.

However, the coca did genuinely seem to give some much-nee[ded] resilience as we approached the first high pass, Warmiwañusqua (D[ead] Woman's Pass), at almost 14,000 feet. Presentación further won my he[art] by carrying my pack for a short while over some of the final haul to [the] pass itself. There followed an equally numbed descent down into the val[ley] of the little Pacamayo, the 'sunrise river'.

We were too tired to take in much of the compact and partially circu[lar] Runcu Raccay site when we arrived. More noticeable was the large pa[rty] of drunken German tourists who were treating the Trail as if it were [an] extended ski-run and had settled down to their schnapps in padded jacke[ts,] woollen hats and, unbelievably, fold-up chairs. A small army of porte[rs] were arrayed around them. One of the party nodded graciously to me ov[er] his schnapps as I limped in. In my halting German I established wh[at] Roddy and I had gloomily suspected: they were on their second night.

We were a modest party by comparison, pitching camp at late twiligh[t] with the shadow of the Inca stonework outlined behind us. David share[d] his tent with Presentación, while Roddy and I struggled to put up our sma[ll] mountaineering Vango in the dark − a good excuse for getting it wrong[.] But that night as we stayed up drinking whisky, looking at a star-fiel[d] unalloyed by the smallest trace of sodium pollution, and as the noise o[f] drunken Germans slowly faded, I began to feel that something interesting was beginning and I was embarking on a period that would bring som[e] surprises.

The next morning, we ate porridge for breakfast (Quaker Oats, or *quaker[,]* pronounced by Peruvians to rhyme with 'mucker'), with a decadent topping of Carnation milk, and set off up to the next pass over to Sayac Marka. [I] felt considerably invigorated and my mountain legs started to kick in[.] Despite a certain amount of idle living in London, I had always walked i[n] the hills, either in the Alps or in the Lake District. When called upon, a[s] now, I could surprise my body into some endurance.

This time, when we came to the top of the pass, we could appreciate th[e] view. And it was a justly celebrated one, for we could see almost the whol[e] of the area that was to become our playground for the coming months[.] Suddenly the whole Vilcabamba Cordillera was spread out before us, wit[h] the hooked Pumasillo and the Yanama pass in the distance, while behin[d] us the Verónica range spread out.

I remembered Bingham's description:

The mystery of the deep valleys which lie in the quadrant north to north-east of Mount Salcantay have long demanded attention. Separated from Ollantaytambo and Amaybamba by the Grand Canyon of the Urubamba,

There was a lower and perfectly well-established route to do this, but David wanted to take a higher route that he thought he could make out against the mountain. In the first ten minutes of hacking our way through, I managed to cut my calf-muscle on a vicious thorn bush, a wound which gave me trouble for days. We started crossing over a rough stretch of pampas grass that was very hard on the ankles and thighs (let alone snake-nerves) because it was impossible to see where you were putting your feet. The landscape was like a Scottish moor gone baroque, purples and magentas gleaming in the long grass.

We were heading for the Abra de las Seis Ventanas, 'the Pass of Six Windows', named after a rock with six holes. Roddy began to feel the effects of the altitude and I experienced the mixture of solicitous concern and pride in one's own performance that is usual on such occasions. Indeed, I felt remarkably good as I stormed up after Presentación. He noticed some stones which had been inexplicably rooted out from the ground, which he thought showed that a puma had been looking for food. It was an explanation that I wanted to believe.

As we arrived at the pass, there was a moment when four condors started to swing around us in great arcs about the peak above, and we had an almost miraculous view right down to the Urubamba river and towards Quillabamba in the rainforest below – miraculous because the mountains all neatly side-stepped each other so as to give a clear sight-line. The valley ridges folded into one another like the waves of a cloud formation. One condor was so high above us that it looked like a plane.

But the prospect immediately below was a different matter. We stared down in horror at the Mesada valley, a tributary valley to the Aobamba and our next destination. A series of hanging valleys blocked out each succeeding drop from sight, making them more sinister than if we were standing on the edge of a sheer cliff, when we could at least have clearly seen the descent.

Up to now we had been following traces of Inca road, immaculately laid stonework, as it elusively traced its way across the landscape, sometimes disappearing completely, then reappearing over precisely the stretch one needed it most, with the intuitive Inca sense for the mountains.

Inca roads are like magic writing. Over the years since that first journey, I've noticed how you can be at the top of a pass and see nothing – but a slight change of angle, a difference in the light, the mist moving across a rock-face, and you suddenly see a line traversing a ridge, usually unnaturally high.

The Incas liked the heights. The Quechuan guides I've worked with always travel instinctively on the high side of any given valley, while the natural tendency of European or American mountain trekkers is to keep to the bottom if they can.

Ever since Bingham made the endearing mistake of coming here in February on his very first expedition in 1909 and so found himself in the middle of the torrential rainy season, explorers have naturally come in the dry, winter season (April to November). Because of this, they have often misunderstood why the Incas built so high on valley walls. In wet-season conditions they would immediately see how impassable and boggy the valley bottom becomes. A further consideration drove the Incas to build their roads high and at times leave empty stretches along the way – the need to preserve as much precious terracing and agricultural land as possible.

But there were other reasons as well for the unusual trajectory of the Inca road. The man who first awoke real interest in the Inca road-system as a phenomenon in its own right was Victor von Hagen.

*

Even in the outsize world of South American explorers, Victor von Hagen shines forth as a personality whose enthusiasm and ebullience carried all before him. In 1952 he set off to follow the old Inca road from Lake Titicaca to Quito in Ecuador, an epic undertaking. There is a picture of him at the front of his book about the expedition, *Highway of the Sun* (sadly long out of print). Somewhere in the desert, von Hagen strides towards the camera along a road which seems to recede behind him to an infinite horizon. It is midday and the vertical sun puts his face almost completely in shade. The impression is of a forceful torso making his way towards you from the back of beyond, and the rest of the book does much the same. *Highway of the Sun* carries one of my favourite dedications by any author, one that many would like to have used but didn't quite have the nerve: he dedicates it 'In all Humility – to Myself'.

There is an equally magnificent opening paragraph:

To travel the whole of this ancient route wherever possible, in an attempt to lay aside the Isisian veils that shadowed this part of my proto-American history, was both my aim – and now my obsession. Then to use another metaphor, was it not like some large-scale mystery played on a gigantic background? We had first the *scale*, the tripartite area of desert, Andes and jungle. There was a *plot* – would we find the road and what would happen to the six of us in the process; and there was *drive* – my demi-urge which pushed against the twin obstacles of distance and finance. There were countless *clues* –

the actual spoors of the road, the remains of bridges, ruins, walls, and the detailed information left by chroniclers and *conquistadores*. There was *drama*: the inherent danger in travelling over the precipitous Andean roads, the over-awing desert, the all-enveloping jungle. And finally there was *suspense*: would we, after all the preparation, find that which we sought, and would there be countless ruins of which so many still remain unlisted and – waiting? [Author's original italics.]

The Napoleonic style is characteristic of the man. It was not surprising that Sir Mortimer Wheeler had given the book a good review. Von Hagen had begun exploring South America young, at about the same age as us, and had first glimpsed the Inca road near its beginnings in Ecuador. He had gone on to become a prolific explorer and writer, following the textbook goals of any self-respecting adventurer – looking for El Dorado, chasing the quetzal bird in Central America and living with remote tribes in the Amazon – before returning twenty years later to follow the road properly. In *Highway of the Sun* he has an endearing habit of reminding readers of the success of previous expeditions and books ('see my *The Realm of the Incas*, which in its different editions and translations now hovers close to the 1,000,000 mark since its publication . . .'). According to his daughter, Adriana von Hagen, herself a distinguished expert on early Peruvian culture, Victor was obsessed by Herman Melville (he even wrote a historical novel about Melville's mistress), and his prose harnesses some of Melville's obsessive, rolling style to the self-taught polymathic skills that von Hagen had acquired in a lifetime of archaeological buccaneering.

The 'Inca Highway' expedition was an arduous one. There are thousands of miles between La Paz and Quito, as the early Spanish chronicler Cieza de León noted when he, like many of the early conquistadors, marvelled at the Incas' road-building skills. But in the intervening centuries, the roads had fallen into disarray. The Spanish preferred less vertiginous routes and abandoned the old system of *mita*, or communal labour tribute, which had kept the roads in good condition. Apart from those sections which had been appropriated by the Pan-American Highway, most of the great road lay forgotten and ignored.

Von Hagen put much of it back on the map. Where his foresight as an explorer was most impressive was in the care with which he had used the early chronicles. Behind some of the showmanship, he, like Hiram Bingham before, had realised that the key to successful exploration was to study the original texts – although as with Bingham, he got someone else to do the work for him. Von Hagen commissioned Dorothy Menzel, a young graduate student from the University of California, to spend a year going through every known reference book for mentions of the road. He then decided to take her on the expedition. Just before coming she telegraphed von Hagen to say she was getting married, to a fellow archaeologist – so von Hagen invited him as well. It must have been some honeymoon.

For while von Hagen succeeded in tracing much of the road over the next two years, it is clear that the expedition was not without its problems: what von Hagen, in a delightfully orotund phrase, described as 'the natural irritations of propinquity. There is always a certain uneasiness when persons unused to each other are thrown together on a continual intimate basis.' He went on to say that 'I was equally irritating to the others, for the altitude seemed to give me more energy (having more than my fair share under normal conditions) and my pushing of the programme certainly strained nerves that were already taut.'

Only three of the expedition were left by the time they finally came to the end of the road, at Cajamarca, where the Spanish conquest of the Incas had begun with the capture of Atahualpa in the main square. Von Hagen celebrated by sending a telegram in thundering hyperbole to the *New York Times*:

EXPLORERS FINISH INCA ROAD SEARCH. WE HAVE MADE OUR LAST RUN ALONG THE INCA ROAD AND OUR LAST DISCOVERY. WE HAVE SOUGHT THE REMAINS OF THE FABULOUS ROYAL ROAD OF THE INCAS BY TRUCK, BY MULE, BY AIRPLANE, ON FOOT. WE HAVE FOLLOWED THE INCA ROADS THROUGH DESERT AND TOWERING ANDES....

In more reflective mood he wrote later in his book that 'we had found that we were dealing with a *master plan*, that the Incas had conceived and put into operation a road system of no less than 10,000 miles of all-weather roads which climbed to heights over which Man had never, until then, maintained communications'.

For the tribes who had been conquered by the Incas, the roads must have been a continual sign of the Imperial presence. As subjects, they had to contribute to the upkeep of those roads as part of the *mita* system of communal labour, even if they themselves were not always allowed to use them. For these were not highways in the European sense, democratically open to all: only those on state business were allowed to use the most important ones.

Indeed, to read the road system of the Incas is to read a different language: they are written with a different grammar to our own. While the Western road typically 'penetrates' through the middle of a territory, with spur-roads branching off, Inca roads were often used as much to 'edge' a territory, to delineate internal boundaries. In the words of Cieza de León, 'the Indians, in order to take stock of what they have in such a large land, comprehend it by means of their roads'. The modern Andean scholar John Hyslop has commented that the roads were not only used to separate people, 'but for thinking, by helping to conceive the relationship of one place to another'.

The four roads leading out of Cuzco to the four quarters of the Empire are well-known symbols of this. Less well known is the peculiar habit which Cieza de León also remarked on, the Incaic tendency to rebuild roads. An incoming Inca Emperor might well order a perfectly usable stretch of road to be replaced by a new parallel stretch of his own, a mark of his arrival and also a reaffirmation of the Inca ownership of the land that the resulting new road system contained. It was also a useful way of ensuring that there were always enough *mita* jobs to keep his subjects busy. Cieza reported Huayna Capac as declaring, 'to keep the people of these kingdoms well in hand it was a good thing, when they had nothing else to do or busy themselves with, to make them move a mountain from one spot to another. He even ordered stone and tiles brought from Cuzco to Quito [a distance of 3400 miles], where they are still to be seen.'

Cieza got lost once leaving the Inca town of Vilcas. He found that three roads seemed to point to precisely the same destination. One had been built by the Emperor Pachacuti, another by his son Topa Inca, and the road actually in use (and therefore kept up and negotiable) had been built by his successor, the same Huayna Capac who believed in a Victorian way about the dangers of 'idle hands'. It was only after several frustrating false starts that Cieza managed to get on the right one.

But there was another little-commented-on factor which makes the grammar of the Inca road system so foreign to us. We are used to a road system designed for the horse and then for the car: a system which tries at all costs to avoid steep gradients and whose ideal (so established by the Romans) is the straight road over flat ground. The Inca needs were very different: the expansion of their Empire was driven by the llama, which as a pack animal could carry their merchandise over long distances. It was the llama which had carried goods as far south as Chile and as far north as modern Colombia. Along the route, Inca *tambos*, the resting houses used by such merchants, as well as by *chasquis*, the Inca messengers, and by the Inca armies, would have plentiful supplies of *p'olqo*, the cloth used for protecting llamas' delicate feet on the stone paths.

The llama was an all-purpose provider. As well as being a pack animal (although it would never accept a rider), the meat could also be eaten, the dried dung used for fuel, essential in some areas of the high *puna* above the tree-line, and the coarse wool woven into textiles.

However, llamas have very specific needs: they are happiest at high altitudes (over 13,000 feet) and, while they can descend for short periods, any road carrying them must deviate frequently to higher ground in order to give them pasturage – a point the conquistadors complained bitterly about as they kept ascending endless mountain passes on their way from the coast to conquer Cuzco. Camelids are far more accomplished climbers than the horse and so can negotiate stairways. The Incas could therefore avoid the lengthy 'zig-zag' technique by which European roads climbed a mountain slope and instead simply use steep stairs to gain height, so reducing road-building to a quarter of the European length. One of the tragedies of the Conquest was that the Incas failed to realise early enough the advantage that this potentially gave them over the conquistadors and their horses. Each time the Spanish dismounted in order to negotiate the difficult mountain roads they could have been slaughtered.

Once, years later with the American explorer Gary Ziegler, I came across a magnificent decayed stairway high up in the Choquetecarpa valley. The stairway rose out of the grass ahead of us, seemingly out of nowhere, stone tread after stone tread, a full twelve feet wide, the width of a royal road – indeed probably the road that the later Incas may have used when they were in exile in the Vilcabamba after having fled Cuzco.

Even higher in the valley were some stone llama pens, built just below the pass at a chilling 13,700 feet: circular buildings, 13 feet in diameter, clustered tightly together to give protection against the wind. Above, a vertiginous stone stairway cut its way directly up towards the pass. No travellers now ever passed along that road – those few that came through would use the modern mule track instead, which wound its course in a more sedate and European style over the other shoulder of the pass. We had found this alternate ancient way because we knew where to look. The Inca instinct for roads is a different language to our own, but it is one that can be learnt.

*

Our own path on that very first expedition was a peculiarly elusive one, sometimes ending abruptly for no apparent reason before restarting further on, while at other times we lost it completely and had to retrace our footsteps (or claw-marks) over a strange sort of Technicolor moss that had a disconcerting spring to it. This was the toughest stretch so far, with Presentación often worried about losing his way. Using a machete to get through the thicker sections of undergrowth became extremely tiring, particularly as our backpacks kept being caught by the hanging creepers: we learned to stow our bulky gear as low as possible in the pack.

Although some of the original pathway we were following may have been lost due to erosion or landslides, the Incas did not always feel obliged to keep a road continuous anyway, particularly if it was not of ceremonial significance – if they came to a stretch where it was either too difficult or, conversely, too easy (and therefore unnecessary) to pave a section, they simply left it. There are records of sections in the desert where the road simply stops for miles at a time, possibly with marker posts in the sand to help the traveller on his way.

After some frustrating hours spent joining up the dots of the elusive path, we finally reached a small oasis of a clearing for the night. Presentación hacked out a space for the tents and then cleverly used the cut grass to soften the sleeping area. But, as Roddy ungraciously commented, 'the sleeping bags still sloped'. Indeed, we spent the night doing that odd form of traction where you continually drag your spine back up a nylon sleeping bag without ever noticing that you are slowly slipping down again.

In the shadow of the great bulk of Mount Salcantay, at 20,500 feet one of the giants of the range, the air was cold and we brewed up tea after tea. It was what mountaineers sometimes call 'a refrigeration camp'. Leaving our packs on the ground-sheet in front of the tent was a mistake and gave us a frozen start as a result.

We picked up what was at least a path, if not an Inca one. A wild steer suddenly erupted out towards us at a narrow bend. Presentación was leading and, with his slight build, could flatten himself against a tree. But there was no such escape for Roddy behind, with his considerably larger bulk, and he was caught square-on by this charging apparition. He managed to twist somehow to ride the blow and the surprised steer crashed off through the undergrowth. Roddy modestly admitted afterwards to having done a bit of rodeo-riding when he was in Canada. We never did discover the truth of this, as with many of Roddy's more straight-faced declarations.

The path up the valley was full of the electric-blue butterflies I had expected to see in a South American forest. The morpho family of butterflies are all named after Homeric characters, improbably and unfairly, given the range of pre-Columbian heroes available. In the Cuzco shops one could see box after phosphorescent box of Morpho Patroclus, Morpho Hercules, Morpho Menelaus, Morpho Peleides, Morpho Achilles and even a Morpho Telemachus, all in slight variants of the shimmering blue that came out of the lush green of the jungle, like sparkles of colour across the retina of an unfocused eye.

Pallcay was a fabulously romantic ruin when we came to it. This was the reason why we (and, for part of the way, the Inca path) had struck off up here. A classical Inca site, it was lightly covered by honeysuckle-like creepers that made it seem like a folly in an English country garden. Although, with the waterfalls of a high valley and the whole of Salcantay behind it, it was pure Inca, I almost expected to find an accompanying wisteria trained up the southern aspect. (Bingham, who said he had discovered the buildings 'by accident', described them as being 'the ruins of a small Inca country-house'.)

A lively Señora lived near the ruin and greeted us with her illegitimate child. Rosilla was a fiercely independent woman who ran a cattle and pig business with her brother, and told me in the first few minutes of conversation that she was only too pleased not to have a husband. She was one of those people, common from Tunbridge Wells to Moscow, who tell you their life stories in the first five minutes.

While talking, Rosilla displayed a lot of gold teeth which were both ornamental and functional, as she, like many of those who lived in the valleys, had dental problems. Her theory was that it was the pressure of the altitude on the cavities. For a worrying moment I thought she was going to open her mouth wider for an inspection. Instead we went on to a general discussion of health issues (like many people in the mountains, she felt that coca leaves were a universal panacea for most problems, including dental ones) and I handed over some aspirin. She brought eggs to share with us over lunch, with potatoes she'd just dug from the ground, welcome after a monotonous diet of processed cheese, biscuits and *quaker*. Rosilla was covetous of our primus stove (which we were not in a position to sell her): she wanted it more as a status symbol than for any actual use, rather like a big food-processor in Britain.

We camped here for two nights, which gave the luxury of a lie-in and the relief of not wearing our packs for a day. The down-side was sharing our camp-site with Rosilla's pigs, which, while companionable, brought us perilously close to pig-worms, parasites which David told us had infected some of the Cusichaca archaeologists. These entered the body both by the feet and the buttocks. 'Archaeologists − serves them right if they're going to sit on their arses all the time,' muttered Roddy. Three weeks into the job and he was already becoming a partisan explorer.

Under the circumstances, it seemed best not to stick around the camp. Walking felt weightless without the packs, as if we'd left the space shuttle, and we wandered further up the isolated valley, which was remarkable more for its waterfalls than for traces of Inca building or paths. The mists rose to give us clear views of Salcantay, a mountain that was usually hidden.

Even more tantalisingly, we were getting close to Llactapata itself, our 'mislaid ruin', or the broad area it should be in if Hiram Bingham's wonderfully vague description was correct. Bingham had emerged here from the hills after finding it. But looking at the miles of dense undergrowth through which he had come and after our initial experiences of the previous few days, it felt like we were going to be searching for the proverbial needle in a haystack. Somewhere high up on the dense slopes of the Aobamba valley was a cluster of a dozen or so buildings, substantial enough for Bingham to presume that 'they may well have been built by one of Manco's captains. It [Llactapata] was on a strategic spot.' It seemed absurd that the place had been lost for seventy years since he had first found it.

Part of the problem was Bingham's own account, which was designed more for armchair readers than anybody following in his footsteps. He starts by saying that his assistant had tried to get up into the Aobamba but had been beaten back by impassable jungle. 'Quite unexpectedly, however, I got into the reaches of the valley about ten days later, and found some interesting ruins ... The end of that day found us on top of a ridge between the valleys of the Aobamba and the Salcantay.' There he finds Llactapata. Even by the standards of the literature of exploration, Bingham is extra-ordinarily passive and vague ('the end of that day found us'), somehow managing to avoid any directions whatsoever. It was an omission we were to reflect on ruefully, just as many previous frustrated expeditions must have done.

We went up towards the ridge between the two valleys in the hope that there might be traces of a path to Llactapata. This took us along a high spur valley and was much tougher than we expected. Nor were there any clues when we came to the narrow pass, the Paso de Pillone, leading over the top. 'Oh well,' Roddy and I reflected over a lunch of wizened dried sausage and some unappetising freeze-dried potatoes that Rosilla had sold us, 'time to head back.' David had gone quiet and reflective, always a dangerous sign. 'Now we're here, I suppose we might as well have a look down into the Santa Teresa Valley as well.' David's 'we might as well' meant 'this is what we're going to do.' But after a brief abortive foray into the unpromising country immediately below, even he gave up.

A bone-shattering descent of 6000 feet to the railway line at Intihuatana was enlivened only by Presentación's discovery of what were clearly puma footprints even to the most jaundiced eye. There was another strange moment when Presentación (with whom I had now strongly bonded as both my coca dealer and fount of Quechua wisdom) took me aside from the others. 'Hugo,' he said ('Hugh' being unpronounceable in Spanish), 'look at this.' He unwrapped the knotted handkerchief he had tied to his belt. Inside was a large snake's head, which he must recently have killed. 'What's it for?' I asked, feeling stupid. '*Por un secreto*, for a secret,' he whispered.

Stumbling into the little shack by the railway lines, Roddy and I asked for a soft drink, but found we had no change. '*No hay crédito*, there's no credit here,' said the Señora, with all the welcoming charm of Albert back home in his pub.

It was with both exhaustion and pride that we arrived at the Cusichaca base-camp, if with substantial worries about our chances of ever finding Llactapata. We discussed the outlook with J.B., who was as sanguine about our chances as only a man can be who has spent a week in camp with nothing to do but eye up the most attractive of the archaeologists and sit in the sun. 'I'm sure we'll find the ruin, if it's there to find.' J.B. was so relaxed about it because he had always been doubtful about the existence of the ruin in the first place. He took the line that he wasn't going to let that get in the way of a fine adventure. More usefully, he had established some inside lines of communication with the cook and with Graham, the genial ex-Army man who fixed up the camp, so that we could get decent supplies of everything from toilet paper to Southern Comfort.

Davina was a little mellower and less like a reproving school prefect now that we had gone off and 'actually done some work', as she put it. She showed us an enticing little rock pool in the Cusichaca, where you could manoeuvre your whole body into a natural jacuzzi of frothing white stream and feel the aching muscles being pulverised. There was a large sloping rock above and, once we had got used to the place, we found that you could slide right off the rock and land up to your neck in the pool below – although the shock of the cold water was considerable. With the carved Inca rock of Pulpituyoc above, it was a fine place to sneak off for a private nude bathe, although I couldn't quite bring myself to wash my hair in the glacial melt-waters. I figured it was generally hidden by a hat anyway.

*

A week later we took the late train down the Urubamba valley, and it rattled away beneath us through the night as we sat slumped against our backpacks. Most travellers got off at the Machu Picchu stop and we started getting food sold to us at discount prices. Roddy ordered us all double helpings on the basis that we might need it.

This was the big one: our first frontal attempt to find Llactapata itself. We were following a hunch. David had met a man who knew a butcher who claimed to have come across the ruins when taking his cattle across the hills. It seemed as likely or unlikely a way to find the ruins as any.

Indeed, the history of exploration by the developed world in the undeveloped is not one of explorers discovering sites by themselves, but rather their ability (or luck) in discovering reliable local guides who could lead them to those sites. Even Cortés had been unable to find a city the size of Tenochtitlán (modern Mexico City) without guides to help him, and Bingham had been led up to Machu Picchu by a local farmer. Any explorer who claimed to have found a ruin by himself was either a liar or very, very lucky.

Finding the right guide was a skill in itself. Once word got out that you were looking for a ruin, and that as gringos you probably had money to spend, there would be a deluge of offers promising *ruinas grandes*, most more wilful than realistic. It was almost impossible to tell who was talking straight. But perhaps this butcher would take us where previous expeditions had failed to reach.

The sleepy shanty town of Santa Teresa sprawled around a bend in the valley line like a set from a spaghetti Western. Local Indians, their hats tipped firmly over their heads, viewed us with complete lack of interest as we stumbled by in the twilight. The kids approached with muttered whispers of '*Hey, mister*' (pronounced '*meester*'). In my diary I described it as needing a soundtrack of 'back-of-the-rail-track blues'.

One look at the beds in the only hostel, and Roddy and I chose to sleep on the floor. J.B., with his sterner Scottish constitution, elected to risk the bedbugs. I dreamt that night of killer cockroaches coming at me over the floor.

At dawn we headed off to the house of the butcher, Juan Ganchos. He wasn't around, but a man called Vincente, who claimed to be his friend, said that he too knew where the ruin was, as Juan had apparently told him about it. Vincente offered to take us instead, although he was recovering from what was clearly a blinding hangover and looked a wreck, unshaven and slurring his words.

Negotiations followed about fees and what we were going to do given the absence of the man who had actually seen the ruins, or said that he'd seen them. '*¿Juan Ganchos? Puede seguirnos*, Juan Ganchos can follow later,' said Vincente, shrugging. 'He knows you're here. We'll probably meet him on the mountain.' It was difficult to argue with a man with a hangover. As I've also learnt since, in South America it's sometimes easier just to give yourself over to the unknown and see what happens.

We started the slog up the valley to Suriray, along a flat exposed path. Vincente seemed none the worse for wear, and led off at a sprightly pace. As we left Santa Teresa, a procession of dogs and small children came snapping at us, intrigued by a bunch of gringos carrying absurdly large packs and wearing machetes.

John Hemming had warned me before I left London that the gnats of the Santa Teresa valley were murderous. He and his men had been bitten so badly that their shoulder glands had swollen. Hiram Bingham, a man who usually brushed such hardships aside, had also remembered them specifically: 'the work of measuring and mapping was made unpleasant by the attention of gnats'. For anyone to notice gnats in an area where it was remarkable if you weren't bitten meant that their attentions must be particularly assiduous, and we too began to suffer almost immediately. At one point there were so many on my arm that it was impossible to dislodge them, and I watched as they dug in, their proboscises back-lit like so many tiny cranes.

At Suriray there was a beaten-up little stall with some brightly coloured bottles of indeterminate Cola gathering dust. They were tepid to drink, but welcome: we had to husband our own water for the climb that was about to begin, and which we could see going straight up towards the ridge between this valley and the Aobamba.

Even after our limbering up expedition, our packs felt murderous and the ascent painful. The only encouragement was that as we looked back towards the Santa Teresa, we thought we could make out faint traces of an Inca road descending and heading west towards the mountains of the Vilcabamba and the Inca site of Vitcos.

It was almost sunset by the time we got close to the pass. The whine of Roddy's anti-mosquito device (designed to imitate the buzz of a male mosquito and so supposedly discourage the pregnant females who bite) was becoming overpowering. We begged him to switch it off, particularly as his legs were already swollen with bites despite the machine, but he refused with the stubbornness of someone for whom life has anyway become unbearable.

Vincente and his little dog kept disappearing into the numerous half-paths ahead of us. He still kept up the pretence of looking for the mysterious Juan Guanchos, the man who supposedly knew where the ruin actually was. This fiction had become ever less likely as we advanced into the monotonous green of the selva and Vincente sensed that we doubted him.

He suddenly gave a loud scream ahead. We had been keeping quiet, out of exhaustion and boredom, and the sound of his machete hitting something and his shouts in glottal Quechua came as a shock. We ran forward and found Vincente proudly holding a small black-and-white snake cut in half, which his dog sniffed at excitedly. It was not what we wanted to see as the light faded, and we moved forward even more cautiously, hacking needlessly at innocuous creepers.

We crossed the pass at about 10,000 feet. It should have been a climactic moment, but there was nothing to be seen on the other side. Usually I found the mountain passes a moment of immense relief. After the long periods of climbing with the perpetual slight shift of the horizon pressing you forward, suddenly to crest a pass and have a complete change of outlook was intoxicating, as if one had suddenly gone into a space-warp. But this pass revealed nothing other than a shrubby falling away on the other side. Demoralised, we staggered on. Even David's shoulders had settled into a hunch.

The ruins themselves turned out to be remarkably close. Vincente gave a melodramatic flourish when we reached the first of them, somewhat spoilt by the fact that it was by far the least significant (a tiny wall). '¡Ven! You see!' he said, in a voice that reproached us for our lack of faith in him. When we got a little further down, we came across more substantial ones, overgrown and silhouetted, looking like one of Catherwood's nineteenth-century illustrations of Mayan ruins from the Yucatan.

I would like to say that we immediately began examining the ruins, but the truth is that we were too tired to take much in. Nor could we be sure in the dark what they really were. Completely exhausted, it was all we could do to get our tents up and tumble into them.

The next morning we woke with a burning numbness of thirst in our mouths and an intense anticipation. Roddy and I went down to find a water-source and our excitement mounted as we came across ruin after ruin in the sunlight. When we finally got to a watering-hole, we came to the most spectacular of all – a large complex of buildings on a flat area, fully deserving the name of Llactapata, 'high town' in Quechua. When we climbed higher, to a large building on the ridge above us, there was the unmistakable outline of Machu Picchu itself folded over the distant skyline. It was a dramatic way to see it for the first time.

Llactapata's position – on a hollow near the Aobamba's own skyline – immediately made perfect sense as a signalling site protecting the great city from the west, yet almost invisible itself. This must have been why Bingham had described it as 'a strategic spot'.

We could only scratch at a tiny proportion of what was a substantial site, arranged as so often with Inca settlements over several levels. Just as in the early pictures of Machu Picchu, before restoration, many of the remaining walls here were only a few feet high. In the thick vegetation, making out where a decayed building ended and the mountain began could be deceptive.

But we were able to clear enough to see the main group of buildings, arranged around two distinct plazas: some of the walls were in good condition and had kept their characteristic Incaic niches intact. David described these buildings as being of classical Inca proportions and detail. The plazas were so close to the edge of the slope that erosion had eaten away at them, and a wonderful view of the Aobamba dropped away into the cloud-forest beneath us.

I found the whole process of discovery not sudden and triumphant, but gradual and disorientating. We worked slowly during the day, stripping the ruins bare of creepers with our machetes, a somewhat futile gesture as doubtless they would grow back before the next party of properly qualified archaeologists came to find them, if they ever did. (It was not just Machu Picchu that remained unexcavated, but a surprising number of other Inca ruins too.) The heat and the sound of parakeets overhead with their curious chiming sound, mechanical like a Stravinsky chorus, made the whole day seem unreal.

Indeed, when we finally descended to the Aobamba valley below, with its coffee bushes and the freshness of its river coursing along beside us, it was possible for a moment to feel that we had hallucinated the whole thing. I understood why explorers in the past had been so irresponsibly prone to bring back samples of the pottery that often lies close to the surface, one of the charges that the archaeologists routinely levelled against them: not because the samples might have any financial or academic value, but simply to prove to themselves that they had actually been there.

What made Llactapata particularly hallucinatory was that it lay so close to the world which was known. From the ruins we had been able to hear the sound of the train echoing up to us from the other end of the valley. It was a reminder that one could be yards from a site and never realise it, so thick was the jungle vegetation that crept up the Andes from the Amazon.

We walked out along the Aobamba river, crossing it by an exceptionally fine swaying bridge (we were becoming connoisseurs), and headed back towards the railway. This was the way we had emerged from our previous exploratory trip with David, and yet there were things I hadn't noticed then, but appreciated now with a heightened sensibility: the beauty of the artificial waterfall created by the hydro-electric station and the golden fields of crops as the valley floor widened. A suspicious policeman stopped us before Intihuatana near the hydro-electric station itself, which was surrounded by wire and was an obvious terrorist target. We persuaded him with the necessary documentation that we were genuine, but he hardly seemed the person to tell of our discovery, even though we were bursting to tell the world.

Waiting in the same little shack by the railway line we had gone to before, I was amazed to discover that among the dusty *refrescos* and limp fruit was a juke-box, which again I hadn't noticed before – indeed, it was one of the few I've ever seen in Peru. Even more surprisingly, I found that they had, along with the inevitable local *huayno* music, a record by Kid Creole and the Coconuts, which I duly played. It was a surreal end to a surreal day.

I remembered John Hemming's words to me before we left: that the process of discovery did not stop with finding a ruin – what really mattered was understanding what that ruin meant. In reaching Llactapata we had been incredibly lucky, with our choice of guide if nothing else. Now what stretched ahead of us was the much greater challenge of putting that discovery in context. It felt like the beginning, rather than the end, of our journey.

CHOQUEQUIRAO:
CRADLE OF GOLD

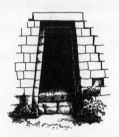

Tell the white men that to get where we live, the roads are so bad that they
will die on the journey, and that we have no chicken eggs to give them.

Message from a village headman
to the Comte de Sartiges in 1834

CORTÉS, ARGUABLY THE GREATEST of all South American explorers, was
famous for never being able to stop exploring. Having conquered Mexico
and then advanced down much of Central America, he didn't seem able
to enjoy the fruits that these discoveries brought – land, wealth and even a
Marquisate – but instead launched various punitively expensive trips up the
western coast of Mexico towards what is now California in an attempt to
find a supposed city of gold. He found nothing, bankrupted himself and
died struggling as a result. The waters between Lower California and
Mexico are still known as the Sea of Cortés as an ironic epitaph. Likewise
Captain Cook was unable to resist the lure of a third and, as it turned out,
terminal voyage, even though he had been offered a well-earned retirement
in Greenwich.

Our surprising success in finding Llactapata had not satisfied our need
to keep on with our own modest expedition. If anything, it was a spur, a
first real hit of the heady drug of discovery, and I could understand better
how Bingham had been so propelled from one lost ruin to the next. What
also had begun to intrigue me more and more was not the idea of finding
ruins, but of tracing the Inca roads between them. Perhaps I'd always felt
the same about mountains, where I'd never particularly needed to get to
the top but had always enjoyed the passes.

The more I walked them, the more the Inca paths became fascinating in their own right, deliberately over-constructed objects of beauty that were a statement as clear as any work by Christo or Richard Long about a love for the ground they walked on. They were emphatically not simple ways of getting from A to B. Nothing was more remarkable than to emerge on some hidden plateau at 10,000 feet and see a gleaming stone road or causeway laid ahead of you, apparently going nowhere, a testament not only to the Incaic skill in stonemasonry but to their extraordinary, almost symbiotic feel for the mountains themselves.

We determined to follow some of the routes that the early explorers had taken in the hinterland beyond Machu Picchu, even more remote than Llactapata, and in particular, to get to the distant site of Choquequirao. This famous and romantically isolated ruin lay by the side of the Apurímac river and we decided to go there not by the only known open route, ascending from the river itself, but by hacking our way across the jungle and the mountain watershed between the Urubamba and the Apurímac basins and seeing what roads lay between. This was a route that Bingham had considered impassable and not attempted, but which an intrepid French aristocrat called the Comte de Sartiges had taken in 1834, with fifteen Indians cutting a path for him through the dense shrub.

David Drew and some of the Cusichaca archaeologists wanted to study the sites in the higher Santa Teresa valley, which lay on our route, and so we arranged to work together with them for a while before then heading off on our own towards Choquequirao.

We arrived with the archaeologists at the Santa Teresa railway station feeling rather proud of ourselves after the Llactapata discovery. Vincente was even prouder of having taken us there, and I stood him numerous drinks as he regaled the villagers and a slightly disgruntled Juan Ganchos with the tale.

This time we had to see the Chief of Police for the various permissions we needed both for a larger party and for our own later trip across to Choquequirao. He turned out to be an affable man starved of company, who ushered us into a study dominated by an enormous gold-and-green banner above the desk: he explained that the banner was for the police football team. Our paperwork had been prepared by Ann Kendall, an expert in Peruvian bureaucracy, and was impressive enough for him to stamp it no less than three times with different seals.

The Chief offered us the use of their football pitch to sleep on. As an alternative to the bedbugs and sleazy hostel we'd experienced before, this was welcome, although the pitch was so compacted by heavy playing that it was still uncomfortable. One advantage of having the archaeologists along, however, was that our supply of alcohol had now increased to manageable proportions. After a few rum-and-apple-juices, even the football pitch couldn't stop me from sleeping.

It was good to have some new blood. Along with the archaeologists came Vaughan Fleming, a photographer attached to the Cusichaca group to document finds, but whose real passion in life was natural history. He had already researched a monograph on Cretan flowers and was now making a collection of Peruvian fungi for the British Museum. As we travelled up the Santa Teresa valley together, he would point out both exotic and startlingly ordinary mosses. In a charming way Vaughan looked a bit like an insect anthropoid, with an engaging, alert head and long, thin legs. He was a fund of strange but true zoological stories, from the rainforest conditions along a section of Welsh coast to the migratory habits of Monarch butterflies, one of which landed on our sandwiches but could equally well, according to Vaughan, have been seen off the Isle of Wight.

I was starting to have problems with a wisdom tooth. This may have been due to the constant supply of Army ration sweets, or perhaps Rosilla's theory about the effect of altitude on the gums was correct, but it was difficult to focus on much else. I increased my supply of coca to try to numb the pain, although by now I was on the equivalent of three packs a day.

That night, at a small village called Miscabamba, I slept atrociously in the tent and staggered out early. The tent was anyway no place to outstay your welcome. J.B. had been in economical mode when he had bought it and the man in the shop had assured him that a three-man tent would be fine for us. What he hadn't told him was that this was a mountaineering tent, and so 'three-man' in the sense that you could get three into it if you were over-nighting on a narrow ledge, or your life depended on it. It was not designed to live in for months on end. As a punishment Roddy and I had consigned J.B. to the very bottom end, where he slept cross-wise with only the occasional understandable complaint about the smell of our feet.

The night had left me debilitated and in considerable pain. The trek up the valley was unrelenting and I looked enviously at the few ponies we had, which were carrying supplies rather than people. By the time we came to Colcapampa, where the various head-valleys met, I was getting behind. David came back for me and gave me a hand with my pack. As the nearest dentist was several days away at Cuzco and going there would mean aborting the whole trip, there seemed no alternative but to persevere.

Colcapampa had one great natural asset – some hot springs that bubbled up from the rock-face right by the path. I stripped off and washed. Holding my head under hot water seemed to help the pain, for no good logical reason. My hat was unable to conceal any longer what was becoming a serious hair problem, and I used a sachet of Johnson's Baby Shampoo that I'd purchased from the shack down by the railroad. Halfway through the operation, a column of Quechua ladies wound down along the track and passed by without a glance at the unusual spectacle of a pale gringo in his Y-fronts, lathering up his hair.

There were some small farming communities at the head of the valley, and that Sunday they had a *fiesta*, with plenty of *chicha blanca*, a drink inherited from Inca times with a wheaty, not quite fermented taste, like a speciality Belgian beer. This was not your all-night-samba sort of fiesta. Most of the participants stayed comatose throughout, slumped against the sides of the hut, and the average age was late forties. Many of the younger men had headed off from the villages to try to get work in Cuzco or at the hydro-electric station. Loosened up by a few glasses of *chicha*, I started chatting to a lively group of older women and one of them, Tía Ollas, invited some of us to stay up the valley near a little hamlet called Rayanpata. This seemed a good base from which to climb to a rarely visited pre-Inca site above on the cliffs, called Unuyoc.

The hamlet was at 10,000 feet, with a mountainside of forest rising up into the clouds behind. We camped near Tía's hut and immediately started to receive generous amounts of hospitality. Tía gestured at some of her guinea-pigs. 'When you leave, we will kill some for you,' she said with a magnanimous if distressing gesture at the little furry creatures around her feet.

The hamlet was tiny. Social life revolved around the watering-hole where the women met in the evening to gossip and by day to weave large peppermint-coloured shawls they could sell down at Cuzco or Chincheros. Within a few days we got to know them all. Indeed, we spent a while at Rayanpata, lulled by their remarkably attractive lifestyle, which included getting good coffee sent up to them from Quillabamba in the jungle. Roddy and I had endless cups as we played backgammon and waited for the clouds to lift.

With us was a young archaeologist called Harvey Lilley, who impressed me by carrying *War and Peace* in his pack. After a week at Rayanpata he had almost finished it, as the mountains were usually covered by mist and drizzle and we could rarely climb them.

When we did get up to Unuyoc, we found it to be again on the end of a ridge, with the characteristic double-bonded circles and spectacular views we were getting used to. We started the job of measuring the site. Whatever the archaeologists might say, it seemed to me that all this called for was the ability to hold a tape-measure and draw an accurate diagram. Bingham had self-deprecatingly described his own initiation into this black art:

'Fortunately I had with me that extremely useful handbook *Hints to Travellers*, published by the Royal Geographical Society. In one of the chapters I found out what should be done when one is confronted by a prehistoric site – take careful measurements and plenty of photographs and describe as accurately as possible all finds. On account of the rain our photos were not very accurate.'

It was early morning and my reactions were slow when Roddy told me there was a bear behind me. It took a while to realise he was joking and then another delay before I realised he wasn't. The bear seemed surprisingly small, like Yogi Bear in the cartoon, and was looking at us with total bewilderment, having wandered up the side of the hill about fifteen feet away. He had dark circles under his eyes which I later learnt are the distinguishing feature of the Peruvian spectacled bear. My surprise was all the greater because, despite Paddington, I had forgotten that there were bears in Peru at all.

The bear blundered away, doubtless surprised at finding us. Pre-Incaic sites are rarely visited, lacking the glamour of the full Inca fortresses. The remains of Unuyoc's walls were thinner than, say, Llactapata and the stonework less impressive. Yet such sites were a useful reminder of the precursors of the Incas. The Inca Empire had grown up rapidly on the back of countless others, many of which, like the Etruscans in Roman Europe, had been subsequently subsumed into their own history and architecture.

By the end of the day the clouds had set in again and we came down through the forests with the damp slowly rising in our nylon waterproofs. We told Tía about the bear and were alarmed to see one of her neighbours, Lucho, immediately head off with a battered shotgun.

Tía Ollas invited us in for a *trago* of rum on the Peruvian National day of Independence. We got talking about the land reforms that the village had seen over the previous decade. For centuries after the Spanish Conquest there had been a system in which certain landowners, the *hacendados*, had feudal rights over large estates, which they often abused. In the late 1960s the government had begun a limited process of land reform which had seen some of the more unpopular *hacendados* either got rid of or paid off by the government. The whole valley of Santa Teresa was now being run on a co-operative basis by an elected president, although Tía commented sharply that if this didn't work they'd just get the old *hacendado* back. But she felt they had a much better standard of living than they'd had before.

In their valley, the campaign to get rid of the local *hacendado*, a man called Ortiz, had been led by the schoolmaster, who had persuaded the various villages to rise up and throw him out of town.

Tía Ollas had a radio in her hut and could tune in to local messages from Quillabamba. It was on while we were talking and when they played the national anthem, the villagers solemnly stood up and the men placed their hats over their chests. This did not seem like fertile territory for the guerrillas of the Sendero Luminoso.

Lucho returned from his search disconsolate at not finding the bear. Despite being relieved at his failure, I gave him a tin of peaches to cheer him up. When I wandered down to wash the porridge bowl the next morning, Lucho greeted me at the watering-hole with a cup of precious fresh milk, in silence. After weeks of nothing but tinned Carnation, it tasted like mother's milk.

I had a pocket Shakespeare, and some lines from *Hamlet* stuck in my mind that night as I watched the moon rise over the mountains and the low mists hanging over the roofs of the village huts:

Hamlet: 'But this is wondrous strange.'
Horatio: 'And therefore as a stranger give it welcome.'

*

We left Rayanpata reluctantly. Indeed, Roddy and I were so sorry to depart that the others went on ahead while we ate a last meal of roast guinea pig with our various benefactors (the skin had a not unpleasant crisp quality, like chicken). It was already late in the afternoon by the time we got off. With the over-confidence of increased familiarity in the mountains (and too much beer), we decided to look for the abandoned Santa Helena silver mines on the way back. We soon lost our way and had a reminder of how quickly conditions could change at this altitude. The cumuli whipped in from the jungles to the east and, as it started to get both dark and windy, we could only just make out the proper path below us, separated by a steep drop over rocks.

We tried to scramble down and quickly realised that this was a bad idea. The scree of the rocks started to give way in the half-light, and we took off our heavy-framed backpacks as the forks kept catching whenever we slid down. Roddy was ahead to one side when I stumbled and fell awkwardly against a boulder, momentarily winding myself. My backpack took on a life of its own and lurched away from me, carrying on to fall some hundred feet down the slope, bouncing against the rocks, with a sound of crunched metal each time the tin pots that were strapped to it crashed against the stone.

In the half-light Roddy couldn't see if I was still attached and started to shout for me. It took a moment before I could get my breath back and reassure him. We found a dried-up stream-bed and managed to pick our way down to the pack, which had unbuckled as it fell and had distributed various of my possessions over the mountain. The orange sleeping bag had burst open like a split body. Disconcertingly, there was an odd buzzing coming from the pack like a rescue helicopter – my little electric razor had switched itself on in the fall.

Battered, we struggled on to the camp at Colcapampa, picking out the path with our head-torches. Worse was to come. In Roddy's own struggles down the rock-face, the tent-frame had fallen off the back of his pack and so we had no way of putting the tent up. Others took us in and I was soothed to sleep by Vaughan as he told me of the various insects he had spotted in my absence.

It was time to leave the main party and strike out on our own for Choquequirao. J.B. had done some more masterly negotiations while waiting for us and we had as many rations as we could manage, although limited by having only two *arrieros* (muleteers) to help us carry them. There was an experienced local guide in the village called Washington Delgado, a man with charismatic eyes and the owner of various pack animals. He decided to send his young son Willie with us, as a blooding for him, and another muleteer called Claudio.

Willie was an extremely self-assured eighteen-year-old. He brought with him his father's white horse (it was never clear if we were entitled to ride the horse as well, even though we were certainly paying for it) and an instinctive feel for the difficult terrain we were going to travel through, despite never having been there before.

When the Comte de Sartiges had first made this journey in 1834, he and his men were forced to burn the brushwood ahead of them in order to make their way through what he described as 'some of the most magnificent scenery in the Americas, but a path that was *détestable*'. The rock was worn away in many places and destroyed by landslides while 'the water which filters up through the granite makes the steps of the mountainous ascents shine like ice'. Sartiges built rope bridges to cross the chasms, and suffered the attentions of mosquitoes: 'I do not believe that man could ever live in this valley, however fertile it is, because of the voracious mosquitoes that have taken possession of it. It was impossible to breathe, drink or eat without absorbing large quantities of these insufferable creatures.' One of his men went over a cliff with a mule. The team drank rum morning and night to keep out the cold.

We were under no illusion about the hardships of the twelve-day journey that lay ahead of us. A perpetual disappointment for the explorer is that jungle paths, once cut, quickly revert back to shrub for the next expedition, and we knew that few had ever come this way since the Count.

But we were also as fit as we were ever going to be and were diet-hardened to the porridge, potatoes and tinned tuna that was probably all we were going to eat over the next fortnight. The luxuries of the Army compo packs had long since been truffle-hunted.

Then I made a chance discovery. The little shack in Colcapampa sold the usual array of subsistence goods that we had been surviving on for weeks. However, something caught my eye, high up on a shelf above the cans of Peruvian tuna fish.

Before we had set off on our expedition we had, as most explorers do, looked for sponsorship. Tate & Lyle had unexpectedly donated us a full crate of their Golden Syrup. As the excess baggage on this alone would have been enough to swallow half our available budget, we had sold it 'off a lorry' to a local catering concern near the North End Road and forgotten all about it.

But here on the top shelf was the unmistakable green-and-gold label of Mr Tate and Mr Lyle, on a tin covered in dust and chicken feathers. The Señora brought it down for me. The seal was broken and the top had been opened, with about a spoonful of syrup taken out, but to all intents and purposes it was a full tin. Apparently a previous expedition had left it there many years before as a barter for potatoes and eggs, and the locals had decided, after one tasting, that they'd made a poor deal.

We tried to conceal our eagerness as we bargained for it ourselves. It quickly became the high point of each day, something to look forward to as we hacked at the undergrowth and plodded along behind the flatulent mules, while our proper supplies of food inexorably ran out and the packs became perversely heavier: the moment when we could each measure out a spoonful of the syrup onto a digestive biscuit, watched carefully by the others, and lie back on the grass to enjoy every honey-soaked crumb.

The first few days were relatively easy. We climbed high up towards the Yanama pass and I sympathised with Willie on discovering that he too was experiencing bad toothache (although mine was finally abating). I bought eggs and an *arroba* of potatoes at the last small-holding near Totora.

We camped just beneath the Yanama pass and struck off early the next day to get over it before the heat came up. It was, to use J.B.'s phrase, 'a bugger of a pass' which seemed to recede further every time you came over a lip towards it. My altimeter had broken in the backpack's fall, so I no longer had a reliable way of knowing quite how well we were doing. But finally we were through to the wild country on the other side (a previous expedition the year before had been beaten back by snow at the top, so we were lucky).

A succession of almost magical days followed. Every night Claudio lit deft fires in the most unpromising of locations and we would reflect on our progress. As Willie had never been to Choquequirao before, he was, like us, guessing at the precise route.

Initially it was easy, for our path lay along a proper Inca-laid road, bringing us down in some style through wild country to a long, shallow valley, irradiated by distant splashes of waterfalls against the green. We saw some curious blue eggs lying in clumps out on the rocks, in the open, as if there were no natural predators for them.

In the first flush of victualling our own journey, we had fine meals of tinned meat and potatoes, or pasta and beans, all surprisingly good for one-pot cooking. The only culinary dispute that began to develop was over porridge. Roddy liked his thin and milky, I liked mine thick and J.B. didn't mind either way as long as it came fast. In the bitter cold of the Andean mornings after sleeping in our cramped tent, this was, as the counsellors say, ground for conflict.

At the small settlement of Yanama we again slept on a football pitch, this time belonging to the school. A quiet girl appeared out of nowhere, bearing potatoes, and we discovered from chatting to the locals that there was another back route from here towards Huancacalle and Vitcos, along narrow mule-tracks and over a high pass. Vitcos was the remote location of Chuquipalta, 'The White Rock', and of Manco Inca's death, a place that intrigued me increasingly as I heard more about it.

Less encouragingly, the locals thought the route over to Choquequirao was impassable in places. We climbed on anyway up towards the next ridge, making our way with considerable difficulty, and after several false detours came to some old mine-workings set into a path along the cliff-face – a path that would have looked like a picturesque set from *The Treasure of the Sierra Madre* if we had not had to walk along it. The path crumbled away in sheer drops at several places, and Willie and Claudio blindfolded the horse and mule to lead them across.

When we came over the next pass, the San Juan, we could see the Apurímac itself, often described as the most magnificent river in the Americas. The name Apurímac means 'the Great Roarer', and this was one of its most impressive stretches as it cut savagely indented canyons in great serpentine arcs through the mountains. With its beginnings deep in the Andes, the Apurímac was thought to be the furthermost source of the Amazon. There were condors close over the pass, one a young bird with the lack of white plumage that showed it to be still undeveloped. The fringed wings of the condors looked gaudy, like the tassels on a moccasin jacket, and they had surprisingly stubby bodies between the huge gossamer expanses. The great birds were catching the thermals up from the valley and doing so in such an elegant way that it was easy to forget that they were essentially glorified vultures, feeding on carrion.

On the other side of the pass there were more mine-workings and some of these seemed to be still operational. Even though there were some hours of light left, we decided to stop early and camp near one of the shafts where there was a useful source of water, as there might be none below. This gave us the chance to have a leisurely fry-up of potatoes. By now we were ready to write the cookbook on 101 things to do with a Peruvian potato and had learnt to identify the six principal different types, from the floury and disintegrating *hariñoso* to the bullet-hard ones that came from the higher ground. The most unusual and, arguably, inedible were the freeze-dried potatoes, the *moraya*, which sustained Andeans through the lean months and which bore the same relationship to their parent potato as the raisin to the grape. Roddy tried to soak his in alcohol to improve the flavour, but they would have defeated an Elizabeth David.

That night we had a full moonrise, the moon lighting up little clouds like powder-snow before it took off from the ridge above us.

A man appeared at the camp-fire and introduced himself as the superintendent of the last lead and silver mine that was still working. We shared some whisky with him. He complained a lot about the local Quechua co-operatives, saying that they had no commercial initiative and only provided for themselves. It was certainly true that the locals didn't have a grain of greed or commercial instinct about them, in a way that I found very attractive: they gave us food without a second thought, and we had to force gifts back on them. It was equally noticeable how avidly the superintendent stuck into our own precious supplies of whisky.

Roddy came up with a delightfully daft hypothesis to explain why the names of all mining communities (Yukon, Yellowhead and now Yanama) begin with a 'Y' – that this might be because they would then come last in the dictionary and throw any other prospectors off the scent. At 10,000 feet and after a couple of whiskies, the theory made perfect sense, and when we explained it to the superintendent he nodded in approval.

When I came back this way many years later, I found the mines abandoned and an ore-cart hurled over the side of the mountain onto the slopes below. The Sendero Luminoso had passed through and closed them down in their usual brutal and total fashion.

On our descent the next day we found to our surprise that the path was really superb, a full Inca path that had been maintained by the miners and descended in tough but disciplined gradients. The Incas did seem capable of miraculous stretches of engineering when it came to mountains. The only other time I'd been so surprised by man's achievements at such altitudes was when travelling on the spectacular curved bridges and roads of the Italian Alps.

A full train of mules passed us as they made their way up to the mine. We had heard their bells tinkling from the depths of the valley long before we had seen them. It was the continued use of the mine which, in a gratifying way, had kept much more of the track open than we had expected, for even below the laid causeway the undergrowth had been trampled by the mules. But our way diverged. From here on the route became harder, and we had to get the machetes out, just as the clouds came up from the valley and enveloped us.

Once out of the cloud, we came to some of the most fabulous landscape we'd seen so far: rich purple flowers against the green of the *selva*, thick peppermint-striped red-and-white bamboo (one of which I cut to use as a switch on the mule), a huge flamboyant red orchid that the trees wore like a carnation, umbrella ferns, tiny shamrock-like flowers. Across a nameless small river, a tributary of the Apurímac, we saw our next day's journey, a stark ascent up a fierce ridge.

The country on this side of the great Apurímac/Urubamba watershed was even more savagely indented by canyons than the terrain on the other side. Coming down, we wandered through neck-high grass-reed that by annihilating our vision to a green shade made the whole trip seem even more dreamlike than normal, particularly when Willie led us to a camp-site that Jules Verne or Kipling would have enjoyed. With an enjoyable flourish, he slipped through a fissure in a seemingly impregnable ring of granite wall that emerged onto a small, perfectly formed plateau for camping, set near the river.

We forced ourselves to bathe in the water. The river was fast and freezing, and immersing the body totally under the tumbling glacial melt-water was like getting into a washing machine. I felt the way surfers do after battling a cold winter swell when they talk of 'an ice-cream head'.

J.B. had been grandly designated in the promotional literature for our expedition as 'Medical Officer', despite his complete lack of any quali-fications to be so (although he assured us that he had been on a first-aid course at school). However, it looked good – indeed, was probably essential – to have a Medical Officer on the letterhead, and J.B. looked the part; he even wore a striped shirt in the middle of the Andes. He also exuded a pragmatic confidence and a list-making ability that gave Roddy and me absolute confidence in his GP's bedside manner.

How wrong we were only unfolded as the trip to Choquequirao got tougher day by day. The Medical Officer's resources became increasingly strained. First we discovered that he'd forgotten the antihistamine. On a trip that took us on an etymologist's tour of the underbelly of insect life, this was a bit like not bothering to bring any water, and Roddy and I put it to him, sternly, that he should at least forfeit a few days' ration of our Tate and Lyle Golden Syrup as penance. Roddy's machine that imitated the whine of a male mosquito had thankfully run out of batteries. We were already scratching like monkeys.

But worse was to come. That night J.B. was cooking and decided to test the temperature of the soup with his medical thermometer. Roddy and I watched impassively with the feeling that he must know what he was doing even if we didn't. The thermometer broke and the mercury swirled around our few potatoes and tinned tomatoes. 'Do you have a spare?' asked Roddy in an Eeyore-like voice which presumed, correctly, that he didn't. 'Ah well, I suppose if we get ill we'll know about it anyway. Antibiotics all round, eh?'

'Actually,' said J.B., a little diffidently by his usual cheerful standards, 'I didn't bother to bring the antibiotics. Big glass bottle, weighed far too much. It's at camp. Left the Lomotil behind too. And the bandages.'

'Jesus Christ,' said Roddy with a heart-felt kick at the embers still glowing under our mercury-poisoned soup. 'We're in the middle of nowhere, at least a week from the nearest railhead, on a path that no one's travelled for hundreds of years – and you've left the antibiotics behind. What precisely are we going to do if we get ghardia or the shits? Did you by any chance,' and he paused to give his words maximum weight, 'bring any form of medical supplies at all?'

'Oh yes, there's plenty of aspirin,' said J.B. 'It's probably better,' he continued with breath-taking assurance, 'just to let any illness flush through the system anyway.'

That night we retired to bed early.

*

Claudio's cry of '*¡Mula! ¡Mula!, ¡Carajo!*' echoed up the hill as we struggled on the next morning. This was the worst section of the journey by far, virtually unpassable in places, and we often had to double back on our tracks. The canyon trapped the heat and all of us were drenched in sweat by late morning.

Claudio had told us that snakes usually bite the second walker in a group (on the grounds that while they might get irritated by the first passer-by, it's the second one that really makes them lose their patience), and this naturally caused a certain amount of jockeying for position as we cut through the undergrowth.

When we did come across a snake, we heard it long before it heard us. There was an unholy sound of hissing and thrashing undergrowth ahead and we rounded a turn in the path to see a skunk locked in mortal combat with a coral snake. Claudio killed both with his machete and the skunk's dying blast against the world stayed with me for the rest of the day, despite all the fragrant flowers we passed. I realised what the medieval writers had meant when they talked of the smell of sulphur in hell.

About one and a half hours up from the river, we found a ruin set back from the path, a site loosely called Espa Unuyoc by someone in Yanama on our return. This was not a site that the Comte de Sartiges had come across and we were not expecting it. There were at least six or seven layers of terraces, with many more stretching into the dense undergrowth, an irrigation canal and one particularly fine room which we set out to clear, with well-preserved doorways and recessed niches (Bingham liked to speculate whenever he saw a recessed niche that it must have been for mummies). We were excited by this and started to measure the site, discovering some intriguing features: a drinking fountain and also a little stone run-off to the actual canal which seemed to be designed as a drinking trough and could presumably have been stoppered and un-stoppered at will.

Because previous twentieth-century expeditions had always approached Choquequirao from the other side, across the Apurímac, no one had recorded this site and (although unaware of this at the time) we were the first to do so. Subsequent years well illustrated the problems that attend such Division B locations: no less than three later expeditions thought that they had discovered, or described, the same site first (the choice of verb is important and can reveal much about an expedition – while explorers will talk of an 'undiscovered' site, archaeologists like to talk of an 'undescribed' site). We were followed by a team of Cuzco explorers in 1985 – the so-called 'Cuzco Ramblers', whose genteel name belied their toughness and achievements – then by the American explorer Gary Ziegler in 1994 and finally by another expedition led by the architect Vincent Lee in 1995 – all of whom thought they were the first to find Espa Unuyoc (later renamed Pincha Unuyoc). Likewise, there may have been people before us who had passed through but had left no record.

There were some oddities in the masonry that we immediately noticed as being atypical – particularly the vertical stacking of stones near the principal gate, which was at odds with normal Inca practice.

After measuring the site, we climbed higher up and looked back to see clouds of smoke rising from the scrub above our camping-place by the river. We suspected Willie and Claudio, as they had lit a second fire after us. The fire seemed to be spreading across a substantial section of the slope, although contained by the walls of the river plateau. We watched gloomily. I thought of Donne's lines, 'And that this place may thoroughly be thought / True Paradise, I have the serpent brought.' We ate the last chocolate with our biscuits at lunch and tried to keep away the flies.

As if to punish us, the next section was very tough indeed. A hard slog up was followed by a vertiginous path skirting above the Apurímac: the river canyon was sometimes hidden by the dense undergrowth, but we could always hear it swirling thickly below. The vegetation changed with bewildering rapidity as we moved from wheat-coloured grass into a dense woody section that could have been a forgotten corner of England, with wood pigeons – *cuculas*, as Claudio called them – crashing out of the trees at our approach.

There was a lot of pushing through the undergrowth as we tried to hack a way for the pack-animals. Considerable damage was done to the baggage when the mule ran into low branches. My jacket got ripped by some vicious brambles. The problem with using machetes was that we were constantly at risk of cutting ourselves when undergrowth gave way unexpectedly and we got tired.

When we first saw Choquequirao, it was bathed in sunlight on its ridge, looking literally like a 'cradle of gold', its meaning in Quechua. It was late and there was no time to reach the ruins themselves, but as I gazed across at them a brilliant red-and-green woodpecker came into focus in the foreground, as if the lens had been pulled. A sheet of green went over us and for once we could properly see the parakeets we had heard so constantly above the trees or glimpsed in silhouette at a distance, flying against the sun or cloud.

That night was clear enough to view the Southern Cross again and we had a triumphant swig of Remy Martin to celebrate our coming.

*

One of the best things about arriving at the ruins was that we could finally sleep in late after days of early cold starts. By the time we wandered over to the site of Choquequirao itself, we were in holiday mood. To get there, we followed an endlessly long wall above which we could make out long terraces and the occasional stairway plunging up into the undergrowth – although some of the stairways had been blocked, for reasons I was to discover much later. The quality of the wall and the monumental size of the terraces indicated a major settlement. Choquequirao was often described as a 'sister-site' to Machu Picchu.

We came to the most visible set of ruins (it looked like there were many more below in the jungle): a long *kallanka* or meeting-hall dominating the side of a plaza, several more beyond and a great trapezoidal doorway leading through to what may have been a sacred enclosure on top of the ridge. It was satisfying to see perfect and well-preserved examples of the architecture that we had previously come across in a much more dilapidated state, even if much of it was still covered by the undergrowth.

Bestriding the mountain saddle, the city centre had a dramatic view down towards the Apurímac thousands of feet below, moving like a grey ribbon through the green as it began its long journey to join the distant Amazon. It was a most extraordinarily isolated site, and while theoretically useful as a look-out post for attacks from the north, it did not appear to have heavily fortified defences.

A large group of gabled buildings had prompted the Comte de Sartiges to think of Egyptian styles when he came here, and there was an ornateness that I had not previously associated with Inca architecture – a profusion of double-recessed doorways, for instance. However, it was not the buildings that intrigued me most about Choquequirao. Rather, it brought home to me a feeling that had been building up over the course of our explorations.

My impression, from having seen some of the hidden sites of the area, was that the Incas in the sixteenth century were a culture unusually obsessed with the beauty of mountains, in a way that European culture would only assimilate hundreds of years later. Why else build Choquequirao – and Machu Picchu itself, another site draped over the fold of a mountain – far from any convenient source of water and with only their superb views to recommend them? Why did they fetishise mountain rock, elaborately carving into it to draw attention to the natural landscape on either side? Why do the Incas' accounts of their origins go out of their way to attest to a symbolic birth in the mountains, rather than in the lakes and gardens of almost every other ancient culture's mythology, both Mesoamerican and Caucasian?

Yet the way in which the Inca sites were located to maximise the mountain setting ('view' seems too tame a word) had been virtually ignored as incidental by those seeking to explain such sites. Archaeologists and explorers may have failed to appreciate the primacy that the Incas gave to mountain aesthetics, for a number of complex reasons.

One was to do with the history of our own appreciation of such landscape, acquired long after the Spanish Conquest of Peru. In the sixteenth century, when Pizarro arrived, Europeans still regarded mountain landscapes as savage wilderness and the Inca attitude towards them would certainly not have been understood. Given that almost all our primary sources for what we know of the Incas are filtered through contemporary European sensibilities (including that of the Inca Garcilaso de la Vega, who wrote a classic account of his ancestors after many years of living in Europe, and seasoned it to please a Spanish palate), there was no reason for an Inca cult of the mountain to be either noted or understood.

Only in the late eighteenth century, with Burke and his theory of the sublime, Wordsworth and his mountains, Rousseau and his thoughts on Nature, did any sense of the romantic appeal of such wilderness areas begin in Europe. But having discovered such a sensibility ourselves, there has always been a reluctance to ascribe it to any other culture, let alone one which might have come to it before us. This and an equal reluctance by the modern anthropological and archaeological disciplines to allow any explanation of different cultures other than a strictly functional or religious one seem to have been powerful impediments to a clear assessment of the Inca sensibility.

It seemed an odd vestige of cultural patronage, as blinkered as the original missionaries who could not recognise the validity of any religious convictions they had not themselves arrived at. Why should we be privileged to appreciate a mountain setting and assume that the Incas could not? Why should the buildings have strictly functional or religious purposes, any more than all buildings in Europe did? From the comparatively little we know of the Incas, theirs seems to have been a culture which worked precisely by not being strictly functional.

We went further down the ridge with Claudio, where we found a small two-roomed building with an outer rampart. Roddy, with his neophyte enthusiasm for Inca architecture, pointed out that the features of the building were neither classic Inca nor for that matter particularly distinguished, but it further confirmed my thoughts, as it had the finest position of almost any building I'd seen in any set of mountains, with a magnificent view down both sides of the ridge to the river.

Roddy and I walked on down the ridge as it became a razor's edge and perched successively on the most eyrie-like position of all as we took photos. It was like sitting in a crow's nest: the river seemed to run right around the vertical pinnacle of the rock we were sitting on.

I felt completely cleansed, a marvellous pure mountain feeling, in the middle of nowhere with only the euphonious river twisting its course thousands of feet below. I noted in my diary 'a feeling of rare and elusive empathy with the Incas, mountain people who pick the most spectacular and difficult of refuges'.

Perhaps the ideal explorers to the area would have been Wordsworth and Coleridge. If Coleridge's scheme for a Pantisocratic society in North

America had been transplanted into a similar scheme for Peru (hardly less fanciful), would we have a 'Lines written above Choquequirao' which, like Wordsworth's poem on Tintern Abbey, managed to ignore the buildings completely and just concentrated on the setting, 'these steep and lofty cliffs, / That on a wild secluded scene impress / Thoughts of more deep seclusion.' Certainly it was the Romantic impulse that brought early nineteenth-century French explorers like the Comte de Sartiges and Léonce Angrand here, weaned on Humboldt's stirring tales of the Americas and their infinite possibilities. Wordsworth's lines about the 'still, sad music of humanity' echoed with me as I squatted high above the Apurímac by the lonely set of deserted buildings.

Señor Lucas Coborubias, the aged caretaker of the ruins, came up from his hut to talk to us when he saw the smoke from our fire. We signed his book, which showed a trickle of visitors over the years. Lucas spoke only Quechua, so Willie translated, and it emerged that Lucas had been at Choquequirao as a young boy when Hiram Bingham first arrived in 1909. Looking at his face, it was conceivably true. Little had been done at the site since Bingham's visit and it had never been properly excavated.

There were many questions to ask about the place. Had the Spanish ever discovered it? Certainly there were no references to it in their literature. Roddy and I had found shards of pottery everywhere, littering the ground in places. Were the ceramics colonial? And was this one of the places that the Incas had retreated to after the Spanish invasion? It was remote enough to deter any pursuit. For the while I was happy enough to stay in a state of what Keats described as 'negative capability', absorbing questions without trying to give answers.

That evening we had a salad of dried peaches and apple soaked in rum, reckless in its extravagance given that we had so little food to make the return journey, as J.B. pointed out. He was the most cautious of us, a necessary counterfoil to Roddy and my sudden enthusiasms, and a natural quartermaster. J.B. amused us by husbanding the toilet paper he'd wrapped his lunch with, just in case he needed to use it later; when supplies of paper did indeed run low, he had the last laugh.

Roddy spent hours trying to coax his potatoes into gourmet perfection over a spitting and smoking fire, much to Willy and Claudio's entertainment. They were relieved to have got here with so little rain, as this section of the Apurímac was notoriously wet even in the dry season. That night I woke to the sound of a heavy downpour and, remembering that we'd left the food out, screamed at everyone to help me cover it with the tarpaulin and the mule's blanket.

They say that for mountaineers going down is always tougher than the ascent, and certainly our own journey back felt harder, now that we no longer had the testosterone charge of getting to Choquequirao.

Conversationally, we had by now speculated about the love-lives of almost all those we had ever known, of many that we hadn't and certainly of all those back at the Cusichaca base-camp. We had wondered avariciously about the high starting salaries given to some graduates we knew who had become bankers, and were doubtless having three-course lunches at shareholders' expense in the City while we ate boiled potatoes. For one particularly strenuous climb, Roddy and I played a game in which we constructed the perfect wine cellar, giving ourselves generous sums to do so: he speculated in vintage claret, I in burgundies. When Roddy moved on to the comparative advantage of white madeira over port, as the butterflies swirled around and the air chattered with the intensity of a mountain forest, I began to feel I was hallucinating. Meanwhile the boiled water flavoured with Stereotabs went tepid in our water-bottles. Once all conversational diversions had been exhausted, there was nothing to think about but the unremitting load of the packs, the thorn-bushes whipping back into our faces and the endless farting of the mules.

When we camped again at the site by the river where the fire had been, the scorch marks traced back with sickening accuracy to our fire, not Willie's, as he was quick to point out. However, the damage to the surrounding vegetation was less severe than we had feared and I went for a swim in the icy water of the river for absolution.

Willie and Claudio worried that supplies were getting low. As morale plummeted, I got out the last 'luxury pack' I had brought from England – a small tin of truffle pâté which had sounded exotic when I had bought it but was now both dull and insubstantial. We had long since finished the Tate & Lyle Golden Syrup. My diary entry for one day's journey was terse: 'The food has become monotonous, we already know the route and the weather is bad.' The constant rain had started to soak through our grimy underwear.

By the time we arrived back at Yanama in the mist, the urge to explore had begun to fall away from us. We had said to David that we would make a detour to look for a possible pre-Inca site he had heard of above the schoolhouse, and we had left this for the return journey. Now our good intentions started to fade, particularly as, after a scramble up, there seemed to be nothing but an endless succession of sprawling cattle-pens. I felt my team slipping away as we discussed the merits of continuing to look.

David himself had been unable to get across the pass the previous year because of snow and I argued that we should at least try to do this for him, now that we were here. In the end I suggested the one lesson in leadership

I had learnt so far – that we stop for lunch. The cold potatoes and our last tin of sardines didn't get us far after a hard morning's walk, but in the meantime Roddy, who had gone to eat by himself and sulk, discovered the pre-Inca site just ten feet below us in the mist. Our earlier mistake was slightly less stupid than might appear, as the site consisted of the simple, low, double-bonded rings we had seen at Unuyoc and, as such, was easy to miss among the cattle walls. We became enthused again and shot off a roll of black-and-white film for David.

Willie and I then toured the Yanama huts trying to barter for potatoes and the odd egg. We were a good double act, as Willie's local connections could play off my novelty value, but we were sent ever higher up the valley by the stone-walling inhabitants. '*Manan kanchu*, there isn't any', was the constant Quechuan refrain. Normally I admired the way the Peruvian Indians would only sell a fraction of what they could – the reticence was appealing. But not now. The superintendent at the Vittoria mine had told us that the Yanama population were *difícil*, but this became infuriating. '*Esa gente son muy cerrados*,' said Willie, 'very "closed" people,' and I could not but agree. Even the local shop had nothing for us.

To make matters worse, one of the mules bolted, at least having the sense to go the right way up the valley, and Claudio disappeared after it. It took us a while to catch up with them. When we did, there was one of those little oases of surprise that Peru sometimes brings. The very last house in the valley, a small one, offered us not only potatoes, eggs and coffee, but some *chicharrones*, hunks of pork ribs. Apart from the odd tinned frankfurter, this was the first meat we'd had in weeks (indeed, since those memorable guinea pigs) and we fell on it with rapacity.

The image of that final night is imprinted on my memory: a strong fire guttering up out of the elaborate stone hearth that Claudio had been teaching me, with much comment on my slowness, to make at each campsite, clouds over the mountains to the north, drinking all of our whisky (as Willie pointed out, there was no point in returning with any) and endless mugs of sweet tea – finally going to bed drunk and happy in the knowledge that there would be an extra egg for breakfast the next day.

*

David was leaning against the doorway of Washington's house at Colcapampa when we returned, looking even more like a Hollywood leading man than usual and swigging on a bottle of beer. '*Buenos Días, Señor Hugo*,' he said with a deadpan expression. Ann Kendall was also there – she had come over from Cusichaca to see what progress had been made. A slight flicker of a smile showed that she thought the expedition had gone well.

The hot waters were a life-transforming moment. After the two-week-long expedition to Choquequirao and back it was hard to get my trousers off, let alone washed. The tough corduroy material had been ripped to pieces by thorns and rocks. I sat in my underpants, in the sun, eating fried-egg sandwiches and having as much hot coffee as I wanted. It was a wonderful feeling. Even the tins of Gloria condensed milk now looked appetising: how could I ever have looked at them with such indifference?

I had an awkward parting from Willie, whom I'd come to like over the journey, and I gave him all we could afford as an extra tip over the agreed amount. Then he asked for my watch as well. It was a Graham Greene moment, in which I felt all the anxieties of inequality, ultimately resolved by the fact that I needed the watch too much to give it away. This did not stop me from feeling guilty, or Willie from feeling aggrieved.

Striding back down the Santa Teresa valley, my pack felt light with the relief of having come through it all so well, and when I arrived at Miscabamba, where I had previously suffered the anguishes of a wisdom tooth, it seemed a different place. The one book I had taken to Choquequirao was a paperback of Robert Byron's *The Road to Oxiana* and I'd been struck by the pleasure he took in revisiting places: that often what was most interesting was not one's initial impression of a site but the contrast between that first impression and one's later growing understanding of it.

I thought of this as I passed Suriray the next day, our leaping-off point for Llactapata. Those ruins, with their surprising hidden sight-line of Machu Picchu, made more sense now that I'd seen Choquequirao. What the Incas seemed to enjoy was not just a view, but a revelatory view.

J.B. and I struck off from the others to investigate a strange report from a man called Andrés who was based near Miscabamba. He told us of a burial cave above the valley and when we got there, at a site called Larmapata, we did indeed find a shallow recess filled with human and animal bones. J.B. and I gingerly cleared a space to get down to work. It was an odd feeling to be sifting through the bones (skulls, a human foot, some vertebrae unstrung like a broken necklace across the cave floor) looking for the really important evidence – pieces of pot – which we were unable to find. The setting stayed with me, though, with the yellow-white bones on a ledge: 'Those are pearls that were his eyes.'

Afterwards we had lunch with Andrés, our informant. He had a small-holding of about 50 hectares sufficiently below the crucial altitude of 8000 feet to enable him to be self-supporting in maize, potatoes, carrots and avocados – he only needed the market for sugar, salt and oil. Andrés was the first person I'd met to be superstitious about old sites, telling us calmly that we were likely to be blasted by thunder and bitten by snakes for our intrusion into the cave. To show that he didn't hold this against us – indeed, he rather pitied us – he prepared a special dish of *cuy* (roast guinea pig).

By now we knew the procedure. First the children would round up the herd until they formed a circling wheel of fluff and fur in the middle of the hut. Then all faces would turn expectantly to us as, Caesar-like, we had to decree which should live and which should die. The decision made, execution was swift and the animals would be spitted over a roasting fire. It was enough to make you vegetarian for life, although the children accepted the ritual sacrifice of their pets with remarkable equanimity. Indeed, the guinea pig is a good example of the pragmatism at the heart of much Andean culture, in the way they serve not only as pets and useful vacuum cleaners around the floors of the huts, but ultimately as food.

Back at the Santa Teresa train station that night, we had to wait for the train which had been delayed downriver. As we sat in the sleazy café, with its Kenwood mixer in a glass case (Kenwood mixers were status symbols in the remote areas of Peru), drinking beer and listening to the rain and dogs outside, Ann Kendall started to talk at length. Up until then, I had hardly heard her utter two consecutive sentences, but the end-of-trip release and possibly the freedom of being away from her responsibilities at the main camp seemed to unburden her. For the next few hours she talked of the discoveries she was making, as outside the rain got worse and the dark set in.

Ann believed in the overriding importance of listening to local inhabitants when it came to investigating sites, an idea that might seem blindingly obvious but was often ignored. I have seen archaeologists jump out of their four-wheel drives, take detailed readings with compasses and altimeters, draw immaculately detailed site plans and then jump back into those same jeeps – without so much as a word to the people who live nearby.

She told a story about the famous rings at Moray, which lay not far upriver. A series of natural hollows in the mountains had been turned by the Incas and their predecessors into a stunning set of concentric terraces that disappeared into the earth below like some physical enactment of the circles of Dante's *Inferno*. Their purpose had puzzled observers for centuries. Studies had suggested one possible reason – that the night-time temperature for each layer of terrace dropped significantly as you went down. This had given rise to a number of hypotheses, the most elaborate being that the Incas had used it as a 'laboratory' to develop different varieties of maize for the extremes of climate found within their empire. It was still a familiar sight outside Quechuan huts to see a pile of corn in a heap of many colours, from the familiar creamy yellow sort to varieties speckled with red and brown kernels, and the jet-black *morada* corn used in a speciality *chicha* drink.

Ann had a simpler suggestion, derived from a local woman who had looked at her as if she was stupid when she asked the question. 'It's for freeze-drying *moraya* potatoes, of course – that's why it's called Moray.'

A drunk swung by the café, lurching towards us and demanding money. We ignored him. Ann continued, her low, quiet voice holding our concentration.

A decade of working on sites along the Urubamba and doing so in a way that kept her inside the community had given her a down-to-earth view of Inca life, especially its secular side. She rejected romantic theories such as Bingham's, who liked to describe Machu Picchu as a mysterious religious hideaway for the Virgins of the Sun.

Instead she described how Pachacuti Inca, the great initiator of Inca expansion out of their Cuzco base, had built the temple-fortress at Ollantaytambo when he had conquered this area, and how he and his successors had expanded their empire down the valley to build Machu Picchu. She speculated that rather than being a religious site, Machu Picchu, with its milder climate, would have made an ideal winter base for the Inca and his court, an attractive retreat from the cold of Cuzco. One of its purposes may also have been as a vast hunting lodge in what was an outstanding area for game – indeed, so outstanding that the area around Machu Picchu is now a protected sanctuary and has the unusual distinction of being a Unesco World Heritage site for both architecture and wildlife.

The idea of Machu Picchu and its surrounding area as a pleasure centre, built by either Pachacuti or his son Topa Inca, was a revelation to us, an idea that made sense of much of what we had seen, and particularly my feelings about the aesthetic supremacy of view and location.

Ann warmed to her theme, as we asked her about the significance of some of the paths we had taken. She speculated that the way the paths seemed to end abruptly on our first trek along the Mesada and Aobamba, which had so puzzled us, was completely consistent with a hunting path – once in the game area, there was no reason to proceed.

Patallacta, the site that Ann and her archaeologists were digging at Cusichaca, offered further evidence for this, as it seems to have been a service town for Machu Picchu, providing the city with crops which its own extraordinary position on top of a mountain made impossible to grow. Patallacta was not necessarily lived in by the Incas themselves but by client peoples, *gastarbeiters*, who may have been shipped in from another part of the Empire to do the job. The Incas, like Stalin and his treatment of the Cossacks, were fond of moving potentially difficult peoples to new, uninhabited areas.

We had to wait until midnight before the train arrived, so we hunkered down in sleeping bags on the platform, trying to ignore the fighting dogs and the sound of drunks bawling along to the tinny *huayno* music that was coming out of the radio. As the train then rattled up the valley through the tourist town of Aguas Calientes, where people stayed to visit Machu Picchu, the sleeping Indians hunched in ponchos along the carriages were lit up by the neon strobing from hotels and restaurants, and I reflected that in an odd way Machu Picchu had returned to its original function of resort town.

MACHU PICCHU

AND ITS BONES

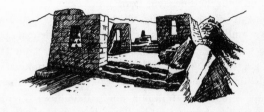

WE HAD DELIBERATELY NOT GONE to Machu Picchu before. Like teenage girls who didn't want to go all the way too soon, we had held back on the greatest and most celebrated of all the Inca ruins until we had immersed ourselves in the area and travelled to ruins that were far more inaccessible, like Choquequirao.

As it happened, we went up to Machu Picchu on 24 July, the exact anniversary of Hiram Bingham's own first ascent.

It remains the archetype of the perfect discovery. As Bingham tells it, they had no suspicion that such a ruin could be found until they met a local farmer, Melchor Arteaga, who told them when they arrived in the valley that there were some ruins on top of a hill. Bingham supposedly treated this bald statement with suspicion for, as he says elsewhere, 'in this country one can never tell whether such a report is worthy of credence'. Still more satisfying for the narrative, in the light of future events, none of his party were at all inclined to go with him, the naturalist remarking that 'there were more butterflies near the river'. So Bingham went up alone, leaving his American team behind, although, as with all explorers, this in practice still meant taking a local guide, Melchor Arteaga himself, and a Quechua translator, Sergeant Carrasco, loaned to him by the local Prefect.

Bingham describes the approach in a style worthy of Kipling or Rider Haggard. First, as he climbs up the hill, there is the ever-present possibility of lethal snakes, 'capable of making considerable springs when in pursuit of their prey' – not that he sees any. There is a sense of mounting discovery as he comes across great sweeps of terraces, then a mausoleum, followed by monumental staircases and finally the grand ceremonial buildings which make him realise that he has come to some of the greatest ruins in South

America: 'It seemed like an unbelievable dream ... the sight held me spellbound.'

He tells the story as a series of *coups de théâtre*, in which his new guide, a local boy (for after a while even Melchor loses interest and passes the job on), presents each succeeding revelation with a flourish: 'Suddenly, without any warning, under a huge overhanging ledge the boy showed me a cave beautifully lined with the finest cut stone.'

And climbing up ourselves, the site still had all the same qualities of dramatic revelation. No amount of tourists or picture postcards can spoil that first breath-taking view of a city almost casually draped over the shoulder of a mountain ridge, with the peak of Huayna Picchu dominating behind.

With Ann's idea of the city as winter quarters for the Inca, a country estate or leisure complex, fresh in our minds, I could see the picture before us as the perfect prospectus for the early Inca nobles: certainly a place where they would be queuing up to buy the condominiums.

Around us I could hear the tour guides handing out the usual guff, in which they painted a scene of endless 'Virgins of the Sun' carrying mummies in ceremonies, like some image from an old Cecil B. DeMille matinée movie. 'Now this,' said the earnest Peruvian girl in a Harvard sweatshirt as she gathered her group around her, 'was primarily a religious centre, a pilgrimage route from Cuzco. They would have come to see the Virgins of the Sun. And on this stone llamas were sacrificed, probably black ones, not white ones, as they were preferred ...' It was the detail about the colour of the llamas' skins that sounded so authoritative, and the tourists nodded as they continued on their way.

Certainly, the innate tendency to ascribe religious connotations to a site whose very dilapidation added to its air of spirituality was understandable, if dubious. I preferred to credit the Incas with an aesthetic which could appreciate Machu Picchu for the sheer pleasure both of its surroundings and its architectural beauty.

The Inca concept of religion was broad-based and can be thought of as a pyramid with three faces, all equally worshipped: the sun and the complex cosmology that surrounded it; the physical earth and the *huacas*, or shrines, that embodied it; the Incas' ancestors, rulers who had left estates and mummies to perpetuate their line and who gave the Inca people a sense of destiny. At the apex of this pyramid, neatly rising from each side, was the figure of the Sapa Inca, the 'Emperor', the direct descendant of those ancestors, the leader of worship at the shrines and the man who was himself worshipped as 'the son of the sun'.

While the Inca state was in some ways a theocratic one, it would be wrong to ascribe to the emperors a total and overriding belief in their own religion. Religion was a tool of state, much as it often was in Europe, and the Incas could as easily have declared that 'Paris was worth a mass' as any French king. The history of the Conquest attests to this. Atahualpa had not the slightest hesitation in offering – indeed, volunteering – to despoil the Coricancha, the Temple of the Sun in Cuzco, of all its gold in order to ransom himself. His nephews, when ruling their rump kingdom in the Vilcabamba after the Spanish victory, often toyed with conversion to Christianity as a part of the diplomatic game, and the very last Inca, Tupac Amaru, gave a famous speech before being executed in which he denounced his own and previous Incas' cynical use of the Punchao, the golden disc of the sun. These were not the actions of men who were slaves to their own religion, however much we would like to ascribe to the Incas a faith that we ourselves no longer possess.

What seems to have had a far more important position in Inca society (in a way analogous to the Roman Empire) was the primacy of the Inca's own pleasure. This was a society, famously and in an oft-retold story, where runners would come in relays of thousands of miles from the coast just so that the Emperor sitting in Cuzco could eat fish from the sea.

Machu Picchu was perfectly placed so that the Inca could enjoy the best of cuisines from both the high and low parts of his Empire: fruits and coca could be brought up from what is modern-day Quillabamba in the jungle, while corn and the more highland produce would be brought down the Inca Trail from Cusichaca. He would have had an excellent breakfast, after what could have been an excellent night.

The excessive and now disputed attention paid to the existence of so many female skeletons at the site has focused on the religious significance that their presumed status as the inappropriately labelled 'Virgins of the Sun' could give to the site. This ignores contemporary accounts that the function of the *mamaconas* and *acclas* was as much to provide the Inca's pleasure as to do religious duty (indeed, the two were indivisible).

One of Bingham's colleagues on his second expedition of 1912, George Eaton, was responsible for the myth that there were more female than male skeletons found at Machu Picchu, a myth that has proved almost impossible to eradicate in the face of the powerful images it conjures up. Eaton based his conclusions largely on an analysis of the skulls of those bodies he found, but gender differences are much smaller in the Andean head than the Caucasian and he therefore misattributed many of his skeletons (he had no prior experience of Andean physiognomy). Later work has been done on those same skeletons, concentrating on the more revealing pelvic structure, which showed that the proportion of the sexes was in fact roughly equal, as one might expect.

What the tour guides neglect to point out (and what may also have misled Eaton) is the fascinating cranial deformation that an examination of the skeletons reveals: it was common pan-Andean practice to bind the skulls of children, particularly those born to the nobility and priesthood, so as to achieve startling deformations of the head that were considered attractive and prestigious. Different Peruvian communities tended to do this in different ways (on the coast, for instance, the tendency was to elongate the skull upwards) and Machu Picchu must have presented a cosmopolitan picture to the visitor strolling on the central plaza: there would have been high-born representatives from all over the Inca Empire who had come to this gathering place of the winter court, many with just such deformed heads.

I liked to think that in the delightfully hypothetical instance of an extra-terrestrial having landed here, as the flakiest of the spiritual tour-guides liked to suggest, that alien would have sent back to his home planet a picture of a world inhabited largely by pointy-headed people. A doubtlessly irreversible stereotype of earthlings as 'pointy-heads' would have been born.

The actual range of cranial deformations was extraordinary, from elong-ated to flattened foreheads. While it seems that certain areas of the Empire tended to a particular style, there was also a certain amount of copying of cranial deformation as different provinces were exposed to each other's influence and to the metropolitan styles of Cuzco, much in the same way that a new haircut in Bristol, Manchester or Glasgow eventually reaches London.

I stood by the unfortunately named 'Funerary Rock', a magnificent rock sculpture the shape of which, as with so many of the stone-workings around the site, was obviously designed to reflect the mountains beyond. Looking down from this high point, the city was like a penthouse estate of the most breath-taking sort, with views off to Pumasillo in one direction as the Urubamba swirled around below in a spectacular curve of canyon that mimicked what we had seen at Choquequirao. It was not just impractical (there was not even a convenient water supply), it was ostentatiously impractical in the same magnificent way as Las Vegas in the desert, or modern-day Cancún with its ninety-three hotels built along a spit of sand.

It seems that the Incas built Machu Picchu on a virgin site, another pointer to a lack of spiritual significance, as pre-Columbian peoples often appropriated already existing religious centres. They certainly chose a building site that could more than satisfy their mountain aesthetic. From the saddle of the hill, there were overwhelming views of almost 360 degrees around the surrounding peaks and ruins. The clouds that hovered above these ranges (due to the close proximity of the Amazon) would occasionally part to spotlight a particular feature, and the continual play of light over Huayna Picchu's shoulder as the sun moved around the back of the mountain provided a set of changing pictures of Machu Picchu itself, like a Monet series.

It was virtually possible to mark the tripod sites around the ruins from where the tourists were all taking the same obligatory shots in wasteful replication: the view from where I was standing, by the Funerary Rock over the city to Huayna Picchu, was the first shot, the 'establisher'; then the cameras would be led to the Intihuatana, 'the hitching-post of the sun', one of the finest of all Inca sculptures, with the power and thought of a miniature submarine arising out of the earth. It stood above some of the most beautifully worked of all the Machu Picchu buildings, those of the Sacred Plaza, where huge ashlars were fitted to one another with the ease of tiles in a luxury bathroom (there was some evidence from buildings in Cuzco that the Incas had used llama grease to slide them together).

Sitting near the exquisitely curved wall of what was now called 'the Torreón' or 'the Bastion' (Bingham had fun naming every feature in the city), I was struck by the precision and playfulness of the water-system. The spring for Machu Picchu's water supply rose 800 yards away from the city and had to traverse the steep slopes of Mt Machu Picchu to get there. This in itself was an impressive enough engineering feat, given the gradients that the canal was fighting. When the water reached the city, there began an elaborate display of fountains that wound down 'The Longest Staircase' of the city, playfully showing off as the water cascaded and changed direction. Each fountain seemed to do a different trick with the way it channelled the water, like a course of crazy golf: some rounded the next basin from behind, or appeared at unexpected oblique angles to the next from hidden run-offs. The basins themselves were far too shallow to be of much practical use, although tour-guides liked to picture a line of Virgins of the Sun waiting to use them, as if it were a village wash-pump. There were sixteen of them, before the final run-off took the water down to the terraces below.

Roddy delighted in the cunning with which different channels could be easily diverted if an Inca noble or priest wanted relief from the noise. This was not a city designed purely for functionality. The sensuality of the fountains seemed closer to the Islamic culture of the Almohavids of Granada or the Red Fort of Delhi than the austerity usually ascribed to the Incas.

We had become interested in the canal system at Cusichaca where, under Ann Kendall's direction, long lines of canals had been successfully restored as irrigation systems for the agricultural terraces. But at Machu Picchu there seemed to be no additional irrigation for the terraces (relatively small in area, they relied on rainfall) and the Incaic skill at hydraulic engineering could be applied solely to providing drinking water in a self-gratifying way that any American shopping mall would have been proud of.

The small extent of the terraces also seemed to support the view that this was a town devoted to pleasure, not work. With only ten acres of agricultural land available on the narrow ridges at the top of the mountain, most foodstuffs would have had to be brought in, with perhaps some luxury crops like herbs, flowers and peppers grown on the terraces themselves: coca was certainly grown in the valley below Machu Picchu and possibly even on the high terraces as well, although the exposure would be quite severe for the plant. The terraces were deceptive: the casual visitor might presume them all to be for crops, but many may have had a more functional role as supporting buttresses for the city at the top of the vertiginous slopes. They certainly fitted with the idea that Machu Picchu was used for only a short season each year when the weather in Cuzco was bitterly cold.

It was unlikely anyway that the city could have supported more than a thousand people at any one time: what was striking (and why Machu Picchu was always referred to as a city and not the village that such a population might indicate) was how well housed so many of them would have been, for the finely worked granite homes extended far beyond what Bingham dubbed 'the King's Quarters'. This was a place for nobles and their households, not the common man. Given the considerable restrictions on free travel within the Inca Empire, very few of the Incas' proletarian subjects would ever have seen the city, or even known of its existence. This might explain the total silence about it by the time the Spanish arrived in 1532. If there had been any substantial religious significance to Machu Picchu, let alone if it had been a place of pilgrimage, the city could never have been so forgotten.

But the idea of Machu Picchu as a pleasure centre did not exclude a further role, and there would doubtless have been a religious side to the site as well, just as Versailles always had its chapel. The Inca would have been expected to continue with the rituals that marked the life of his subjects wherever he was, and there were plenty of ceremonial buildings at Machu Picchu for him to be able to do just that, many of them aligned on some of the peaks that the Incas held sacred.

There were also fine gates and walls encircling the city, although these may have been as much for ostentation as defence, like a Victorian mock-Gothic castle. The expedition led by Paul Fejos in 1940 had concluded that the role of Machu Picchu and its attendant sites was not primarily defensive, although this did not mean that there was no military role at all. The emperors, and particularly Pachacuti, would have been particularly aware of the threat from the Chanca in the north-west across the Apurímac, as it was just such an attack which had almost destroyed the Incas at the start of his reign. It would have been foolhardy to allow any ambush from that direction.

Having been to Llactapata, so clearly positioned as a connecting look-out post for Machu Picchu, and given the network of sites nearby, it seemed evident to me that the city must have had a limited military purpose, if only for intelligence. Even if its fortifications were light compared to others in the Inca Empire, it could have served as part of the early warning system for Cuzco's own defences. There is one approach to Machu Picchu from the west which has a 'missing' section of path over a precipice that can only be crossed by a log, in effect acting as a drawbridge about a mile before the city (we were told that the path had been recently closed to visitors as a tourist had carelessly fallen down the precipice).

Treading carefully, we climbed instead up to the top of Huayna Picchu, the mountain behind the city, to see the little signal station on its top. One could easily imagine the lit beacons flashing from here as a message went to Llactapata and on hundreds of miles into Antisuyo, the North-eastern Quarter, or back to Intipunku, the site that was just visible on the next pass, to be relayed on to the Inca's regents in Cuzco, left in the cold of the plateau while the Emperor enjoyed his winter sun.

Sitting up there on the precipitous pinnacle, I felt that there was no reason why the various theories about Machu Picchu's purpose should be mutually exclusive. Why should we presume that the Incas were any less capable than us of a multi-purpose site which, like Rome, could combine military and religious functions with that of a pleasure centre?

The guides below were concentrating naturally on the buildings, many of which still had the fanciful names first given to them by Bingham: 'the Royal Mausoleum', 'the High Priest's House', even one called 'the House of the Princess', for which there was no conceivable evidence other than that it would have been a very nice house for a princess to have lived in.

It was not only the quality of individual examples of stone-masonry that amazed, but the quantity. If a single building in the sacred complex had survived, it would still be the finest example of Inca masonry in existence. To have a whole city of such buildings was a surfeit that few could digest.

Just as at the start of my journey, in Sacsahuaman, what struck me was not so much the strength with which huge stones were dry-mortared together, impressive as this was, but some of the finer, more oblique work that had been done around the edges. The way in which the Incas had taken raw boulders of granite, sculpted into that granite and then, in some instances, built an extension to that natural stone reached its apogee with the area under the Torreón, in what Bingham dubbed 'the Royal

Mausoleum': this, in European terms, would technically have been called a grotto, but it bore the same relationship to the domesticated kitsch of Neuschwanstein Castle as an Alessi kettle to a plastic one. It was, to use an over-worked term, a masterpiece. On one side the natural rock cut savagely into the hill, but on the other the Quechuan stone-masons had crafted a series of steps, curves and impossibly angled masonry that fashioned the space in a unique way. The effect was to make the cave feel like a receptacle of pure sensation. John Hemming had already described it for me: 'a hollow sculpture of great beauty, three-dimensional and plastic, with strange shadows and a deep sense of religious mystery'.

I sat in the evening sun, by the Intihuatana stone, and looked at the city. I thought of Pablo Neruda's description of it as the '*alto arrecife de la aurora humana*', 'the high reef of the human dawn', where 'the mother of stone and the sperm of condors' met. His poem '*Las Alturas de Macchu Picchu*' ('The Heights of Machu Picchu') was partly an elegy for the poor, bloody infantrymen of the Inca world who had been forced to struggle up the hill to build this monument, whatever its purpose.

In the poem, Neruda had thought more of these slaves than of the stonework, however grand; he had invoked Juan Splitstones, Juan Coldbelly and Juan Barefoot, the anonymous serfs of such architecture, sleeping with their mouths open, half-dead from exhaustion.

It seemed as if explorers and archaeologists had always been remarkably blind to such sentiments and, conversely, forgiving of the totalitarianism that had given them their finds, and which they could likewise turn into monuments to their own discoveries. Perhaps, I thought a little subversively, this was because they shared similar autocratic dispositions to such master races. Was their covert acceptance of draconian social policies (Bingham spoke of 'the benevolent despotism of the Incas') because the same despotism at least meant that the buildings had been finished for them, whatever the human cost? Napoleon is said to have admired the pyramids for similar reasons when he conquered Egypt.

I liked Neruda's attitude. When he visited Machu Picchu, an attendant coterie of Peruvian intellectuals had followed him around the site, with the sycophantic respect that Latin American poets often seemed to command. Coming to a particularly fine carved stone, the great man paused, as if lost in thought and contemplation. Finally one of the hangers-on dared to ask him what he was thinking about. 'You know,' said Neruda, 'this would make a wonderful place to lay out barbecue meats.'

It had also been a place of regeneration for Neruda, after a fallow patch in the thirties when his poetry, like that of Auden and some British poets, had become almost overwhelmed by the force of its own political rhetoric.

He remembered later that in 1943 at Machu Picchu he had found '*una profesion de fe para la continuación de mi canto*', 'a source of faith to help me continue with my song', and the resulting poem, '*Las Alturas de Macchu Picchu*', is often seen as the start of his poetic comeback.

I found some buildings that were completely ignored in the guidebook descriptions, the buildings that some of the same workers whom Pablo Neruda had described would have used. They had a simplicity that moved me as much as any of the grander monuments nearby: small, round structures of the sort we had seen on the way over to Choquequirao, only a few feet high and probably covered originally with a temporary roof from a central pole. Although not far from the majestic ceremonial buildings of the Sacred Plaza, they were easy to miss as they were virtually inside the jumble of excavated rock that served as a quarry for the city – the workers living on site, presumably on some sort of rota as they worked out their *mita* service.

Doubtless they would have laboured right through the hell of the wet season to get as much ready as possible for the arrival of the court each summer. I could imagine the sopping tent, the clouds drenching the workers as the quarry stone was worked with agonising slowness, and the meals of simple maize being ground on the large mortar-stones, with their circular depressions that could still be found in the centre of some of the huts. No wonder so many of the simple tombs of the worker-class that had been found nearby revealed bones with symptoms of malnutrition. To add a final insult, many of these same tombs had been bulldozed when a road was constructed up to the ruins in 1948.

*

Almost as soon as Bingham saw Machu Picchu, he began the ceaseless stream of hypotheses that have flowed ever since about its origins. The sheer audacity of the site encourages free-wheeling speculation. Even the normally sober John Hemming seems to have had a rush of blood to the head when confronted by it. He speculated that one set of buildings might have been the prisons for the complex, while the vaults and basement below could have been 'the subterranean buildings that once held dangerous beasts' such as snakes, pumas and bears to which the prisoners would be fed alive.

What was so attractive about Machu Picchu was that this theory could be both irrefutable and unsubstantiated at the same time, could even co-exist in the imagination with Bingham's explanation for precisely the same building, that it contained niches in which mummies could be kept and venerated (having been reared as a boy on tales of Egyptology, Bingham was obsessed by the idea of mummies). The place was a blank canvas on which explorers could superimpose their pet theories.

Hemming had noticed a curious feature of one of Machu Picchu's most famous buildings, the Temple of the Three Windows, and it was one which particularly intrigued Roddy and me. The windows were trapezoidal, as we by now had come to expect, but the corners were rounded and the sides just slightly curved to widen the perspective of the view. The effect was to frame the landscape of the Urubamba beyond as if it was a sequence in a story.

Bingham had wondered, from the evidence of this same building, whether this could have been the birthplace of the very first Inca, Manco the Great, who, according to legend, had ordered such a set of three windows to be built at the place of his birth. This would have made Machu Picchu an early site. But at the same time, Bingham was reluctant to let this get in the way of his determination to find Old Vilcabamba, the 'last city of the Incas' to which they had retreated when on the run from the Spanish, and he proceeded with some tortuous theorising to try to confirm this. As late as 1948, almost forty years after his original discovery, he was still asserting, with revealing over-emphasis, that 'no one now disputes that this was the site of ancient Vilcapampa.'

No one now would dispute that he was wrong. Sadly, his vision of the site as both the cradle and the grave of the Inca civilisation, while a magnificent one, doesn't hold up. The last city of the Incas, 'Old Vilcabamba', actually lies a hundred miles away in the depths of the jungle. Every available architectural indicator shows Machu Picchu to have been built at the time of Pachacuti (c. 1438–71), during the expansion of the Empire, and so at the midpoint of their brief history. What has more credibility is the idea that a three-windowed building of such prominence (designed to dominate the central plaza below) may have been intended to resonate with that same myth about Manco the Great.

One further question that has continually perplexed visitors, historians and archaeologists alike is why the site seems to have been abandoned before the Spanish Conquest. (The over-used joke among the tourists around the site was that it must have been due to the midges.) Here the argument for Machu Picchu as a *moya*, a place of relaxation for the Emperor, is particularly strong. It is hard to credit the idea that the Incas would simply abandon a religious site, given their steadfast use of religion as an instrument of the State. Likewise, if it was primarily defensive, any perceived threat from the north would certainly not have abated after Pachacuti. But it would have been far easier to leave a pleasure centre that no longer suited the needs or desires of his descendants, who perhaps felt that as a gigantic hunting folly it was both too impractical and ostentatious, a huge old country house that required enormous upkeep to run.

Machu Picchu may have been the Biarritz or Brighton of its day, a pleasure resort built on the grand scale at the height of Empire and then left to fade away as royal tastes changed and fashion moved on.

*

Seeing Machu Picchu had made me question the nature of its discovery, given our own previous experience of looking for ruins. Back at the Cusichaca camp, I returned to Bingham's account, reading it with mounting suspicion now that I had travelled so closely over the ground he described.

Bingham's story of how he found Machu Picchu, as he recounted it in the evocatively titled *Lost City of the Incas*, had great appeal, an appeal which had led to almost every guidebook quoting it as absolute fact ever since:

> For centuries travellers could not visit it ... the Grand Canyon of the Urubamba, where Machu Picchu is ... because a sheer granite precipice, rising 2000 feet from the banks of the river, defied all efforts to pass it. The planters who raised coca and sugar in the lower valley could bring their produce to market only over a snow-covered pass as high as Pike's Peak (14,109 feet). Finally they persuaded the Peruvian government to open a river road by blasting it across the face of the great granite precipice. They had been using it for several years without being aware that on top of a steep ridge 2000 feet above them were the ruins of a great Inca sanctuary.

He goes on to say that

> Raimondi, greatest of Peruvian explorers, was ignorant of them [the ruins], as was Paz Soldan, although their existence had been rumoured in 1875. Charles Wiener, an energetic French explorer, had looked for them without success. They had been visited by several energetic *mestizos* [half-castes] and a few Indians. Quite a number of ambitious treasure-hunters had tried to find the last Inca capital. The new roads made possible the discoveries of the Peruvian Expeditions which are herein described.

The whole paragraph is full of the most disingenuous reinvention. The seductive idea that only the new road had opened up the area to travellers does not stand up to much scrutiny – if planters could manage a pass at 14,000 feet, not much by Andean standards, so too could any of the hardy travellers who preceded Bingham – and indeed he goes on to list some of them. But here again he angles his account to point up his own achievements at the expense of any predecessors. He fails to point out that even though Raimondi never went there, he had placed a '*Cerro Machu Picchu*' on his map, in approximately the right place – a map which Bingham elsewhere reveals he had with him. After the delightfully vague 'their existence had been rumoured in 1875', he then neglects to mention that Wiener had specifically mentioned the names of the sites (Machu Picchu and Huayna Picchu) in the following year – and clearly said that there were ruins to be found there. The actual visits by various Peruvians are artfully conflated with the attempted visits of 'a number of ambitious treasure-hunters'.

Most invidious of all is the way the earlier Peruvian visits are passed off as having been by 'several *mestizos* [half-castes] and a few Indians', a phrase which could probably have applied, if pejoratively, to any group of Peruvian discoverers. Don Enrique Palma of Cuzco had visited the site in 1902, ten years before Bingham, and left an inscription on a wall commemorating it, while in 1911 a local landowner had written to the Cuzco archaeologist Dr Alberto Giesecke (who was himself originally from the States) telling him of Machu Picchu and inviting him to visit the ruins. Giesecke passed this intelligence on to Bingham himself, as evidence for the sites. Bingham's response was constantly to denigrate 'the academics of Cuzco' in his book, something I had always thought curious until I discovered the background.

Bingham knew of the ruin long before he met Melchor Arteaga. When he went down a route now made easier for him by the cutting of the famous new road, he went, like us, to look for a ruin that had already been found. His achievement – and it was a considerable one – was in publicising that discovery and his many later finds. I had noticed that the authorities at Machu Picchu had come up with a particularly tactful euphemism to gloss over any discrepancies in Bingham's account: he was described on a plaque as being 'the scientific discoverer' of the site.

The notion of discovery is a fluid concept. The question of Columbus' arrival in America has focused minds on all the potential incongruities. With South American ruins, rather like ideas in Hollywood, credit goes not to those who discover them first, but to those who succeed in putting them on screen. As one Peruvian commentator wryly put it: 'Dr Bingham discovered Machu Picchu and made it known to the whole world, just as many others had discovered it for their own pleasure.'

Bingham's character had much to do with it. He was born in Honolulu, from a well-known line of American missionaries, from whom he inherited an evangelical flair that mixed passion with a touch of hucksterism. I liked to think of him surfing the Waikiki break off Honolulu (then a celebrated wave, now curtailed by alterations to the harbour into a tame affair for tourists). He learnt his love of mountains from his father, who took him up some of the Hawaiian volcanoes, and Bingham was fond later of comparing some stretches of the Urubamba valley to the islands of his birth.

He must have stood out at Yale as a showman amongst the solid law-students and future bankers, who clearly admired him enough to back his expedition later. Bingham describes with characteristic forthrightness how he obtained their support at a 1910 class dinner in Yale: 'I was called upon for a speech. Naturally I spoke of what was on my mind.' What was on his mind was to launch an expedition not only to look for the lost capital of the Incas, enough for most men, but at the same time to make a complete cross-section of Peru from Urubamba to the Pacific along the seventy-third meridian, uncharted and wild territory. Along the way, presumably to provide diversion, he proposed to climb Mt Coropuna, which he thought (erroneously) to be the highest mountain in the Americas.

The only book of his still in print was *Lost City of the Incas*, which he wrote in 1948 when he was seventy-three, almost forty years after the events he was recording. A certain amount of self-aggrandising and retrospective legitimising was therefore perhaps inevitable. However, it was impossible not to forgive a man whose 'breath was taken away' by his own discoveries on such a regular basis.

There seemed to be some curious time-delay at work in general among the chronicles of South American adventures: Garcilaso de la Vega, the best-known chronicler of the Incas, had been in Europe for forty years before he wrote his account of the civilisation he had left behind; Pedro Pizarro wrote his memoirs of the Conquest of Peru as an old man; similarly, the great chronicler of the Mexican campaign, Bernal Diaz, had only recorded his eyewitness account of that parallel conquest some fifty years after the event.

Was there something that made the continent peculiarly difficult to assimilate in the present tense? Did it carry a sensory overload which could be best interpreted only years later, when the glitter and noise had fallen away to reveal structure underneath? Many of Gabriel García Márquez's novels depend on just such an almost optical effect in which events of the distant past are foreshortened and looked at with startling clarity. W. H. Hudson's classic memoir of Argentina, *Far Away and Long Ago*, also relies on the passage of time between the writing and the remembered events for its nostalgic power. Or was there a simpler explanation – that young men inclined to go out into the jungle are equally disinclined to sit down at the desk and write about it immediately afterwards?

Years later, in Amsterdam's Rijksmuseum, I saw a seventeenth-century picture by the Dutchman Frans Post which had a powerful fascination for me. It was a picture of Brazil, then a partially Dutch colony, and showed the buildings at Olinda in their surrounding countryside.

What intrigued me about the picture was that it was painted a full eighteen years after the painter's return to Holland from Brazil. And yet, despite some liberties taken with geography (Post had transposed the beautiful and still-standing monastery at Iguazu, in reality some twenty miles away, so that it could nestle into the same landscape as Olinda), it remains one of the most powerful portraits of the continent.

Heavy clumps of white clouds break up both the sky and the ground, so that the shadowy and shrubby foreground contends with a brightly lit temple, and there is a sense of the landscape as an infinite and unyielding recession. The only human figures are distant and completely overcome by the land, as seems appropriate on a continent where man has at best often only managed to scratch a presence.

In the foreground are a few animals lying replete with either heat, illness or a languorous self-satisfaction. The animals feel allegorical and the whole picture could be taken as a commentary on the memory of travel and on travel-writing: experience recollected later in tranquillity, with not too much attention to factual detail but much to atmosphere and the sense of a different, slightly unreal world that does not work to our rules. It mocks the notion that travel-writing should replace the photo-journalist.

Bingham realised this. He wrote his book for a public who knew what they wanted from an epic of South American adventure and he made sure that he gave it to them. In the same year that Bingham excavated Machu Picchu, Conan Doyle published *The Lost World*, with its ringing declaration that 'the more you knew of South America, the more you would understand that anything was possible – anything'. Bingham's writing plays to this. There are plenty of waterfalls, misty mountains and narrow rope-bridges. Some nicely turned literary effects ensure the constant presence of potential danger (like the snakes with the lethal spring he had speculated about as he went up to Machu Picchu but never in fact encountered). Enjoying the view from a mountain,

> we were discovered by a huge condor, who proceeded to investigate the invaders of his domain. Apparently without moving a muscle, he sailed gracefully down in ever narrowing circles until we could see clearly not only his cruel beak and great talons, but even the whites of his eyes. We had no guns and not even a club with which to resist his attack. It was an awe-inspiring moment, for he measured about twelve feet from tip to tip of wing. He finally decided not to disturb us....

The 'finally' is masterful. The likelihood of a condor really attacking, unless its young were being actively threatened, is almost non-existent.

Yet Bingham could be likeably honest as well, admitting at one point to be far too out of condition to manage a 6000-feet climb, and without pretence to any great archaeological knowledge – an admission the archaeologists have patronised him for ever since. His energy propelled him through the Urubamba in a rolling maul of enthusiasm and sheer drive which more circumspect academics would never have managed. He opened up the Urubamba far more than any road.

*

Weeks passed as we continued to explore the area, using the Cusichaca camp as our base. Since that first nervous descent down the valley on our arrival, the Urubamba train had now become our regular lifeline to Cuzco for supplies and we knew each bend by heart. There were two trains a day along the valley, an 'up' train and a 'down' train, and they timetabled our daily life, for there was always something being brought or taken, if not by us then for us.

We would swing aboard it at Kilometre 88, with our stubble and ripped trousers, giving scant regard to the Machu Picchu tourists whom we, with all the arrogance in the world, thought of as 'day-trippers', although for all we knew they may have gained as much insight into Machu Picchu in a day as we could in weeks of looking.

I still dream of that train. I used to hang out of the door (you could travel on the roof for all anyone seemed to care) watching the terraces and mountains of the Urubamba slide by in the sun, as the vendors whisked endless delights past your nose: hunks of deep-fried pork (*chicharrones*), stuffed *tamales*, guinea pig, boiled corn with cheese, fruit, roasted nuts, once even a whole side of suckling pig that a hefty Quechuan woman cut open for customers with a machete. She splattered Roddy's shirt with the blood.

It was the perfect embodiment of a boy's dream of freedom: the little coloured train cutting through the valley, with its cow-catcher at the front, no rules, endless food, the wind in your hair and not even a timetable to remember. The train guards gave us commuter-status and we would get free coffee from the coffee-lady, while we ate sweet popcorn and *pastillas*. The vendors would ask after Señora Kendall's health, as Ann had become a well-known and popular figure in the valley.

One day I got on at Cusichaca, going upriver to Cuzco, and was surprised to find a tall figure with dyed blond hair sitting in the carriage, wearing an immaculate blue denim suit and clutching a small leather writer's briefcase. He looked out of place among the *campesinos* and the backpackers, an apparition – the blue denim suit was pressed as if he'd just stepped out of a Culture Club video or one of the New Romantic parties that had been sweeping London when I left.

Having acquired the Peruvian habit of immediate and inquisitive interrogation, I asked him what he was doing. It emerged that Marek was a London journalist for *The Face* and other style magazines. For unspecified reasons of his own, he had decided to head off to Peru – he had a line he kept repeating about how Paul Morley (at the time a cult music journalist on the same paper) had supposedly come here and got lost. Marek was acting in the Stanley character, travelling to see if he could come across the missing Livingstone. It was strange to be plunged back into the world of London record companies and media hype, and doubtless I was an equally curious spectacle for Marek. He couldn't get used to the way that I kept looking at my altimeter, not my watch, in order to know when we would arrive.

But in the way of travelling friendships (so attractive because there is no commitment on either side for friendship to continue beyond the next stop), we hit it off, and once in Cuzco we went to an Argentinian restaurant on the Plaza de Armas celebrated for the size of its steaks and the quantity of its chips. I had a large kebab of *anticuchos*, beef-hearts, as he plied me with rock-and-roll gossip and I held forth excitedly about the journeys we had made.

Food had started to become both an obsession and a problem. I was suffering from what I later discovered to be a common phenomenon for those who had spent a long time in the mountains – a form almost of bulimia in which sufferers would compensate for the long weeks of dried potatoes and tuna fish by stuffing themselves with every imaginable product once a city like Cuzco was reached.

I had already, after exhaustive research, discovered where the best chocolate cake could be obtained (a small Italian café produced one topped with a chestnut-and-coconut icing). Lunches would be spent in some little sun-filled *quinta* in San Blas, reflecting on the difficult choice between house specialities and having double helpings of *lúcuma* ice-cream (the jungle fruits were often at their best in desserts). And the Argentinian restaurant was becoming a regular in the evenings.

The inevitable consequences followed and I had to resort to cocktails of codeine phosphate and Imodium to get my stomach back on course. With bulimic addition I would then return to the fray.

No one would ever claim, however, that Peruvian cuisine was a particularly fine one. It relied too heavily on cheap meat and quick frying for that, with plenty of rice, potatoes and bread as starch. It was a favourite fantasy – what if the French or Italians had colonised South America? The food would almost certainly be better (I still remember the baguettes and fresh coffee I had in a little Senegalese village), and the church art less tortuously baroque, but the Spanish also had advantages as conquistadors. They were in the main the bastard sons of a tough country, coming from around Extremadura, an area that in its aridity and toughness can hardly be matched in Europe. It was good training for the Andes.

Take this description: 'a mountainous country, with imposing geography, dependent on its wealth for the extraction of minerals and with an under-developed agriculture and few other natural resources'. Peru? Of course it could be. But the writer (the American historian Irving A. Leonard) was in fact describing sixteenth-century Spain.

The Spanish also had one immense advantage over other Europeans: they brought with them a knowledge of the cultural tactics needed to confront another civilisation, a storybook of bold moves and brutal betrayals they had learnt from their wars with the Moors and with the Nahuatl of Mexico. Pizarro would never have seized Atahualpa in the main square of Cajamarca and thereby held a nation hostage if Cortés had not done precisely the same with Moctezuma in the previous decade.

I spent a restless night at the little hotel by the railway station, one of the cheapest in town and where the volunteers from Cusichaca generally stayed. By one o'clock in the morning the place would resemble a French farce as the Cusichaca revellers, fired up by pisco, would creep from bedroom to bedroom in order to carry out assignations that were too difficult or embarrassing under canvas back at the camp.

I had once read a short story by a young Argentinian writer, in which the protagonist becomes so irritated by a cock crowing every night that he finally goes down one dawn and strangles the offending bird with his bare hands – only to find the next night that he's killed the wrong cock. I not only had a similarly persistent crowing cockerel, but diarrhoea, a sagging mattress that itched in a suspicious way, the noise of trains from the nearby station and what sounded like two men completely demolishing a car under my window at three o'clock in the morning. When they finished, a processional band came by on the way to early mass before the market opened.

Even by the usual standards of Latin American noise pollution, where your ears were never alone (in the most remote of mountains there was usually a transistor somewhere), this was extreme. Then, as the first stall-holders set out their wares for the market, the *huayno* started.

Musical anthropologists may tell you that *huayno* music is a rich tradition from the sierra, but to those who have been over-exposed to it (particularly on cheap radios), it has an almost limitless capacity to grate on the nerves –

a thin, high voice over thin, high instruments, like country and western played at 78 r.p.m. In any Peruvian musical contest, it is *criolla*, the sultry music of the coast, which wins hands down. At four in the morning the *huayno* was unbearable.

I went off for a restorative coffee with David Drew. I was telling him about the spectacled bear we had seen at Unuyoc, when a bearded American at a nearby table became more and more agitated by our conversation. Finally he could contain himself no longer. He was a naturalist and I had just badly spoilt his day. For three long field seasons he had been trying to get a glimpse of a spectacled bear in the region, without success (his nickname was 'Bernie the Bear'), and tyros like us had beaten him to it by accident. Once he'd recovered from his irritation, he did tell me more about the bear's endearing Paddington-like habits: one reason for its survival in hostile terrain is that it will eat almost anything, though it does have a particular passion for bromeliads, the startlingly colourful sucker plants that grow on trees. The bear has been known to construct rudimentary platforms out of fallen branches so that it can climb up to them, like Paddington reaching for the marmalade. Once it has feasted, and with few predators (other than man) to worry about, the bear often falls asleep.

The 'Wiracocha' café was a celebrated Cuzco hang-out, not least because it was one of the few places in the city that served real as opposed to instant coffee (there was a prevailing Peruvian feeling that instant coffee, *café americano*, was somehow more advanced because it came in a tin). Sitting there was a reminder of why the Spanish surrealist Buñuel had found his natural home in Latin America: one moment you could see a solemn procession of a Virgin going past, the next a mule-race would charge through in the opposite direction.

David and I wandered over to the Cuzco Archaeological Museum, which he knew well. There was a wealth of material, with *tumis* (cutting knives) and *tupus* (pins used by Inca women to hold their clothes in place) scattered indiscriminately in great piles. Much of the exhibition was either unlabelled or woefully misleading. Our favourite was a plain oval polished stone, described over-enthusiastically as '*una papa ceremonial*', 'a ceremonial potato'.

What the museum did give was a striking sense of the way the Incas had adapted – or rather, radically deviated from – the pottery of their pre-decessors. While much of the earlier Moche ceramics was elaborately zoomorphic and the blackened Chimú pottery featured representations of monkeys, Inca pottery was more restrained (some would say less achieved) and tended towards the abstract. It was not a point that I had considered before, but it was striking how much of their aesthetic was in fact abstract, in a way that chimed with our own, late-twentieth-century impulses. The 'stripes and chequers' patterns of Inca pots were Mondrian-like in their rigour and simplicity (other predecessors of the Incas, the Huari, were also abstract but in a more playful, Klee-like way).

And the same was true of the buildings of Cuzco. It was only when you came across some small representational figure on a Colonial building (the snakes weaving across the Palacio de Culebras, or the busts of the Pizarros) that you could see how rigorous was the classic Inca adherence to abstraction, in a way that would have made even Clement Greenberg happy. An occasional curve was the most luxurious release allowed from the clean line of the ashlars that dissected the city. Only in their last days, with the coming of the Spanish, do the rules seem to have been relaxed and artisans had what we would call 'the creative space' to start carving figuratively – in the eyes of the surviving old guard, probably a decadent fall from grace.

The abstract nature of Inca art had encouraged the common misconception that they themselves were necessarily abstemious and rigorous – a fallacy no more true of them than of the New York abstract artists of the 1950s.

Cuzco had continued to be a productive artistic centre for long after the Incas, with its own style of Christian religious art, the Cuzqueña school of the seventeenth century, producing dark oils full of the shadows that Cuzco itself was falling into as a 'forgotten city'.

But the work I really wanted to learn more about was that of the greatest of all artists that Cuzco had produced in the intervening centuries, the photographer Martín Chambi.

*

I had first come across Martín Chambi because of his magical early photos of Machu Picchu. Chambi had travelled there in 1925, when much of the vegetation had grown back after Bingham's initial discovery and it was almost a virgin site. In Chambi's picture, only the most prominent buildings – like the Torreón – emerge clearly above the vegetation, but the shape of the city is enticingly clear under the blanket of shrub. Chambi died in 1972, but I managed to get an introduction to see his daughter Julia, who still lived in the street where her father had always had his studio, the Calle Marqués, not far from the main square.

It had turned into one of those brisk Cuzco days when a chill wind from the *altiplano* descends on the city, and Julia Chambi tugged at the sleeves of her cardigan as we talked. The studio's small office still had a large print of one of Chambi's most famous and odd images, the giant of Paruro, an Andean Indian some six foot eight tall in threadbare clothes, looming over us as we talked.

As she spoke of her father, Julia's face became more and more animated. She told me that her father had made many of his trips into the mountains alone, or with just one trusted companion, Doctor Luis Aragón Velasco, who provided horses and mules from his hacienda. Of the many self-portraits Chambi did throughout his long career, the most famous was that of him on a bleak mountainside with a mule. In it, his handsome Indian features stare straight ahead while he holds the mule at arm's length, while behind is the raw landscape near Puno, where Chambi had originally come from. It is the very essence of the photographer as lone explorer, carrying his huge camera and 18-by-24 plate-glass negatives to the remotest corners of the Andes.

Many explorers had wanted to photograph Peruvian ruins previously but had baulked at the effort involved. Raimondi, for instance, the indefatigable nineteenth-century geographer who travelled all over the country mapping as he went, wished that he had been able to photograph the innumerable ruins he came across, as 'there are some areas of Peru where one can't take a pace without finding some interesting remains of an ancient civilisation'. However, Raimondi couldn't face the actual business of hauling fragile glass plates over mountain passes, with all the bulky equipment entailed. He went so far as to order a customised smaller camera from England for one of his final pioneering journeys *adentro*, into the interior. Sadly, the camera proved to be not quite so portable as he had hoped when it arrived, and he still had to leave it behind.

Chambi was a tough enough man of the mountains both to travel with all the heavy equipment needed and still to have the energy to produce superb, shining images of the ruins that went far beyond the 'archaeological record' taken by Bingham's photographers. In an interview published in a magazine in 1936, he could already say:

> in my archive I have more than two hundred photographs of diverse aspects of Quechua culture. I have travelled and re-travelled the regions of the Andes on this pilgrimage. In particular I have scoured every corner of the palaces and fortresses of Cuzco with the lens of my camera. Here are Sacsahuaman, Ollantaytambo, Machu Picchu, Picchu-Picchu, Pisac, Colcampata, the valley of Urubamba, the entire region in which that empire flourished....

What really seized my imagination – and surprised me – was what Julia told me next. Apparently some of Martín Chambi's expeditions had also been made with a group of artistic friends who constituted the glittering Cuzco café society of the 1920s and 30s. She went into the archives and came back with a small box of unpublished prints and produced them one by one as she continued to tell the story.

There was Chambi standing beside two friends on a mountainside, one of whom was dressed immaculately in an Edwardian frock-coat with a velvet collar, the other in an equally fine suit. Both were casually smoking cigarettes. In another picture, Chambi held a machete and was leading a party, stripped to his waistcoat but still wearing a tie, with gaiters of fine cloth wrapped around his knees. In a late photo of Machu Picchu (Chambi returned obsessively to photograph it – there are over a thousand negatives of the ruin alone in the archive) he shared the narrow top of Huayna Picchu with two companions: one friend pretended to sketch him, another to view him with binoculars from four feet away.

A troupe of Cuzqueños would accompany Chambi on expeditions which became social and intellectual events. An average expedition might include plant-hunters, doctors, café intellectuals and often those who wanted to combine the search for a ruin with some good hunting, rather as Topa Inca might have done (a picture Julia showed me had a line of shot deer beneath the explorers). The tents they used were the upright ones fashionable at the time, shaped more like pillar-boxes than pyramids. There was a wonderful photograph of Chambi shaving in the morning, laughing as he lathered himself up with a tiny and ineffectual mirror. In another he puffed on a pipe as the clouds covered the peaks below him.

'And then,' said Julia, 'there was the millionairess.' One year a wealthy young Cuzqueña, Señorita Ricarda Luna, wanted to fund a trip of Chambi's to Machu Picchu, which he readily agreed to. However, the offer had strings attached: she also wanted to bring her friends along (a party of some thirty Cuzco socialites), with plenty of live chickens and pigs for the commissariat and a full troupe of musicians. The 'millionairess' was determined to live in the manner to which she was accustomed. 'It was a circus,' laughed Julia. The trip would take over a month to complete.

Chambi amused himself with the bright young things of Cuzco, many of whom had never been into the mountains before, by killing snakes with his machete for dramatic effect. A photo survives of the party when they finally arrived at the ruins: the musicians play in the background as couples tea-dance in the overgrown and deserted buildings. It is an intensely romantic and unreal image. But this is perhaps the most distinguishing feature of a photographer whose work tried to document the light shining through the mundaneness of Peruvian daily life.

Chambi's own life had been an extraordinary one. He was born in 1891, if not in poverty then certainly in simplicity, to an Indian family living in a small village near Puno, close to the frontier with Bolivia. Peru was undergoing one of its periodic bouts of financial insecurity. The country had recently lost the disastrous War of the Pacific (1879–83) with Chile, and so foreign capital had been invited in to help. The British sent a team of engineers from the Santo Domingo Mining Company to prospect a mine near Chambi's house. With them came a photographer. Young Martín was befriended by the photographer's children, who were about his age, and he was very taken by what he saw of their father's photography. Interestingly, it was not the pictures produced of his own surroundings that apparently inspired him, but those of the photographer's home back in England, the sense of a world different to his.

He begged his own father to take him to Arequipa, a city with a photographic studio, run by a Señor Vargas. According to Julia, the young Martín even paid for their tickets with a small amount of gold he had managed to pan in the local river – 'He was always very *ágil*, very quick.' Once at Vargas' studio, he secured first a menial job and rapidly a valued position as Vargas' chief assistant for the studio portraits and weddings that were the stock-in-trade of such a business. But Arequipa had its limitations. It was a predominantly white, or *mestizo* city, and as a pure-blooded Indian it was difficult for Martín to make his way. He went instead to Cuzco, a city which by definition might have been expected to be more open racially.

He arrived in the 1920s, at a fortuitous time. As Julia put it, '*Cuzco se desalumbró*, Cuzco woke up.' The town was enjoying a boom after the long sloth and neglect of the eighteenth and nineteenth centuries. The railway had arrived and with it opportunities for textile factories and other foreign investments (one of Chambi's funniest pictures is of three gentlemen from a German beer company seated around a table, each with a glass in hand solemnly advertising their product). Cuzco began to enjoy itself and Chambi was there to capture the revelry that this wealth brought. In one picture a group of party-goers recline after a night's party, the girls wearing flapper dresses, with fashionable white make-up to lighten their skin colour, the men in carnival costumes: reclining in the foreground is a student dressed as a skeleton.

Julia said of her father, '*Se enamoró de Cuzco aun antes de llegar*, he fell in love with Cuzco before he'd even arrived.' It was easy to see why. Cuzco was becoming known throughout Peru as a town of intellectuals, who were attracted by the freshness of approach at its universities and its symbolic value as the centre of Peru's pre-Columbian past. In the new climate of *indigenismo*, when Peruvian intellectuals were bending over backwards to promote the Indian cause, Martín Chambi's background could now give him an advantage. To be Indian in Cuzco in the twenties was like being black in the New York art scene of the 1980s – a badge of honour. He became friendly with Luis Valcárcel, the Peruvian archaeologist who worked at both Machu Picchu and Sacsahuaman, while José García Uriel, a key figure in the *indigenista* movement and author of *The New Indian*, hailed him, rather worryingly, as being 'an autochthonous exemplar of the race'. It may have helped that the royal mace the Incas used to carry into battle with them was called a *chambi* in Quechua.

Martín Chambi began his commercial career with a bold stroke. He invested all his savings in processing free portraits of all the city's great and the good, and then exhibited the results. Julia paused at this point in telling the story. 'It seems like an easy thing to do,' she said, 'but he risked everything.' The sheer cost of plates and chemicals involved was astronomical. Luckily the magistrates, doctors, dons and businessmen were delighted and commissions followed. His natural sociability – 'my father was a great dancer' – helped him fit into Cuzco café society and his reputation was made. He also developed a lucrative – and pioneering – line in postcard sales. (After his death he was described as having been a distributor of postcards, in the same way that Orson Welles was remembered in some tabloid obituaries as having been best known for sherry advertisements.)

He continued throughout his career to take formal portraits, but almost immediately went for the first time to Machu Picchu and took his first, hallucinatory pictures of the site. He experimented constantly with lighting. '*A mi padre, le encantó la luz*,' said Julia, 'my father was enchanted by light.' The cloudy conditions of the Urubamba valley allowed for sudden shafts to pick out detail and stone, as in the picture of the Wiñay Wayna complex he took soon after its discovery and clearance by the Fejos expedition of 1941. Very few of his pictures of the ruins are in full sun.

His self-portraits at the time are also remarkable: in *Autoretrato con Autoretrato* (Self-Portrait with Self-Portrait) he looks at an image of himself in a plate-glass negative. In another he is back-lit to an almost solarised extent, like the images that Man Ray was experimenting with at about the same time in Paris.

Earnest young Peruvian academics have tried to claim Chambi as a champion of the indigenous cause against the land-owning classes, but it seems more as if, like many artists, he used his art as a way of escaping from the constraints of both class and position. As a photographer he could equally well take pictures of bare-footed Indians waiting patiently in the judgement dock or of the rich engaged daughter of a grand house posing on the stairway (looking carefully, one can just make out the figure of an attendant maid hidden in the shadows below).

His openness allowed him to become a chronicler of Cuzco for the remaining fifty years of his life: the initial impetus of the twenties fell away in the city as foreign investment was distracted by the economic crises of the thirties and then the Second World War which, while distant, impinged considerably on South American trade. Cuzco fell back to sleep.

Chambi's archive constitutes an almost Gabriel García Márquez-like account of life over half a century of relative solitude in what was still a small town: the turgid flow of a provincial society still gripped by hierarchy (a self-satisfied *hacendado* surveys his field of llamas; beggar boys stare at the camera in the Plaza de Regocijo), interrupted by sudden flashes of events, some public, some private: the coming of the first motorbike to Cuzco, owned by his friend the dashing Mario Pérez Yáñez; the disastrous derailment of a locomotive, with a crowd of concerned onlookers peering down at the wreck below; even the unexpected arrival of Edward, Prince of Wales, in 1931, being escorted across the Plaza de Armas by a pompous priest and wearing a double-breasted suit that was to be much copied by the Cuzqueño dandies of the day.

Chambi had his studio on the upper floor of the house on the Calle Marqués specially designed with a complicated series of blinds and shutters, so that he could control the natural daylight. There he built up an extraordinary dossier of commemorative pictures from those who came to him: a young society Señorita posing in her bathing suit; the town's basketball-hockey team; two boxers squaring off against each other; a magistrate with a medal and absurdly formal headgear, like an operatic miner's hat; a female bullfighter holding her cape triumphantly aloft; finally the giant of Paruro, the strange image that hung over us as Julia and I talked, a man with holes in his clothes and short trousers that seemed to exaggerate his enormous height. It was a kaleidoscope.

Guaman Poma, the eccentric seventeenth-century chronicler of Inca life, described Cuzco as '*un espacio mágico*' and Chambi created just such a magic space in his images of the city in the twentieth century. In the same way that some images of Doisneau or Brassaï have become emblematic of Paris, so it had become difficult to see some parts of Cuzco without Chambi's images in mind: one print shows early dawn at the Plaza de Armas, the Cathedral soft in the background, impermanent, while the hard shadow of an Indian woman falls across the foreground; in another the massive supporting wall of the Incas' great Sun Temple, the Coricancha, rears up above the camera – the wall is one of the few visible remains of the Coricancha, as the church of Santo Domingo was built over it. At the bottom of the stupendous masonry sprawls his friend Luis Aragón Velasco, although whether to give scale or for a laugh is not clear. (Chambi had an idiosyncratic fondness for photos of people lying down – some of his group photos are remarkable for his clear insistence that many of the subjects lie flat on the floor, like sardines radiating away from the camera.)

Julia had started to work with him in the studio as he got older, doing hand-coloured prints of the debutantes of fifties Cuzco, who looked more staid than their wild mothers of the twenties. She said some had never been collected by their subjects, 'although I don't know why, as they had plenty of money to pay for them!'

Chambi retained his enthusiasm for Machu Picchu right up to the end. 'On my birthday in May, or his in November, Papa would sometimes say, on impulse, "*Te invito a almuerzo a Machu Picchu*", "How about lunch in Machu Picchu", and we'd be off.' They would take shrimps and champagne in buckets of ice. With the laying of the railway-line, this was by now a much easier business than in the days when he had left Cuzco with a set of mules and beautiful people in tow. The only thing Chambi deplored was the volume of visitors that the railway brought to Machu Picchu. 'Why can't they all wear slippers?' he would complain, as he saw the boots go up and down the chiselled stonework.

Some of the most moving of the unpublished prints Julia showed me were those of her family holding such parties in the middle of the ruins. Chambi was messing around, posing in traditional costumes for exaggerated *indigenista* effect and playing the pipes he loved. He unaffectedly enjoyed the more sentimental side of Andean life and could quite happily do pictures of llamas silhouetted against the skyline or pan-pipers, with titles like *La Tristeza Andina* (*Andean Sadness*), pictures which the intellectuals of Lima decried as a patronising of Indian values, as indeed they might have been if they had done them themselves.

Then an event shattered both Cuzco and the life of the Chambi family. Julia remembers the precise moment of the earthquake, at a quarter to two one afternoon in 1950. 'When it happened, Papa couldn't bear to go upstairs to the studio. He knew what had happened. I had to go for him.' It was not the large glass windows of the studio that he was worried about, although these were of course shattered to pieces. Rather, as Chambi had feared, it was the broken remains of some of the fragile glass negatives he had built up over a lifetime.

A true professional to the last, Chambi forced himself to go out and photograph the damage. 'He photographed with tears in his eyes,' said Julia. What he saw was a city that had been desecrated, with buckled and contorted houses and with the long lines of red roof tiles that cut across the city grids suddenly made soft and plastic. The homes of 35,000 people were destroyed.

But the earthquake had an unexpected positive side-effect. Many of the colonial façades fell away, revealing the better-built Inca stonework beneath. At the Coricancha, the old Sun Temple, where Chambi had photographed his friend Don Luis so many years earlier, some of the church collapsed.

Behind were walls of the most perfect Inca stonework, impossibly elegant, close-fitting stone of a standard worthy of Pachacuti and the highpoint of the Inca Empire. On the main square, a façade of tawdry tourist shops also broke open to reveal the stonework of the great hall of Casana behind, thought to have been lost since the chronicler Garcilaso de la Vega had been there as a boy and described it as 'capable of holding four thousand people'.

In some way it was as if the Spanish had been unable completely to bury the Inca past. And it happened at a time when Peru had come fully to recognise itself as a country with a pre-Columbian heritage, indeed almost to define itself as such. An argument flared up after the earthquake between those who wanted to rebuild the convent of Santo Domingo and those, the inheritors of the *indigenista* tradition, who wanted to expose yet more stonework of the Sun Temple beneath, even if the church was left incomplete. The *indigenistas* won the day. The Sun Temple can now be seen nestled incongruously within the cloisters of the convent, rather like the great mosque that has had a church built around it at Córdoba. The effect is like one of those odd medieval dishes, where an entire pigeon is roasted inside a pig's head.

Chambi was already almost sixty when the earthquake happened and the later years of his life saw a decline as he went into virtual retirement. Julia had a simple contact sheet of the very last photos taken of him in the studio, his last self-portrait, when he was already ill. In one he poses with Julia, in another he stares at the camera alone, and then with his loyal assistant. In the final contact picture of the four, he has fallen asleep on the chair. He died in 1972, still known only in Cuzco, and there primarily for the black-and-white pictures he sold in the arcade and his work as a commercial photographer – right up to his death he would still take the odd passport picture for identity papers.

Only posthumously did he start to enjoy fame. A group of Peruvian photographers and an American, Edward Ranney, together with Julia and her nephew Teo, succeeded in mounting substantial exhibitions of his work, first in Lima, then abroad. He quickly became one of the icons of twentieth-century photography, with exhibitions at MOMA and around the world. Even now the sheer range of his work is still barely touched. There are 14,000 negatives in the archive.

Julia gave me an original print of Chambi to take with me – the one I had most liked, of the young Martín Chambi stripped to his braces and holding a machete, on a mountain path. We had talked for hours and as we left the cold little room, the sun hit us in the courtyard. 'Go out and enjoy it,' she said.

*

I strolled through the Plaza Regocijo, watching the old men taking their siestas and the shoe-shine boys doing their rounds. Cuzco was now a place I felt at ease in: I had my set places to eat, was a regular at the same hotels and restaurants and had finally worked out how the *poste restante* system did (or didn't) work if you wanted to collect mail. It was a city that felt like a town, with an intimacy that absorbed the visitor.

In 1952, only a few years after the earthquake, a young traveller arrived in Cuzco. He had driven up from the south, from Chile and Argentina, on a Norton 550cc motorbike which he had christened *La Poderosa*, 'The Powerful One', and he was crossing the continent after having just taken his medical exams. He was only twenty-five. His name was Ernesto 'Che' Guevara.

The city that Che arrived in was still recovering from the destruction of the earthquake. Guevara was immediately struck by the image of the Chapel of Belén, its twin towers toppled, lying 'like a dismembered animal on the hillside'. But he was also overwhelmed by the city. For the young Argentinian, it had a symbolic power as the centre of a genuinely American culture pre-dating the Spanish and certainly the 'false' American culture, as he saw it, of the United States. In his diaries and letters from the time, he unfavourably compared Argentina (where there was no indigenous culture to speak of) with the Quechuan and Aymara cultures of the Andes. 'Cuzco invites you to turn warrior and, club in hand, defend freedom and the life of the Inca,' he wrote, while he was also open enough to admire the conquistadors' colonial architecture and the 'gentle harmony' of the city.

Guevara had already been travelling for some months when he arrived. He had left his girlfriend, his studies and Argentina behind to take off with a fellow medical student, Alberto Granado, on a free-wheeling and delightfully irresponsible tour of the continent. With hardly any money, they begged meals off fellow doctors in the countries along their way, most of whom amiably complied – although eyebrows were raised at their scruffy appearance. Che admitted that the only difference between the clothes they wore at night and during the day was that they took their shoes off in bed.

They also fell off the bike a great deal, not least because bits kept falling off the bike (Alberto, who was the more mechanically minded, apparently had a strong belief that wire was better than screws for holding components together). After a while the bike fell to pieces completely and they started hitching. In Chile they had to flee a village when Che made advances to the wife of a drunken farmer, which she welcomed but the farmer did not. Later they stowed away and would have sailed right up the coast to Peru, but their greed in consuming the ship's produce gave them away: the captain spotted tell-tale melon skins floating downstream from the boat.

Che was in Cuzco when the María Angola bell was rung from the Cathedral for the first time since the earthquake. The bell, one of the largest in the world, was made with twenty-seven kilos of gold and was a Cuzco icon that Martín Chambi had repeatedly photographed (he liked to shoot from inside the bell-tower, looking out over the main square). It had recently been restored by a donation from General Franco's government in Spain. When the band were ordered to start up with the Spanish national anthem at the rededication service, much to Che's amusement they played the Spanish republican anthem by mistake: 'As the first notes sounded, the bishop's red hat turned an even deeper red as he waved his arms in the air like a puppet. "Stop, stop, there has been a mistake," he cried.'

He then travelled down the Urubamba and along the Sacred Valley. His archaeological comments were often misinformed, as was his history – he imagined conquistadors storming the nearby 'fortress' of Pisac, which they hadn't – but his response to Machu Picchu was emotional: 'It doesn't really matter what the origin of the fortress was or rather it is better to leave that debate to the archaeologists. The undeniable thing, the most important thing, is that we have before us a pure expression of the most powerful indigenous race in the Americas, untouched by contact with the conquering civilisation.'

Che was not yet as politicised as he was later to become, although his experiences on the road made him sympathise with 'that race of the defeated', as he called the Quechuans. He was uncomfortable at the way he was constantly prioritised over Indian travellers – when it rained, for instance, he and Alberto were invited to take shelter in the truck-driver's cab, while the driver's native passengers were left to shiver in the open back of the truck.

His experiences in the Andes sowed the seeds of an empathy which brought him back years later to Bolivia, when he was already a successful leader of the Cuban Revolution and a man who could quite easily have rested on his achievements. He was to die there, fighting in the Santa Cruz mountains for the rights of those self-same Indians.

So struck was he by Machu Picchu as a place which 'drives any dreamer to ecstasy' that he wrote about it for his first published article, in 1953: '*Machu Picchu; Enigma de Piedra en América*' ('Machu Picchu, a Stone Enigma in America'). In this he made the perceptive point that 'Machu Picchu was to Bingham the crowning of all his purest dreams as an adult child'. He also raised an issue few academic critics had liked to consider: 'Where can one admire or study the treasures of the indigenous city [Machu Picchu]? The answer is obvious: in the museums of the United States.'

Che's question was one which would be increasingly asked as a politics of liberation began to spread across the continent. There was a natural tendency to conspiracy theorise and to presume that Hiram Bingham had stripped Machu Picchu in a way analogous to American behaviour elsewhere – like their support for the right-wing *coup* in Guatemala that Che was shortly to witness in 1954. Certainly the organised trade in smuggled antiquities and the activities of *huaqueros* had become almost institutionalised in Peru and stemmed from official attitudes dating right back to the time of the Conquest. Many such finds did make their way to rich collectors in the States. But the story of what happened to the archaeological finds that Bingham excavated at Machu Picchu is a complex one.

Bingham's team did little more than explore on that memorable expedition of 1911 (and given that in that one short season they found the three biggest remaining Inca sites, that seems a reasonable enough limitation). They took few objects back with them. For their return journey in 1912, when they planned to excavate Machu Picchu, Bingham tried to arrange to ship all his findings back to Yale. He even drew up an extraordinary contract which proposed that Yale should have the exclusive right to export any archaeological find 'convenient to them' made over the following ten-year period. Unsurprisingly, the Peruvian government baulked at this – as did the American government, if for different reasons, as they saw no cause for Yale to be given such exclusive rights over other American universities.

Bingham did manage to get some material back to Yale, including the bones that Eaton had discovered in the tombs. However, for the final expedition of 1914–15, Bingham was forced to return any new finds. Che seems to have been unaware that very few metallic objects were ever found at the site, a curiosity that Bingham and George Eaton had commented on, while better ceramics have been found elsewhere, so the bones were and still are the principal find of interest.

The distinguished Peruvian archaeologist Sonia Guillén recently made a search to determine what had happened to those same bones. To her understandable dismay, she discovered at Yale's Peabody Museum that some of the skeletons recovered from the Machu Picchu tombs had deteriorated from poor storage and were being used, of all things, in osteology demonstration classes.

Nor was the situation necessarily any better at the National Museum of Anthropology in Lima. Sonia Guillén finally, after a great deal of effort, again managed to track down the wooden boxes marked as containing skeletal remains from Machu Picchu. When they were prised open, they were empty. The bones of the under-nourished workers who had built Machu Picchu had gone missing.

I stood again on the heights of Sacsahuaman looking down at the city, my head swimming with tales of Cuzco. From above, the trapezoidal shape of the main plaza, echoing the principal Inca architectural motif, was even more apparent. The hills behind undulated gently away in ridges of overlapping contours, burnt to the red, ochre and umber colours usually associated with Tuscany. Late-afternoon sun was sweeping sideways across the great stones of Sacsahuaman, casting hard quadrated shadows across the parade ground.

When I had first come to these immense fortifications, the image that had stayed with me was that of the final battle with the Spanish, when Manco Inca had been driven from Cuzco for ever and the last real hopes of the Incas had died. This was the symbolic value of Sacsahuaman, as a pyre for Incaic values: the condors circling overhead, the bodies buried in the battlements. But after my journeys into the interior, I had also become fascinated by the Emperor Pachacuti, the man who had supposedly built Sacsahuaman long before the arrival of the Spanish.

In the Inca version of their own history, as recounted to the first Spanish chroniclers, two episodes were clearly pivotal to the way they understood themselves as a people: the first was their origin myth, when they were led towards the valley of Cuzco from a cave somewhere near Lake Titicaca (this was shadowy pre-history, so accounts varied as to the precise location); the second episode was far more precise, from the century just before the Conquest, and concerned Pachacuti.

Pachacuti (originally known as Inca Yupanqui), was a younger son of the Emperor Viracocha. During Viracocha's reign the Incas, according to the chronicles, were no more than one of many small tribes dotted around this area. Then, some time around 1438, the Chanca, a rival tribe to the north of Cuzco, attacked the Incas with such ferocity that Viracocha and his designated heir, Inca Urcon, fled the capital. Only a small band of captains led by Inca Yupanqui remained to give a last-ditch defence. Although facing seemingly hopeless odds, they managed to defeat the enemy with the help, so it was said, 'of the very stones of Cuzco', which rose up from the ground to fight alongside them. Not only were the Chanca sent packing, but Inca Yupanqui (who now adopted the soubriquet Pachacuti, 'Transformer of the Earth', and took the throne from his disgraced father and brother) embarked on an ambitious programme of conquest that initiated the imperial phase of Inca culture. Within a generation they had grown from an anonymous small tribe of the Cuzco valley to become the dominant force of the Andes.

From this account, which the Spanish chroniclers had gathered from many Inca sources and which modern archaeologists had by and large followed, Pachacuti deserved to be as celebrated as Alexander the Great or Napoleon. Like them, his achievements seemed almost to beggar geographical comprehension. He led the first wave of conquests over to Bolivia and Lake Titicaca. His son Topa Inca, working under his direction, followed with further expansion north up to Ecuador, until the whole chain of the Andes from Colombia to Chile was under Inca control, a distance of some 3000 miles and an area the size of continental Europe.

Pachacuti's achievement was not purely military. After his victory over the Chanca, he is supposed to have gathered the stones that had helped him in his fight and set them in places where they could be worshipped, in gratitude for the assistance they had given – like the carved rock, or *huaca*, that I had admired on my very first visit to Sacsahuaman. He enthused the Incas with the idea that they were a people of power, of destiny, and created an elaborate hierarchy devolving down from his own position as the *Sapa Inca*, the Emperor. The nobility became a separate tier in this hierarchy and were allowed to wear ear-plugs as a distinguishing feature. Tribes living close to Cuzco were accommodated within this concept by being made *Incas de Privelegio* ('Honorary Incas').

Pachacuti erected impressive monuments to this idea of an imperial destiny. Inca leaders had always been expected to build (one of the slurs perpetuated about the disgraced Inca Urcon, the brother that Pachacuti had usurped, was that he was too weak to leave a building to his name). But Pachacuti took this principle to new, grandiose extremes. He ordered the construction of Sacsahuaman, of the temple-fortress at Ollantaytambo and, it seems likely, of Machu Picchu. He built great roads across the continent. He was a true Emperor.

According to later Inca accounts, he was said to have laid down all the basic framework for the institutions of state over his long reign of approximately forty years – institutions which his successors were ritualistically to preserve in his name. For the first time, the peoples of the coast and the mountains were given a unified administration, a *pax incaica* that allowed peaceful trading and co-operation, with Quechua as the *lingua franca*. Where there had previously been darkness, so this story went, the Inca Empire brought order.

However, this account of Pachacuti needed to be treated with enormous care, and certainly with more caution than the Spanish (and indeed some later archaeologists) had given it. It was a seductive idea – an empire carved out by the sheer will-power of one individual, single-handedly turning the tide of a nation's destiny – and as such appealing to Spanish chroniclers reared on just such chivalric exploits themselves. But it was also very much the 'official version' of the history, carefully propagated by Pachacuti and his descendants. As a usurping family, they had an interest in denigrating the achievements of their predecessors and postulating a Year Zero for their own dynasty (Pachacuti also set a precedent for usurpation which was to be followed disastrously by his great grandson Atahualpa a century later, when he plunged the Empire into civil war).

Later discoveries have shown that the Incas were not the first to bring ordered government to large stretches of Peru – other civilisations had done so before. Many of the institutions which Pachacuti is supposed to have initiated had also been previously invented – even in the Spaniards' time, it was known that the Chimú on the coast had done much the same. Yet the power of the Pachacuti myth, the idea of the miraculous birth of an empire from almost certain defeat, has been so strong that even academic archaeologists have succumbed to it, and it remains as pervasive as the idea that Machu Picchu was a retreat for the Virgins of the Sun.

Curiously, there was little archaeological evidence to help show exactly how the Inca State did expand into an Empire. Apart from the excavation of Sacsahuaman itself, hardly any work had been done in the 'pre-Empire' Inca territories around Cuzco (Ann Kendall's work at Cusichaca was outside this area). The whisper among the younger archaeologists at Cusichaca was that this was where the next challenge lay. They suspected that any such excavation would probably show a much more gradual change from the quiet subsistence farmers of one generation to the Empire-builders of the next.

I had begun at the centre of the Inca Empire, in their heartland close to Cuzco. But I now began to feel that to understand the Incas better, to get a measure of their real achievement – and of quite how much they had indeed borrowed from shadowy predecessors – I needed to travel to the limits of their domain: first to Bolivia in the south, then up to Ecuador in the north.

Our initial expedition was officially 'over': I had left Roddy back at Cusichaca; J.B. was returning to London and a contract. But I had no reason to head back home. Indeed, as no job awaited me, there seemed every reason to stay in Peru, and with good Spanish and low expectations I could easily live on a few dollars a day. If the money ran out there was always teaching.

The decision made, I headed back down the hill, as night set in and the dogs of Cuzco started to howl from the skyline.

On reaching the first houses of the upper town, I was struck by an intense blue colour, a cobalt shade, that the citizens of Cuzco seemed particularly attached to and which shone out in glimpsed patios and the shuttering of white-washed houses with intense relief. The Inca use of colour on buildings is something about which little is known – most of their coloured plaster has not survived centuries of the rigorous Andean climate. Only down at the coast, at sites like Tambo Colorado, can one begin to get a sense of how vibrant the buildings must have looked at the time. The whitewash applied since is a purely colonial style.

Cuzco was a lovers' city, like Florence or Venice, and like both those cities it was at its best in winter, when a cold light threw the red rooftops into sharp outline against the mountains behind. Towards sunset, there was a turning point (which later I would spend many hours trying to catch on film in various parts of the world) when the light was low enough to darken the sky but still strong enough to make out detail in the city shadows.

In the narrow alleys wheeling down the hill from Sacsahuaman, as I hurried along with my head down, I could see shapes pressed into the wall, trysts and assignations between the students of the colleges that now filled the old city. These were the boys with their *novias*, that Spanish word that hovers with useful indecision between meaning 'girlfriend' or 'fiancée', and in the back streets the long courtships and secret meetings could be conducted out of the prying sight of families.

I had a couple of pisco sours to compensate for my own single status, and an extra one to help me successfully sleep through the dawn cock crow and the *huayno*. Early the next morning, exhilarated and with the clear head that too much alcohol can sometimes perversely give, I stumbled off to the station and bought a ticket to Bolivia.

TO BOLIVIA AND
COLLASUYO

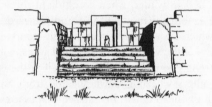

I WAS NOW FOLLOWING in the path of the Spanish chronicler of the Conquest I most admired, Pedro de Cieza de León. He too had ridden out from Cuzco towards modern-day Bolivia in order to explore the further fringes of the Inca Empire. In 1549, a few decades after the Conquest, he had reached Lake Titicaca and the monumental ruins of Tiahuanaco nearby. He was the first European to leave an eyewitness account of them.

Cieza de León had been hooked on the idea of the Inca Empire since he was an impressionable thirteen-year-old living in Seville. In 1534 he had seen one of the first ships of booty brought back from Peru by Hernando Pizarro. When Cieza came to write his great Chronicle twenty years later, he recalled 'the rich pieces of gold that I saw in Seville, brought from Cajamarca, where the treasure that Atahualpa promised the Spanish was collected'. The sight of the beautifully crafted Inca treasures must have been magnificent, particularly as it was such a transient one – the treasures were immediately melted down to feed the coffers of the Emperor Charles V for his endless European warfare.

Fired up by what he had seen, the young Cieza de León managed to secure a passage on a boat heading to the New World. However, it was not until 1547, by the time he was twenty-seven, that he finally arrived in Peru, as part of a Royal Army that had been sent to put down an insurrection of settlers led by another Pizarro brother, Gonzalo: the settlers were revolting at the so-called New Laws from Spain, designed to give the Indians more rights and prevent them from being treated like beasts of burden by their new owners.

During the intervening years Cieza had been blooded in campaigns in

Colombia, had searched for a passage through to the Atlantic, narrowly avoided being killed by Indians using curare poison and had gone looking for El Dorado – in short, all the usual training grounds for a budding conquistador.

But Cieza differed from most of his contemporaries in one essential way – by the time he reached Peru he had got into the habit of taking copious notes of all that he saw. This was not a common characteristic among the 'second generation' of conquistadors who headed down to Peru after the first gold rush of Mexico had subsided. They were an altogether rougher and less educated group of men. While Cortés had been a skilled writer whose letters to the Emperor about the Conquest of Mexico are impressive literary documents, Francisco Pizarro could barely sign his name. (Perhaps as a consequence, Peru has always taken a surprisingly benevolent stance towards *analfabetismo*, illiteracy: there are still lesser legal penalties for those who 'could not read, so knew not what they were doing'.)

Cieza's great virtue as a chronicler was that he had no political or religious axe to grind, other than a mild, understandable aversion to Gonzalo Pizarro, and his account is fresh and forthright as a result – so much so that when it came to publication many years later, the Inquisition suppressed most of it. Lines like 'for wherever the Spaniards have passed, conquering and destroying, it is as though a fire had gone, destroying everything in its path' were not popular at a time when Spain was trying to live down the *leyenda negra*, 'the black legend' that was beginning to accumulate around its doings in South America.

The slow progress which the Royal Army made down the coast enabled Cieza to describe the Inca Empire in great detail. He wrote his account as a travel book in the true sense, in that it interwove reflections on Inca history and customs with a physical description of the country as he passed through it. I found it amazing that he had been able to preserve his increasingly bulky manuscript over the years, as he fought in battles and crossed and re-crossed the old Inca Empire (he was upset when he lost a few sheets in a climactic victory over Gonzalo Pizarro's forces – he really did seem to carry the whole manuscript with him in a knapsack).

The point that he returned to again and again in his Chronicle was what brilliant administrators the Incas had been and how inferior the Spanish were by comparison. The Incaic road system, their communal labour projects and their ability to coax terraces and irrigated fields out of the toughest of conditions filled him with nothing but admiration. He was careful also to refute some of the more common slanders that were being used by the Spanish to justify the Conquest – for instance, that the Incas encouraged sodomy, which as Cieza pointed out, was far from the case:

they actively persecuted other tribes, like the Chimú on the coast, for practising it.

He was impressed by the way in which the Incas had so often won over subject tribes without warfare. Their technique was first to send in spies. Then, after carefully weighing up the local situation, the Incas would let the old chiefs know that they could still keep their positions if they joined the Empire. Judicious bribery with concubines and textiles (cloth had enormous value in the Andes) further lubricated the transition.

Above all the Incas made it clear that they would win whatever happened, because they always did. Cieza reported one Inca Emperor as saying to a prospective new tribe, 'These lands will soon be ours, like those we already possess.' Given the Indians' often fatalistic turn of mind, this proved effective diplomacy and many tribes gave in without a fight.

The Incas were adept at incorporating such new tribes into the Empire. Pachacuti had instigated a typically efficient method for achieving this. Local populations had always carried out works of communal labour, or *mita*, for their own infrastructure. Now large numbers of people were taken from their homelands to serve as tribute labour elsewhere, in a new system called *mitamayo*. The workers themselves were known as *mitimaes*. To take their place in their own community would come other workers from other tribes: 'In this way all was quiet and the *mitimaes* feared the natives, and the natives feared the *mitimaes* and all occupied themselves only in serving and obeying.' It was a system of divide and rule that appealed to Pachacuti – he seems also to have instigated the Inca practice of splitting towns into two halves, a lower and an upper sector called *hurin* and *hanan*, who would compete with each other in providing services to the State and to the town itself, like some glorified version of 'house-teams' in a school.

As part of the process of absorbing new peoples, the place-names of conquered towns would be changed to Quechua ones. And just as Pachacuti had effectively created a dynastic myth for his own succession, there is some evidence that the Incas also substantially retold the history of preceding civilisations to down-play their achievements, and in some cases to ignore them completely. Cieza reports, quoting his Inca sources, that before them there were only naked savages and that 'these natives were stupid and brutish beyond belief. They say they were like animals, and that many ate human flesh, and others took their daughters and mothers to wife and committed other even graver sins.'

This manipulative distortion of history (common to other conquering pre-Columbian cultures like the Aztecs) was so successful – the same myth was repeated by other chroniclers like Garcilaso de la Vega in the early seventeenth century – that the truth has only emerged comparatively recently. Far from imposing order on an unruly bunch of savages, the Incas were merely the latest dominant tribe (and a short-lived one at that) in a series of Andean civilisations that had flourished over the preceding 2000 years: the Moche in the north of Peru, with their magnificent pottery, the Huari of the central states and the Tiahuanaco culture near Lake Titicaca (whose capital I was travelling to) were just a few of the cultures that had attained a high level and on whose achievements the Incas had often built.

It was a German archaeologist, Max Uhle, who first began to reveal how literally deep the roots of Andean culture were. In dig after dig in southern and central Peru in the early twentieth century, he showed conclusively that the Incas had been preceded by earlier cultures and that some of them had built up similarly far-flung empires. In the north, the doyen of all Peruvian archaeologists, Julio C. Tello, had in 1919 excavated the even more ancient culture of the extraordinary Chavín de Huantar, with its jungle iconography of snakes and jaguars dating back as early as 500 BC – two millennia before the *arriviste* Incas.

Cieza de León would have appreciated the conservationist change that was sweeping over Peru as a result of increased pride in this rich heritage. After centuries in which ancient tombs had been seen as a legitimate source of plunder – the early Spanish had even issued mining licences to prospectors to extract gold from them – they were being protected and restored. Cieza had deplored the way in which Sacsahuaman was vandalised by the Spanish conquistadors after the fall of the fortress-temple at the time of Manco Inca's rebellion in 1536: 'I hate to think of those who have governed in allowing so extraordinary a thing to have been destroyed and cast down, without giving thought to future times and events and how much better it would be to have it standing and cared for.'

His main complaint – which won him few friends, not least because it was grounded in truth – was that if you let illiterate conquistadors govern countries, you were going to get disastrous results. No wonder that he died embittered and dismayed in 1553, only a few years after returning from Peru, in the knowledge that while he had successfully published one book, the rest of his great manuscript would almost certainly be suppressed. He had given the better part of his life to the dream he had seen on the quay-side of Seville, and when he died at just thirty-three (some said of a broken heart after the death of his beloved wife, or of a sickness he had picked up in Peru), it must have seemed as if for all of those years he had been chasing a chimera.

I liked to think of him, though, on that day when he first took the High Road south out from the Great Square of Cuzco towards Collasuyo, the

Quarter of the South, with the knowledge that every writer craves – that he was going to be the first to report on all that he saw.

*

Above Cuzco, the upper Vilcanota river was viscous and sluggish as it meandered along the valley: it had carved great curved gorges that were monotonous in their regularity. As we got ever higher into the *puna*, the landscape became more barren, with plains of yellow and gold that looked as if they ought to be wheat but were in fact pampas grass.

I remembered Cieza's words: 'The excessive cold of this region is a handicap, and the grass that grows here is good only for the *guanucos* and *vicuñas*.' We passed a section where there had recently been some burning and the whole valley was patterned yellow and black as if it had been kiln-fired.

Having been away in the mountains for months, it was a shock to be back on a tourist route. The railway between Cuzco and Puno was a funnel-neck for travellers from Peru to Bolivia and the city of La Paz, who then went on to Argentina and Brazil. For what was an enormous continent (the width of South America being greater than that of the Atlantic Ocean), there were surprisingly few transverse routes. As a result, a sort of 'Gringo Trail' had been established, helped by a guide-book of the same name, which had become self-fulfilling: many travellers never deviated from it.

There was a group of Spanish travellers in the carriage with me, complaining loudly about the Indians as '*maleducados*, badly brought up,' and insisting that I moved my rucksack so that it was directly above my seat – very different from the easy-going behaviour of those same Indians on the mountain trains. That night in Puno, I dined on fresh-water trout from Lake Titicaca with an Australian girl and an American couple I met. The talk was all of muggings in Colombia, of hepatitis, dollar exchange rates, getting ripped off and of marathon journeys across half the continent. They couldn't believe that I had spent so many months around Cuzco. 'Cuzco is a five-nighter, maybe eight if you do the full Inca Trail – but no more,' said the Australian girl in an authoritative tone. She was a big, full-breasted, athletic girl and looked like she would brook no argument.

Puno was generally considered a 'one-nighter', if that, but I wanted to hang around and in particular visit the 'floating islands' of Lake Titicaca, which had intrigued me ever since I was a child.

I went first to see the nearby ruins of Sillustani. I knew nothing about them other than a few lines in a local guide-book stating that they were there and Cieza de León's description of 'the tombs of the native chiefs of this place, as high as towers, broad and square, with doors towards the setting sun'.

What I saw, scattered over the hills above Lake Ayumara, was a host of stone monuments, standing upright against the skyline on otherwise barren ground: they were *chullpas*, burial chambers, some big enough to take a score of bodies and built with huge blocks in the style that originated around Lake Titicaca.

Sillustani was mainly the work of the Colla, one of the tribes whom the Incas had suppressed in their conquests here and after whom they had named this quarter of the Inca Empire (Collasuyo). Some of the outlying monuments were crude, smaller structures. But the four or so principal towers at the centre of the complex had a powerful if skeletal presence, with the shimmering lagoon behind: the magnificent desolation of the Altiplano stretched out ahead of them, like the desert around Ozymandias' prostrate head.

However, as I got closer I realised that not all of these central towers were Colla, for they gave a fascinating example of how the Incas could sometimes directly copy the work of others.

One of the four, the largest, was indeed Colla, built with massive cubes of a warm ochre stone and similar to the many smaller monuments on neighbouring hills. Some of the cubes had spilled out from the coiled tower, revealing that they were hollowed on the sides, perhaps to allow adobe bonding between them. But the three other principal towers were clearly Inca, while modelled on that of the Colla. They had followed the same unusual shape (the towers widened as they ascended, in contravention of every architectural instinct), but used blocks of grey granite in the usual Incaic way, irregular but precisely fitting and with some of the strange projecting bosses which I had seen on other Inca buildings and which always caught my attention. They shared the same small plateau with the Colla tower, and overlooked the Ayumara lagoon. Were the Inca towers imitation as flattery or were they a boast by the conquerors – anything you can do we can do better?

The Incas certainly took the monumental style of building they found in Collasuyo back with them to Cuzco and assimilated it as their own. Because they suppressed so much of the history of the tribes they conquered, what little we know of such cultures – and what, therefore, the Incas borrowed from them – tends to come not from Inca records but from enquiries by the conquistadors. The Spanish didn't conduct these out of anthropological curiosity but rather to prove that the Incas were unlawful rulers of conquered territory and could therefore themselves be legally usurped – a typical bit of pedantic legalism on their part.

The warm stone used on the towers glowed against the sombre backdrop of the Altiplano – a backdrop made more sombre by the build-up of storm-clouds behind, which unleashed not only rain but a dust wind of scratching ferocity, a wind that had me running for my taxi with my head huddled in a coat.

As I drove back into town, I passed a mortician's with an advertising logo: '*Funeraria – Servicio Permanente*' ('Mortuary – Permanent Service'). Puno was not a cheerful place. Exposed to the Altiplano, it seemed to be forever raining – no wonder that most visitors, including the Incas, had always preferred the more secluded climate of Cuzco. To keep warm, I was forced to buy an alpaca jersey (something I had vowed always to resist), and even though I managed to find one that had no llama motifs and wasn't *cardado*, 'combed out' to look like a moulting hamster, it still felt like a garment John Denver would wear to play songs by the fireside.

The wind lasted for days and turned the waters of Lake Titicaca sheet-metal grey. It was like Weston-super-Mare in the off-season.

*

The 'floating islands' of Uros did not live up to my expectations. 'Floating' is anyway an erroneous description (they are more properly 'anchored'). The islanders were said to have originally fled from Spanish occupation and enforced work in the mines. They had constructed the islands out of reeds and now spent most of their time cutting new reeds to add to the surface as the islands continued to sink. This had acquired more urgency in the previous few years as changes in river-distribution from the sur-rounding Andes and the receding snow-line were causing the water-level to rise. Titicaca is a volatile lake and the changes in its levels may well have precipitated declines of civilisations like that of the Tiahuanaco.

Indeed there is a theory that many of the pre-Columbian civilisations (with some exceptions like the Chimú, who were conquered by the Inca) may have ebbed and fallen as a result of climatic changes rather than colonisation by another power. The occasional eruptions of *el Niño* phe-nomena – droughts, landslides and floods – every century or so caused such widespread disruption that entire dynasties could perish.

On the 'floating islands' there was an overpowering smell of rotting and fermenting vegetation. Walking around the islands was like negotiating endless puddles on a muddy lane. The novelty of an unstable surface did not give the same tactile pleasure as bog-moss or sand, for one's feet neither bounced back nor felt any resistance. They just sank a little.

The islanders led a wretched life, their existence centring around the

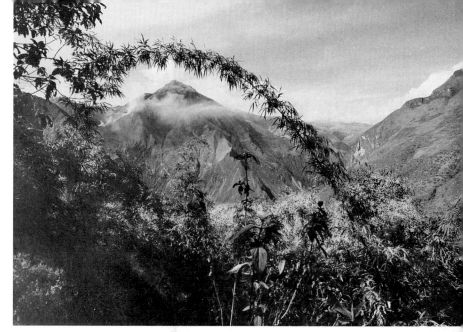

'The mountains of Eastern Peru, where the cloud-forest washes up the sides of the Andes from the Amazon.'

The Cusichaca camp, near the confluence of the Cusichaca and Urubamba rivers, with the site of Huillca Raccay in the foreground and Patallacta to the left: *'It was the Inca world in miniature and it was to be the base for all our future exploration.'*

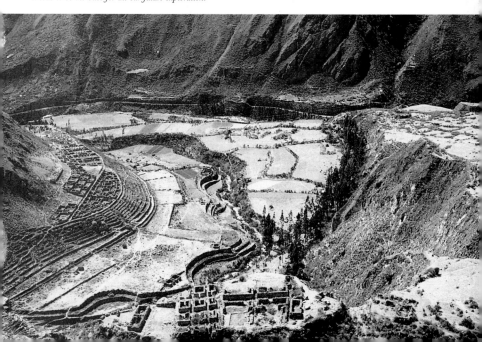

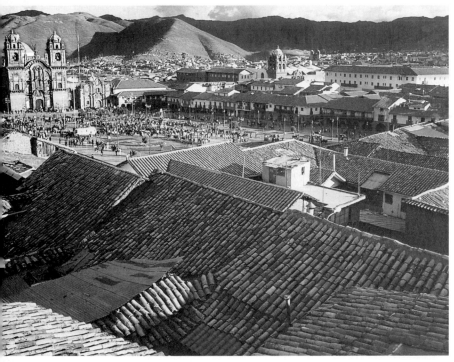

Cuzco: *'From the great central square, roads radiated out to the four quarters of the Inca empire, Tahuantinsuyo.'*

Struggling up at altitude, with the Vilcabamba range behind me.

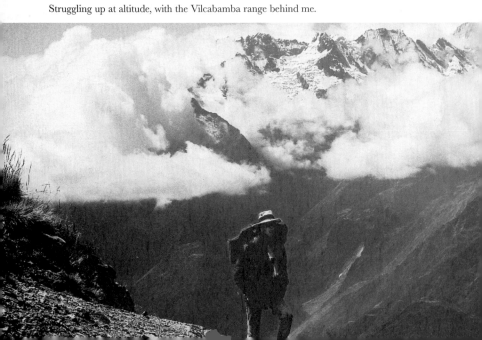

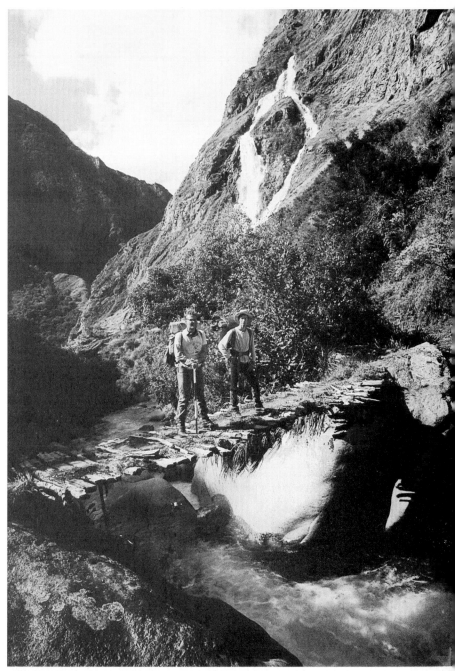

With J.B on a bridge over the Río Aobamba after descending from Llactapata.

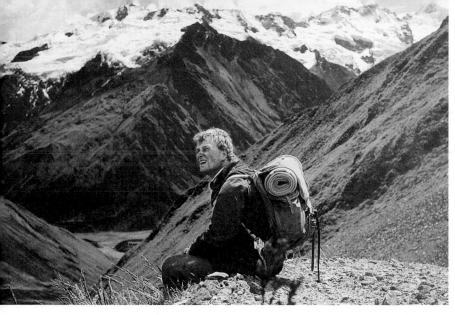

J.B. getting his breath back on the pass above Yanama, on the way to Choquequirao.

The view from Llactapata: *'The unmistakable outline of Machu Picchu was folded over the distant skyline.'*

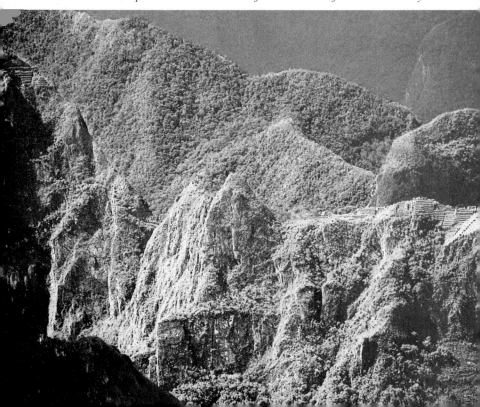

Villagers at Rayanpata.

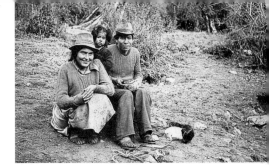

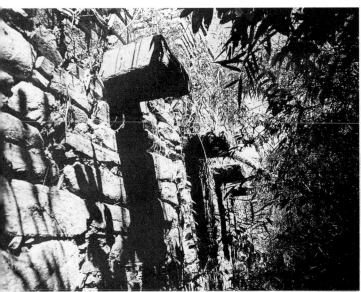

Left and below
Choquequirao: the
great *kallankas* of
the Main Plaza as
we first saw them
in 1982, covered in
undergrowth.

Following page
Machu Picchu.

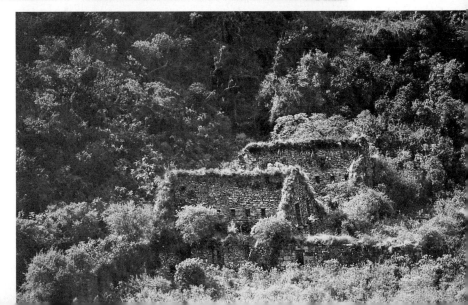

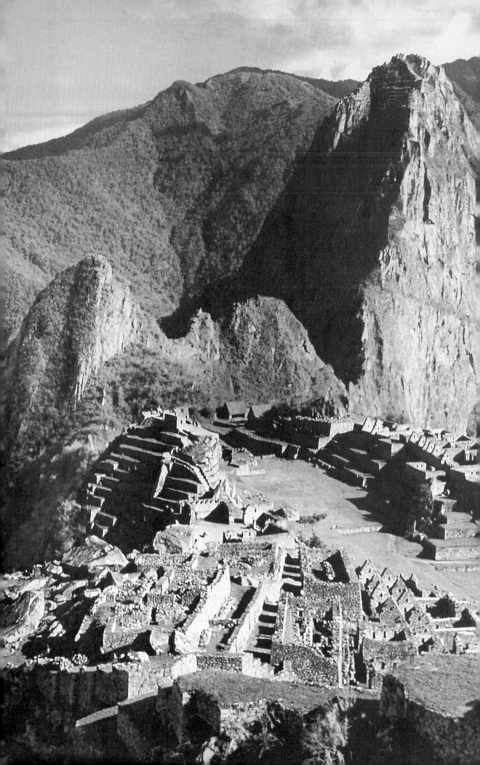

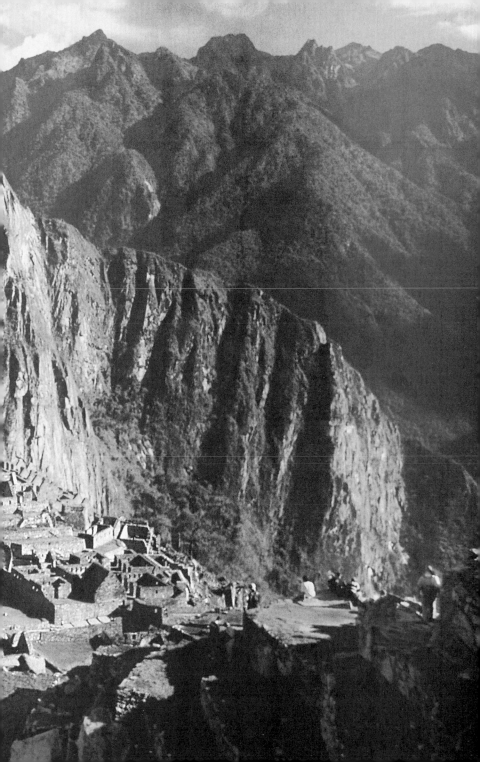

Machu Picchu: the area under the Torreón, which Bingham dubbed The Royal Mausoleum: *'a receptacle of pure sensation.'*

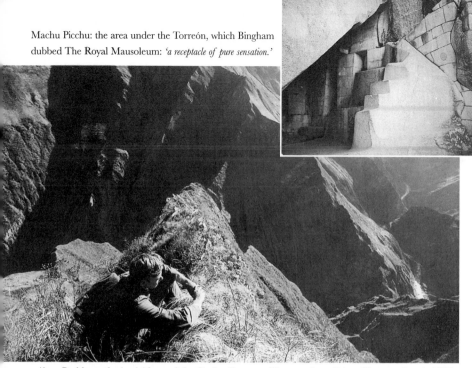

Above Roddy on the 'eyrie' beyond the Outlier Group at Choquequirao. *Below* Choquequirao in 1999, after clearing and restoration. The *kallankas* of the previous plates can be seen beside the Main Plaza.

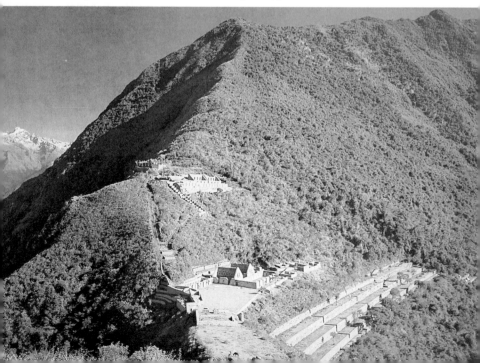

arrival of the local tourist boat from the mainland and desperate attempts to sell crude handicraft and weavings. The schools (there were three, all run by Seventh Day Adventists) were the only buildings with corrugated iron roofs – the others had more of the decaying reed.

I wondered what Swift would have made of it. This would have been a fitting destination for Gulliver, with plenty of scope for parallels to be drawn – men forever trying to shore up the ground they walked on.

By contrast, the little island of Taquile, further out beyond the bay, was a far more hopeful analogy for the human condition. Everything was in harmonious proportions. An island about the size of an English parish, on mercifully firm ground, it had enough hillocks to have 'hidden places' and enough people to be prosperous without intermarrying. The land was quite fertile enough to live off without tourism and the islanders had worked out a sensible communal arrangement for taking visitors. There were no hotels so each family would offer accommodation on a rota system. Nor were there, as the islanders pointed out with considerable pride, any thieves or dogs. Certainly there were no police, and the only goods I saw being sold were all worked with impeccable craftsmanship. The islanders lived mainly on fish and vegetables, with little meat. Their traditional dress was flattering – loose trousers, a rough white shirt, black-and-white waistcoats, a red cap.

Both men and women would spin continuously, using small hand looms, and did so even when they walked around the island. I would meet them as I circled the entire shoreline in a few hours and climbed the little summit hill, from where you could see the patchwork of small allotments spread over the island, divided by simple stone walls. To prevent footpath erosion (for each small plot was only about fifty square yards), the island was translaced by carefully walled paths, paths that sometimes contoured, sometimes darted down to the water's edge and sometimes went up and around the small hillocks, like cut apple peel. With the lake beyond, it looked like a Mediterranean idyll.

The boatman I was staying with, Fortunato, had lined the walls of his adobe hut with bamboo and I slept on a pile of rugs in the centre of the room, with a candle to write by as there was no electricity. His children would sometimes come in, both to watch me writing (which they felt was an odd occupation for a grown man) and to ask for one of the oranges I had brought from Puno. My only problem was that few of the islanders spoke Spanish, keeping to Quechua, of which I understood little. This would have been the savage twist for Gulliver – that having arrived at what seemed, in microcosm, to be a perfect balanced society, the Houyhnhnms, he was unable to communicate with them. Lévi-Strauss had a similar parable of the perfect uncontacted tribe in the Amazon who, while a paradigm of all that the civilised world wants the 'savage' to be, were unable to communicate any of their knowledge to their finders, as their language proved impenetrable.

It was with real regret that I left after a few days, and considerable relief that I arrived back in Puno. The crossing of the lake was not a good one. When we left, there was sun on the island and the islanders waiting on the curved jetty were silhouetted heavily against it, like symbolic figures. Once underway, however, a storm quickly began. In a small boat on a big lake this was no joke. We began to pitch. The captain was disconcertingly alarmed and brought out a large pile of oilskins and life-jackets, but rather than issuing them to the passengers, these were lashed to the stern in a heap. One of the islanders told me that the last time there had been a bad storm, the ferry had sunk only a hundred yards from shore and five people had been killed – not helped by the fact that, like so many islanders in different parts of the world, they had never learnt to swim. In the distance we could see the two lighthouses that marked the approach to Puno, winking alternately as if in complicity at our plight. We still had some way to go before we reached them.

I like the sea and have since made films about off-shore sailing, but that trip across the inland lake of Titicaca remains a low point. It was not so much the height of the waves, although the pitch was extreme, but the feeling of total insecurity. The light day boat we were in wasn't equipped to deal with storms. Some of the plastic fittings ripped off in the wind. A woman started to cry. The water was dripping from the roof as the passengers huddled together in the tiny, rolling cabin.

Up ahead beyond Puno, the sun was setting in a red gap between the black storm clouds. The reeds to either side of the lake were being lashed by the wind, looking like fields of wheat that had been trampled on. It was with a communal feeling of thanks that we finally passed through the channel between the lighthouses. An Italian man who had been staying on the island with me said a prayer. I needed a drink.

I had got talking to three Swedish girls on the boat, day-trippers, who were reserved when I first saw them but became more approachable under the duress of imminent shipwreck. One was tall and striking-looking, with a Garbo profile and blonde hair. After months in the mountains and on my own, this seemed an unfair provocation to my deprived hormones. That night I went with them all to a small *Peña*, a folk-club, where we were serenaded with the song '*Abra la Puerta*' ('Open the Door'): this turned out to be the plea of a despairing man who needed to enter a house not, as I at first assumed, for his girl, but in order to get a drink. An Argentinian guitarist came on who was introduced as being deaf: he played with ferocious intensity, hunched over his guitar and stopping frequently for taut moments; he even played '*El Condor Pasa*', turning it from the over-familiar pan-pipe lament into something with the emotional lacunae of a tango.

I tried chatting to Garbo, but she preferred to let her smaller brunette friend do all the talking. After a while, what with the noise and the difficulties of speaking in Swedish English, I concentrated on the music and the excellent *ponche* they served, a mixture of hot milk and pisco brandy.

Garbo and the third girl peeled away back to their hotel, leaving the brunette and me. It was only when she put her hand on mine that I realised, with the usual male slowness, that I had very discreetly been 'switched' without realising it. I also realised, now that Garbo wasn't casting such a shadow, that the brunette was extremely attractive in her own right. Unfortunately the *ponches* chose that moment to kick in savagely, with the slight delay and extra potency that altitude seems to encourage, and it was all I could do to get back to my hotel, let alone take anything further. I woke up with a hangover and considerable regrets (how often in life was one going to meet an available Swedish girl high after a life-threatening experience?). But at least the boat hadn't sunk.

*

Later that day I became more seriously ill and remembered the last time I was ill after one of those same *ponches* – from the milk rather than the alcohol (I thought of the Arctic explorer who alone among his crew never got ill because he refused to mix his whisky with what turned out to be contaminated water). I got onto a serious antibiotic diet and rested for a while before heading on towards La Paz.

When I finally hauled myself onto the bus, I found an engaging Dutch anarchist called Alfred. He was a welcome relief after all the South-America-by-numbers travellers and a good companion for the journey to La Paz. I had already met him wandering around Puno market: at six foot five, with bleached hair and a nose ring, he stood out, to say the least. He was in the process of buying a heavy-duty catapult – to use, so he said, in the Amsterdam street battles that he and his squatter friends fought with police. Alfred had worked there as a male nurse, but the constant carrying of patients had damaged his back and after cashing in the insurance he'd started travelling the world – albeit very slowly. He had spent six months just in Nicaragua, before heading south.

Alfred's main comment on Nicaragua was how wonderful it had been to have such a thriving black market in dollars – not perhaps a particularly left-wing sentiment, but he reminded me that as an anarchist he didn't need to follow any dogma. This was what was luring him to Bolivia now. 'The exchange is going through the roof,' he cackled with delight. 'We'll be able to live like kings.'

Within a short while we were over the border into Bolivia.

*

The name Copacabana was precisely right – a pastiche name for a resort town, a friendly place on top of a hill, looking out over the Bolivian side of Lake Titicaca. It bore about as much resemblance to the Brazilian beach of the same name as Bournemouth does to St Tropez. I felt as if I were suddenly on holiday, in a new country and with different food: there were delicious *salteñas* in the market, hot pasties stuffed with chicken or egg, and I washed them down with *api*, a kind of teetotal punch.

Alfred and I established ourselves in a sleepy *pensión* near the waterfront run by a Señor Ramón, which had chamberpots in the rooms and a decayed balcony looking out over Lake Titicaca. Señor Ramón took one look at us and stated the house rules with all the firmness of a Blackpool landlady: 'No drinking in the rooms, and no women – or you're in the street.'

It was a Sunday, and the weekenders were out in force: pleasure cruises were coming back from the Islands of the Sun and Moon, while a photographer was using a box camera straight out of Lumière to take pictures of Bolivians in their Sunday best. The odd kid bicycled along the shoreline. A large family gathering had spilled itself over the shores of the lake, the women bowler-hatted, the men in racing trilbies, and beside them were packets of food in white muslin waiting to be opened. It was a nineteenth-century scene, some Breton seascape for a Boudin or a Monet.

A full Bolivian admiral was promenading with his family, in a magnificent uniform with enough medals to have their own auction at Sothebys. His family kept a discreet ten feet behind him. The admiral probably felt he had to make up in attitude for the lack of any sea-going fleet. The Bolivian navy had been sadly curtailed ever since the War of the Pacific a hundred years before, when the country had lost all access to the sea (Chile had taken the Atacama Desert from them, with British assistance). They now had to make do with elaborate ceremonies on land and the odd ride over Lake Titicaca to scare the smugglers, for whom the political division of the hundred-mile lake was a contrabandists' charter.

The Copacabana Cathedral was as ornately decorated as the general, Byzantine in style and with a magnificent mosaic roof. Inside the bishop shuffled along with the liturgy: it was only with the sermon that he became rhetorical and forceful, knocking the gilt psalter over in his excitement. It is difficult for the Spanish language to achieve the powerful plainsong effect of an English liturgy, being too inflected, and so church services often oscillate between hastily mumbled intonation and full-blown rhetoric. However, the Church is a powerful force in the Andes. After the violence of the Conquest, the two cultures discovered they had much in common when it came to religious temperament. The mordancy of the Spanish met the fatalism of the Indian, and the resulting combination is a powerful one, a peculiarly Andean form of Catholicism that mixes a fierce eschatology with pastoral images of the *cantuta* flower and the lily.

Beside the cathedral was a simple *capilla de velas* ('chapel of candles'), a narrow concrete trench of a place with a darkened Christ figure at the back. Compared to the gilt and pomp of the cathedral, it was a humble affair. Worshippers had lit candles for the *difuntos* (a fine Castilian word for the deceased), and also for their patron saints. A woman I had met on the bus came over and poured her heart out to me: she came here regularly as a pilgrim, she had lost her husband, this time she had come with her eldest son, the next day was a fiesta so she had been able to come over from Cochabamba for a long weekend, they had a fiesta there in March when childless men prayed for children and men with too many children prayed they would have no more.

We were interrupted. Outside the usual Sunday brass band had been parading, although with more of a military presence than I was used to in Peru. There seemed to be soldiers everywhere. Suddenly one of them produced a machine-gun and fired off a round into the air in front of the cathedral. If this was to attract attention, it was spectacularly successful. The noise was deafening. Some kids ran forward to retrieve the spent cartridges off the cathedral steps. The soldiers, satisfied that they were now being noticed, continued on their way.

I had known that Bolivia was in political turmoil, but this helped focus my attention. Later that day, over some beers that we had smuggled into the *pensión* past the disapproving eye of Señor Ramón, Alfred gave me his critique of the Bolivian political situation.

'The generals want to give up power – by force if necessary.'

I thought that Alfred's usually excellent English had failed him. 'You mean "take power".'

'No, give up power. The situation has become so impossible to manage that the generals are prepared to force the democrats at gunpoint to take over from them. Of course the democrats don't want to run Bolivia any more than anybody else wants to. This country is impossible, you see.'

Alfred clearly relished its impossibility. Bolivia was the role-model for an anarchist state. It was said to have had over a hundred changes of presidents in the past century. Now the military government had closed the banks and tried to limit foreign exchange to a few government agencies, trading at a fixed rate. It was an invitation to a thriving black market, as I realised when changing a few *sucres* outside the bus station, a traditional spot for money-changers. The *sucre* was named after Antonio José de Sucre, the very first of Bolivia's many short-lived presidents and a man who had done as much as Simón Bolívar to throw the yoke of Spanish colonialism off the continent.

I could afford to travel in a luxurious leather-seated Pullman rather than the bone-crunching wrecks I was used to: we pulled out of Copacabana and the narrow ridge road wound across the Tiquina peninsula that juts out into Lake Titicaca. The road was a delight, slipping and sliding across the top of the ridge, with alternating views of both sides of the lake and the small fishing communities that dotted the shore. There were oxen grazing in the shallows of the water.

I sat next to a fit and brisk looking *mestizo* in shirtsleeves who pointed out to me with some relish the small island where Bolivian prisoners were incarcerated, a ferociously humped Alcatraz that looked menacing even at some distance across the lake. This was Coati, the Island of the Moon.

The Incas made pilgrimages along the peninsula to visit both this and the nearby Island of the Sun. On the Island of the Moon, they built a convent for *mamaconas* ('holy women') which directly copied many of the features of the earlier Tiahuanacan buildings already on the island, like the step-motif which was to the Tiahuanaco culture what the trapezoid was to the Incas. Some Inca legends described the Island of the Sun as their birthplace and one could see why it would fit so perfectly into their aesthetic – the high lake (an altitude of over 12,000 feet), ringed by mountains, with excellent sight-lines and legitimised by the worship of an ancient culture whom the Incas admired.

I felt the heat on my face from a few days sun-bathing by the lake. My body was still feeling the powerful antibiotics that were working their way through my system. The inside of the bus was like a furnace. It would have been a brave gringo who attempted to open a window. Andean peoples may be forced to endure a cold climate, but they still hate it, just as in India the inhabitants complain endlessly about the heat, and the mountain coaches were always compensatory fugs of condensation and stale air as a result. Sitting in the central back seat, I was staring straight down the length of the bus at the neon display over the driver's windscreen, which was flashing '*Dios es Amor*' ('God is Love') at me in saturated red. The driver sounded the horn by pulling on a bell-rope suspended over his head – and he sounded his horn at every corner, car, truck, dog or sheep.

My companion started to talk to me about the dollar rate (not surprisingly, a national obsession). I worried at one point if he was going to try to change money for me, but instead he told me, very usefully, how to exploit the situation – where I could get the best black-market rates for dollars, where the best markets for contraband were in La Paz. After a while I asked out of politeness what he did. 'I'm a customs official.'

We came to Tiquina and the straits, the narrow section of water dividing the northern and southern halves of the lake, which the customs man was prompt to tell me 'have a depth of over 800 metres' (Latin Americans love statistics), and a curious crossing began in which the passengers were transferred separately onto small launches while the coach itself was strapped onto a large raft. Once over the straits, the Bolivian Altiplano widened out in front of us. After months of being in the narrow Andean valleys, it was like finding oneself on a prairie, albeit one at 13,000 feet. The horizon was made even emptier by the few houses scattered across the plain like broken building bricks, their brown adobe walls even drabber than the land. I found the Altiplano desolate but not in a spectacular way – it seemed rather to be the landscape showing its complete neutrality and indifference.

Beyond the lake, I had already seen the Cordillera Real rearing up. The first sight of a mountain range from afar is always a deceptive one (I remembered when we had first flown over the Peruvian Vilcabamba on arriving in Cuzco). A new range can seem both more anonymous and more clearly visible than when one gets entangled in the valleys and each mountain becomes a looming presence, often unseen behind a cloud or ridge. It felt wrong to see the mountains so exposed – they seemed naked, lit by the bleak afternoon light of the Altiplano.

It was a stage-drop suitable for what was the bleakest passage of all in the Spanish Conquest of South America. If Peru had seen the climax of the conquistadors' achievements (victory over a powerful Empire had at least been a brave achievement, if a brutal one), Bolivia saw the squalid end-game, the almost Beckettian reduction of their aims to the annihilating extraction of wealth, whatever the human cost, where the only words to be heard were 'More silver, now.'

When the original conquistadors had set off with Columbus in 1492, they carried with them some of the aspirations and ideals of the Renaissance they had left behind. They searched for wealth and glory as well, of course, but it was also true that some saw the New World as a canvas in the same way as the ones being painted in Rome and Venice, a setting for the best in man to emerge. For the humanist, America could be seen as an Arcadia, a Golden Age setting as envisaged by the classical sources that had only just been rediscovered.

Likewise, many of the first wave of Christian missionaries who went to the West Indies and Mexico genuinely thought they were converting lost souls, re-establishing a prelapsarian state in a land where God had clearly been bountiful in his distribution of riches. The natives, wrote the great campaigner Bartolomé de las Casas, were '*tablas rasas*', 'blank slates', on which a new faith could be inscribed.

Thus Cortés, in conquering Mexico, could mythologise his achievements into a compendium of dashing military conquest, religious conversion and fairytale wealth. His letters back to Charles V are full of optimism about the 'New Spain' he had established. Thirty years later, by the time the silver mine of Potosí was found in Bolivia, much of this early idealism had fallen away. The Spanish could no longer play at being romantic heroes in some chivalric epic – now they were not dashing *conquistadores* but land-owners, extracting as much as they could from Peru and shipping it back to a mother country which increasingly distrusted their attempts at independence. The priests had made the disillusioning discovery that the natives of the New World were remarkably like Europeans in their capacity for sin and moral turpitude – and that far from being '*tablas rasas*' for a new re-birth of Christianity, they held deep religious views of their own that were almost impossible to erase or at times even recognise, such was the cultural gulf between master and servant race. This feeling of increased disillusionment, of a dystopia, was to reach its apotheosis at Potosí.

Potosí was one of the richest silver mines that has ever been discovered. At first the silver was so plentiful that it lay on the ground and could simply be gathered by hand. Around 1550 the Spanish began extensive mining down into Potosí hill, the *Cerro Rico* or 'Rich Mountain'. Indians were brought forcibly from hundreds of miles away to work the mine. A horrific number of them lost their lives.

The image of the mine as described by contemporary witnesses seems Dantesque, the great central shaft of the mine descending endlessly into the mountain, with three crude ladders hung from the sides: a 'down' ladder, an 'up' ladder and a third for use if either of the other two broke, as they frequently did. The Indians would carry enormous loads from the perpetual darkness at the foot of the shaft – one authority quotes 45 kilos, a tremendous weight (even a fit Himalayan porter will rarely carry more than 25). As many as 4500 men could be working in the mine at any one time, with twice that number waiting outside to take their turn. The mine consumed the labour-force of Bolivia's Altiplano. If they didn't die, they were ground down by the apology for a wage that was paid to them. Within a generation, the population of those parts of the Altiplano used for mine conscription had halved. Within another generation it had halved again. And still Potosí continued to exact its quota.

Any pretence that this was being done voluntarily by the Indians – a pretence that had been sustained at some of the lesser mines elsewhere – was simply washed away by the enormous wealth that Potosí created for the Spanish Emperor, a wealth which fuelled further misery in Europe with the prosecution of Spain's European wars. Potosí is a terrible reminder of how the Dark Ages continued past the Renaissance and of how the Spanish Conquest ended. It was to the sixteenth century what Auschwitz was to the twentieth. The great Uruguayan writer Eduardo Galeano put it succinctly in his book *Open Veins of Latin America*: 'Potosí remains an open wound of the colonial system in South America: a still audible *"j'accuse"*.' Much of the sadness and instability of the country seemed still to well up from the destructiveness of that early greed.

*

We seemed to circle around the rim of La Paz before finally dropping into it: it was an odd vertiginous feeling to be in the suburb of a city and look down over a precipice at its centre. I was used to city centres only revealing themselves from the tops of skyscrapers or spires – La Paz alone seemed to resemble a plug-hole into which the whole city drained.

'*Dios es Amor*' was still blinking at me in red from above the driver's seat. It was twilight and the bus was alternately flashed by the city's sodium light and the washes of coloured neon from the shop-fronts. We stopped at some traffic-lights and hawkers came by with newspapers, which the passengers bought anxiously to read about the political situation.

Alfred was looking very wired, either from amphetamines (his nurse's duties had left him with a collection of chemical habits) or from the impending excitement of possible street violence and confrontation. I had already heard and wearied of his many stories of fights with the Amsterdam police. 'This revolution will not be televised!' he announced suddenly in a loud voice. The Bolivian passengers looked startled. There was already an odd, tense mood in the bus as we circled down through the empty streets.

Outside the diaspora of the bus station, the dim figures of street-sellers and commuters swirled by us in the dust. A big car pulled alongside us. '*¿Dólares?*' The thick-set Bolivian inside had seen too many Hollywood movies. He was wearing a trenchcoat. Short of having a sign on the roof saying 'Black Market Exchange', he stood out a mile. I received an obscene amount of money for just a few dollars. 'Let's go drink to the death of capitalism,' said Alfred.

There was a roof-top restaurant at one of the hotels that was said to be one of the best in the city. The *maître d'hôtel* looked in horror at my battered backpack and Alfred's dyed blond hair and nose-ring. But he was in no position to turn us away. We were about the only people left in La Paz who could afford to eat out. Around us were a few other travellers who looked like they couldn't believe their luck. 'This is even better than Nicaragua,' said Alfred appreciatively as he ordered the largest steak they had.

It left me feeling uneasy. I checked into the sort of hotel I normally went to, downtown near a market, and left Alfred to his luxury suite. I fell asleep with the scurrying of city traffic below and an unexpected full moon shining down on me, as if blessing a lost orphan.

*

La Paz was a small city with a small centre. I quite often ran into my friend in the big black car and the trenchcoat over the next few days. He would cruise up behind me and idle along until I noticed him. Because it was pointless changing more than a few dollars at a time (the rate would have doubled by the evening), I needed him: the official exchanges were usually shut or trading at yesterday's money and the business of continual inflation and trading up prices was addictive. Sometimes he would have a woman beside him, wearing bright-red lipstick and playing moll to his gangster. She would count out the money. Trenchcoat (I never asked his name) was my only reliable source of information about what was happening. I knew a curfew had been declared and that the military were on the streets, but that was all. The newspapers were useless. In my hotel the staff knew nothing (instead the bell-boy asked me to record some passages from Graham Greene onto his tape-player so that he could listen to them for his English course).

Political correspondents reporting on a *coup* are usually close to the sources of information and each other, so can follow the rapid political changes of a crisis hour by hour. But for the actual inhabitant or less informed foreigner in the middle of a *coup*, for those on the ground, the process is continually hidden. In La Paz in the autumn of 1982, the newspapers didn't report what was happening, the television was a closed circuit and the only copies of *Time* were weeks out of date. No one I knew had a short-wave radio to listen to a foreign station – and if they had, would not necessarily have heard that much. Another *coup* in Bolivia was hardly news-worthy.

I discussed the situation with Brian, an Australian car-battery salesman who had taken time off to travel the world and was bemused that he had ended up in a *coup* that was bloodless yet also paralysing. 'I wouldn't mind it if there was anything to bloody *do*,' he wailed. This was the problem. Even the limited range of activities that travellers kept themselves busy with – hanging out in cafés, trying to negotiate the Byzantine complications of the *poste restante* system, haggling for souvenirs – were denied.

One day I watched as 'a general and indefinite strike' took to the streets, called for by the trade unions who, despite (or because of) a history of exploitation and corruption since Potosí, had become a strong voice in Bolivian politics. The strike was proclaimed from the Plaza San Francisco and spread with impressive speed into every working sector, both public and private. To the Bolivians it made little difference that most of the shops were shut – they had reached the position where they couldn't afford the goods anyway.

The only outward sign of any political urgency was the shrill '*Ultima Hora*' cry of the newsreaders, usually choked off into '*Hora*'. Each edition told as little as the previous. The strike had turned La Paz into a dead city. I watched as some riot police set up a barricade; they seemed embarrassed and were trying to stop their Dobermans from barking. One Doberman defecated right in front of the barricade and a policeman stepped forward with a scoop to remove it.

La Paz was a city drawn in charcoal, with washes of brown and grey. The clear light of the Altiplano above seemed to have sucked all the colour out of it. Just by the market and my hotel were rows of soup-kitchen stalls, smoking in the dark like some image from Depression America. I would eat *chairo* there and watch as the *Tránsito*, the officious transport police, patrolled the soup-sellers in their long, khaki, buttoned-down overcoats for any signs of sedition. There were police and military of every sort and it took a while to learn how to distinguish them. Once I passed a stall selling masks of gorillas in different types of Bolivian military uniform: although incredibly ugly, the gorilla masks were intended as a sign of masculine strength and were done affectionately rather than pejoratively.

In the streets, the women sat immobile for hours over a pocket hand-kerchief of goods – a little pile of bootlaces, or rolls of toilet paper – for returns so minuscule that it broke my heart. Bowler-hatted and impassive, they seemed a Latin caricature of English reserve.

Coming down from the Prado, I crossed the end of a big demonstration march by the opposition Left, a hunger march, and followed them towards a large square. The crowd was too big to fit in the square itself and funnelled backwards into the narrow streets. An amplified speech echoed around the walls, distorted by a bad microphone and feedback so that it was impossible to make out any words. Rival trucks were circling the city with megaphones. I felt like I was sitting right behind the speakers at some very bad festival, without being able to see the band.

It was difficult to tell when (or if) the crowd's jostling and whistling stopped and an actual riot started. Suddenly there were police coming towards us and people running away. The police had gas canisters strapped to their belts. A kid with some scales was screaming, '*Pésense, pésense, tienen que saber su peso*' ('Weigh yourself, weigh yourself, you must know your weight'). In the mêlée along the narrow side-streets, I was sometimes unsure if people were hurrying to get away from the police or just to catch a bus to get home. Everyone always hurried in La Paz. It was a cold city. Later I learnt there had been some savage beatings of the demonstrators.

The army curfew meant that I was holed up every evening in the little hotel by the market. I had been carrying Lévi-Strauss's *Tristes Tropiques* around with me since the start of my travels, but had always resisted reading it. Given the notoriously circular and somnambulant style of the book, being confined to a small room by military action was one of the few ways I was ever going to do so. It was worth it, for Lévi-Strauss had flashes of brilliance that punctuated the book's occasional monotony and in his overview of a decaying world slowly becoming more and more homogeneous, a 'mono-culture', he made me realise how much more precious those areas of true difference – like the culture of the Incas – were to become.

I could hear the lorries with their amplified and distorted speeches patrolling the streets long into the night as I read of Lévi-Strauss's expeditions into the interior of the Amazon in the thirties, his nights spent with a tribe sleeping in the ashes of the fire they had lit, the bees which could lodge themselves in a man's nostril, trees that smelt of excrement, and the slow distillation of all these memories as he wrote the book twenty years later.

Paradoxically, given the famous opening ('I hate travellers and explorers'), the book is one long and intense meditation on the need for both travel and exploration, even if he argues that exploration should be as much mental as the physical crossing of a space. His own mental travel can be, to say the least, circuitous, and reading the book at times felt like travelling up a particularly turgid Amazonian tributary. Just when I was about to give up on him he would produce some brilliant firework of a thought that would irradiate the page – often a thought that ran completely counter to what he had previously been arguing. For a man who could say that 'the first thing we see as we travel around the world is our own filth, thrown into the face of mankind', he was also prone to an extreme romanticism: 'Dreams ... have always slipped through my fingers like quicksilver.' The mixture of world-weary traveller and poet was intoxicating.

He also helped me define one constant of my own travelling experience – that travel is the perpetual difference between what you expect and what you get.

I couldn't leave La Paz because of the strike and the only book I had was *Tristes Tropiques*. Inevitably I resorted to the restaurants. I ate my way through the menus of the fine clubs of the city – and there were many of them, tucked away down side-streets and with verandas looking out over the city, often decorated as if in a parody of a gentleman's club, with leather armchairs and prints on the walls: the Club Hogar Austriaco (the Austrian Club), the Club de la Paz, the Club de la Prensa, the Club Alemán. All of them had a declining roll of members, peeling wallpaper and furniture that was too large. They felt like a Hapsburg had died in them.

It was in one of these clubs that I met Felix. I was his sole customer and, as there was only so long you could read *Tristes Tropiques* on your own in an empty restaurant, we fell to talking as he served me the long lunch that was the standard fixture at such clubs: the aperitif, the hors d'oeuvre, a soup (lobster was a favourite, although I tried not to think where it had come from), the *segunda* (the entrée), and finally a groaning trolley of deserts. My only strength of will came with refusing the liqueurs that Felix would always press on me.

Felix looked as if he had been there as long as the furniture, but I discovered that he had travelled extensively as a young man and had worked in many different European restaurants: 'I always got work because my comportment was correct,' he told me proudly. He stood upright, with a shock of white hair and a face so grained and mottled that it stood out against the smooth pressing of his shirt and suit. His Spanish was some of the most formal I had ever heard and I kept trying to keep up with the elaborately courteous phraseology. 'Would you, Sir, desire some wine with your meal?' he would say as he showed me a leather-bound volume that groaned with musty Argentinian and Chilean vintages. Even when I ordered a pisco with ginger ale (a *chaufflay*), the rough solecistic equivalent of ordering a Babycham, he would take it on the chin without a flicker of disappointment at my failure to single-handedly keep the flame of Bolivian gourmet dining alight.

He had worked in the Netherlands, in Italy, even in the Tottenham Court Road, but the place he remembered most fondly was Basle. I asked him if he had ever been to the mountains when he was in Switzerland and he shrugged politely, as if to say why on earth should he have, given that La Paz itself was higher than many Alps. He was, however, terribly impressed by the Swiss. When he mentioned them he always made a gesture straight ahead, as if to say just that: '*Los Suizos fueron siempre muy rectos*, the Swiss were always very correct.' Then he would shake his head and mutter about '*la situación*', as he called the political impasse. 'Things aren't right at the moment. There is no respect. Sir, would you like the *crème brûlée* or the diplomats' pudding?'

Every day I would return to Felix and his steaks done '*a la inglesa*' ('English-style' meant medium-rare for some reason), and he would tell me more of his travels and of those who had not appreciated his manner, but were the poorer for it. One day he announced that the strike had finally been lifted. The assembly who had been elected a full two years earlier but had been usurped by the military could now finally take their seats in government, led by Hernán Siles Zuazo, one of those who had instigated the land reform movement of the 1950s.

I could leave La Paz.

*

Looking back from the bus, La Paz looked like a premonition of a moon-city, packed into craters, rent by fissures and cracks, a red-and-brown terrain. The journey became more lunar as we travelled east, a desert landscape unlike anything I had ever seen. There was not even a cactus to relieve the wide expanse of red-brown rock and dust-bowls, with Mount Illimani looming up ahead of us.

I was heading for one of the old Inca roads that I knew descended towards the jungle, a spectacular path called Takesi that fell from a 15,000 feet pass down to an old mining village some 8000 feet below. It was good to get out of the city. I had felt myself starting to get corrupted by my artificial wealth (eating fine meals while out on the streets there were hunger marches) and there had been an incident that had crystallised this the day before I left.

One of the few other guests who had been marooned with me in the hotel was a Bolivian woman in her forties or fifties. I had found a watch left in the communal shower, a cheap watch with a plastic strap, and guessed it might belong to her but wasn't sure. I took it back to my room, meaning to hand it in to reception, but then absent-mindedly forgot about it. Later that day I was sitting reading when I heard a commotion outside, with the woman claiming that I had stolen the watch, that I was a '*delincuente*', that my room should be searched. The management hammered on the door. I panicked, opened the window and threw the watch as far as I could out of the window. It was not exactly my finest hour, but there was something in the city that was beginning to get to me, a state of moral inertia.

Getting back on the trail was a good corrective – and now that I was travelling on my own, with the same tent and stove but no one else to help carry it, this would be a truly Calvinist shedding of any excess fat.

If this was a pilgrim's progress, I had hardly taken two steps before being way-laid by Temptation, in the form of an engaging, moustachioed Argentinian called Antonio, who turned out to be the controller of the local coca industry. He first stopped me to sell some gold that one of the locals had panned out of the river, but we fell to talking and quite soon I abandoned any thought of walking further that day. He was at the legal end of the coca business – some was allowed to be grown on a quota basis – and had some interesting stories about the smugglers (he himself had elaborated a cunning scheme where he traded any confiscated 'non-quota' coca leaves for gold). He also had the first bottle of whisky I had seen in months. It was a compelling mixture. I had been fascinated by the mythology of coca ever since my induction by Presentación and here, clearly, was the man to tell me more about it.

The irony involved in the whole business of coca leaves was so big that it was easy to overlook. Here was a product that provided the recommended daily allowances of iron, calcium, vitamin A and phosphorous, just like it says on the cereal packet. It also gave enormous stamina to those Indians working in the extreme climate of the Andes. For centuries it had been one of their few reliefs from the cold, the mines and all the small potential miseries of daily life. In its natural state, as ingested by them (either by chewing or in a tea), it had no addictive qualities, only positive ones. And in lower climates, it was even easy to grow, potentially providing three good harvests a year. The coca plant, or *Erythroxylum coca*, to give it its botanical name, was a dream crop and a dream product.

In a different world, the West would have been actively encouraging Andean peasants to cultivate it and coca tea would be promoted as an effective, healthier alternative to our more normal caffeinated varieties. Yet because of our perverse taste for cocaine, a highly processed product of Erythroxylon which contains less than 1% of the actual coca leaf, the whole plant had been tarnished. The United States had poured money (and threats) into the eradication of the crop. Such was the hysteria surrounding the drug and its derivatives like crack that the States had even made it an offence to import coca tea into the country – as absurd as arresting people for drinking camomile. It was miraculous that Coca-Cola, which had originally promoted itself heavily as a 'healthy drink' because of the coca content, had somehow managed to maintain a licence to export the leaves from Peru.

Coca-Cola's involvement had prompted all sorts of elaborate conspiracy theories from some of the long-haired gringo trailers who had hung around the bars of Cuzco. One Canadian had held forth at length to me about it over breakfast in the Wiracocha café: 'Think about it, Hugh. Coca-Cola are only allowed to export coca leaves if they extract all the cocaine first. Now what do you think happens to all that cocaine they extract? Do you think it's just sitting in some locked customs warehouse in Callao?' He leered. 'Why else should the CIA bother with trying to run down the illegitimate cocaine smugglers if not to help boost their own smuggling business? The CIA, Coca-Cola, ITT, they're all in it together.' It had been too early in the morning to argue the case with him. (I found nothing sadder than to hear these same travellers muttering over their beads about how the *real* psychedelic high was to be had from sniffing datura lilies.)

What was certain was that attempts to close down on the trafficking were leading to some very strange happenings in the more remote jungle. Antonio told me a little about the wilder side of things as he stroked his moustache and managed to imply that while he knew of these things intimately he was at the same time distant from them.

Now that the Americans had more or less managed to close down air-traffic in the drug, the dealers had turned to the remote rivers on the far side of Peru and Bolivia, with their 8000-mile network of Amazonian tributaries. It was almost impossible to stop the dealers getting shipments of coca leaves to Colombia by the back door, where they would be processed into cocaine. In a wonderful example of military-speak, the senior US commander in Latin America had said, 'Riverine interdiction is the heart of the next important step in disrupting the supply.'

To help 'riverine interdiction', the Americans were providing Bolivia and Peru with a hundred patrol boats outfitted with M-60 machine-guns, together with satellite-linked tracking equipment. US military personnel were also using planes to guide local forces in the water below. But as another American official candidly admitted, this time off the record, 'What we are talking about is impossible to control, over areas that the central governments have never controlled.' Antonio put it even more succinctly: 'It's wild, wild country. You could float a circus from here to Colombia and nobody would notice.'

Coca leaves had always been fought over, even in the time of the Incas. The Emperors had sometimes given symbolic presents of a bunch of coca leaves to conquered rulers, a gift that was double-edged, as it was a sign both of benevolence and of the less symbolic and extremely onerous gifts they expected in return. Substantial amounts of coca leaves would have been part of any tribute given by a lowland tribe.

I had already come across examples of *poporas* in museums, the ceremonial coca-dippers which nobles would have used to break down the leaf with an alkaline substance for chewing. They were elaborate affairs and a reminder that for the Incas coca was a jealously guarded royal prerogative, although it is hard to see how they could have restricted its use, given the ease of cultivation and consumption. Coca leaves were burnt at religious ceremonies as a demonstration of conspicuous and extravagant waste (they are still burnt by the people of the mountains as auguries for the weather).

With the coming of the Spanish, the use of coca leaves was no longer restricted and the wider population took it up with a vengeance in what must have seemed at first like a pleasing democratisation of an aristocratic pleasure. However, the consequences were to be disastrous.

This was due not to any harmful side-effects of the drug, but to the greed with which the Spanish grew it. It had previously been cultivated in more low-lying areas as a specialist crop for the nobility and delivered in tribute. To mass-market coca, the Spanish now needed a considerably greater work-force and, given that there was little available man-power for them in the jungle, they pressed highland Indians into service. This had predictably miserable effects on the health of men unused to the diseases and diet of the jungle. Half of those forced to work in the *cocales*, the coca plantations, are thought to have died as a result. Despite attempts to limit the death-rate, the coca business, like tobacco today, was inevitably fuelled by the staggeringly good economic returns. For the conquistadors, coca was as good a trade as silver mining, and, unlike silver, the veins would never run dry. But its reputation as a danger to society was growing.

Coca had always been intimately connected with the Quechuan priest-hood, and there were various ceremonies in which it was worshipped in pre-Columbian times. The arriving Spanish clerics were horrified by its perceived power over the nation and the process of its demonisation began – even the normally sympathetic Cieza de León thought it 'a disgusting habit'.

John Hemming in his book on the Conquest quotes a commentator of the time, Diego de Robles, who declared, 'coca is a plant that the devil invented for the total destruction of the natives,' and the drug was officially condemned at the first ecclesiastical council of Lima in 1551. The US Customs Service and DEA would doubtless have concurred.

Yet the enormous and disruptive amount of money spent on trying to eliminate coca leaves in Peru and Bolivia – with very little offered by way of a replacement crop – was particularly absurd given the potentially far more effective use of the same money on prevention and rehabilitation work in the States. Cocaine was a problem of demand, not of supply. It was easier and more politically expedient to blame the peasants of the developing world than to try to address the acute social problems in American inner cities.

Given the enormous symbolic weight the leaves had come to acquire, I found it all the more moving to see the simplicity with which gifts of leaves were made, particularly on the remote mountain trails where quite often a few leaves would be handed over on the strength of a casual meeting and a feeling of fellowship.

There was a nice description of coca from the nineteenth century, by a Peruvian doctor called Hipólito Unánue who had prepared it for a lecture in New York, perhaps in an early attempt to convince the American public of its efficacy:

> The Indians believe that the use of coca is indispensable. They must chew it or die. They find that coca is capable of restoring lost strength, of resisting the attacks of age, of surviving the attacks of the elements and at the end of the day of giving a real lift to the spirit in moments of anxiety so as to put aside the troubles of the world. Just as in *The Odyssey* when Helen prepares a drink for her guests:

> 'Into the wine of which they were drinking she cast a medicine
> of heartsease, free of gall, to make one forget all sorrows,
> and whoever had drunk it down once it had been mixed in the wine bowl,
> for the day that he drank it could have no tear roll down his face,
> not if his mother died and his father died, not if men
> murdered a brother or a beloved son in his presence
> with the bronze, and he with his own eye saw it.'

It took me a while to get used to the process of chewing the leaves. Many travellers, particularly those expecting the instant gratification of a hit, gave up after a few attempts. The idea was to take the leaves very slowly into the mouth, one by one, and coat each with saliva before adding it to the slowly accumulating cud in the side of your mouth. This gave the chewer the comical appearance of a ruminating cow: I kept my chewing for tough treks, because that was when I really needed it and because no one could see me look stupid while walking ahead of me. The trick seemed to be in timing the amounts of bicarbonate of soda needed to break down the alkaloids in the coca leaves, without which nothing would happen. The Indians used a powerful alkaline substance made out of the ashes of cacao pods to do this. It was called *tocra de montaña* or more traditionally *llipta*, and could take the side of your mouth off if you got the amount wrong (bicarbonate of soda was safer for the 'light user'). Then you swallowed the small amounts of green liquid which the leaves produced.

Disconcertingly, there was always a considerable time delay before any effect really kicked in and perhaps this was the reason why the Spanish, used to more instant satisfaction, never really took to it. ('The Spanish use it simply as medicine, or when the inclemency of the hill stations inclines them to take up Indian customs,' noted one early chronicler.) The results often only began two hours after you'd started to chew, so you could be left unsure as to whether anything was going to happen – but if it did work, there was a real lift and energising effect that could take you over mountains other soap powders wouldn't. The *cocada*, as this was known, could last for an hour and the sense of anaesthesia and euphoria was very different from cocaine. Indeed, it would be hard to think of a less suitable drug to take in the mountains than cocaine, which, with its febrile bursts of energy and mild paranoia, would leave the taker exhausted after five minutes and petrified of possible snakes.

*

I needed all the coca leaves I could get the next day. It was not so much the ascent to the pass – although a steep one – but the extraordinarily heavy pack I was carrying. Used to having companions to share the burden with, I had badly over-loaded. I realised it was all getting too much when the kerosene bottle burst and flooded the rest of my belongings.

I gave half my food to the gold-diggers working the river below. A week's work would produce six or seven grams for them, if they were lucky. Their main irritation was the groups of picnicking families from the cities who came along at weekends to try their luck at panning. 'They're such *amateurs*,' one woman told me indignantly.

Above one village was a decaying church (the tombstones stuck up like matchsticks) and a group of bowler-hatted picnickers enjoying themselves. '*¿Anda solito?* On your own?' they asked solicitously after laughing at my lack of Aymará, and offered me *chuño* with an egg and *ají* dip. 'Already twenty-one? You need a wife.'

The Inca stone path branched up from the road and took a characteristically frontal approach to the pass. It was a stunning path, as good as any I'd followed in the Vilcabamba, stone-laid, purposeful and heading directly up between the rock-teeth towards the skyline – and it gave me heart to be following in the footsteps of the Incas again. The villagers below had told me that few people, if any, ever passed along the old road. At the top was a small *apacheta*, a cairn, which travellers had added stones to: a custom that the Incas were already following before the Spanish arrived. It seemed the instinct both to show that you have been and to guide those who are coming behind was a universal one from the Himalayas to the Atlas to the Andes.

From the pass at 15,000 feet the path fell away towards the jungle areas, the Yungas, and looking down made me think about the dynamics of the Inca Empire. It was not for nothing that so many of their great roads were in areas like these on the fringes of the Andes, where they dropped to the Amazon. This was where the trade and agricultural dynamic was at its most intense – what the academics liked to call the principle of 'verticality'.

Climatic conditions can be very harsh in these areas – just after I was there an exceptionally bad drought wiped out half the potato harvest. However, such a period of hardship would not necessarily affect each altitude in quite the same way. While the fields of the *puna* might experience a drought, in the jungle they might be having a normal harvest. From the earliest times, the Andean peoples had adapted to this by keeping land at different levels precisely so as to be able to ride out these climatic variations. Many *campesinos* of the area still worked the system in which they cultivated land at high altitude, where they could grow potato and quinoa, but also had holdings in the nearby lowlands where they could grow maize or coca.

The same principle applied on a larger scale with trade: the peoples of the jungle and of the highlands needed each other's produce (and not just for subsistence: the jungles could provide splendid feathers for decoration, the highlands woven wool from the alpaca and the llama). Paths like the one I was travelling on were a necessary part of the Inca drive to weave together the peoples of the area in a mutually beneficial exchange of goods.

Not far over the pass there was an old mining shaft near a lake where I could shelter for a while, with snow at the entrance and the Cerro Mururata framed beyond. Below was a small highland farming community, the village of Takesi, which had given this path its name. At 12,500 feet, it was a good height for farming potatoes, while the villagers had pasturage higher up for their llamas. The adobe huts of the village blended so perfectly with the surrounding landscape that I almost stumbled into it without realising.

There was enough evening sun to have a bathe in a rock-pool in the Río Takesi that passed nearby, and the next day I descended even further down: the path was a supremely intelligent one, roller-coasting down the gradients and letting the miles drop away under my boots. I felt terrific – sun on my face, downhill all the way and even the pack started to feel lighter. It was the first time I had walked on my own in the Andes, and it was liberating.

The mining village of Chojlla, where the trail ended, pulled me up short – a brutal place, with shanty huts all around. It was dusk when I arrived and Radio Yungas was blaring from all the shacks, so that I could hear the same disc jockey's voice as I walked along the line of huts. He was making a memorial announcement for someone who had died at precisely the same time the previous year. The faces that looked out at me were the most indifferent I had ever met in the Andes, unable even to reply to my greeting or do more than stare, telluric in the way the cold had carved raw cheekbones out of their mottled skin.

There was nowhere to stay, and precious little to eat, but a grumpy school caretaker let me sleep on one of the school desks, and I laid out my belongings on another as the floor was infested by cockroaches. My last oranges I lined up along the rail below the blackboard where the chalk went. There were old posters pinned up on the wall, exhorting the children of Bolivia to love the *patria*, the 'fatherland', to be honest, to learn how to tell the time and not to leave chewing-gum on their seats.

The windows of the school-room were broken and open, and I woke before first light, determined to leave as soon as possible. The only bus had been sold out days before, but there was a truck driver leaving who was selling standing-room only in his pick-up (at the same price as the bus, but no one could afford to argue with him). He kept us waiting for an hour as he loaded as many people and as much produce as possible into the pick-up: I wedged my pack upright against the press of pigs and sacks of potatoes spilling around me.

The light was blue and I was cold. I could only just make out the faces of some of my fellow passengers, huddled into their shawls. Some of the women were swaying on their feet, and held small children against them. The smell of old clothing and of pig was overpowering, and around the truck-stop was another strange, sickly smell like regurgitated fruit, rotting and dying. But as I stood wedged against the side of the truck, the cold burning against my face, I felt a strong affection for the people around me. It was impossible not to feel their stoicism, the capacity of the Andean Indian to endure punishment, and it was impossible too not to feel angry at the punishment they were still being given.

One passenger was better dressed than the rest. He had gold teeth and a small leather bag which he held tightly to his chest. He noticed me looking at him and we fell into a desultory conversation. He was an engineer and told me that there were plenty of gringos like myself who got interested in mining. After letting this sink in, he came up very close and whispered in my ear, 'I could sell you a small gold-mine, if you like.' The sun was not yet up, and I was being sold a gold-mine.

Finally the truck took off into a swirl of continuous dust from the road and we were coated in it, the women pulling their shawls around themselves. I saw the sun come up over the jungle of Yungas, burning its way through the dust and the opalescent green before the truck finally dropped me at a crossroads in the middle of nowhere and a shack-owner offered to sell me a beer.

'It's too early to drink,' I told him.

'What do you mean, too early? It's already ten o'clock.'

He was right. I had the beer and felt better for it.

*

A few days later and after some tough travelling by roads that bounced over the mountains, I was standing in yet another empty Bolivian street. The only difference was that this was the village of Tiahuanaco and nearby were the ruins I most wanted to see in Bolivia.

The ruins of Tiahuanaco were described by the nineteenth-century American traveller George Ephraim Squier as 'the Stonehenge of the Americas' and they had a reputation for antiquity that impressed even the Incas. Squier, a careful and precise observer who had been inspired by his friend William Prescott's recent book on the Conquest, was one of the first to arouse interest in the site when he visited it in the 1870s. I had read his long-forgotten *Incidents of Travel and Exploration in the Land of the Incas* at the Royal Geographical Society library before setting out.

Squier had a painful arrival in Tiahuanaco. His Irish photographer died suddenly as they approached the village, suffering from feverish hallucinations and 'murmuring something in the Gaelic tongue, in which only the endearing word "mamma" was intelligible'. Then later, in the village cemetery, he had witnessed a pack of the wild dogs that roamed the *puna* digging up the bodies of corpses, particularly of young children. When Squier had remonstrated with the local priest, the *cura* had shrugged his shoulders, ejaculating, 'What does it matter? They have been baptised and all Indians are brutes at best.'

Squier was not a man to be dissuaded by such experiences. When again in the cemetery, this time for the burial of his photographer, his eye was caught by a fine Tiahuanacan gateway which he tried to photograph himself, 'with no instruction except such as I could gain from Hardwick's *Manual of Photographic Chemistry*'. He spent a further week at Tiahuanaco photographing and making plans, noting with quiet satisfaction that most of his predecessors had been wrong in their measurements, a practice that modern academics liked to continue. From studies here and elsewhere in Bolivia, he was one of the first to make the scholarly proposition that the Incas had been preceded by many earlier civilisations – a fact we take as self-evident today. Max Uhle, as a young German archaeological student, was inspired by Squier to write his own book about the site a few years later, *Die Ruinenstatten von Tiahuanaco*. Uhle then spent the rest of his life trying to prove, successfully, that the Incas were by no means the first civilisation to spread out across the Andes.

A fellow passenger saw that I was looking lost and bore me off to the house of his mother-in-law (or '*madre política*' as he called her), who turned out to be a neighbour of the custodian of the ruins himself: Señor Ribero was an engaging fellow who looked Borgesian in a sober suit, trilby and briefcase, and when I explained that I'd been working at a site in Peru, he invited me to stay with him and visit Tiahuanaco in the morning. 'How clever of you to have arrived for the equinox,' he said politely. 'I was expecting more people to come – particularly the French – but you seem to be the only visitor in town.' I had no idea it was the equinox – indeed, would have been hard pressed to define precisely what an equinox was – but felt obscurely pleased to have timed my arrival so well, although I was a little unclear why it was so propitious.

I strolled around the village in the remaining light and the dust that seemed not to have left me for days. Outside the village church were two so-called 'guardians of the gate', pitifully dilapidated compared to the fine examples I had seen in the museum in La Paz, but a reminder that the Tiahuanacans were far more interested in the human figure than the Incas ever were. Their stone faces were goggle-eyed and strong, like Elisabeth Frink sculptures.

'We'll leave tomorrow an hour before dawn,' Señor Ribero told me that evening as he solemnly waited on me, to my embarrassment, bringing the dishes out of the kitchen: a bachelor's meal of rice soup followed by egg and chips and then a dessert made with condensed milk, all washed down with the unusual Bolivian stout, 'Bicervicina'. He told me about his children who had left for the United States, of the new government, of other foreigners he had met. As a young man, he had fought in the disastrous war of the Chaco against Paraguay in the 1930s, when Bolivia had lost yet more land. The history of Bolivia over the previous hundred years had been one of steady loss: after the disastrous War of the Pacific at the end of the nineteenth century there were various boundary disputes with Argentina and Peru (in which Bolivia came off worst) before this final, pathetic war with Paraguay, when almost 100,000 soldiers died.

Señor Ribero told me the story of the Chaco War sitting in the small *comedor*, by the light of a simple desk-lamp he had on a table. 'Most of those fighting with me were *analfabetos* [illiterates] from the highlands. They hadn't the slightest idea what it would be like down on the Chaco [the semi-tropical plain that sweeps down south from Bolivia towards Paraguay, often badly swamped in the wet season]. The whole war was fought for "El

Standard Oil". That's why so many of us died. For "El Standard Oil".' He held out his arm towards me, from under the sleeve of his suit. I had not noticed that he had served the meal with one hand. The other had been mutilated to a withered stump.

We set off together a little after four in the morning, with some coffee in a thermos and a large antiquated torch. Despite wearing every item of clothing I possessed, it was a bitterly cold wait when we reached the monument. As a site for the capital of an empire that at its height stretched all the way to the Peruvian and Chilean coast, it seemed distinctly unpromising. However, climatic variations around Lake Titicaca have always been extreme, and it may have been a more welcoming climate in the first millennium AD when the Tiahuanacan culture flourished. They were adept at farming around the shores of Lake Titicaca, using a system of irrigated raised fields (known as *waru waru*), canals and causeways in a remarkably successful way that, just like the canal-system at Cusichaca, had been largely lost after the Conquest. The Tiahuanaco civilisation had declined after 950 AD, when a prolonged drought seems to have set in around the lake, destroying the system of irrigation canals. By the time the Incas arrived in the area in the fifteenth century, they would have been a distant folk memory, if that.

We sat waiting in front of a monumental gate. Señor Ribero and I were the only people there and I felt privileged and virtuous to have made the pre-dawn start. I had assumed that the sun would rise in the centre of the gate, but when a faint glow began below the horizon it seemed off kilter. In the almost pitch-black, I could hardly make out any surface detail, but I was also puzzled that the gate did not have the dramatic split to one side that I had seen in all the illustrations of the Gateway of the Sun. I asked Señor Ribero. He looked at me in an astonished way.

'That's because this isn't the Gateway of the Sun. It's the Gateway of the Moon.'

I looked at him open-mouthed.

'I wanted to see if this gateway lies on any particular solar axis. The Gateway of the Sun is just over there,' he pointed over the mound of the Kalasasaya platform, 'and of course is set along the line of the equinox. I'm so sorry. I thought you'd realised.'

Feeling distinctly foolish, I stumbled over to the Gateway of the Sun in time to join a large group of French tourists watching the sun rise directly through its centre.

My main impression during the long wait for the sun had been of wire everywhere, put up, said Señor Ribero, to prevent *delincuentes* from removing any more stones than had already been vandalised from the ruins. But as the light came up over Tiahuanaco I could see that it was not, like the ruins of Sillustani I had visited earlier, a monument to desolation, but a monument to active mutilation. From the Spaniards, who had carted pieces of stone as far as Copacabana to use in the pretty Cathedral, to the modern inhabitants, Tiahuanaco had been savaged and its stones removed for houses, bridges, churches and the railroad. Far worse, in a way that was childishly spiteful of time, the noses of the statues had been broken off and their features ground down into stumps. Max Uhle, when he first visited Tiahuanaco in 1894, found the Bolivian army regiment stationed there using the statues for target practice. Even those who had attempted some form of restoration had been destructive – the large supporting rods used to prop up some of the stonework had themselves caused holes. Many of the structures had simply been moved around like furniture in an outhouse: it felt like an archaeological building-site.

This was all the more poignant given the fine work that had survived. The famous figure over the Gateway of the Sun, which Squier had described in such detail, was a tantalising taste of the quality of stonework that must have extended over what was a vast ceremonial centre (there were estimates of between 20,000 and 50,000 inhabitants). The few stelae and monolithic figures that remained stood up like isolated pawns on the chequered quadrants. The enormous man-made hill that had impressed Cieza de León at the time of the Conquest had been so shredded by *huaqueros* and brutal excavation that it required a considerable effort of the imagination to picture it as it must once have been, with seven great layers of terraces lifting it above the plain. Nearby, around the Puma Punku temple, great ashlars now lay scattered on the ground. Some fragments of doors that had survived showed the Tiahuanaco step-motif ascending their sides. Much of the reconstruction work which had been done was Stalinist in its brutality.

Nor was this vandalism necessarily all post-Columbian. There was some evidence, from artefacts found at the site, that it may have been the Incas themselves who moved many of the stones at Tiahuanaco. We know that they were impressed by the ruins and thought them the work of giants. They would have appreciated the positioning of the city, playing as it did to their own mountain aesthetic (the top of the man-made hill was positioned so as to give sight-lines of the distant Mt Illimani in one direction and Lake Titicaca in the other). Pachacuti, who conquered the area, borrowed many of the architectural themes in his great works of state around Cuzco. It would have been in keeping with the Inca sense of destiny to have simply 'rearranged' these monuments in a way that suited their own religious preoccupations – for one of the principal conundra was that the monumental gateways seemed almost certainly to have been moved from their original locations. I could almost hear the Incas saying, 'What a shame the giants didn't build this gateway in line with an equinox or solstice – let's move it so it is,' and few lords of the Altiplano since would have had the manpower or motivation to do so.

Just as they re-wrote history, so too the Incas seem to have been quite happy to destroy the buildings of preceding civilisations. They were abrupt in their treatment of the ancient temple of Pachacamac on the Peruvian coast, a shrine holding the position that Delphi had in the ancient Greek world, which they almost encouraged the Spanish to despoil. At Nazca, they brutally built a 24-foot-wide road straight through many of those famous desert lines, an act of cultural vandalism that would now have earned them a savage rebuke from Unesco. It would have been wholly in keeping for Pachacuti and his successors to have used Tiahuanaco as a glorified theme park and to have employed *mita* labour from their newly conquered tribes to work on it – by rebuilding walls and moving gates – in a way that glorified the Incas rather than their predecessors.

TO ECUADOR AND
CHINCHASUYO

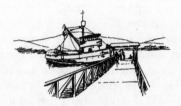

I WAS THOUSANDS OF MILES to the north of Tiahuanaco, where the Andes swept down towards the desert and the sea in great swathes of folded rock that, seen against a clear blue sky, had the uncanny precision of a geographical table-top model.

The Peruvian desert stretched away ahead. I had been in the same bus for thirty hours and before that in many other connecting ones since leaving Bolivia, so experiences were becoming hallucinatory. I remembered getting out one grey early morning after a cold night and seeing a solitary man standing still on the horizon, in silhouette, as I emptied my bladder into the cold: I remembered crossing the deep canyon of the Apurímac and stopping at a wayside shrine where the passengers got out to pray, clutching at the robes of the Peruvian national colours that the Christ-figure was wearing; and those robes in their turn gave way to the image of the road itself, draped across the folds and ridges of the valleys ahead of us as we had passed through Abancay, Ayacucho and out towards Nazca.

This was bandit country, the breeding ground for the Sendero Luminoso, and a policeman rode shot-gun with us, a pistol tucked nonchalantly into his back pocket. There were checkpoints every hour. The bus was a small (and cheap) family one, run by a husband-and-wife team: he was proud of his demonic reputation for getting passengers to their destination on time and resented the constant police stops; she bundled the passengers on and off, collecting fares in a small black leather bag she kept tightly pressed to her stomach. In one town we were delayed when some passengers were taken by the police for not having the right papers. Our bus trundled loyally after them around the streets of the town, from the police station to a notary's office, until they were safely retrieved.

I was heading towards Ecuador and Chinchasuyo, on the trail of the Incas as they swept north after conquering Bolivia. Pachacuti and his son Topa Inca had advanced with enormous speed, absorbing empires and forging trade alliances. However, the coast presented them with different possibilities and problems than those they had faced in Bolivia. Right in the north of the coast of modern-day Peru, they also found a rival empire, that of the Chimú, whose capital at Chan Chan was as extensive as anything the Incas had built themselves.

Someone had traded me a copy of *Anna Karenina* at a bus depot and I was letting the desert stand in for the immense distances of the Russian steppes as I crossed them. The desert was far more beautiful than I had expected, at least from a bus: there were little lush groves of cacti and curved dunes. I realised that this is what I had missed in the Andes – the eroticism of life and the fire in Vronsky's eyes. The desert burnt in reds and yellows, and each oasis town lay in a sudden pool of green.

The bus arrived in Pisco, near the coast, and I relished the sudden warmth of the night air as we got off the bus: there were people *paseándose*, promenading around the tiled square, with its benches painted a fresh lime colour, and *mulatas* walking from the hip, not the waist.

I had hooked up with a friend called Judy, who had worked at Cusichaca when I had been there, and we were travelling to Ecuador together. Judy was older than me and had seen more of the world: she had followed the Afghan trail when it was still open, spending time in India and Indonesia. As we crossed the desert, she looked out of the bus and told me that the layer of civilisation felt so much shallower in the Americas than in the East – that while in India the land was soaked by the many succeeding civilisations that had occupied it, in South America it all seemed surface deep.

Her comment made a strong impression on me. Because South America is still a 'new world' in comparison to Europe or Asia, because it is still a paradisical landscape that in relative terms man has scarcely begun to populate, human strengths and weaknesses tend to stand out in greater relief than they do elsewhere. The scars of mankind's occupation are more recent and the landscape has not yet had time to assimilate them. Unlike much of Europe, where town and country have merged into an indivisible blur, here a settlement really looks like an occupation of the land and probably a temporary one.

There were, of course, extraordinarily ancient civilisations in Peru, but you had to look for them – and many had only come to light in the twentieth century. The next day we went out along the coast to Paracas, the centre of a culture that seems to have pre-dated even that of Tiahuanaco, flourishing from around 300 BC. It was here that the Peruvian archaeologist Julio Tello made a fabulous discovery in 1925: endless mummies, sitting in a foetal position, wrapped in the most beautiful textiles and some with gold masks. The textiles (and the mummies themselves) had been perfectly preserved in their subterranean tombs by the dry climate of the coast.

Even now, wandering along the scraggy dirt desert alongside the highway, Judy and I came across bits of human bone wrapped up in scraps of fabrics, uncovered by the wind, the bones bleached white as the shells around them, and the odd fragile skull or rib poking from the sand, often caked in salt deposits. Many seagulls had also been embalmed by the sand, with their feathers still intact.

They say that Peru is one of the most archaeologically rich countries in the world, despite the ravages of the *huaqueros*, so that a discovery which would merit a headline if found in the States will only get a mention in the *Lima Times*. (This was particularly true of the Peruvian coast – the distinguished Andean scholar John Rowe once suggested that the reason it had taken such a long time for archaeologists to venture into the mountains and excavate Inca sites was that it was so convenient for them to investigate the abundance of sites near Lima.) But Julio Tello's discovery here at Paracas was a truly momentous one: in particular it focused attention on the accomplishment of the Paracan early weavings, richly embroidered with wild feathers they had traded with the jungle tribes and with zoomorphic figures, particularly fish.

Paracas was a culture that drew all its strength from the sea. A boat trip out to the nearby Ballestas islands showed even a non-fisherman like me that the marine life was in hyper-drive: the colossal shoals of anchovies and the fish that followed them brought predators of every sort, from cormorants to sea-lions. As the boat approached, the barking of the sea-lions in the hollowed caves was amplified and projected to us over the waves, an inhuman sound like a radio with its volume too high. Some of the rocks of the island were invisible behind the sheer density of sea-lions and birds. (The accompanying guano became of enormous commercial value to Peru in the nineteenth century, when they exported to the West the pre-Columbian custom of using it as fertiliser – the word 'guano' comes from the Quechua *huanu*, meaning 'dung'.) This wealth of marine life had fuelled the growth of the Paracas and other later coastal cultures along what might otherwise have been an inhospitable desert.

The whole dynamic of Inca and pre-Columbian expansion in this area was determined by the Andean countries' unique geography and consequent food supplies. The great desert kingdoms of earlier millennia, like the Paracas, the Nazca and the Moche had arisen because of the riches of the sea along the coast. However, the climatic conditions that gave rise to the rich seas – colder surface waters and an 'upwelling' from the ocean deep – also precipitated very little rainfall, which was why the desert coast itself was one of the most barren on earth.

For other foodstuffs, the coastal peoples were forced to turn to the valleys and the mountains, and the mountain peoples in their turn looked to the jungles for tropical fruits and coca. Out of the dynamism that resulted from these trade exchanges and the obvious advantages of an integrated market grew various successive dominant cultures and finally the Inca one of Tahuantinsuyo, which contained all three of the productive zones: jungle, mountains and coast.

Tahuantinsuyo was in some ways, I began to realise, more like a huge trading association than a formal empire in the monumental sense. Indeed, one of the archaeologists had described Tahuantinsuyo to me as being 'archipelagic', an expansion by the Incas which did not necessarily try to control all the land within a set area, to 'fill the borders in with red', but instead established key strong-points in different ecological zones which could supply useful produce, connected by Inca highways threading these outposts together. This also explained why not all Inca conquests were military: Tahuantinsuyo was more like an aggressive modern corporation that offered overwhelmingly compelling reasons to each client tribe why it had to join – consumer benefits.

The Inca sitting in Cuzco could have his famous fish for dinner (which would probably have been salted to make the journey from the coast), accompanied by the finest of freeze-dried new potatoes and some pineapple or papaya to finish. The Inca store-houses, the *qollqa*, would have put a Sainsburys or a Wal-Mart to shame with the sheer range of produce available both in and out of season. Traders were sent out to the furthest stations of the Empire and beyond to obtain luxury items. The 'first contact' Pizarro and his men ever had with the Incas – indeed, what made them realise there must be a rich empire for the taking – was when their preliminary expedition down the coast from Panama encountered an ocean-going Inca balsa raft travelling far from shore, in search of prized commodities like coral and crimson fish shells.

This was a consumer society and the Incas were merely building on the acquisitive nature of earlier civilisations. When Tello found the wrapped mummies along this stretch of coast, he realised that some of the textiles were woven with camelid hair (like llama) acquired in trade with the highlands. Another highly valued product amongst the coastal peoples was the feathers of jungle birds, which they loved to weave into their rich tapestries.

all spill out and follow us down the street until it was lost in the salt spray that hung over the jetties of the portside. Here there were just a few old boats – the *Simón Bolívar*, the *Don Quijote* – on which pelicans sat beside clutches of netting-buoys that sprawled onto the decks like gutted fish-roe. We would come here when we wanted a break from the frenetic town life, and drink cold beers, sitting on the jetty with the Bahía de Caráquez soundtrack turned low in the distance.

We explored Bahía lackadaisically, slowed down by the Bahian habit of chatting with everyone you passed in the street and by the need for protracted siestas. Some friends of Judy's had lent us an old beach house a little way out of town. They were artists and the big, open beach house, set on stilts, was filled with light and unframed canvases. Judy wandered the shore collecting shells, with which she filled the plain bamboo walls of the house. Sometimes we would come across black-and-yellow sea-snakes washed up high on the beach.

In town, Tío Guillo's was our centre of operations. Tío Guillo was one of the only anglophiles I had met on my travels (given that the Falklands/Malvinas war was comparatively recent, this was not always surprising). A young forty, he had a fine, thin face with a broken nose. '*Yo me siento joven pero me falta una mujer. Cada noche voy solo a la cama.* I feel young but I need a woman. Every night I go to bed alone,' he told me. Part of the problem was that he worked an eighteen-hour day just to keep up with '*la competencia*, the competition', an exactly similar bar on the other side of the street. But he had time to read: he had, for instance, studied the history of the Second World War, so he said that he had always known that Britain would beat Argentina.

Judy asked him if he smoked. '*¡No!*' Did he drink? Guillo gave a smile. '*Tomo de repente*, I drink all of a sudden.'

I helped a fisherman prop up his reed boat after a morning's fishing. The reeds became waterlogged and heavy after prolonged use, so the technique was to stand them upright on the beach to dry, before dragging them up the beach to safety (this also allowed the fishermen to have a cigarette and shoot the breeze with one another while they were waiting).

It was with boats such as these that the Incas expanded right along the coast, both for trade and conquest. They were tremendously effective ocean-going vessels, as Thor Heyerdahl showed when he sailed one to Easter Island in an attempt to prove an early South American colonisation of that distant Pacific outpost. Topa Inca and his descendant Atahualpa led fleets of such rafts on naval engagements. That first tell-tale Inca trading vessel which Bartholomé Ruiz came across when he guided Pizarro was far out

One of the Spanish chroniclers not long after the Conquest, Bernabé Cobo, was amazed at the profusion of such feathers that had been found in the storehouses:

> The gloss, splendour and sheen of this feather cloth was of such exceptional beauty that it must be seen to be appreciated. Upon entering the land, the Spaniards found the storehouses of the Incas well supplied with many things; one of the most important ones was an abundant supply of valuable feathers for these textiles. Almost all of the feathers were iridescent, with an admirable sheen which looked like very fine gold. Another kind was an iridescent golden green. And there was an immense amount of those tiny feathers which are found on the chest of the little birds that we call *tominejo* [humming-bird], in a small patch about the size of a fingernail.

There was a luxury hotel sitting incongruously along the shore. Judy and I could see rich *Limeños* sitting by the pool or taking off on windsurfers from a private beach. After days of travelling (and a night in a two-bit hotel) it was a tempting vision. Unfortunately to the bouncers on the door we must have looked like two escaped members of some disturbed sixties cult – frayed clothes from months in the mountains, long hair, collapsing packs. They were adamant that admission was for 'residents only'.

We managed to find a hole in the barbed wire that surrounded the complex and (having hidden the packs and most of our clothes behind a bush) tried to stroll nonchalantly towards the *piscina*. In our underwear and pale mountain-deprived skin, we must have stood out like a sore thumb, but we made it to the pool and it was a good moment. I felt months of mountain travel fall away from me in that one long dive into the crystal-clear water. As I surfaced at the other end, a flunkied attendant approached and I prepared to be ejected.

'Can I get you anything to drink, Sir?'

'How kind. I'll have an orange juice and soda, with ice, and a Pilsner for my lady friend. Put it on Room 101.'

I had a feeling I was going to enjoy the coast.

*

The Humboldt current sweeps up most of Peru, making a desert pavement of the coast, but right at the north, near Ecuador, it peels away into the Pacific and the land explodes with relief into a riot of palms and tropical beaches. Pizarro's pilot Bartholomé Ruiz, when asked how future travellers from Central America would know that they had arrived at Peru, simply said, 'When you no longer see any trees, you are in Peru.'

It was near here that the Chimú built their immense capital of Chan Chan. The Chimú were rivals of the Incas and established a powerful empire that spread 800 miles down the coast. The Incas had finally managed to defeat them some seventy years or so before the Spanish Conquest.

The Chimú inherited all the exuberance of the coastal cultures that had gone before them, particularly the Moche. They too celebrated life with elaborate textiles and pottery in which the most noticeable quality for me, particularly after the Inca rigour, was playfulness – well, perhaps not the most noticeable. The sheer inventiveness of the sexual variants shown on the ceramics could still fascinate the least prurient of modern-day onlookers. At the museum in Trujillo, I had met a clean-cut couple from Canada (both physical education instructors at their state college) wearing shorts, trainers and matching day-packs. They clearly did not quite know what to say about the graphic depictions of fellatio, sodomy and sexual diversity that the potters had depicted so realistically.

Hearing I had come from Cuzco, Michelle asked, 'So what did the Incas think about heterosexuality?'

James: 'You mean homosexuality, Michelle.'

Michelle: 'Yeah, all that stuff. I'm just curious.'

I told them what I knew: that the Incas seem to have treated some of the Chimú practices with puritanical disdain and portrayed themselves as highland reformers cleaning up a veritable Sodom and Gomorrah on the degenerate plain. Like so many conquerors, they claimed the moral high ground.

The Incas had a few curious sexual attitudes themselves, however. Victor von Hagen had recounted the story, with some relish, of how orphaned children of the nobility 'would often be given to childless women who instructed them in sexual techniques and brought them up in exchange for this "servicing" of the old by the young'.

James: 'Older women, huh? Now that really is kinky.'

The actual site of Chan Chan nearby was a peculiarly hard one to assimilate. An open-plan city, which was thought to have spread over eight square miles, it was vast: even the ceremonial centre comprised a full two square miles of adobe buildings. The adobe had deteriorated badly in a way that stone seldom does, and it was difficult to tell at times if these were ruins set in a landscape or a ruined landscape.

After the Incas conquered the Chimú in around 1465, they set about destroying them with the tactics they reserved for those tribes considered to be 'difficult': the people were dispersed as *mitimaes* around the Empire or as artisans to work in Cuzco, and their history was not incorporated into the Incas' telling of it. To all intents and purposes they ceased to exist, and

the city of Chan Chan seems to have been abandoned. It is only because the Spanish arrived within living memory of the Chimú that we know anything about them.

The Incas didn't stop with their victory over the Chimú. In the next generation, a further wave of conquest, largely driven by Topa and his son, Huayna Capac, pushed on up the coast into what is now modern-day Ecuador. Huayna Capac was reportedly very taken by the riches of these new territories and tried to consolidate them as a northern power-base for the Empire.

On arriving in Ecuador, I could see why the Incas were so impressed. For these mountain men, used to the austerity of the Andes, the experience must have been like eighteenth-century British seafarers landing on a South Pacific island. It was no wonder they wanted to stay. From the moment we crossed the border, I felt a tremendous lifting of the spirit: kids swarmed into the bus, bringing chilled coconut milk and pineapples as big as pumpkins; there was salsa playing all around us and I could see the palms. We were truly leaving the desert behind.

Judy and I made a bee-line for Bahía de Caráquez, a small town on the coast which she knew well and wanted to show me. Within a week I knew she was right – it was an entrancing place.

Bahía de Caráquez lay almost dead on the line of the Equator, a slow centre to the turning world. Once an important coastal port, built near the pre-Columbian site of Cojimiés, over time it had become delightfully side-lined, even by the languid standards of the tropics: it lay on no main route, was never visited by foreign tourists and existed on some desultory fishing and the occasional weekend visitors from the capital who came to promenade and eat ice-cream by the side of the empty swimming-pool (a pool no self-respecting Ecuadorian would ever swim in, given the close proximity of the sea).

Over the years since, my memories of Bahía have crystallised and grown clear and hard: at the time, there was so much life all around me that it was difficult to take it all in.

At night, the tall wooden shutters of the town would swing open, and women leant out into the street. The sidewalks filled with silken-lipped *mulatas* and ranchers from the hills, spitting with a vigorous rasping of phlegm to draw attention to themselves. A few bars of piano-music would come from somewhere, changing at an abrupt tempo to salsa: the bars themselves had discreet swing-doors to conceal drinking men from their families.

The cumulative noise of televisions playing at too loud a volume, fighting kids, chickens roasting on great spits and the unquenchable music would

at sea and would have been almost directly off Bahía de Caráquez, as it was just after they had crossed the Equator. One curiosity about the winds off the coast was that while they easily carried people up from Peru towards Central America, it was much harder to return, so the conquistadors would have had a difficult job to arrive in the first place. The first sight of that Inca raft came after a journey of immense privations.

That evening Judy and I sat by the beach, watching the little red crabs as they scuttled up the shore and wondering if they crawled back into their own, personal crab-holes or just any convenient hole that happened to present itself as they escaped from the waves.

I thought of that first landfall by the conquistadors and of the strangeness of the land they had come to – so strange that many of the most honest admitted that it was beyond their powers of description, as was so much of the New World. Fernández de Oviedo, for instance, wrote of a bird of brilliant plumage: 'of all the things I have seen, this is the one which has most left me without hope of being able to describe it in words.' The Incas may have lacked a system of writing, but the Spanish were often just as inadequate when it came to leaving an account of the Empire they conquered, particularly if it did not fit into their usual framework of reference.

Perhaps because of this, there was a fascinating delayed reaction to the discovery of the Americas. We tend to assume now that it must have been like the moon landings, a moment when mankind realised that some boundary had changed, but it actually took almost a century for the reality of what had happened to sink into the European consciousness.

The very fact that America was indeed a New World caused Renaissance man an unexpected problem of intellectual absorption: there were no references in classical literature to America, at a time when scholars were trying to re-shape their intellectual maps in the mould of a rediscovered classical world; nor were there any biblical references to a new continent. For long after Columbus, many maps still pointedly ignored his discoveries. And when the outline of the American coast was included, there was still uncertainty as to whether it really was a separate continent from Asia or merely its eastern shore: a good century passed before the Bering Strait was crossed to prove it.

All these factors, amplified by the delay in getting news back across the Atlantic, gave ample opportunity for sceptics in Europe to play down the fantastic reports coming from America, as if they were today's exaggerated headlines for the *National Enquirer* or the *Sunday Sport*: 'The Longest River in the World', 'The Highest Mountains', 'A Gold Ransom Big Enough To Fill A Room', 'Snakes That Can Swallow A Donkey Whole' – all must have seemed far-fetched and Rabelaisian to the sober burghers of Europe, who anyway mistrusted the conquistadors as deeply unreliable witnesses.

The historian J. H. Elliott has described these first reactions to America: 'It is as if, at a certain point, the mental shutters came down; as if with so much to see and absorb and understand, the effort suddenly became too much for them, and Europeans retreated to the half-light of their traditional mental world.' No wonder that any attempt by Renaissance man to understand the Inca mentality should have been so limited, at a time when they were finding it difficult enough to understand themselves.

*

Judy headed into Quito for a while, but I had become rooted to the slow rhythms of Bahía. When she was away I would sometimes sleep in a *pensión* in town. Lying awake in my room, feeling the small 'pic-pic' of the gnats, I could hear the salsa and voices blaring out from the other side of the street. Through the thin walls I could hear the owner's family talking or stirring in their sleep, and in my room there was the smell of the mosquito coils burning and the noise of the electric fan.

After a month or so of this idyllic life came, simultaneously, the time of mangoes and of the annual Bahía de Caráquez beauty contest. A line of vendors outside the cinema sold slices of the fruit, along with papaya, fried banana crisps and lollipops, while the local 'tough eggs', as P. G. Wodehouse would have called them, lined up outside and watched the beauty contest talent arriving: the girls were whisked past these onlookers by fat, bustling aunts with sequinned dresses under their arms.

Inside the President of the local Rotary Club stood four-square to his audience to introduce the contest and delivered a standard South American speech about '*la dignidad de todos los seres humanos y de la patria*, the dignity of all human beings and of the fatherland', a little incongruous given the clearly prurient motives of most of the male onlookers. Then the National Hymn was introduced, everyone stood and nothing happened for about five minutes. When it finally started up, sounding like a Victorian composition for the pianoforte, it was obvious that no one knew the words, although the audience tried half-heartedly to mouth some.

For the first *desfile* or procession, the girls walked across stage in their 'day dresses' and introduced themselves nervously into the microphones: '*Me llamo Anna y quiero trabajar como higiénista dental*, my name is Anna and I want to work as a dental hygienist.' One by one they were taken down into the auditorium by a handsome young escort whose sole function was to negotiate five or six steps with each girl and lead her on a lap of honour around the hall, during which the girl would hold her flushed head high and occasionally flicker a glance at her friends.

The final parade was in evening dress. The girls appeared in new dresses of rich reds and blues, slit to the waist and with the fuller figures often preferred in South America, high cheekbones charcoaled into their dark faces.

I left with Tío Guillo before the judging. Something about the contest – the sheer fecundity of available pulchritude, so near and yet so far – seemed to have depressed Guillo unutterably, and we sat up late into the night after his bar had closed discussing which of the girls would have made him a suitable wife and whether the taste of lobster was preferable to that of oysters. It was so late by the time we finished that I simply slept on his bar.

The next morning, Sunday, dawned with the strange grey light I was becoming used to in the tropics. Guillo woke me with a sweet roll and some coffee. 'It's time for me to do my show,' he told me. 'Come with me, Hugo. I need an assistant.' We bicycled off unsteadily through the still waking town.

I had heard of Guillo's show but had never been awake early enough to hear him deliver it. Each Sunday he would broadcast from Radio Grande de Bahía, the tiny local radio station that operated from a small back-room off the main drag. It was only just big enough for us to sit in the booth. All his records were kept in a set order ready to play.

Guillo's show was billed as *La Música Romántica de Hoy, Ayer y Siempre* (*The Romantic Music of Today, Yesterday and Forever*), and it was a repertoire of ballads that elided as smoothly together as a London radio programme I remembered as a child, *Gerald Harper and his Sunday Affair*. The virtue of Guillo's show for his listeners was in its familiarity. With such a small constituency, Guillo had evolved a system where he would simply play the same tune each week for the same dedicatee. 'This is, as always, for Eduardo from his wife Jacinta, with great tenderness,' and he would lay the needle on the record very gently, as if making a sacrament. Some of the records he had been playing weekly for over a decade: the sleeves had yellowed and faded from the tropical climate.

Although I never asked him, Guillo seemed to take infinite pleasure in the contemplation of all those others who had found romantic happiness, even if it had eluded him. I can still picture him (I became his regular helper on the show), his wiry body hunched over the little turntable as he tried not to pop the microphone: ' "*Te Quiero, Lo Juro*" ["I love you, I swear it"], by Los Padrinos,' and the rich velvety vocals then floating out over the Sunday morning town.

*

I had my own curious romantic incident one morning. I often breakfasted at a small restaurant that doubled as a *pensión*. The owner was an amiable if occasionally melancholy middle-aged man, who spent his time flicking at imaginary specks of dust around the restaurant. We would usually chat as he gave me the breakfast ham and eggs, but on this particular day he seemed strangely silent. Then he declared himself: 'The thing is, Señor Hugo, my daughter has fallen in love with you.'

I would have been less nonplussed if I had known that he had a daughter. It was embarrassing to admit this to a father who, however melancholy, was still Latin and presumably capable of stirring himself to patriarchal fury. For once, I found myself at a complete loss as to what to say. 'You know that Meylin is just fourteen,' he said, turning mournful and reproving eyes on me, as if I were the personification of Humbert Humbert.

Back at the hotel I found a love-letter from Meylin and a special cassette of romantic ballads she had recorded onto a tape for me, many of which I knew well from Tío Guillo's *The Romantic Music of Today, Yesterday and Forever* show. Feeling the situation might be getting out of control, I went to consult with a girl called Marcella, a worldly-wise eighteen-year-old who hung out at Guillo's bar and seemed to know the local score. '*Ay, ay, ay,*' she laughed, sounding exactly like La Lupe in her dance records, '*Hugo, ¡que cabrón!*' I demurred at the implication. I still hadn't the faintest idea what this girl looked like. Marcella described her to me and I remembered a group of schoolgirls who'd hung around when I was eating the night before. 'Every fourteen-year-old girl with a little red blood in her likes the idea of a foreigner as a trophy boyfriend. This girl Meylin just wants to show you off a little, from afar. She'd have a fit if you actually came within a mile of touching her – so don't worry, *Hugito*, you'll be safe from the ravages of an Ecuadorian woman!'

I ignored this. 'Fine, Marcella, but what am I going to do? I don't want her father drumming me out of town.'

'Get a photo taken at the arcade and give it to her – that's all she wants.'

That night there was an all-night salsa party in the street, just outside Guillo's bar. It wasn't a perfect dance venue, as the sidewalk sloped badly to one side and over-enthusiastic dancers ended up sliding into the ditch, but it more than made up for this with the sheer energy of the music. Guillo had moved some of the gear out of Radio Grande de Bahía's back-room and rigged up a rudimentary, if loud, sound-system.

Meylin approached me with the embarrassment that appearing in person after declaring yourself in letters can bring. I couldn't help noticing that she looked worryingly well developed for fourteen – and that her father was hovering in the background – so after an awkward exchange of addresses, I quickly handed over the photo. Marcella's advice had been spot-on. Without so much as a backward glance, Meylin rushed off with her prize and I was left to get on with the dancing.

After patient coaching from Marcella and friends at the bar, I had begun to master the deceptively difficult art of salsa. The trick, contrary to what one might expect, was to keep the shoulders and chest relatively still and relaxed: the arms and hips did most of the work keeping the rhythm, while the legs snaked out all around the place in subtle dislocations of the norm. Some of the best dancers by far were the middle-aged couples with a bit of hip-fat to roll and a relaxed intimacy with each other. By midnight, the street was heaving with dancers and Guillo and his boys were working full-time to keep the chilled beers coming.

One particularly hard-core dancer, a muscular guy in his thirties, had stripped to the waist and was dancing mesmerically on his own, letting his back bend backwards almost double and then very slowly limboing back up, at times almost seizing up completely before uncoiling with spasmodic intensity – like the strange dance they call the *columbia* in Cuba. The girls from the brothel down by the waterfront had taken the night off and were having a wild time dancing with each other while slurping at brandy from the bottle. By three o'clock I was fading and slumped on one of Guillo's chairs, nursing a restorative coconut water-ice to my forehead, but everyone else was still going strong.

I went down to the waterside again. It was a clear night, with a moon, and the waves of the Pacific looked phosphorescent as they massed and swirled in the black water. A little way off I could hear the laughter of the brothel girls as they tried drunkenly to throw bottle-caps at a bottle at the end of one of the jetties. I felt one of those rare moments of complete equipoise, a balance of early morning light with exhaustion after the dancing, and the sound of the salsa in the distance: the ocean and its present tense calmed and filled me.

*

'He's won, he's won,' Guillo shouted excitedly. I couldn't think what he was talking about. The bar was filling up with excited revellers ordering brandies, even though it was only eleven in the morning. Gabriel García Márquez had just won the Nobel prize. It had been announced on Radio Grande de Bahía, so it had to be true.

Although he was Colombian, the town was treating him as if he were a local boy. Guillo was particularly impressed that he was using the money to fund his own newspaper. He had read all Márquez's books – they were piled high in the local stationery shop, along with the comics and murder stories.

Márquez was writing of their world, with its perpetual *llovizna*, that wonderful word for a soft drizzle of rain playing over the dampness of the *platanales*, the banana-plantations, while the *oceano nítido*, the bright ocean, stood off in the distance. The predominant mood in his books was one of nostalgia, '*tratando de recomponer con tantas astillas dispersas el espejo roto de la memoria*' ('trying to reconstitute so many scattered shards of the broken mirror of the memory'), a nostalgia weighed down with decay. In his most recent book, *La Crónica de una Muerte Anunciada* (*Chronicle of a Death Foretold*), the townsfolk had not been able to find a fridge big enough for a dead man's body; there was a police colonel who took a correspondence course in spiritualism; the gold coin they found in the dead man's corpse was one that he had swallowed when he was six years old; and the favourite dish of the archbishop was a soup of cocks' crests.

Even more than Lévi-Strauss, he wrote of the *tristes tropiques* – the feeling that the earth was so fecund and imaginative that man could not compete and instead sank back into the set ways of tribal customs. The only moments that 'gave' at all in his world were in the smells of the early mornings and the drunkenness of dusk – high noon seemed to wash out all reflection, thought and movement.

After a while something of this started to affect me in Bahía itself, a creeping *añoranza*, homesickness, perhaps brought on by constant idleness in a working town. One day, walking along the beach and seeing the ice-cream vendors with their bicycles leaning up against one another and the mud-flats of low tide, I felt that if I stayed any longer I would start living, like the town, perpetually out of season.

I left, but with much the same regret as Cook's men left Tahiti with or as Inca Emperors and their troops had whenever they were forced to return to Cuzco.

For it is clear that the Incas had a prolonged love-affair with the warm climate of Ecuador: fertile lands, the trade in exotic desirables like sea-shells and the attractions of the local girls combined to make it irresistible to the aesthetes from the highlands. Successive emperors spent more and more time campaigning there. The rhythm of such campaigns allowed plenty of time to enjoy the place: the normal, very civilised practice of pre-Columbian peoples was for fighting to pause during harvest-time to allow both sides to gather in crops (when the Spanish arrived, they disconcerted the natives by ignoring this convention). Cieza de León reports that the Incas often found it too hot to fight in the summer anyway.

During these long campaigns, Topa Inca founded the city of Tumipampa, modern day Cuenca in Ecuador, where his son Huayna, the future Emperor, was born. When he succeeded to the throne, Ecuador clearly appealed more to Huayna Capac than the harsher climate of the Inca heartland. He chose to stay for many years in his birthplace of Tumipampa, and was said to have preferred it to Cuzco as a capital.

By Inca standards Huayna seems to have been a bit of a *bon viveur*, perhaps because of his Ecuadorian upbringing: he was said to be able to drink three times as much as any of his subjects. When asked how it was that he never became intoxicated, he replied that 'He drank for the poor, of whom he supported many.'

*

The small tributary of the Amazon drove its way through the forest, the water like sheet-grey tarmac, while each turn of the river revealed precisely what we had just seen: an equally grey sky, with a curtain of green vegetation hung alongside the banks and no other colour visible. It was like being in an endless vegetable suburb. The effect was intensely claustrophobic. The greenery was so dense and compact that it was difficult to distinguish individual plant forms in the morass. After five days on the canoe, we had yet to see a single form of wildlife, other than the odd fish: any self-respecting animal could hear the hum of our motorised canoe from miles away. I found it disorientating in its tranquillity and lifelessness.

The Andes were at their most compact in Ecuador, spilling out to the Pacific on one side and the jungle on the other. It was an ideal place to venture down towards the Amazon, not least because it was not far from here that early conquistadors like Lope de Aguirre had made their epic descents to the Amazon, the image from Werner Herzog's film, *Aguirre: The Wrath of God*, that had so attracted me before I came to South America.

I had made my own preparations to go downriver, although I was unsure what to take. My main impression of the jungle was from a memorable *Thunderbirds* episode in which the gallant puppets were marooned on a sinking raft, with various snapping crocodiles waiting for their descent into the water. I felt competent in the mountains – but in the jungle, all I knew was that everything was waiting to bite you. A French girl I met on the road who was heading out of the jungle gave me her mosquito net: 'You'll need it,' she said.

There was little choice but to join up with a group, not something I would ever do in normal circumstances. I had met few other gringos as I passed some of the new oil towns that were springing up on the fringes of the Ecuadorian Amazon: Mera, Puyo, Puerto Napo. But at the final road-head, Misahuallí, a half-dozen or so travellers had congregated, waiting until there was a large enough group to hire a guide and a canoe.

Most of us hardly knew each other, or wanted to, and after the first day there was little attempt at communication as we floated downriver. The monotonous sublime of the upper Amazon was relieved only by gaps in the jungle where the undergrowth had been trampled back in broad avenues leading away from the river. This was where locals had rolled *chota* palms down to the water, to use the hard wood for canoes. Sometimes we would hit a more turbulent stretch of the river and spray would be sent up into our faces as the boat bounced across the waves.

On the banks we saw gold-panners, swilling out water and sand in large wooden bowls that had been worn smooth by countless such swirls to a fine finish. If the panners were successful, a few grains of gold would settle to the bottom. We stayed one night at one of their settlements. They had some sad, caged, capuchin monkeys as pets, looking like pictures of old Chinese eunuchs, with their hunched and shrewd faces. Sometimes they would be brought out and carried on a man's shoulder, attached to him by a chain and looking like some emblematic representation of an infernal punishment – a man with his conscience chained to him.

I talked to one of the gold-panners down by the river's edge that night, and shared some *guayasu* with him, a drink made from *aguardiente* and herbs. As with the gold-panners I had met in the mountains in Bolivia, he stressed to me (in a Spanish so thick that the words stuck to his gold teeth) that he was not a 'prospector', which he saw as an inherently risky and rather immoral profession – he was a gold-washer, a regular worker, who was applying method to the job and worked on a calculated percentage basis.

We sat in silence for a while, letting the *aguardiente* burn down into the stomach. He wasn't much interested in where I was from and it seemed phoney to try to make small-talk with a man who was living in the middle of nowhere. He was a short man, just over five foot, with intensely black eyes.

'*Oye*, listen,' he said. I waited for what I thought was going to be a story. But he meant the river. 'It sounds like an *arrullo*, a lullaby. I listen to it all the time.'

Over the days that followed, I got used to the way the river's noise changed. Lying in the sun in the canoe with my eyes closed, I could tell if we were approaching some shallows, or a faster stretch. The Napo, one of the Amazon's main tributaries, extended ahead of us, seemingly without end or variety.

I was cheered in my mission by the thought of Charles Waterton, one of the most engaging of all Amazon explorers, who had gone there in 1812. I had come across his memoirs by chance in a second-hand bookshop in England. Called *Wanderings in South America*, it had evidently been popular enough with the Victorians to stay in print throughout the nineteenth century at least: my edition was 1898.

There was an introduction by the celebrated Regency wit Sydney Smith, who described the hero of the book well: 'Mr Waterton is a gentleman of Yorkshire, of good fortune, who, instead of passing his life at balls and assemblies, has preferred living with Indians and monkeys in the forests. The sun bit him by day, the mosquitoes bit him by night; but on went Mr Charles Waterton!'

Certainly Waterton managed to combine a tremendous energy with an equally bluff Yorkshire enthusiasm for the rare and the strange. Setting off through the wild-lands of South America, he was fascinated by all the jungle had to offer, from the nocturnal habits of the sloth to the precise poison that Indians used on their blow-pipes. (Waterton subsequently introduced curare to Europe, thinking it would cure rabies. It didn't, but it has since been used for heart surgery and to treat multiple sclerosis and cerebral palsy.) And these were not just idle jottings, but the result of obsessed study. He kept a sloth in his room for three months 'in order to have an opportunity of observing his motions'.

He delighted in the *campanero* bird, the size of a jay yet with a voice more powerful than a cathedral bell and audible at three miles. Waterton also admired the king vulture before whom 'all the common birds would retire from the carcass. When his majesty has satisfied the cravings of his royal stomach with the choicest bits from the most stinking and corrupted parts, he generally retires to a neighbouring tree.' This was my sort of biology, direct and uninterested in any species unless it was either striking or glamorous.

But Waterton's *tour de force* came with the capture of a boa constrictor, inimitably and enticingly glossed by Sydney Smith in his introduction:

> Everyone knows that the large snake of tropical climate throws himself upon his prey, twists the folds of his body around the victim, presses him to death and then eats him. Mr Waterton wanted a large snake for the sake of his skin; and it occurred to him that the success of this sort of combat depended upon who began first, and that if he could contrive to fling himself upon the snake, he was just as likely to send the snake to the British Museum, as the snake, if allowed the advantage of prior opportunity, was to eat him up.

So Waterton tracked down a huge *coulacanara* of fourteen feet, having engaged two unwilling locals to help him in the enterprise. They became even less willing when Waterton insisted on removing their guns before getting too close, as he was worried they might shoot the snake and so damage the skin. 'I told them to follow me and that I would cut them down if they offered to fly. I smiled as I said this; but they shook their heads in silence and seemed to have but a bad heart of it.'

With his hesitant team, Waterton crept up and threw himself on top of the startled boa constrictor. Understandably, a struggle then ensued. When even the redoubtable Yorkshireman's well-built frame was unable to keep the snake down, he called on one of the natives to jump on top of him so that their combined weight would do the trick. 'I contrived to unloose my braces and with them I tied up the snake's mouth.' They finally got it into a bag and returned to the hut, where Waterton insisted on sleeping with the boa constrictor under his bed. 'He was very restless and fretful; and had Medusa been my bed-wife, there could not have been more continued and disagreeable hissing in the bedchamber that night.'

I felt under-powered beside Waterton. Explorers of his time had little room for doubt or uncertainty. Determined as he was to experience what it was like to be sucked by a vampire bat, he would sleep with his foot stuck out of the hammock in order to entice them.

Not made of such stern material as Waterman, I spent a great deal of effort preventing any mosquitoes, let alone bats, getting near me. Most nights we camped out in clearings on the side of the bank, doubling up in order to share the tents. It was a decidedly mixed group, mainly of Germans and Austrians. Some had already naturally paired on grounds of sex or friendship and I found myself left with Rolf, as none of his compatriots wanted to share with him.

I had already noticed Rolf. All the Germans, of both sexes, wore identical shiny white nylon Adidas shorts with curved hems and a slit up the thigh. In the jungle, as in real life, this was not always a sensible fashion choice, and the mosquitoes had quickly found them. Rolf was red-headed and in addition to the mosquito welts that he had acquired up his legs, sunburn had left dry blotches rubbing against the shorts. Together with his stubble, this had left his skin a sickly red and white.

I had followed his legs closely on a foray into the jungle, when our guide had led us off to look for the elusive wildlife. Indeed, given the claustrophobic tunnel that the path quickly became, Rolf's legs were almost all I ever saw. The synthetic material of his white shorts made an abrasive sound as he brushed against the fallen trees.

It was clear that while the jungle might lack any visible wildlife, it made up for this with its insect population. There were long trains everywhere made by termites, worker ants and great *saltamontes* or grasshoppers. Rolf's legs began to resemble a quilt of insect traces (he particularly attracted the sweat bees), and his skin became almost phosphorescent against the green, as he itched and scratched ahead of me.

Any sympathy I might have had for his discomfort was forestalled by the annoying nature of Rolf's conversation. Whatever anybody else had done, Rolf had always done it better. Been mugged in Colombia? Rolf had – 'And listen, I was so badly beaten up that even the police couldn't believe it.' Spent a week in Oaxaca? Rolf had been there for two. Bought a souvenir somewhere? You could be sure that Rolf had negotiated a better price. All travellers were prone to do a little of this, but in Rolf's case it was pathological. A chance encounter with him would have sufficed to establish this in a few minutes. Stuck in the middle of the jungle, it quickly became unbearable. His fellow Germans could shut him up with some choice Germanic put-down, but I was constrained by some built-in English inhibition about being rude to people in a language that was not their own. By the time we finally came out of the trail and returned to the river, I was ready to throttle him.

After stumbling around in the jungle for a prolonged period, coming back to the Amazon, even one of its tributaries, felt like emerging onto the ocean: the eyes had to readjust to take in the concept of distance again. For a brief moment the river looked beautiful. Then it looked like it normally did, grey and monotonous.

That night we all turned in early, tired by our futile jungle walk. I was not looking forward to an evening's chat with Rolf in the tent, but he had a pleasant surprise. 'Would you like to share a joint? You look like a man who enjoys smoking.' As it happened, I wasn't particularly, but anything was going to be better than an evening of Rolf's normal competitive banter. He beamed at me as he rolled up two remarkably solid-looking joints which, if they were cigars, would have had gold tips. 'Enjoy.' I almost started to like the man as I puffed meditatively and listened to the sound of the river making its gentle *arrullo* outside. Rolf was saying something, but I was having problems tuning in. 'Yes, you see I have spent two years travelling through South America looking for the strongest *marijuana* [he pronounced the '*j*' as if it were a guttural '*g*'] I could possibly find.' He let this sink in. I knew what was coming. 'It took me a long time. A very long time. And you have just smoked it.'

For once I believed him. The hallucinations were starting to come at me in waves. This was not your average grown-on-a-window-ledge European home-cultivated joint. It was not even like the more potent Moroccan or Jamaican blend that might have filtered its way into England for a special occasion. This was an altogether different animal, soaked in some dark tropical psychic resin and carrying an accompanying psychotropic punch that already had me knocked out on my sleeping bag, my legs curled in the air and words emerging very slowly from my mouth.

There was an accompanying paranoia. This was how my trip was going to end: either in a brain coma after being the guinea pig for some *vorsprung durch technik* experimentation (I noticed that Rolf had only taken a few token puffs himself), the victim of a 'super-export special' that Rolf planned to flood his home market with once he had got it down to manageable strengths; or, more simply, I would end up being sodomised, robbed and murdered by this mad German, who would be left with my money and the camera that he had secretly admired while making derogatory remarks about it.

But the paranoia was left behind by the strength of the hallucinations, which had a mesmerising intensity. At one point I was back in an English garden. It was mid-summer. Although a hot day, the leaves of the *Alchemilla mollis* – lady's mantle, a standard in every English border – still held water droplets from the previous night's rain. I watched as each droplet rolled to the edge of the leaf and then rolled over. Each droplet was very large and moved with great slowness. I could hear myself breathing and feel my own sweat running down my forehead.

Then I became aware of people around me. It was morning. Rolf, in a caring, considerate sort of way, had simply struck the tent from around me and revealed my prone body to the rest of the group, still lying in the standard tortoise position. One of the girls told me later I was whimpering slightly.

The guide bent over in a concerned manner and managed to get me to focus. 'Is there anything you want?'

After twelve hours of hallucinations I was in no state to have a meaningful conversation. 'Yes,' I replied. 'I want to get the fuck out of here.'

*

The Incas had paddled rather warily around the edges of the descent into the Amazon jungle – it was not their natural territory – but the Spanish had been far more reckless, lured on by tales of cinnamon trees, a spice that brought great wealth and by the legend of El Dorado: this told of a tribe among whom gold was so common that the native king covered himself in gold dust at an annual ceremony, and to find this tribe became the obsessive quest of many a party of *conquistadores*.

Gonzalo Pizarro had been the first to hear rumours both of El Dorado and cinnamon when he was made governor of Quito in 1540, a few years after the Conquest. He immediately set off down the same tributary of the

Amazon, the Napo, as I was travelling down now, but despite finding a few cinnamon trees and torturing Indians to reveal the location of El Dorado, he and his men met nothing but disappointment. The Indian tribes would tell them that, while they had no treasure themselves, the next tribe downriver assuredly did, and the gullible Spanish were led ever further eastward.

At one point Pizarro sent an advance party ahead under the leadership of his second-in-command, Francisco de Orellana. He was supposed simply to reconnoitre and then report back. Instead, in one of the most spectacular instances of military insubordination on record, Orellana just kept on going until he and his men came out on the Atlantic coast some thousands of miles away. The journey took them a harrowing two years. In the process, they were the first Europeans to travel down the greatest river in the world.

Not much is left to commemorate their achievement in discovering the Amazon. Near to the road-head at Misahuallí was a town named after Gonzalo Pizarro (who, after kicking his heels in the jungle for a while, got bored of waiting for his lieutenant and headed home to file complaints against him), while Puerto Francisco de Orellana was just downstream and there were a few other small settlements named after him scattered over the Amazon basin.

The rewards of discovery are fickle: Sir George Everest, Surveyor General of India, famously never went to the mountain named after him, but has been immortalised, yet who now remembers Francisco de Orellana, the discoverer of the Amazon? Perhaps it was because he named the river not after himself but after one of the tribes he encountered, recognising in a way not usually done by colonising explorers that they had been there first.

And there is a fascination in the way that the river should have been called after a Greek myth, on the most spurious of grounds. Orellana and his conquistadors noticed that among the Indians of one tribe they were fighting there were many tall women, attacking as fiercely as the men: this particular tribe successfully drove the Spanish away. It is from this small incident that the River Amazon was named. The defeated conquistadors captured an Indian from another tribe and interrogated him about these female attackers: he told them (or as sceptical later commentators noted, his answers confirmed all their questions in the manner they doubtless wished) that, yes, these women did all the things the original Amazons did: they cut off their right breast the better to draw a bow (the word Amazon means 'breastless') and had intercourse only once a year.

His answers fed the conquistadors' fantasies about the myth they had grown up with, the idea of a tribe of women warriors with super-human strength. This myth had been given enormous fuel in the Spanish mentality by the success of *Sergas de Esplandián*, the sequel to *Amadis de Gaul*, in which the Amazon legend figured prominently. Indeed Sergas, a sort of Zorro figure cast in the mould that every Spanish conquistador liked to see himself as, had not only defeated the Queen of the Amazons in combat, but had made her fall in love with him as well. As myth, it hit every button on the conquistador console. That the native women might share the mythological power of their classical predecessors also soothed any wounded pride at having been defeated by female fighters – not an easy concept for the conquistador mentality to accept.

Their wilful and gullible acceptance of this story is a good example of the power that literature still had over these men, who had been lured out to the New World in the first place by fantastical stories. Drifting downriver, enduring terrible starvation (they cooked the soles of their shoes at one point), living constantly with the threat of death at the hands of hostile tribes, or disease, or starvation, they reached out for a myth to reassure themselves that somehow, contrary to all the evidence, they were engaged on an enterprise as bold as that of Theseus.

Yet the Amazon was where this myth of chivalric endeavour became truly impossible to sustain. Orellana's men at least succeeded in getting down the river and emerging sane at the other end. The expedition led by Pedro de Ursúa twenty years later in 1560 had a far less happy outcome. By then the quality of conquistador stock had degenerated after years of civil war and easy living off the land: Ursúa had a rabble to lead and was quickly murdered by the psychopathic Lope de Aguirre, who proceeded to kill most of the rest of the men as they sailed downriver (Herzog's film presented, if anything, a sanitised version).

He was finally killed by his own bodyguards, but not before he had run his daughter through with a sword and caused the deaths of hundreds of conquistadors and of their Andean porters.

Lope de Aguirre's famous last, mad letter about the Amazon, addressed to the King of Spain himself, was as near to bleak existentialism as the sixteenth-century mind could get. It told him that 'If a hundred thousand men came here, none would escape. For the reports are false: there is nothing on this river but despair.'

The Incas could have warned him of the dangers of the jungle long beforehand. They had never penetrated far into the Amazon – it was not their natural terrain. Their name for the disorientating network of tributaries that twisted into their Empire was *Amaru-Mayu*, 'Great Serpent-Mother of Men'.

Even the push up into Ecuador by the Incas can with hindsight be seen as an expansion too far. In just three generations, under first Pachacuti, then his son Topa Inca and finally his grandson Huayna Capac, the Inca Empire had grown from an enclave around Cuzco to one that stretched several thousand miles along the Andes. In the process it had become fatally distended.

There has long been a debate, both among chroniclers of the time and modern scholars, as to whether Huayna Capac may even have fathered Atahualpa by an Ecuadorian princess, which would have made his son illegitimate by the Inca rules of succession: whatever the truth of this, the mere attribution shows the extent to which Atahualpa has always been inextricably associated with the North. The endless campaigns that Huayna waged in Ecuador left a permanent standing army in the North, with powerful generals, a disruption of the normal Inca convention that armies were temporary and centred on Cuzco.

After Huayna Capac's sudden and disastrous death in around 1527 from an epidemic which swept the country, killing as much as half the population, the cracks in the new Inca Empire of Tahuantinsuyo quickly started to show. Huayna had been away in the North for over ten years. His legitimate successor, Huascar, was based back in Cuzco. Now a contingent of Incas in Quito led by Atahualpa decided that they were far enough away both from Cuzco and Huascar to declare independence.

The resulting civil war between the Ecuadorian and Peruvian sides of the Empire was devastating. It was the turning point in Inca fortunes, much more so than the Spanish Conquest of 1532, which simply exploited the wreckage it caused. The two sides were evenly matched: as the legitimate contender, Huascar had all the resources of the Cuzco state behind him; Atahualpa was the more experienced soldier, with a strong Ecuadorian power-base and a ruthless streak. Far from being the passive and noble Indian of Millais' famous picture or Peter Schaffer's play, Atahualpa was one of the most brutal of all Inca Emperors, and this in a category where he had stiff competition – he was more of a Richard III figure than a Richard II. Atahualpa eventually defeated Huascar, but not before the country had been laid waste.

Like the Moghul civil war between Aurangzeb and Dara Shukoh a century later in India, with which it has many points of comparison – both dynasties allowed their emperors the sexual licence to produce too many competing heirs – the success of the unscrupulous usurper was to precipitate the decline of the Empire he won, a dramatic nemesis that Shakespeare would have enjoyed to the full if he could have used it. (One sad result of Elizabethan and Jacobean politics was that the delicate relationships between England and Spain did not allow Shakespeare and his contemporaries to write the wonderful drama that the Conquest of the New World would have provided, and that Spanish contemporaries such as Lope de Vega were indeed producing. Middleton was forced into hiding after writing about Spain in *The Game of Chess*. It was safer by far to set your plays in Italy.)

The great Inca civil war so weakened Tahuantinsuyo that by 1532, when the Spanish arrived, they could simply walk in and take it. The conquistadors, as so often, were incredibly lucky. After landing on the coast at Tumbes, they travelled south down the Royal Road towards the Inca capital, moving through a civilisation which had been fatally weakened first by disease and then by internal divisions.

I was now going to follow them on that route. Having travelled the length and breadth of the Empire, I felt it was time to return again to the Inca heartland near Cuzco and in particular to see where the very last Inca Emperors had retreated after the Spanish Conquest.

*

It was dawn as we came up the crest of the hill from Limatambo, with the clouds hanging underneath us and the mountains of the Urubamba massif ahead: I could see the familiar outline of Mt Salcantay, which had dominated some of our earlier exploration. We were approaching Cuzco.

As I had travelled the long road from the North, I had tried to imagine what it must have been like for the conquistadors when they first penetrated this enormous country, following the Royal Road, the *Capac-nan*, that must have seemed to them to deviate wilfully into every obscure mountain fastness.

While there were stretches of landscape that were biblical in their bleakness, the avaricious eyes of the conquistadors would also have settled on the fertile valleys between mountain ranges. Just below, at Limatambo, I had been taken in by the family of an old estate who had offered me their house as their own ('*mi casa es su casa*', the habitual South American form of greeting). In their garden grew fruits of a wonderful diversity, from *aguaymanto*, the sharp cape gooseberry, to rich custard apples, strawberries and papaya. Beyond in the fields were rich crops of maize and, higher up, potatoes. Truly, it must have seemed like God's own land to the Spanish.

They had managed the journey with remarkable ease, after the first dramatic gesture of seizing Atahualpa in the main square in Cajamarca. The psychological shock of this – kidnapping the Emperor was simply not in the Inca rule-book of how to wage war – had been so immense that the forces of the Empire had found it hard to regroup.

We are used in the West to a considerably sanitised version of this story:

the Pizarro brothers and a handful of Spanish managing to take the Inca by surprise at Cajamarca, emerging suddenly from a *kallanka* to capture Atahualpa. There is a well-known pre-Raphaelite portrait of the moment by Millais, which hangs at the Victoria and Albert Museum in London. The Inca has been tipped forward on his litter by his fallen bearers, so that he reclines gracefully on a jaguar skin. He is half-naked, with a simple white loin-cloth (a depiction that the Inca himself would have particularly objected to, given his obsession for fine woven fabrics – where was his bat-fur?). Francisco Pizarro leans forward and puts an almost comradely arm on Atahualpa's shoulder, as if to say, 'Don't you think, old man, that the sensible thing is just to come with us?'

It was a far more savage affair. Francisco Pizarro's men fired cannons into the unarmed crowd of Indians, and then hacked at their bodies until, according to one commentator, 'the bodies formed mounds and suffocated one another'. Pizarro managed to seize Atahualpa in the mêlée, but only after a fierce struggle: even after the Spanish had cut off the hands of those supporting the Inca's litter, the bearers continued to carry him with their shoulders until they were finally mown down completely. Such was the scrum of horses and escaping Indians that one wall of the plaza was knocked over by the press of bodies against it.

There was an interesting historical theory that liked to draw back from the actual moment of capture and see the success of the Conquest as due more to 'bacteriological determinism' than to Atahualpa's capture or the superiority of conquistador firepower over Inca defences. According to this argument, the crucial engagement between the two cultures was not between steel swords and clubs of jungle palm, but between European livestock and the Andean llama.

This was not just a battle to ascertain which was the most effective beast of burden or fighting animal – a battle which on most criteria the horse won hands down. What mattered was the disease pool the animals brought with them. The smallpox that came from European cattle battered down the Indians far more effectively than European arms ever could, as did the waves of diphtheria and measles that swept through Peru in the years before and after the Conquest (European disease arrived before the Europeans, carried down the coast from Panama, and almost certainly caused the epidemic which killed Huayna Capac in around 1527). The Incas could fight back with syphilis, an unwelcome American stowaway back to Europe with the returning conquistadors, but by then the battle had been lost.

As the bus climbed above the lush valley of Limatambo, I remembered that this was the one place where the Incas almost managed to stop the Spanish in their tracks. After the capture of Atahualpa at Cajamarca, the conquistadors advanced with extraordinary and brave decisiveness, right to the heart of the Empire. The Incas failed to realise that while their fearsome horses were formidable on the flat, they were vulnerable on the ascent. But on this last ascent into Cuzco, they attacked the leading contingent of Spanish as they clambered exhaustedly up the slope and almost wiped them out. Pedro Pizarro noted, with his usual eye for detail, 'The Indians surrounded them [the conquistadors] in such a manner that they even laid hold upon the horses' tails.' Only the chance arrival of reinforcements prevented a massacre of the Spanish. But the Incas had left it too late to exploit their new tactical knowledge. This was the last great pass before the Inca capital. Within the week, the Spanish had entered Cuzco and taken control of the Empire.

OLLANTAYTAMBO

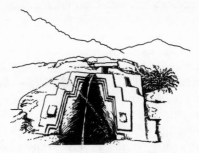

COMING BACK INTO CUZCO BUS STATION first thing in the morning after a night on the coach had a nightmarish quality. I'd come thousands of miles and was dirty, tired and lugging a heavy pack past a notorious training ground for pickpockets. I had no money left to buy myself a moment of luxury, yet wasn't sure where I was going to stay. And half my insides felt like they were hanging out.

'Hey mister, why you got holes in your trousers? Your *cojones* will start to show,' said one of the local guys leaning up against a wall. His friends leant forward. The market ladies laughed raucously. Like coyotes sensing weakness, I was quickly surrounded by what seemed to be every con-artist in Cuzco. 'Hey mister, want a hotel?' 'Wanna good *cambio* for your dollars?' 'Taxi, taxi!' One of the registered deaf and dumb beggars chose this inopportune moment to press a card stating his case on me. I was supposed to read it and then he would return and accept a donation. Some blond Mormon missionaries were standing by impassively, watching in pale suits and ties. They looked like they were part of a completely different movie.

Then out of the mêlée of voices I heard someone calling for passengers to '*El Valle Sagrado*', the Sacred Valley. I had one of those moments that travellers sometimes need where you instinctively just let go. There was no need to spend more time in Cuzco, so why not head straight out again? The Sacred Valley bus would take me to the great site of Ollantaytambo, which I had never seen and which played a key role in the last days of the Incas. I heaved my pack up onto the roof to be strapped down and was away, with some relief.

By contrast to Cuzco, the arrival at Ollantaytambo was one of the best welcomes to a town I've ever had. The local bus I'd taken turned out to be full of weekenders and we'd stopped in the little town of Urubamba to eat at a small *quinta* called *Los Geranios*. Urubamba had a reputation for being a bit of a tourist town with some large government resort hotels, but this *quinta* was the real thing, a sun-filled courtyard with *criolla* music drifting around and huge plates of beans and *chicharrones*, deep-fried chunks of pork rib. There was a wedding party in full swing off to one side and the band were pumping it out. After a couple of Cristal beers I was well away, dancing with the bridesmaids and a pretty college girl from Lima who was visiting her relatives. The cares of the road fell from me.

By night-time, the band were playing one of my all-time favourites, the lament of '*Mi Guajirita*', in which the singer implores his love to '*Quiereme, quiereme, más*' ('Love me, love me even more'), with a mournful tone that seemed uncertain where it was all going to end. My bus had long gone without me and two truck-drivers offered me a lift to Ollantaytambo in their large pick-up. As they'd drunk at least as much as I had, it was an unsteady journey along the rest of the valley, but with a full moon and a clear night I could see the imposing silhouette of Mt Verónica ahead as I stood on the back of the pick-up and let the wind hit me in the face. I was serenading the drivers with my own versions of Elvis songs and, during an impassioned rendition of 'Good Rocking Tonite', my hat blew off. The truckers were becoming almost incontinent with laughter and screeched unsteadily to a halt in the ditch.

With the assistant, Justo, I went back to look for the hat. We scrabbled around half in and out of the ditch looking for it, with trucks looming out of the night and blaring their horns in characteristic Andean style. As we walked back Justo turned to me and said, 'Look at the mountain. Look at Verónica. *Este es un momento nítido*,' using a word I'd only ever seen in literature and meaning that this was a moment of intense clarity. It was one of Borges' favourite adjectives, which he used when describing events of hallucinatory sharpness in his mythologies. I looked again at Verónica, a cone of a mountain that looked like a Japanese wood-cut, such was the neatness of its silhouette.

They dropped me by the square and I swayed down the path to the little railway station and the river. I knew that there was a small *albergue* nearby, a hostel where members of the Cusichaca project would sometimes stay. A dog barked as I pushed the gate open into total darkness. A woman with long black hair appeared and seemed unfazed by receiving a drunken hiker in the middle of the night. Wendy lit a candle and showed me into a room. 'I'm sorry it's dark, there was a power-cut earlier. In fact, why am I doing this? We have the electricity back on now,' and she flicked a switch to show a room totally unlike any I'd seen in Peru, with a bed fashioned out of the bare rock and simple tapestries hanging on the whitewashed walls. The *baño* (which I badly needed) was nearby, a toilet set over an off-shoot from the stream, with the white porcelain gleaming over the pitch black of the waters. You could hear the current swirling below as you sat on the can, a disconcertingly fluid experience which my bowels were mirroring.

Wendy and her partner Robert Randall had come to Peru at the end of the sixties and, together with some other friends, had set up a little bit of Woodstock in the middle of the Andes. The *albergue*, with its simple frontier-style buildings and, I discovered the next day, a sauna off to one side, had been built by them: they were activists in the local community, helping both with the school and with campaigns to preserve the village's heritage. Robert had studied Quechua and led trips to obscure parts of the area, while Wendy knew much about the weaving techniques of the high villages. The place was full of the closely woven dark-red cochineal cloth associated with Chincheros and the pieces had the patina of age and hand-weaving.

Ollantaytambo was a good place to come not just because it had a lower altitude and mellower climate than Cuzco (and some magnificent ruins), but also because it marked the beginning of the final Inca retreat into the hills of the Vilcabamba and the subsequent deaths of the last Emperors. It was this route I now wanted to follow, out of conflicting emotions of piety, curiosity and completism: I wanted to see the story through to the end.

In the late afternoon I climbed up Ollantaytambo's impressively fortified buildings. After losing Cuzco to the Spanish at the great battle of Sacsahuaman, Manco Inca had brought his troops here. From the top of the fort, one could see why it was the natural place for him to come.

Ollantaytambo had a dominating geographical position, being on the edge of the Urubamba plateau where the river began to channel down to the narrow gorges that curled around Machu Picchu and all the sites I had travelled to earlier. But the site also gave access to the north-west and the Vilcabamba over some high passes behind the town, giving Manco a good escape route if he needed it.

The tourist coaches that sometimes passed through Ollantaytambo for a cursory ten-minute stop on the way back from Machu Picchu had all left and I had the place almost to myself. Over the steep crags that fell away to the west, I could see a solitary goatherd in a baseball cap trying to round up his herd, as the sun set behind him.

I was high above the town. From the top of the ruins there was a peculiar acoustic effect. The bowl of the valley made the tiniest sound below reverberate: a child's laugh from somewhere down by the river, echoed by another child; the hooting of the up-train as it made its way back to Cuzco; the thwack of feet hitting leather as a football was kicked around by the off-duty staff at the small bull-ring directly below me.

I noticed a funeral procession starting up from the small church in the square at the bottom of the hill. Half the town seemed to be following the coffin and the brass band that accompanied it. The music seemed effortlessly to transpose the melancholy of the Andean flute to the Western instruments, with a trumpet that floated the sadness up to me.

An early traveller in the nineteenth century had described the chants he had heard the Quechuan Indians making at such a funeral: 'Why have you abandoned us? What have we done for you to leave us like this? Will we not see you again? *¿No beberas ya la chicha con la familia?* will you no longer drink *chicha* with your family?'

From the top of the ruins I watched as the procession wove its way through the grids of the tight chequer-board pattern the town had retained since the time of the Incas. The funeral was for a Señora Juana, who I later discovered had lived down by the bridge across the river all her life. Again the acoustic was so clear that I could hear the mourners' voices rising along with the brass band.

It must have been extraordinary for the Indians on that day in 1536 when the Spanish followed Manco here in an attempt to put the native rebellion down. The leader of the Spanish party was Hernando Pizarro, Franciso's brother and 'the evil genius' of the Conquest, according to the historian William Prescott, whose 'ambition and avarice were insatiable', even in a group of men where such attributes were commonplace.

The *conquistadores* approached across the river-plain at early morning, and the Quechuans from their defences on high would have heard the amplified sound of the horses and the guttural swearing of the Spanish as they fired off the odd arquebus, more for effect than anything else as the range would have been insufficient.

However, no amount of bravado could quite disguise the Spaniards' dismay at first seeing how impressive the defensive position of Ollantaytambo was (bizarrely, none of them had ever seen it before, although only a day's journey from Cuzco) and the strength of forces that Manco had accumulated. A series of stepped terraces, built with the usual Inca flair for a steep slope, led up to the fortifications that clung to a knife-edge ridge. The only possible approach was at an angle that could leave a fit hiker breathless, let alone anyone trying to ride up on a horse, even in the light armour that the conquistadors had taken to wearing in Peru.

The Spanish would have seen rows of soldiers on every terrace stretching away above them, including many of the ferocious jungle tribes whose precision as archers was much feared by both Spanish and Indians alike. And at the top Manco Inca himself would have been riding up and down on a horse he had captured, showing himself defiantly to the Spanish enemy and rallying his own troops.

This was certainly in character. Manco Inca is the sometimes forgotten hero of Inca history. His predecessor Atahualpa is remembered as the Emperor whom Pizarro and his men first seized and ransomed for his weight in gold and silver before executing him, while the name of Tupac Amaru, the very last Inca, lives on for its symbolic value and has been sporadically revived as the focus for later resistance groups. But Manco was a more admirable character than either of them. At the time of this engagement at Ollantaytambo, he had survived both a brutal civil war and the Spanish Conquest, which along with a smallpox epidemic had managed to lay waste one of the world's great empires in less than ten years. The world he had known had crumbled around him. Out of the ashes, and with some consummate political manoeuvring, he somehow managed to rally a rebellion which, if not ultimately successful, at least gave heart to his people.

Manco had been born a full (i.e. legitimate) son of Huayna Capac. After Huayna's death, Manco backed Huascar in the disastrous civil wars between his brothers and so suffered for being on the losing side against Atahualpa. When there were subsequent reports of strange bearded men arriving on the coast, who seized and killed Atahualpa, Manco and the surviving followers of Huascar at first thought this was divine retribution on the usurper and welcomed the conquistadors on their arrival in Cuzco.

Indeed, so pleased was Manco with the Spanish for having killed Atahualpa that he voluntarily surrendered himself on the outskirts of Cuzco. Francisco Pizarro was very taken by this young prince who was so quick to do the Spaniards' bidding. Needing a suitable puppet Inca to install on the throne, he chose Manco from the range of available brothers. For some years this worked satisfactorily, if uneasily, with Manco manoeuvring through the complicated net of Inca alliances left after the civil war. Many of Atahualpa's old troops were still stationed in Cuzco, and some of his surviving brothers did not take kindly to Manco's succession. But then, disillusioned by Spanish brutalities, he rebelled, took Sacsahuaman and nearly destroyed the Spanish in Cuzco.

Despite having been driven from Cuzco after the fall of Sacsahuaman, Manco still presented a formidable threat when he came to Ollantaytambo, and he had carefully forged alliances with many of the wild jungle tribes to the east, the Antisuyo quarter of the old Empire. He also had an effective plan. Manco used the town's impressive system of channelled waterways to advantage. On a pre-arranged signal, just at the moment when the Spanish stopped in dismay in front of the great walls above them, water was released to flood the plain below. At the same time archers attached from either side. It was only with luck, as so often with the conquistadors, that they managed to ford the now swollen river and escape.

Still, it must have been wonderful for Manco and his troops to see their enemy retreating both humiliated and wet. That night there would have been much *chicha* drinking in the square. Even the Spaniards, no mean drinkers themselves, were always impressed by the prodigious capacity of the Incas to consume alcohol. At Manco's own coronation earlier in Cuzco, the drains of the city were reported to have run continuously with the urine of the revellers, so bacchanalian was the consumption. I've since seen Quechuan muleteers put away enough sugar-cane spirit or rough *aguardiente* after pay-day to be medically anaesthetised, yet still manage to get home, if unsteadily. However, as Prescott mournfully remarks in his history, 'This was the last triumph of the Inca.'

The following year the Spanish returned in larger numbers. Manco had lost many of his followers, who were taking the usual campaign sabbatical to return home for the harvest. The Spanish had caught a group of jungle archers out in the open and massacred them, although not before the archers had wounded many of their horses. Realising the hopelessness of his position, Manco decided to withdraw. He is reported to have given a speech worthy of Bonnie Prince Charlie's departure from the Highlands. He told his followers that 'he felt compelled to give satisfaction to the Antis [the tribes of the jungle] who had so long desired to see him, and so would visit them for a few days,' although all who heard him must have known that the Inca was abandoning the homeland of the Cuzco plateau for ever.

The conquistadors had been lucky, but they had also brought their own luck. Time after time in the annals of the Conquest, one comes across moments when the occasional fatalistic impulse of the Incas led to their worst moments. Why did Atahualpa's main commander Chalcuchima meekly and voluntarily surrender himself to the Spanish on their arrival when he could easily have annihilated them, 35,000 men against a handful? Why did the Quechuans allow the Spanish to make the fearsome ascent of the Royal Road from the coast to Cuzco without picking them off as they exhausted themselves on the high passes? Why had Manco himself fatally hesitated at the siege of Cuzco and waited for yet more troop reinforcements to arrive, thus losing the momentum of surprise – a momentum the Spanish intuitively understood as being necessary for war and used so impressively when they took Sacsahuaman?

It is too easy to ascribe the conquistadors' success purely to superior technology, as romantic sympathisers with the Inca cause are prone to do. Pizarro's men were also outstandingly brave and determined, however greedy and brutal they may have been. They grabbed every chance offered to them with both broad hands. The Incas did not.

I thought of Conrad's great line in 'Heart of Darkness' – that the strength of conquerors is 'just an accident arising from the weakness of others'.

High above the main site of Ollantaytambo was a small ruin that faced the setting sun and the mountain fastnesses that Manco would have retreated into. There were some holes in the walls and the usual fantasy had arisen that these might have been used to secure prisoners before some sort of ritual sacrifice (Charlton Heston would have played the role of the captured white man to perfection). In the unlikely event of this having been true, the sacrificial victims would at least have had a superb view before their deaths: the platform faced due west towards the mountains beyond Machu Picchu. As I sat there quietly in the last of the sun, I wondered if the Incas' positioning of their sites was as much for the aesthetic qualities of stone, so that it caught the most flattering light of the day, as for the reasons of 'sacred geography' that were often given.

Like Sacsahuaman, it was easy to forget that just because Ollantaytambo was used as a fort in an hour of need, it was not necessarily constructed as one. This was in fact another of Pachacuti's great buildings and carried many of his trademarks: the insistence on the highest quality of stonework and of ornamentation, with a spectacular setting. It could have been used as much for religious reasons as military ones, and its purpose may also have been to impress the peoples of the valleys below, whom Pachacuti had recently conquered. There was a noticeably redundant defensive wall, built behind the site on what was anyway an impregnable flank, but which greatly added to the grandeur of the place. Ollantaytambo was 'decoratively military', like a Victorian mock-Gothic castle. Manco's enforced use of it might be compared to Balmoral being pressed into service for a last-ditch defence of the realm if Hitler had invaded Britain.

The most celebrated feature of Ollantaytambo were six stones. These great upright monoliths of pink porphyry were almost all that remained of the sun temple. They were arranged so as to face the rising sun, and had some of the strange bosses and protuberances that had so intrigued me elsewhere with Incaic stonework.

These stones revealed much of the Inca relationship and debt to conquered nations. Having now visited Tiahuanaco, I could see the clear connection between Ollantaytambo and that ancient site. There was the same distinctive Tiahuanacan stepped motif on one of the stones, and the Ollantaytambo masons had used thin strips of stone to joint the monoliths – a technique even more difficult than the usual dry-pointing and one which Señor Ribero had shown me at Tiahuanaco.

I had learnt from John Hemming some fascinating details relating to the building of Ollantaytambo. After the original inhabitants of the area had refused to submit peacefully to the Incas, Pachacuti had conquered them with a large army and burnt their town. He had then erected this magnificent memorial to Inca occupation which the Spanish had found so frightening and which modern tourists now admire. To do so, he had shipped in another client tribe from a different part of the Empire, the Colla near Tiahuanaco, whose burial towers I had seen at Sillustani. The Colla brought their stone-building techniques with them, if under duress: they must have suffered enormously in the transportation of the huge Ollantaytambo stones from the quarry across the valley. From records left by early Spanish chroniclers, who interviewed their descendants, we know that at one point they rebelled and fled back to modern-day Bolivia.

This certainly cast the building in a different light from 'romantic Ollantaytambo', described in such glowing terms by nineteenth-century travellers such as Charles Wiener and George Squier. Squier had even compared it to a 'castle on the Rhine'. Yet this was a site built by an army of occupation, using forced slave labour who had been transplanted from their homelands to do so. Those sympathisers with the Inca cause, who picture a noble culture being decimated by the imperial West, sometimes forget that the Inca culture itself could be a cruel and colonising one.

*

I wandered down the hill and traced some of the waterways that still coursed around the town, some dividing the streets as they would originally have done in every Inca city and in Cuzco itself. The usual playfulness of Inca stonework was fully in evidence, particularly around the bases of the ruins themselves, where various fountains chased around corners and delightfully oblique carvings could appear if the rock was looked at hard enough. In a smaller way it echoed the ability at Machu Picchu to blend raw granite with cheeky curlicues of integrated sculpture − a niche here, some steps cut there.

In a rash moment I had revealed to Wendy at the hostel that I had occasionally done magic tricks for kids at parties, on a strictly amateur basis. One of her sons was having a fifth birthday the next day and she persuaded me against my better instincts to put on a show. I agreed before I realised quite how many friends young Nathan had. Standing behind my makeshift magician's table, there was a sea of little Peruvian and American faces staring up at me expectantly, with an attendant phalanx of parents outnumbering their offspring.

It was a cheerful scene. A clown (a charming gay friend of Wendy's) was wandering through the audience pouring water over people, to the children's great amusement. Meanwhile the adults, the men with their beards and ponchos and the women in hippy dresses, looked like a festival audience after a mellow afternoon's spliff-taking. I warmed them up by taking a few chocolates out of children's ears, did some tricks with a balloon and the usual card-sharping stuff. It was time for the *pièce de résistance*. I borrowed a bowler hat from one of the Quechua women watching and then (with an impressive sweep of a cloak, the inappropriate spell of 'Hey Geronimo' and my own slight surprise at pulling it off) managed to produce a white dove out of the empty hat, which flew up startled into a completely blue sky. The audience of five-year-olds were so surprised by this that they sat there with open mouths. It was, to use Justo's phrase, '*un momento nítido*'.

What with the extremes of the Andean climate and my travels through the deserts of the coast, it had taken me a while to realise that it was now spring here. As I climbed up the other side of the valley from Ollantaytambo and the *albergue*, I noticed how green the valley of the Urubamba had become. The pisonay had flowered in magnificent and shameless scarlet and the strawberry season was imminent. Against the green of the fields, the red-and-black ponchos of the workers stood out in sharp relief. It was a cheating spring, an October spring.

I was walking up to see the old Inca quarries above the town. The quarries were themselves remarkable not so much for what stones were left (there were several partially finished blocks) but for the view back to the town: from above, in the sunlight, one could still make out the route the stonemasons must have used to transport the stones, a track ghosting across the crops in the fields to the bottom of a ramp leading up the side of the temple-fortress site.

Much energy had been expended on various crackpot theories about how the Incas managed to construct their extraordinary buildings. The question asked was how they managed first to cut the blocks and then transport them into place with such uncanny precision, given that they had no metal tools or wheels to do so.

Colonel Percy Fawcett, the overrated British explorer who had disappeared up the Amazon in mysterious circumstances in 1925, had first started this trend. Before doing a Lucan, he had reported as gospel fact the wild rumour that a sort of 'jungle-juice' was able to dissolve solid granite. For a public who were as credulous then as now about any form of jungle medicine and who were also inclined, illogically, to put great credence on the words of a man who had since disappeared, this started a long and continuing search for the plant concerned. Others speculated that the Incas, so obsessed with the sun, might in some way have learnt to use parabolic reflectors, so concentrating the sun's beams enough to act as a laser through the stone.

A more prosaic and infinitely more likely solution had been demonstrated by the academic Jean-Pierre Protzen, who had actually taken the time to test his theories out on site. He had shown that it was perfectly possible to shape the blocks using simple hammer stones from the river that had been rounded by the current. With these he could achieve the smooth bevelling characteristic of good Inca masonry. It seemed equally possible to drag the blocks considerable distances, given the enormous amounts of manpower the Incas had at their disposal through the system of *mita*, or annual labour tribute, from the locals and from client tribes like the Colla.

Along the path the builders must have used were some great blocks that had simply been abandoned along the way. In a nice phrase, these were known as the *piedras cansadas* or the 'tired stones'. One was sitting placidly in the middle of a cultivated field. No one knows when or why this happened: they may have been abandoned when the Colla left, or when Pachacuti died and the estates passed from royal interest, or in the smallpox epidemic of around 1527. In any event, I liked to imagine the moment when a foreman took a break: 'OK guys, let's take five. We'll pick up from where we left off next week, once we get a bit more help on the case.' Five hundred years later, the job was still waiting to be finished.

There was a trio of brown-skinned boys splashing around in the Urubamba, and I went in for a swim after the climb. 'Swim' was perhaps the wrong word as the current was too strong to do much more than push back against the water like a jacuzzi. But up to my neck in the surging water, and with the mountains of the west still touched by sun in the distance, it felt pretty good.

I had the same view as I waited for the train at the station. There were files of uniformed school-kids waiting in lines along the platform: they had just processed around the village to mark the tenth anniversary of the village school. I was gratified when some swarmed around and recognised me as '*el mago*', 'the magician'. They were all swinging lanterns at one another and the air was lit up as if by glow-worms. At one point the teacher led the girls to one side of the track to urinate in the normal Andean way, using their full skirts to preserve modesty as they squatted down in a long line beside the railway tracks. (It was quite possible to come across streams of urine in Cuzco streets from Andean ladies caught short on the way to market.)

I swung onto the train and it rattled away down the tracks way beyond Machu Picchu and on towards the mountains of the north-west. If all went well, I was going to follow Manco to his final retreat in the heart of the Vilcabamba.

*

To my delight, the train was full of old friends from the Cusichaca Project who were heading back there to pack up at the end of the season. They had a crate of beer and we drank cold Cristals standing by the open door to the foot-plate, with the phosphorescent waters of the Urubamba swirling away below in the night light. Each time the train turned from side to side on the tight valley corners, the articulated links would stretch and sway us violently from side to side.

They had news of Roddy, who was not at Cusichaca as I had expected but was right down in Quillabamba at the end of the railway line, in the jungle, and I determined to go straight down there to meet up with him.

The beer and the end-of-dig feeling loosened tongues. In the enclosed world of the Project, the volunteers had always tended to be reticent with any criticism, as the canvas was thin and there was a feeling that somehow any comments would always get back to Ann. One of the volunteers now told me a story which stuck in my memory. They had just been in Cuzco to deliver this year's huge collection of pottery found at the Cusichaca sites to the INC (the *Instituto Nacional de Cultura*, the government department responsible for archaeological sites). In passing, they had looked into the room where the pottery from previous years was stored, in rows of cardboard boxes marked '78', '79', '80', '81', like so many vintages. Apparently the place smelt like an old potting shed and there was a general feeling that Ann was becoming the victim of her own success: the scale of the digging had produced such an amount of pot that it was becoming impossible to assimilate an avalanche of samples.

An added problem was the narrowness of the time-scale involved in dating the pottery: the difference between a classic and post-Inca pot was only a hundred years, which could pose problems in delineating clear changes of design. From my own brief observations, classical archaeology did seem to be a discipline that could grind to an uncertain halt under the momentum of its own scrupulous thoroughness. The work that Ann had done with the local community – the restoration of canal-systems along Incaic lines and a feeling of pride in the past achievements of their ancestors – seemed much more profitable, perhaps the face of archaeology in the future.

The inevitable tensions of a long dig had also surfaced and many had quarrelled with Ann or her lieutenants about arrangements – there was a rumour (or threat) that in future seasons they would get diggers from an American organisation called Earthwatch who would actually pay to come down and work on the Project, supplanting the current volunteers. Personally my sympathies were with Ann; trying to run a camp that size, for the fifth successive season, would have tested the patience of a saint, let alone an archaeologist.

Davina, the camp administrator, had been through a terrible time while I had been away: her father had died suddenly in England, from a riding accident; at the same time she had contracted severe hepatitis. Despite a rocky start, I had become fond of her, and I was not surprised to hear that she had borne these misfortunes with quiet bravery.

There was tragic news of Graham, the ex-army organiser who had been looking after all the arrangements at the camp. Driving back to Cuzco at the end of the season, he had been involved in a head-on collision and died instantly: the fifty-gallon oil drum he was carrying on the back seat flew forward and broke his neck. During that hot, long season at the camp, Graham had been the good-humoured butt of our endless jokes for his 'Carry On Up The Andes' approach to life and his way of adjusting the solar-powered showers with bits of string. It made me feel worse about his death.

The Cusichaca lot bundled off at Kilometre 88 and I carried on alone, heading down the Urubamba river, past Machu Picchu, past Santa Teresa where we'd always got off for our exploring trips and on towards the Vilcabamba.

Passing beneath Machu Picchu reminded me that I was back in the footsteps of the man who'd started me on this journey. Indeed, one of the many curiosities about Hiram Bingham's discovery of Machu Picchu was how quickly he'd left it and carried on downriver, just as I was doing. In his own words, he 'pushed on down the Urubamba asking for ruins, offering cash prizes for good ones and a double bonus for any that would fit the description of the Temple of the Sun'.

Bingham had good reason to press on down the Urubamba in 1911. A Peruvian academic called Carlos Romero had alerted him to the recent discovery of a remarkable manuscript: a report dictated by one of the rebel Incas, Titu Cusi (Manco's son), in 1570 as he led his people in their final resistance to the Spanish. It was the only eyewitness account of the Conquest by any of the major protagonists, Spanish or Quechuan, to have survived, which made it unusual enough. But to Bingham's intense interest, Titu Cusi had dictated it for the King of Spain's benefit from a city he called 'Vilcabamba'.

The term 'Vilcabamba' was confusingly used for both an area and a city. The whole area of Vilcabamba was the last redoubt of the Inca defence against the Spanish, as was already well known by Bingham's time, and the area is still known by the same name after the river that runs through it. It extended over several valleys to the north-west of Cuzco, between the rivers

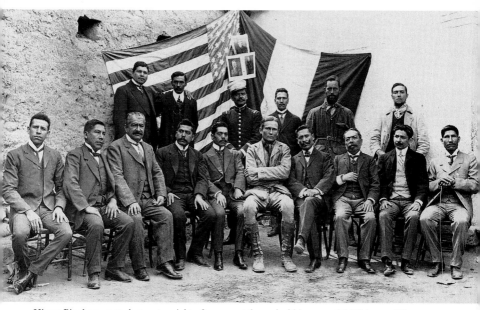

Hiram Bingham, seated at centre right of group, at the end of his successful 1911 expedition.

Hiram Bingham in characteristic pose (and boots): *'His energy propelled him through the Urubamba in a rolling maul of enthusiasm and sheer drive.'*

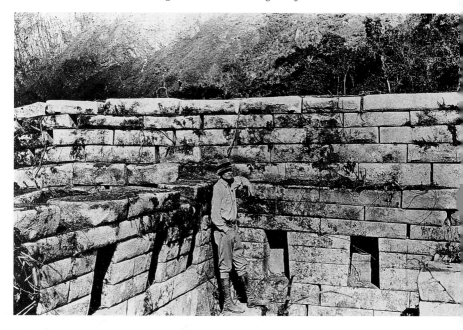

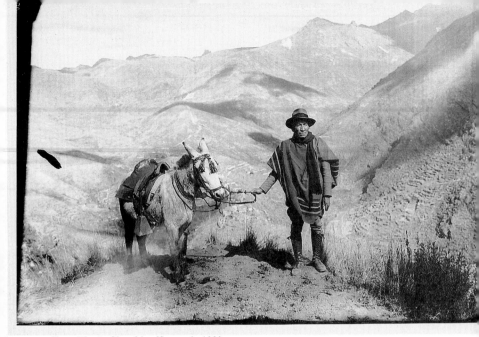

Above Martín Chambi: self-portrait, 1930:
'the very essence of the photographer as lone explorer.'

Below Martín Chambi *Autoretrato con Autoretrato (Self-portrait with self-portrait)*, 1923.

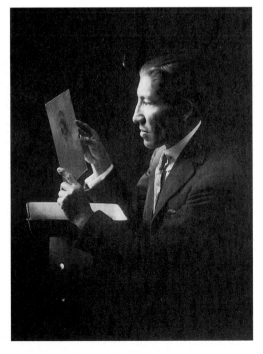

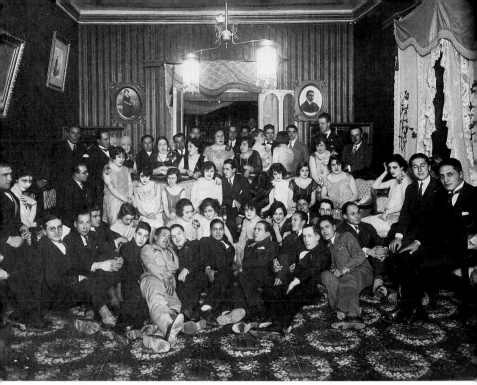

Martín Chambi *Party-goers in the 1920s*. '*Cuzco se desalumbró*, Cuzco woke up.'

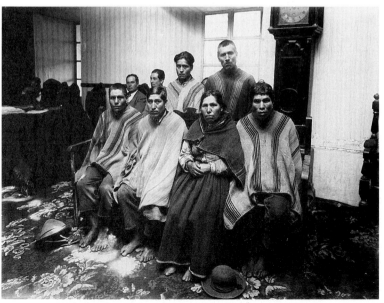

Martín Chambi *Juicio Oral, Corte Superior* (Judgement in the High Court, Cuzco), 1928

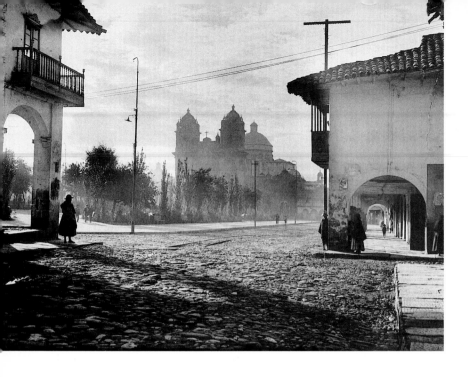

'Martín Chambi was a chronicler of Cuzco for the remainder of his long life.': (above) early dawn at the Plaza de Armas 1925; (below) Cuzco after the earthquake in 1950, with Incaic walls visible beneath the colonial structure.

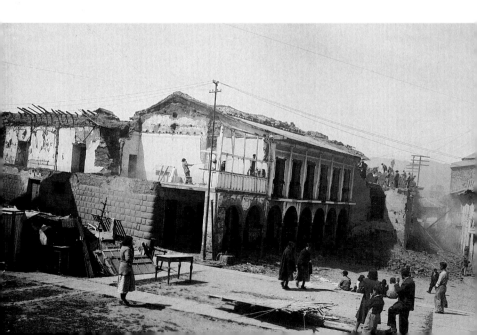

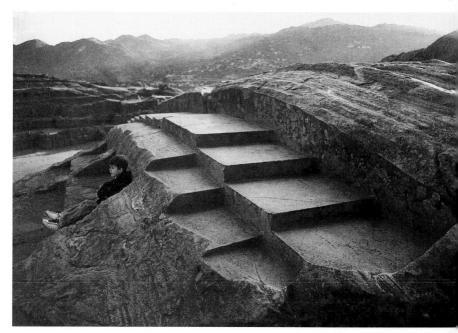

The carved steps of the Throne of the Inca on Rodadero hill above Cuzco, with Sacsahuaman beyond.

The Coricancha, or Sun Temple, in Cuzco after its post-earthquake restoration. *'Nestled incongruously within the cloisters of a Spanish convent, the effect is like one of those odd medieval dishes, where an entire pigeon is roasted inside a pig's head.'*

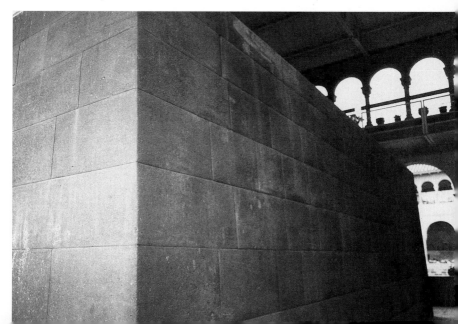

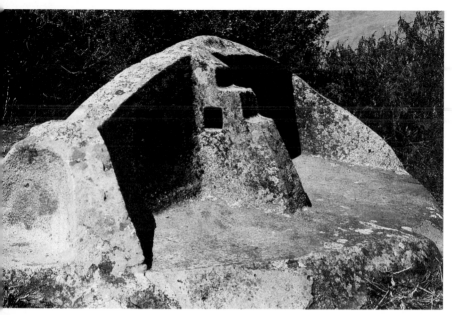

Above and Below Martín Chambi: Carved *huacas* at Sahuite.
'The Incas worked stone with more facility than they did clay.'

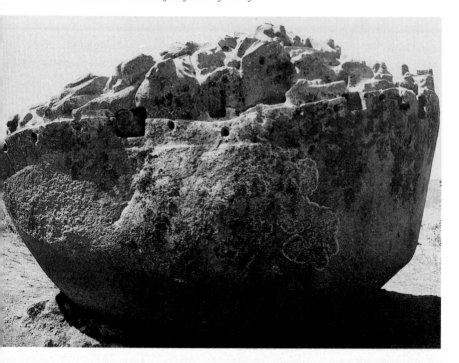

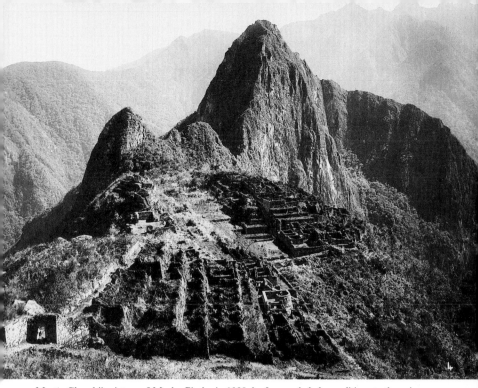

Martín Chambi's picture of Machu Picchu in 1925; he frequently led expeditions to the ruins.

The Funerary Rock at Machu Picchu.

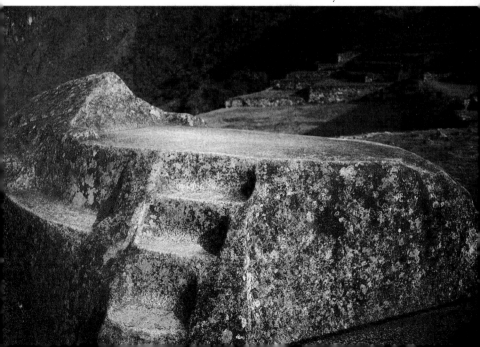

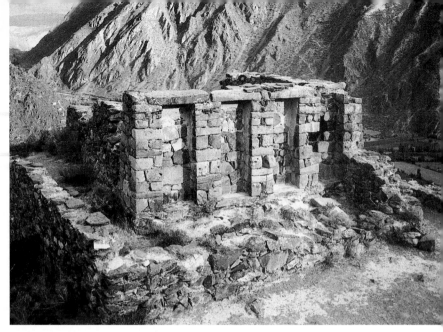

The so-called 'Incahuatana' (hitching-place of the Inca) above the main site at Ollantaytambo: *'a small ruin that faced the setting sun and the mountain fastnesses that Manco would have retreated into.'*

The carved stone of Qenko above Cuzco.

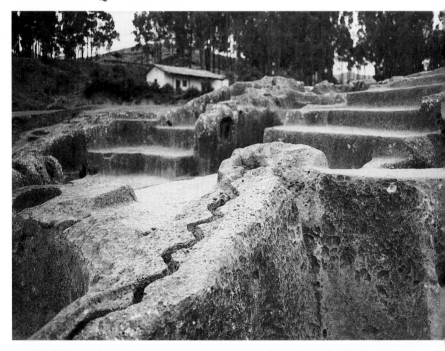

Urubamba and Apurímac, in the quarter of the Empire the Incas called Antisuyo, and was centred on a mountain site called Vitcos, near the White Rock of Chuquipalta.

This was the area into which Manco led his people after leaving Ollantaytambo (referred to by Prescott as 'an obscure fastness in the depths of the Andes'), and as a rump kingdom it long survived attempts by the Spanish to destroy it. However, in case even this proved vulnerable to persistent Spanish attack, the Incas decided on a last place of retreat, down towards the Amazon where they could lose themselves in the jungle. There they built the actual city of Vilcabamba, from which Titu Cusi dictated his memoirs, and which, confusingly, was not in the area of Vilcabamba. (To avoid such confusion, I have followed the convention of referring to the city throughout as 'Old Vilcabamba'.)

Manco's choice of the Vilcabamba area as a retreat from the Spanish was an inspired one. It was to be a full forty years after the Spanish Conquest and Atahualpa's murder before the last Inca, Tupac Amaru, was finally caught and brought out of the mountains, to be publicly executed in Cuzco in 1572.

This gave time for a genealogy of Inca Emperors to flourish in Vilcabamba as pretenders over the mountains. Manco Inca was succeeded by his sons Sayri Tupac, Titu Cusi and Tupac Amaru, and it was Titu Cusi who dictated the remarkable document that had only been rediscovered shortly before Bingham's arrival. In it the Inca told the life of his father Manco and gave a full account of what it was like to be on the receiving end of the Conquest, a useful corrective to the many European versions. Importantly, he also gave many new details as to the actual location of the city, Old Vilcabamba, in which he was living and which the Incas had made their base. From these details it was clear to Carlos Romero that a mistake had been made.

For the previous two centuries, all explorers to the region – the Comte de Sartiges, the geographer Raimondi, the traveller Charles Wiener – had assumed that Choquequirao must have been the great final city of the Incas, Old Vilcabamba. They were swayed to this judgement by Choquequirao's magnificent position, the fact that no other major Inca sites were known of and, in Sartiges' case, doubtless by the very human fact that he himself had managed to get there. But from Titu Cusi's description, Romero was able to assert categorically that Choquequirao could not be Old Vilcabamba. It was, apart from anything else, too high.

Spurred on by the Titu Cusi manuscript, Romero, a dedicated scholar who deserves more recognition for his part in the Machu Picchu discovery, also re-examined the long account left by Father de la Calancha, an

Augustinian monk, who had given many details about Old Vilcabamba in an epic account of the doings of his fellowship in Peru.

Romero published his findings in 1909, the year Bingham first arrived in Peru. Bingham's timing, as always, was almost beyond luck, yet few men would have been so opportunistic and daring as to act quite as decisively on such information as he did. Romero reported from his reading of Titu Cusi that Old Vilcabamba lay at a low altitude, that it enjoyed the fruits of the forest, and he named various places near it which were a long way from Choquequirao. So when Bingham careered on down the Urubamba, he had that most intoxicating of documents figuratively under his arm, in Long John Silver style: a manuscript, which few others knew about, with good clues as to the whereabouts of an archaeological treasure. The Titu Cusi manuscript could show him the way and Carlos Romero had supplied some other detailed and scholarly pointers as to where to look for Old Vilcabamba, which, as Bingham constantly reminded his readers, was the real 'lost city of the Incas'.

The search for Old Vilcabamba became his great obsession. One reason why he pressed on from Machu Picchu with such indecent haste after first discovering it must have been his quick realisation that however wonderful, Machu Picchu, like Choquequirao, did not fit particularly well with Titu Cusi's account of the city of Old Vilcabamba. It was too high and also too close to Cuzco to offer any real escape from the relentlessly following conquistadors.

So Bingham left his colleagues behind to clear and map the Machu Picchu site (like many an explorer, he preferred the excitement of the search to the cleaning up) and pressed on down the valley in search of this city of Old Vilcabamba, accompanied only by the delightfully named Professor Harry Foote, who sounds like a character from Conan Doyle's *The Lost World* or Spielberg's *Jurassic Park*.

Bingham made the journey on foot and with mules. I felt no shame about sitting in a comfortable train to do the same, particularly as the food vendors kept jumping on at each stop: I filled up on coffee, cakes, *tamales* and chocolate (the best of the local varieties of chocolate bar was called 'Sublime', pronounced with three stressed syllables like 'cor-blimey').

As we left Santa Teresa and started to descend, the Urubamba widened into what felt like a major river, with wide pebbled shores that made it look coastal in the moonlight. The climate quickly changed from the brisk chill of an Andean night to a jungle moistness, and all the passengers started to disrobe. I watched with some fascination as an old Quechuan woman unwrapped herself like a mummy, each succeeding layer revealing more foodstuffs tucked about her person. By the time we got to Quillabamba, the vendors were getting on in shorts. One cheerful woman flashed a smile full of gold teeth as she waved papaya slices at the carriage.

Roddy was sitting morosely in Quillabamba's only hostel when I found him. A few days of Quillabamba's delights had clearly exhausted him. It was good to see him again. We headed out for a meal, passing a hairdresser's nearby called the 'Peluquería Beatles', with photos of the 'Fab Four' in the window in their early-sixties 'Beatles cut' days: it was a style that many of the Indians in Quillabamba still followed. Next to it was a stationer's with an array of comics outside: Roddy pointed out to me some of the more lurid titles such as *El Sadismo* and *La Ninfomanía*, illustrated in photo-romance style with caption-bubbles coming from the characters' heads; they were from a series called *Psicológico Trauma (Psychological Trauma)*, with equally lurid covers, and sat oddly with the children's notebooks and sets of pencils.

For a town with a wild reputation, Quillabamba seemed quite stately. There were wide streets and a large market, to which vendors would come from hundreds of miles around. Yet this was a place that back in the 1960s and 70s had been on the frontier. The state in which it lay, La Convención, was then a byword for terrorist activity, and the guerrilla Hugo Blanco (later, like all good guerrillas, to become a senator) had led his men in fierce resistance to central government. Gunmen were regularly seen on the streets. In those days, it was not a good place to be in if you were a government official and we had heard that those days were returning with the Sendero Luminoso, the 'Shining Path' movement.

It was also a bad place to be a chicken. I had never seen so much chicken being fried. Every sidewalk, bar and restaurant seemed to have a rotating spit of birds. The standard dish, to go, was a quarter of chicken, chips and a beer. As they ate this, the citizens would perambulate around the square on a gentle *paseo*, taking in the evening air and the other chicken eaters.

There were little bars set up in the open doing a brisk business. Each stall had a TV attached, blatantly hitched up to an illegal feed from the mains cable above. In a scene reminiscent of the recently released *Bladerunner*, the bar-women were cooking and serving food in a cloud of smoke: a cluster of clients around them were watching mesmerised as poorly receiving televisions played video hits from Europe and the States. We ordered a bottle of rum and washed down some *lomos americanos* (steaks with banana, eggs, chips and cheese), as Rod Stewart sang 'Maggie May' on the screen. It was difficult to know what the average Peruvian would make of lines like 'All you did was wreck my bed / and in the morning kick me in the head', although they were not that far from some of the *criolla* ballads about '*la negra*', who did her man wrong.

A vendor came by with a fabulous array of jungle ice-creams: mango, tangerine, coconut, even avocado. The best (Roddy had done extensive pre-sampling) was *lúcuma*, eggfruit. As we sat eating ice-cream, an old Scotsman seized on us as the first Europeans he'd seen for five years. He had been living in the jungle prospecting for gold and looked it, wearing a battered check shirt and some thin Peruvian tracksuit bottoms with elasticated legs that cruelly showed the swellings and abrasions around his ankles. His stubbled face was pockmarked with sores and rashes. He came into Quillabamba occasionally when he got lucky to cash in his finds and buy some chicken and beer.

The Scotsman told us dolefully that the amount of metal he was 'taking' was diminishing each year. 'Heard of any rich spots?' he asked hopefully, and refused to believe that we hadn't, or our protestations that we weren't there looking for gold. 'Why else come to Quillabamba?' was his attitude.

He told us more about the Sendero Luminoso. Up until recently they had been a distant rumour, an impending storm, centred around Ayacucho in the south. Now they were building up strength in La Convención, particularly along the Apurímac, for the same reason that guerrillas since the time of Manco Inca had come here. It was ideal country to mount a campaign, with many inaccessible valleys both to hide in and launch sallies from. 'These guys aren't like the old terrorists,' said our Scottish friend (we never learnt his name), with some regret. 'The old ones would cut you a bit of slack, leave old-timers like me alone. But these guys ...' He made a gesture of a neck being cut.

We gave him more rum. 'Have you heard of the cult of Fatima?' he asked. We hadn't. 'Well, let me give you one piece of advice. Make sure, when you get back to Europe, that you investigate the cult of Fatima.' And with that he hobbled off into the night.

Roddy took me off the next morning for a fortifying breakfast at a market stall he had discovered. The ladies greeted him like a regular prized customer, as well they might: Roddy had a prodigious breakfast appetite and I had once seen him eat six bananas on the trot within five minutes of awakening. Roddy ordered two *jugos especiales* for us, long fruit juices made up of orange, papaya and pineapple, mixed with lime juice and raw egg to give *sabor* and beer to give *fuerza*. The ingredients were solemnly prepared for us in one of the big Kenwood mixers that were such status symbols in the remote areas of Peru.

It seemed a good time to sell Roddy on my plan. My idea was that we should travel into the heart of the Vilcabamba, to Vitcos and the famous White Rock nearby. I'd already tried once to get a permit to do this, without success, as the government was worried about the growing Sendero

Luminoso presence in the region. The only way we could do it was to travel without papers and risk getting caught by the police. After another *jugo especial*, Roddy was game for it, although such was the kick of the *especiales* that I could by then probably have got him to dance naked in the town square with a live chicken, if such a thing existed in Quillabamba.

THE WHITE ROCK

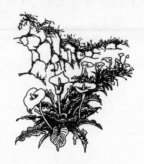

WE FELT NERVOUS as we approached Chaullay, the jumping-off point for the Vilcabamba: without papers or maps, we were heading into new, unknown territory. This wasn't helped by the complete inability of anybody on the train to tell us where to get off. Chaullay apparently had two stations. Some said we should disembark at the first, others the second, leaving us in one of those classic travellers' dilemmas – uncertainty not quite strong enough to resolve itself into paranoia. We got out at the first stop and found the train had left us in a one-track railway town with the entire population staring at us. It was the wrong station.

My trousers didn't help. At some point during a past trek, I had split the back seam and all attempts at repairing them had failed miserably: that morning I had discovered a neat line of mosquito bites running down an exposed part of my buttock like fine stitching. They had come irreparably adrift at some point on the train journey and I was all too conscious of the spectacle I presented, an unshaven gringo stumbling around in the mid-day sun, looking lost because he was. It was pitiful enough to arouse a certain amount of sympathy. One lady gave us some fresh bread (a rare commodity), another some avocados, and we were told of a truck-driver who might be able to give us a lift right into the heart of the Vilcabamba.

Below was the site of the celebrated Chuquichaca crossing: a large rock in the centre of the stream had allowed the Incas to build one of their most famous and strategically useful bridges across the Urubamba river near its confluence with the Vilcabamba. This was the bridge that Manco and his men used when they retreated from Ollantaytambo into the hills. Manco left orders that it should be held (or simply demolished) if the Spanish tried to follow them, just as they had already destroyed much of the road they had taken down from the Panticalla pass. This did not deter the Spanish who pressed on after them, led by the glamorous and determined Rodrigo Orgóñez.

Orgóñez was a conquistador who had come from humble beginnings as a quasi-bastard to become one of the New World's great soldiers. Battle-hardened by campaigns in Chile, where he had survived a disastrous expedition, Orgóñez was quite prepared to make do without a road and ford a few rivers if it would bring him the last Inca's head. A small contingent of his men managed to cross the bridge before Manco's men were able to destroy it. Now Orgóñez could follow Manco right into the Vilcabamba itself.

It is tempting to see Manco's retreat into this area as being as romantic as Bonnie Prince Charlie's into the Highlands of Scotland – a king on the run, returning to his natural heartland, chased by a heartless enemy. But just as Stuart and Highland politics were infinitely more complicated than this, so were the politics of the Andes. The assumption that the Inca Empire was necessarily inhabited mainly by Incas is a common mistake – strictly speaking, the Incas were a relatively small group centred around Cuzco. The larger Empire was comprised of other ethnic groups who had been subjugated by either treaty or war and were variously compliant with the continuation of that Empire. The *pax Incaica* was a forceful one: the names of cities were changed, while local gods (and human servants) were taken back to Cuzco as hostages. And as I had seen in my travels, they had used the system of *mitamayo* to move tribes from one end of the Empire to another for imperial projects, as Pachacuti had done with the Colla at Ollantaytambo. Those particularly prone to rebel would be most at risk of this forced migration.

This brutal policy finally caught up with Manco as he passed through here on his retreat from Ollantaytambo, with Orgóñez snapping at his heels. When Pachacuti's son Topa Inca had expanded the Empire northwards, he had in the process conquered the Chachapoyans, a noticeably bellicose tribe who had built a series of great fortresses in their country beside the Marañon (fortresses which have been the focus of intense exploratory and archaeological activity in recent years). The Chachapoyans had rebelled frequently, both against Manco's father Huayna Capac and Manco's brother Atahualpa: each Emperor had put down the rebellion with severity, killing local *caciques*, and they had started to move the Chachapoyan population by way of reprisal.

It is estimated that almost half of the Chachapoyan population were deported from their homeland as *mitimaes*. On the eve of the Spanish invasion, Atahualpa, who had clearly decided to rid himself of these troublesome fighters for ever (they had made the mistake of backing the wrong brother, Huascar, in the civil wars), ordered a mass migration of all the surviving male population to his power base in Quito. As he had already slaughtered most of the Cañari tribe for a similar offence, the Chachapoyans must have feared the worst. Their *cacique*, Guaman, led them to the Marañon river which defined their boundary. As he was about to lead his people into permanent exile, slavery and possible execution, news came of Atahualpa's capture by strange, bearded invaders, the *barbudos*. It must have seemed extraordinarily providential.

By chance, Manco's route now took him through a large community of these Chachapoyans in Amaibamba. They had been brought here from their homeland many years before under the *mitamayo* policy to build a palace for Topa Inca and had remained even after the Spanish invasion. Not unnaturally, they now gave Manco a hostile reception. The Chachapoyans harassed their old oppressors continually and vicious fighting ensued: Manco was finally driven to throw the local Chachapoyan leader off this very same Chuquichaca bridge as a warning to the Chachapoyans (and other subject tribes) that while the Incas might be on the run, they still had teeth.

Surprisingly, given this episode, Manco still nursed the illusion that the Chachapoyans further north in their original homeland might now forgive old grievances and find common cause with the Incas in the fight against the Spanish. He was to be quickly disabused. The messenger he sent, one hapless Cayo Topa, was taken captive with all his men and brought back to face the Chachapoyan *cacique* Guaman – the same chief who, Moses-style, had once been ordered by Atahualpa to lead his entire people out of their country. Guaman reacted as one might expect, and his words to the Incas were recorded:

'Because the *barbudos*, the bearded ones, are clearly never going to return to Castille but will always be here, we are all going to have to become Christians. And since you have always betrayed us, you are now going to die.' It was an admirably succinct exposition of *realpolitik*. Cayo Topa was then burnt alive, Castilian-style.

The same pattern was repeated elsewhere. Part of Manco's problem in ever leading a successful pan-Andean uprising against the Spanish was that half of the relevant tribes hated the Incas far more than they did the new invaders – just as in Mexico the Aztecs' habit of extracting large numbers of human sacrifices from their client states had prevented them from playing the loyalty card when they too needed support against the Spanish. And for the Incas, this was not simply a passive lack of support. The Cañari, whom the Incas had treated even worse than the Chachapoyans, went so far as joining forces with Orgóñez in chasing Manco and were to prove particularly relentless in doing so. As one of my Peruvian friends graphically put it, 'It just shows that you should never piss in the air, because the wind might change.'

Wandering up from the bridge, we came to a small hut where the truck-driver was laying into the *cerveza* in a committed way before setting off. He suggested that as it was now late (three o'clock), and we wouldn't make Yupanqa before dark, we should sleep the night at his house, which lay along our route. We were more worried about whether he'd make it round the first bend.

The suggestion of prolonging the journey with an overnight stop turned out to be a mixed blessing, mainly because of the driver's assistant, an irritating overweight adolescent who insisted against all evidence to the contrary that he could speak a little English. After a couple more *cervezas* (for it was Saturday night and the truck stopped at every grocery store we passed for another quick one) he insisted on prefacing every sentence with 'Yes, yes, I speak English.' He irritated Roddy enormously, if enjoyably, by calling him '*el enamorado*', 'lover boy', and as a result the tips of Roddy's ears were reddening slightly, a dangerous sign. I didn't fare much better. He told me that I could buy plenty of women at the market the next day, particularly, for some reason, American and Argentinian ones, whom he had mythologised as the most sexually desirable.

By the time we arrived at the driver's house, our normally affable relations with Peruvians had become strained. I asked what the speciality of the region was: they thought I was questioning the quality of the driver's cooking. Things worsened with the sleeping arrangements: many of the truck-drivers used the house as a regular stopover and we all slept together in a filthy dormitory room, in an atmosphere of dirt and dirty jokes – the first time that I'd felt really sordid in Peru, although I'd slept in worse conditions. The drunken drivers joked about *maricas* and *maricones* ('homosexuals' and, literally, 'great big homosexuals') and sneered at us for being gringos.

We were woken at 4.30. After trying to sleep in the damp and sweaty room, it was a relief to be out in the night air, and Roddy and I rode on the cross-bars at the front of the truck. I suddenly remembered when I was a kid riding on a farmer's night delivery van and taking the milk to a depot – the same rush of stars and night about the head, and that sense of having to work the road oneself with each unexpected turn, as the cold concentrated the body. We were driving into what the dawn slowly revealed to be a stunningly attractive valley, with the small Vilcabamba river below us.

The one advantage of travelling with our driver and his obnoxious assistant was that we cleared the various checkpoints without difficulty, lying down in the bottom of the pick-up truck each time one approached: the driver was a regular and knew all the guards. We arrived in the little village of Yupanqa numbed with cold. The driver charmingly doubled the agreed price for the drive on the grounds that otherwise he would inform the police of our presence. We paid up grudgingly and hunkered down at a market stall for a coffee, keeping a low profile in case word got around that we were in town.

As it happened, we got lucky. A young broad-faced woman with a cowboy hat, who reminded us of *Annie Get Your Gun*, offered us a lift to Vitcos. If neither American nor Argentinian, she was certainly the proverbial angel. We explained that we wanted to avoid the road-blocks and Annie just laughed, 'You'd better pretend you're Cuzqueña Pilsner, then.' She was delivering beer to the Vilcabamba valley and we arranged ourselves uncomfortably among the crates in the back of her pick-up truck, stopping at every house along the way to off-load bottles as she gathered gossip and messages to pass on higher up the valley. Beer was a major currency in the mountains and I was amused by the sheer incongruity of the posters advertising it (usually some bare-nippled blonde beauty arising from the sea with an ice-cold bottle of Cristal or Cuzqueña held to her chest). These posters dominated the dark, dusty shops of the mountains, with their tins of tuna fish or packets of Quaker Oats.

We sailed past the biggest police checkpoint at Puquiura, with a nicely judged bit of innuendo from Annie about how good the guard looked in his uniform. An hour later we had arrived at Huancacalle: both Vitcos and the White Rock were only a short distance away. I couldn't believe that we'd made it – so many of the travellers I'd met in Cuzco had been turned back.

I have been back to Huancacalle several times since, but nothing can quite compare with that first arrival, with Annie playing *huayno* on her radio and Roddy and me crouched down in the back of her truck feeling like extras from *The Great Escape*. A frisson of illegality added to the pleasure of the experience, just as Robert Byron had enjoyed dressing up in disguise in order to enter his Persian mosques.

The village had an idyllic setting – groves of eucalyptus, trout pools and a wide street that curved over a hill. It was market day and we passed many clear-faced, smiling women, with an independent air about them. This was also a village of horses – they were everywhere, tied up to the posts outside houses and grazing in the nearby meadows, while horsemen down from the hills drank outside the shacks that passed for bars.

We asked a couple of boys to take us up first to the old palace of Vitcos and then on to the White Rock. Alfredo and Wilfredo can't have been more than about seven or eight. We stopped by the river to wash — the boys were fascinated by my electric razor. Then they led us up a winding path above the valley, spinning tops as they went, and after an hour or so we came round a corner to see the old palace of Vitcos ahead.

The ruins of the palace lay on a ridge which rose like a throne in the very middle of the Vilcabamba valley. From the rounded summit, Manco and later his sons could survey not only the valley, but the many passes that led into it from almost every point of the compass: this was the Incas' centre of operations while in exile.

A narrow spit of land led us out onto the summit and the main buildings — and we could see at once that these had been Inca buildings of the first order, although now dilapidated and covered with tangled weed and some plants that looked like overgrown cabbages. The plaza was surrounded by fine gateways and ashlars worked with the almost casual ingenuity the masons liked to display, as if to show how many sides a stone could have and still be made to fit with another. Large lintels were still in place over the doors, although treasure-hunters seemed to have repeatedly excavated beneath the doorways themselves. The building that fronted onto the plaza was a full 250 feet long. There was no doubt that this had been a palace.

It is probable that much of it had already been built by Pachacuti and earlier Incas when Manco arrived here with some relief, thinking that he had outrun his pursuers. He ordered that a new house be built for himself and organised a festival at which to parade the mummies of his ancestors before the locals and his jungle allies.

If Manco thought that he had reached sanctuary, he was to be rudely disabused. His pursuer Orgóñez, once he had crossed the bridge at Chuquichaca, made good time and caught the Inca unawares. It was a rout. The Incas, according to Manco's son Titu Cusi, were as drunk as they were accustomed to be at such festivals and were completely taken by surprise. Manco himself was only saved by the Spaniards' greed. They were so excited by the amount of gold and loot they found (much of it on public display for the festival) that he was able to get away over one of the passes that led from Vitcos. Before Orgóñez could mount a further chase, he was recalled to Cuzco to take part in the interminable civil war that was rumbling on between two factions of the conquistadors (a civil war in which Orgóñez later lost his life) and Manco could return to Vitcos, although he had lost many of his treasures and troops.

He was not able to relax for long — a second punitive expedition was launched against him a few years later by Gonzalo Pizarro, the same Pizarro brother who was later to try to sail down the Amazon. Gonzalo was the youngest brother of the four who had come to Peru: Francisco led the expedition, Juan died at Sacsahuaman, while Hernando, the only legitimate son and Prescott's 'evil genius', was eventually imprisoned in Spain for his crimes, although for those against his fellow conquistadors rather than against the Indians. Gonzalo was as tough as his older brothers, if not always as intelligent. In 1539, he chased Manco even further than Orgóñez had – over the mountains beyond Vitcos and right down into the Amazon. Again Manco managed to escape and was reported to have shouted defiance at his persecutors as he was borne off into the depths of the jungle.

So once more Manco lived to return and rebuild his kingdom. He was nothing if not a survivor. So confident did he become in his Vilcabamba stronghold that he launched punitive raids against the Spanish on the old Royal Road from Cuzco down to Lima and mounted an effective guerrilla campaign. He was helped by the continuing civil war between the conquistadors, in which Gonzalo Pizarro was eventually executed and his brother Francisco assassinated. Manco, always a cunning politician, welcomed the assassins of Francisco Pizarro to his palace at Vitcos on the grounds that any enemy of the Pizarros was a friend of his (understandable given that Francisco had tortured and killed Manco's wife, then floated her mutilated corpse down the Urubamba river so that Manco could see it).

But Manco's kindness to the Spanish refugees was to be his undoing. Standing in the plaza, with a gentle wind blowing up from the valley below, it was impossible not to remember how Manco had finally died on that same spot.

Manco sheltered Pizarro's assassins for a few years. After a while, they decided to curry favour with the Spanish authorities and obtain a pardon by killing Manco. Although kept unarmed while they were at the Vitcos palace, they somehow managed to obtain a dagger. While playing a game of quoits with Manco, one of them produced it and stabbed the Inca to death.

Manco was only twenty-nine when he died in this final act of Spanish treachery. He had been a great leader. Prescott put it well in the nineteenth century when he wrote (perhaps surprisingly for a North American at the time): 'Manco did not trust the promises of the white man and he chose rather to maintain his savage independence in the mountains, with the few brave spirits around him, than to live a slave in the land which had once owned the sway of his ancestors.'

Vitcos was a theatrical setting for a death – a stage playing to the amphitheatre of the valley. How Manco's unarmed assassins thought they would get away with it when they were so exposed, virtually unarmed, and a hundred miles inside enemy territory, is unclear: they were promptly chased down and burnt to death. It was a strange result of the twists and turns of politics in the tumultuous years after the Conquest that the same assassins should have killed both the Spanish and Inca leaders.

Vitcos had never been reconstructed (spared the fate of Machu Picchu, the purists would argue) and had been only partially excavated. There was a sadness to the few items which had been found there by Bingham: 'a mass of rough potsherds, a few Inca whirl-bobs and bronze shawl-pins, and also a number of iron articles of European origin, heavily rusted horseshoe nails, a buckle, a pair of scissors, several bridles or saddle ornaments, and three Jew's harps' – a sense that the refugees had been forced to use the scrapings of the culture that had displaced them.

Unlike the Aztecs, whose poetry is at least preserved, we have only a few fragments of the cultural remains of the Incas – most of their great epics and the plays we know they used to perform have been lost. As a civilisation with no writing or hieroglyphics, it was uniquely vulnerable to the confident cultural attack of the Spanish. The world of the Incas has been obliterated as thoroughly as they themselves tried to obliterate that of their pre-decessors – only a few broken shards and some magnificent buildings remain as hints of what their Empire must have been like.

We followed our young guides over the shoulder of the hill and on towards the White Rock itself, passing some lesser buildings of rough *pirca* in the overgrown woods.

Just as the monumental carved rocks or *huacas* around Cuzco had attracted worship in the heyday of the Empire, so now did those in the rump kingdom, and none more so than the White Rock, or Chuquipalta, as it was known by the Incas. If Vitcos was the political capital of the surviving Inca state in exile, then Chuquipalta was the spiritual epicentre. The more I had read of it in the histories, the more I had wanted to see this great shrine.

A Spanish priest, Antonio de la Calancha, had left a scandalised description of it as 'a temple of the sun, and inside it a white stone above a spring of water. The devil appeared here, and it was the principal *mochadero* – the common Indian word for their shrines – in these *montañas*. There was a devil, captain of a legion of devils, inside the white stone called Yurac-rumi, within that Sun Temple.'

Hiram Bingham had followed this description when he found it, although he was more interested in the site as a signpost to the nearby ruin of Vitcos (which he then subsequently found). He knew from his friend Carlos Romero's reading of the chronicles that one lay near the other.

This was Bingham's own account of his discovery:

Here before us was a great white rock. Our guides had not misled us. Beneath the trees were the ruins of an Inca temple, flanking and partly enclosing the gigantic granite boulder, one end of which overhung a small pool of running water. Since the surface of the little pool, as one gazes at it, does not reflect the sky, but only the overhanging rock, the water looks black and forbidding, even to unsuperstitious Yankees.

It was late on the afternoon of August 9, 1911, when I first saw this remarkable shrine. Densely wooded hills rose on every side. The remarkable aspect of this great boulder and the dark pool beneath its shadow had caused this to become a place of worship. Here, without doubt, was 'the principal *mochadero* of these forested mountains'. It is still venerated by the Indians of the vicinity. At last we had found the place where, in the days of Titu Cusi, the Inca priests faced the east, greeted the rising sun, 'extended their hands towards it and threw kisses to it, a ceremony of the most profound resignation and reverence.'

Little visited, this was still a strange and melancholy place. It lay in a side-valley, in the shadow of the ridge on which the palace of Vitcos stood. The smallness of the valley helped to emphasise the presence of the rock, the shape of which seemed consciously to have been sculpted to reflect the sky-line of the mountains directly behind it (there are numerous examples of this style of reflective sculpture in Inca work, at Machu Picchu and elsewhere). We came to it from above, so we could see the layers of terraces stretching away beneath it, many filled with arum lilies and grazing horses.

The White Rock itself was perfectly formed, rather than monumental: the length was about fifty feet. As a sculpture it was magnificent. Because it was carved from the natural rock, it was asymmetric and almost impossible to photograph from any angle without reducing it. Not all the rock had been carved, but there were sweeping planes that had been smoothed on some sides, including the top, planes emphasised by the steps that had been cut to meet them.

Under the rock was a spring and the water was carefully channelled away from this and through a small *baño*, a ceremonial bath, before flowing off down the meadows and past many other smaller rocks, also partially sculpted.

Because we stayed for a full twenty-four hours, we were able to observe the way the light played off every facet as the sun moved around the rock, including a high wall that featured some ostentatious stone bosses studded across it, on the eastern side (first light brought out the bosses in strong relief, just as it did for similar stonework at Ollantaytambo). Around the rock were scattered elaborately carved boulders and the remaining foundation walls of the temples that had been built here, although none were high enough to show the ornamental niches they probably once had.

The rock had been called many things by many different people: 'The White Rock', 'Chuquipalta', 'Yurak Rumi', 'Ñusta España' – the very profusion of different names for the place gave a sense of the talismanic qualities it held.

We are used to the idea that the Incas quite literally worshipped stone, but few question why. There is an idea in the West that stone must imply some notion of permanence, but this is not necessarily true in the Andes, which is not a static landscape. An area of incipient volcanic activity and landslides, with recurring and violent El Niño activity over the millennia, the landscape has always been changing. For the Incas, stone was a much more volatile, organic medium.

In an Inca creation myth, Lord Viracocha formed the first man out of stone. Later, when Pachacuti successfully defeated the Chancha at the birth of his imperial Inca dynasty, he was said to have summoned the very stones around Cuzco to rise up and fight with him in a desperate defence of the capital against the invaders. This sense of stone as a life-force is crucial to understanding the Inca architectural and sculptural aesthetic. That old, tired phrase about 'the living stones' of some great site suddenly becomes a powerful, resurrected cliché.

The sheer primacy given to monumental stonework by both the Incas and the earlier Andean civilisations from whom they arose is also remarkable. Whereas in most nascent civilisations, including those further north in Central America, such building only occurred after an earlier stage of experimentation with ceramics and smaller-scale fabrication, in the Andes monumental architecture pre-dates even the earliest pottery to have been discovered. The Incas worked stone with more facility than they did clay (their pottery is functional rather than memorable).

Stone worship naturally seemed the height of idolatry to the friars who first came as missionaries to the Vilcabamba, and it was not long before Chuquipalta became the centre of their objections to native religion. In 1570, when Manco's son Titu Cusi was ruler of the province, two Augustinian friars led a party of local converts to the White Rock and proceeded to burn and destroy all that they could. Although Titu Cusi's captains wanted to kill the Christians, Titu was of a forgiving disposition, like his father Manco, and allowed them to live.

What one saw now at Chuquipalta was the aftermath of that destruction. A few blocks lay toppled to the ground and the nearby temple buildings had been razed to just a few feet in height, but the priests were unable to destroy the rock itself. Like a bombed church, the spirituality of the place remained. The White Rock was part of what had survived the Spanish Conquest – the heart of old Peru.

Cooking by candle-light with our shadows thrown back against the rock, we had an eerie meal crouched under the giant Inca stone, the petrol-flame of the cooker guttering in all directions. The frogs started croaking from the water under the rock, their noises amplified into an echo. We used our torch to pick out their coal-black eyes in the water. Outside in the night, the fire-flies hung over the banks of the water-channel, twitching with static.

In the morning I woke early and sat on one of the large carved seats that surrounded the rock itself. The sun rose at full strength from behind a hill, as it does in the mountains (there are no soft sunrises). I felt suddenly an intimation of mortality. Like most twenty-one-year-olds, death had always seemed at most a remote possibility and something that happened to other people. But in the cold of the morning and surrounded by the stone *disjecta membra* of the monument, with the white arum lilies against the green of the meadows, I felt a chill.

Wilder commentators had speculated on this place as a possible burial site for Manco after he had been murdered on the hill above. This seemed unlikely. However, I couldn't help feeling some satisfaction that at least Manco had without doubt died in sight of the high mountains that he and the Incas loved, a free man near the lily-fields, rather than down below in the foetid jungle city of Old Vilcabamba, where his successor Emperors were often forced to hide from the Spanish and where the very last of them, Tupac Amaru, was to be ignominiously captured.

That jungle city of Old Vilcabamba was the one place I had yet to visit. From here it was at least a four-day descent, and a tough one for which we needed mules, supplies and most of all permission. I felt that we had, miraculously, got away with penetrating into the heart of Vilcabamba and had reached the White Rock, which for me was the climax of our journey – but to go further down into the jungle and deeper into the Sendero Luminoso territory seemed foolhardy. It would have to wait for another year. I did not then know quite how long I would have to wait.

*

It was a cold spring day a few weeks afterwards, the start of November, and the clouds started to swirl high over the bowl that Cuzco lies in. From way above the city drifted the sound of the revellers, increasingly raucous as the day wore on. They were making their way to the cemetery on the hill beyond, taking *chicha* to drink and *lechón*, the roast pig that is specially prepared for *El Día de Todos los Santos*, All Saints' Day, more familiarly known as the Day of the Dead. Whole families carried flowers and picnics to the graves of their relatives, the little girls in white dresses as if going to first communion. Outside in the streets I had passed groups of youths who were already well tanked up on *chicha* and *cañoso*, the lethal sugar-cane spirit, and were stepping out deliberately in front of slow-moving cars to intimidate the drivers.

Juan Letona shook his head as he stood in the little patio of his Cuzco house. He was a quiet, gentle man in a cardigan. '*Hay muchos delincuentes arriba, hacen conmoción*, there's a lot of racket up there, too many delinquents,' he said, using the favourite disapproving word of the pious for the great unwashed. Juan was the guardian of the El Niño Mario shrine, one of the most important in Cuzco, if also one of the smallest – a tiny chapel that he and his family had made out of their living room. This was an important day for him, as a priest from the nearby parish of San Cristobal had come to hold a mass in the presence of El Niño Mario ('The Child Mario').

Mario was a controversial figure. Juan Letona led me in to see him as the mass was about to start: a tiny skeleton, with apparently preserved flesh and long black hair, a crown and long red cape, who sat over the altar in the Letonas' little living room, his face smiling in the rictus of death and with piercing glass eyes.

The setting was bizarre. To one side were the fridge and television, covered with cloth, to the other the priest wearing his green robes and lighting his incense, while El Niño Mario dominated the centre of the room. As many people as possible began to crowd inside and those that couldn't enter stayed out in the courtyard with the chickens, peering in. The smell of the incense and the denseness of the press of people began to overpower me as I listened to the priest intone about the dangers of *purgatorio*, of *delincuentes*, and of how the devil's main trick was to make people think that he didn't exist.

It took me a moment to realise what was most disconcerting about the seemingly mummified remains of Mario: the proportions. His head looked only about four inches long – and yet he was supposed to have been a boy of about thirteen. Although he was said to have a full body underneath, the cloth effectively covered everything below his face, which therefore stared out with an intensity increased by the glass eyes and eyelashes he had been given.

The cult of Mario had grown in Cuzco substantially over the previous thirty years. At first he had been a private object of worship for Juan Letona's mother and her family, but as the efficacy of petitions to him had increased and his fame had grown, they had accepted more and more visits from outsiders. By the early seventies he had thousands of visitors queuing for hours to file into the living room: at night there were candle-lit vigils in the patio outside.

This attracted the attention of the Catholic Church, who began to have considerable doubts about El Niño Mario. In 1976 a new bishop arrived in Cuzco and one of his first actions was to denounce Mario in ringing terms as being not only heretical but probably the skeleton of a monkey.

What happened next was described to me by one of the communicants after the mass, a quiet, small man with deep-set eyes, who took me aside to one of the quiet areas of the patio.

Cuzco had been thrown into an uproar. The bishop, Monsignor Luis Vallejos, was from the coast and had a small group of similarly minded clerics who advised him, particularly a French priest called Louis Dalle. They were immediately assumed to harbour all sorts of prejudices against the Quechuan version of Catholicism which had grown up around the fringes of Cuzco, of which El Niño Mario was the outstanding example. By some, this was thought to be yet another example of Lima's centuries-old disdain for the mountains.

Mario went into hiding. His followers (including the communicant who was telling me this) would carry him from house to house at night, while letting it be known that he had been moved to another town altogether such as Quillabamba or Puno. But his followers were convinced that he should never leave Cuzco and he appeared to them in dreams to tell them so. Secret ceremonies were held in his presence at night.

He had originally been known as El Niño Compadrito, using the emotive word *compadre* which has no direct translation in English but is used of intense friendships between people of the same sex – to be a *compadre* or *comadre* to someone is to be a partner of theirs in life's problems, in the same way that a godparent is to a child. Now in those same dreams he appeared to many of his followers in this time of need and told them his actual name was Mario. 'At about that time, our relationship with him changed,' my informant told me. 'It became deeper, more *íntimo*.'

Part of Mario's appeal was that so little was known about his origins. He was thought to have died in around 1850, at the age of thirteen, and his body had come into the possession of the Letona family only after the Second World War, when the previous family who had guarded him, apparently dissatisfied that he had not prevented the death of their mother, had passed him on to her *comadre*, Juan Letona's own mother. Then his cult had taken off.

Six years of persecution had followed the bishop's decree in 1976. El Niño Mario's followers argued with the Church, saying that the figure of Mario was always surrounded by objects of more traditional Catholic veneration – pictures of the Pope, of the Virgin Mary, of saints – and that he was not heretical. But the bishop and his close advisers were unyielding. Their comments about the Niño Mario probably consisting of the bones of a monkey were particularly insulting to the Niño's mainly Indian adherents. The city's religious community divided into two bitterly opposing factions – the *pro-Niñistas* and the *anti-Niñistas* – along a fault-line that had already grown up between those priests who believed in trying to accommodate local beliefs – the so-called *re-educadores*, the 're-educators' – and those who, like the Monsignor, wanted to enforce absolute orthodoxy.

The situation had been dramatically resolved only shortly before the mass I was attending. In May of that same year, Louis Dalle, the French priest who was widely seen as having been behind the bishop's decree, had died suddenly in a terrible car accident. His mother had also died almost immediately afterwards, 'not from natural causes', the communicant told me. At the same time, Father Luna, one of the most virulently *anti-Niñista* priests, had also died – again, in a sudden accident.

The bishop, Monsignor Vallejos, had been shaken to the core by the sudden deaths of those in his close circle. Only two weeks after Father Luna's death, the bishop went to visit some parishes south-east of Cuzco, near Sicuani. Driving on the steep mountain roads, his brakes apparently failed. With his death, the *anti-Niñista* campaign collapsed.

The city was still shocked by this extraordinary sequence of sudden fatalities. Juan Letona himself was far too diplomatic to comment on these deaths – not least because almost immediately afterwards, with a new bishop, a rapprochement with the Church had been reached: Mario had been allowed to come out of hiding and a *pro-Niñista* priest had been allowed to officiate at the special service on the Day of the Dead that I had just attended. But my informant, who was remarkably accurate about the details of the deaths (which I later confirmed from other sources), drew me even deeper into the shadows of the patio and made the point more bluntly.

'*Mira, Señor. El Niño Mario se escondió exactamente seis dias después del decreto del obispo.* Look, Mario went into hiding exactly six days after the bishop's decree. And exactly six years later these deaths have occurred. So far only four of them, but *ya ve*, wait and see, two more will follow.' And he shrugged, with the clear implication that if he were of the *anti-Niñista* persuasion he would not now be sleeping easy in his bed.

High over the city the light was suddenly shutting down, as the sun made its abrupt departure behind the mountains to the west: the dogs barking on the skyline mixed with the sound of the revellers returning from the cemeteries. I stepped out of the bright blue gate into the quiet Cuzco street feeling intoxicated by the incense, the intensity of the mass I had witnessed and the emotional charge that the Niño had for his petitioners.

Juan Letona had been at pains, for obvious reasons, to stress to me that Mario was not a mummy but a 'sacred relic' and, given the recent history of controversy surrounding him, I could see why. But there were some fascinating parallels with what had happened to the surviving mummified bodies of the Incas.

When each Inca died, his estate (or *panaca*) continued to maintain his household as if he were still alive – he remained 'resident' in his old palace in mummified form, to be brought out on feast days or for the coronation of his successors, and each of those successors would therefore have to build themselves a new palace. When Manco Inca had been crowned by the Spanish (a decision they had such cause later to regret), contemporary accounts describe how the mummies of the whole dynasty of dead Inca Emperors were carried in procession alongside him (along with their fingernail and hair trimmings, which had been scrupulously preserved while they were alive). The sense of a living dynastic succession must have been overwhelming.

At the time of the Conquest there were twelve such *panacas* in existence. Each mummy would have its own litter, bearers and attendants from that *panaca*, and a pavilion would be erected for them on the main square where the coronation took place. In a ceremony that extended the traditional consumption of vast quantities of alcohol by the Inca's new subjects, the incoming Emperor, the 'Sapa Inca', would also exchange toasts with each of his dead ancestors, with the mummy's attendants drinking on behalf of the corpse.

It's clear that the 'mummy lobby' had grown very powerful towards the end of the Inca Empire and precipitated a divide in Cuzco as bitter as any caused by the bishop's later decree. Huascar Inca, who had a reforming agenda during his brief tenure as Emperor, tried to limit what he saw as the abuses that had grown up. The problem was that the mummies' attendants had free licence to 'interpret' what the needs of the mummy might be: if he was said to need more provisions, *chicha* and concubines to keep him happy, then these had to be provided.

According to Father Bernabé Cobo, 'So many nobles were involved in serving these dead bodies, and their lives were so licentious, that one day Huascar Inca became angry with them and he said that there should be an order to have all the dead bodies buried and to take all their riches away from them. He went on to say that the dead should not be a part of his court, only the living, because the dead had taken over the best of everything in his kingdom.' It must have been particularly galling for each new Emperor that the mummy of his predecessor got to keep all his land, wealth and particularly palaces, so that the incoming Inca would have to build a new one. The main square of Cuzco when the conquistadors arrived was witness to this: each side was lined with the palaces of past Incas, still inhabited by their mummies. Indeed, there had been no space left for Huascar on the square itself and he had been forced, to his fury, to build a new palace on the hill above (he caused outrage at one point by threatening to confiscate one of the palaces of his dead forebears instead).

Huascar, like the Monsignor, met a bad end – quietly killed in the mountains on his way to meet the Spanish, when supposedly being protected by an escort provided by his treacherous half-brother Atahualpa. The story has a further twist: Huascar himself belonged to the *panaca* of the dead Emperor Topa Inca, and so to further attack him, Atahualpa arranged for Topa Inca's mummy to be burnt – an act which must have seemed deeply sacrilegious to the Inca population and evidence of how savage the civil war between the brothers had become.

Neither Huascar's attempts at reform nor Atahualpa's actions quenched the power of mummy worship, which was flourishing again by the time of Manco's coronation. Manco used the emotive power of the mummies during his exile, carrying the surviving bodies of previous Inca Emperors with him into the Vilcabamba. Even though the mummies were captured by the Spanish and brought back to Cuzco, they passed back into native hands and continued to be used by the underground resistance movement for the next twenty years.

Only in 1560 did the Spanish finally manage to get hold of the most important surviving ones (of Pachacuti and Huayna Capac), and they quickly removed them from Cuzco to Lima. By then, they had fully realised their importance as symbols both of resistance and of what they saw as native idolatry, and the mummies were destroyed – Bernabé Cobo speaking for many when he talked of 'the beastly act of venerating the bodies of the dead'.

Bernabé Cobo was a priest sympathetic in many ways to Inca traditions, and it is interesting that his principal problem with the tradition of the mummies was not just the worship of the dead itself, but the fact that the Incas could worship mummies yet at the same time not believe in an afterlife. He saw this as being incompatible and complained that 'It is impossible to go into this matter among them without giving offence. It is not even possible to pressure them into making an analysis of the rationale upon which this practice is based.' Cobo, who had seen one of these royal mummies in the flesh (noting that the placing of a calabash skin under that flesh had given it 'a nice gloss' over the years), also commented on the practice of giving mummies artificial eyes – the detail that had so struck me about El Niño Mario.

None of the mummies of the Inca Emperors have survived – unlike those of the Egyptian pharaohs, which are some 3000 years more ancient – and so we are completely dependent on eyewitness accounts such as Cobo's.

After Manco's own death at the hands of the Spanish, his own mummy served to give inspiration during the reigns of the three sons who followed him as Inca: it was not captured until the very final fall of Vilcabamba. For twenty-five years the mummified body would have been carried through the wild landscape of that mountain redoubt, as resistance to Spanish rule was perpetuated – a symbol of defiance and of the man who had ridden successfully into battle on horseback against the Spanish themselves.

*

The taxi driver swore profusely. Compared to, say, Mexicans, Peruvians swear very little, so it came as a shock. He had been forced to pull in to allow a pick-up truck to pass and the humiliation had left him gasping. 'These fucking Indians. It's because there were four of them in the truck. If you get one on his own they go all timid and *manso* [he made a begging mouse gesture], but get four of them together and, *carrajo*, they think, "There's a white face, let's have a go."'

We were crossing over the high country between Ollantaytambo and Cuzco, a beautiful stretch of the high *altiplano* with Mt Verónica behind us and the great plain of Anta ahead. It was from these heights that curious Indians could have seen the Spanish split into two rival factions during one of the civil wars that erupted so often after the Conquest. The cavalries wheeled around in great circles to attack one another across the plain, a spectacle that Cervantes would have savoured both for its absurdity and final futility. The leaders of the losing side would usually have been executed – it was how Diego de Almagro, Francisco Pizarro's original partner who rebelled against him, and then later his own brother, Gonzalo Pizarro, both met their ends.

Peru had always been a place of instability and it was tempting to see its rape at the time of the Conquest as setting up waves of violence which the country was still paying for. There were more stigmata of conquest here than in Mexico, where I had also travelled, perhaps because the second generation of conquistadors who landed in Peru were an altogether more brutalised bunch. Cortés in Mexico, with his complexity and ambitions, was a tragic, Napoleonic figure: Pizarro and his brothers were nothing but thugs, if occasionally brave ones.

Yet it was perhaps unfair only to blame the conquistadors. As I had discovered during my journey, Peru had been equally violent during the time of the Incas and their predecessors. The country was a victim of its own impossible geography: the coast would always have a different agenda to the mountains and communication between the two would always be partial, let alone with the jungle areas of *adentro*. Conflict was always likely, if not inevitable.

The taxi-driver was wearing a baseball cap and had already played me his entire collection of Vangelis and Eric Clapton tapes on the long drive. He returned to his mutterings about Indian drivers. 'You see, there's a lot of racism in Peru,' he said, blithely unconscious of his own contribution. 'These Indians have been so downtrodden, so repressed for so long.' He said it as if it had largely been their own fault. 'So now they have all this *antagonismo*. I tell you, this country is like a champagne bottle – do you know what champagne is? – all corked up and waiting to explode.' He made a masturbatory gesture with his hand.

I looked out of the window to try to shut him up. The light shone over the plain with hallucinatory clarity. The mountains I'd spent so many months in were all uncovered, one of the first times I'd ever seen the range without cloud. It seemed still and calm and inviolable. I flew out that day.

*

It was to be almost twenty years before I was able to return. The growing police presence in the Vilcabamba, which we had laughingly evaded on our way to the White Rock, was in hindsight a first sign of the vicious decade that was about to begin.

In 1984, just two years after I had left, noted hard man John Ridgway travelled through the area. Ridgway had rowed across the Atlantic single-handedly and led a legendarily tough outward-bound school in Scotland, where participants were allegedly tossed out of boats into the North Sea if they were not up to scratch. He and his party came across multiple examples of the increased activity of the Sendero Luminoso, particularly along the Apurímac, and were forced to alter their planned route. His closest Peruvian friend, Elvin Berg, was killed by them. As another South American explorer, Gary Ziegler, put it to me: 'There had always been terrorists around the Vilcabamba. But the difference was that the old guys in the sixties would only kill you if they felt they really had to, and then they'd do it politely and a bit apologetically. The Sendero Luminoso would make sure to torture you first, then kill you out of hand.'

The Sendero Luminoso were in some ways a historical curiosity. In the rest of the continent, the guerrilla movements inspired by Marxism had largely come and gone in the sixties and seventies: the upheavals in Argentina and Chile that had elicited such a savage over-reaction from the military dictatorships, the peasant war in which Che Guevara had died in Bolivia, the uprising in Nicaragua. Peru too had experienced unrest then, although nothing comparable. The Sendero Luminoso were perversely a direct result of Peru's relatively liberal policy towards land reform compared with its neighbours.

The changes I had seen at first hand in the mountains, with wealthy landowners being deprived of most of their holdings and land redistributed to the community (policies one might assume a Marxist movement would at least be sympathetic to) had actually been put in motion by an enlightened military government, who had despaired of such necessary social reforms ever being pushed through by the corrupt democratic parties. They had taken power in a 1968 *coup*, led by General Velasco, and had set about the changes with great vigour. By the time I had arrived in Peru in 1982, almost three-quarters of the land was under community management, a staggering achievement after so many centuries of the cruel *hacienda* system, although community farming brought its own problems.

However, the very success of the land reforms had created a dispossessed middle class, who no longer had their land to fall back on, and it was from the children of these dispossessed, particularly the university graduates, that the Sendero Luminoso had drawn some of its strength: Abimael Guzmán, the Sendero leader, drew many of his cadres from students he had taught when he had been a teacher at the University in Ayacucho, and gave them a Maoist zeal for total solutions that led to the brutal slaughter of all who disagreed with them. This provoked an equally brutal military response from the Government, which was by now (such being the looking-glass world of Peruvian politics) a democratically elected one.

Ayacucho became the centre of guerrilla operations that over a few years extended right across the highlands and down to Lima itself. It was ironic that Sendero should have grown out of Ayacucho – a town founded by Francisco Pizarro (and originally called Huamanga) specifically to stop Manco and his guerrillas harassing the Spanish on the main road to Lima.

The Sendero Luminoso presence, and even more the perceived threat of them, made travelling in the deep Vilcabamba increasingly difficult during the eighties. I had managed to get into the area only just before it was cut off, although there were a few intrepid archaeologists who were still able to get permission to go there.

Other areas of life had also finally imposed themselves on me. I could not travel the Andes indefinitely and needed to get a job. Back in England

I began the long haul up the film-making ladder, with an apprenticeship first as a cameraman and then as a director. No one would ever let me make a film in Peru, so to sublimate my obsession with mountains and with Latin America, I led filming expeditions to the Himalayas and across the badlands of Mexico, following the route of Cortés' invasion there.

Meanwhile I obsessively read every bit of source material about the Incas I could lay my hands on. In Los Angeles (ostensibly to interview rock and roll stars) I was able to see the opening of the stunning Sipán exhibition at the Fowler Museum, which first revealed the extent of the buried Moche treasure that the archaeologist Walter Alva had uncovered in northern Peru.

These were good years for Inca scholarship, as more and more of the original chronicles became available in translation and a new, younger generation of scholars questioned some of the received wisdoms. The growth of the Internet also finally allowed explorers to share information after decades of working in self-publishing isolation.

Finally, by the end of the 1990s, the situation in Peru stabilised again: the Sendero were effectively squashed with the startling arrest of their leader Guzmán in a Lima suburb, who was seized together with detailed accounts of the group's safe houses. The rump revolutionary movement that followed, Tupac Amaru, took its emotive name both from the last Inca, beheaded in Cuzco by the Spanish, and a subsequent revolutionary movement in 1780 that had been equally viciously suppressed.

In 1996, the Tupac Amaru group seized the Japanese Embassy in the middle of a diplomatic cocktail party and held the 490 international guests hostage. President Fujimori, a Peruvian strongman, sent in the paratroopers in a style that had Margaret Thatcher cooing in admiration (they tunnelled under the building). All the Tupac Amaru members inside were killed. Whatever Fujimori's detractors might say (and his autocratic style attracted many, with justification), by 1999 he had rid Peru of terrorism and managed to achieve some industrial growth. And I had read intriguing reports over the Internet and from friends in the field that new discoveries were being made in the Vilcabamba. It was time to go back.

PART 2

RETURN TO CUZCO

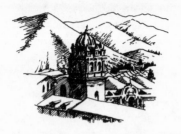

LANDING AGAIN AT CUZCO in 1999 was a shock. The population of the city had tripled since 1982. The old airport had been in an isolated field: the new improved one was already surrounded by fast growing suburbs.

My young taxi-driver Carlos was intrigued that I'd been away for so long (he couldn't have been born long much before I left). 'The city used to be *chiquíssima*,' he said, using the affectionate diminutive, 'now it's *grandota*.' But the heart of the city, the area around the Plaza de Armas, was much the same as ever, a mixture of stately colonial architecture and tourist opportunism. It was with some embarrassment that Carlos gave me his card, emblazoned with the slogan 'Magical Mystery Tours'. 'It's just the name of the travel agency I work for,' he explained, 'nothing to do with the Beatles.'

The hotels had changed out of all recognition, as had my need to stay in the cheapest. I checked out a few. The El Dorado looked like something out of Las Vegas: in the entrance hall, the lift-shaft was completely free-standing and had been plastered to look like a tree rising up into a cavernous space – the corridors ran like branches off the 'tree' to bedrooms that were lit with startling neon pinks and reds. Soft new-age muzak was piped into every room. '*Algo un poco diferente?* A little different, isn't it?' murmured the porter who showed me around.

In The Royal Inka, a colonial building on Recogijo Square, there was an enormous mural stretching the length of the dining room which showed a sort of Body Shop fantasy of pre-Columbian life: dusky, bare-breasted maidens were bathing in an idyllic Amazonian paradise, probably using jojoba soap and surrounded by luxuriant greenery and compliant jungle animals; the only thing most were wearing was a pendant of vaguely Incaic design. The artist, for reasons of his own, had chosen to make them all extremely nubile young women and the effect, in an otherwise conventional dining room, was startling.

This was the way Cuzco now liked to sell itself, as an ecological gateway to the jungle resorts of Manu and the Madre de Dios, with a little bit of Inca Golden Age mythologising thrown in: a prelapsarian alternative to the evils of the fallen West. The small ads in the press offered tourists the services of 'local shamen' who could guide you to 'places of fulfilment, on journeys of the spirit'.

Cuzco (or Qosqo, as the hippies liked to spell it) was traditionally thought to mean 'navel of the world' for the Incas, and 'Qosqo: Navel of the World!' was emblazoned on many a T-shirt for travellers to buy. Unfortunately this attractive idea had been undermined by an American anthropologist, Denise Arnold, who had shown after extensive research that Cuzco really meant 'placenta of the world', a slogan which had yet to make its way onto the T-shirts.

I had arrived in the middle of a four-day music festival, sponsored by Cuzqueña beer. All weekend the sound of amplified *techno-cumbia* echoed over the city. The purist European travellers in the Plaza de Armas, huddled over their pisco sours and listening to piped flute music, complained that it was a sign of things changing for the worse. But I enjoyed it and went back for two nights of the festival, which was playing to an audience of 20,000 or more in downtown Cuzco, way off the tourist loop.

There was a palpable feel-good quality to the crowd, which was new. Teenagers were wearing American clothes, with hip-hop style razored haircuts. The girls were showing a lot more leg. Hardly anyone was wearing the baggy alpaca sweaters which had been the unprepossessing youth uniform of the early eighties, despite the fact that it was the middle of winter and a cold night. The crowd were downing plastic mugs of Cristal by the gallon (drinking habits at least hadn't changed) and girls were swaying on their boyfriends' shoulders, copying what they felt was right from the self-perpetuating American concert films which MTV had brought to Peru. Scarves were being waved in time to the poppy stadium-rock music of one Pedro Suarez, a smooth-voiced lead singer with tight leather trousers and dark good looks – his guitarist henchman was even wearing a full-length glitter trench-coat, something I hadn't seen since the heyday of Slade or The Sweet.

But Pedro was only the warm-up. The crowd had really come for La India, one of the most popular South American singers and an inheritor of Celia Cruz's mantle as the Queen of Salsa. Like most *salseras*, she was a creature of the coast and no sooner had she launched into her first rumbustious vocal assault than the mountain altitude got too much for her.

After a discreet word with backstage support, an oxygen bottle was rushed onstage and the show could go on, with La India taking big hits of gas between each song.

A Limeña woman I'd met had told me that this was becoming a common fashion accessory: now that Cuzco was a hip destination, city folk from Lima would fly up for the weekend and carry a little oxygen bottle with them to puff on when their unaccustomed lungs couldn't take the altitude. Fortified by the oxygen and the roars of the crowd, La India belted out her next song about what she would do to 'the other woman'.

I crossed town to the offices of COPESCO, the Peruvian state archaeological department, for an appointment with a man I was anxious to meet: Perci Paz, the archaeologist who had been working at Choquequirao in the years since I had first visited it.

At that time Choquequirao had been unexcavated and I could remember how intrigued I had been by the many unanswered questions it posed. There were some obvious similarities to Machu Picchu (the extraordinary position, the altitude) and also some less obvious ones, like its lack of extensive agricultural terracing or easy water supply. And again like Machu Picchu, there was no mention of it in any Spanish accounts of the Conquest, or in Inca chronicles such as Titu Cusi's. Who had built it and was it still in occupation when the Spanish invaded, a hide-out for Manco Inca and his men?

It was dark by the time I arrived and Perci was waiting for me at the COPESCO reception. He was an enthusiastic, squarely built man in his late forties, wearing a brown donkey jacket and with black Brezhnevian eyebrows and hair swept back. He could hardly contain himself with excitement about Choquequirao, as he led me to his office. None of his findings had yet been published and, given the scale of his responsibilities at COPESCO, he was not sure when they would be.

Perci was an archaeologist who seemed genuinely to enjoy field-work (and surprisingly few senior archaeologists do). Between 1992 and 1996, as the Sendero problem died down, he had dug at Choquequirao every season. Now he was tied to a desk job in Cuzco and was envious of my planned journey down to Espíritu Pampa and the old city of Vilcabamba, the one site I had not reached and which he likewise had never been able to get to.

He was also fascinated by our pioneering early route to Choquequirao, and I described in detail to him the state of the roads (more used then than now, as the old Vittoria mine had still been active – it had been abandoned soon afterwards as the grip of the Senderos on the region increased). He was particularly interested in the little site we had discovered and measured on the last day before reaching Choquequirao, the site we had named Espa Unuyoc and which Perci had renamed Pinchiyoq Unu. I asked him about the unusual architectural details we'd noticed at the time.

'Yes, it has some architectural aspects that are clearly not Inca but Chachapoyan. Rather than being upright, the stones are laid at geometric angles to one another,' and he did a quick drawing of a herring-bone pattern, 'what we call *tejando con piedra*, weaving with a stone – very clearly Chachapoyan, not Inca. And this would make sense, because I'm sure that the function of this site was to serve Choquequirao with satellite housing for workers, much as Machu Picchu had its satellite towns. So the Chachapoyans would have been imported as *mitimaes* labour to service the Inca nobility and priesthood who must have lived at Choquequirao.'

It was an exciting idea and I could immediately see the implications: 'So whoever built Choquequirao presumably did so only after the Inca conquest of Chachapoyas – which was by Pachacuti's son, Topa Inca?'

'Exactly.'

If, as seems likely, Pachacuti built Machu Picchu, then his son Topa Inca might well have built Choquequirao as his own rival winter palace – one reason why Machu Picchu could have fallen into disuse. Choquequirao was very similar to Machu Picchu in so many ways – the staggering view, the elaborate and playful water-channelling, the ostentatiously impossible position – but a few architectural details, such as the profusion of double-recessed doorways, argued for a later construction.

The need for Topa Inca to duplicate his father's building was simple. The Incas had an unusual habit of inheritance which largely accounted for the aggressive territorial expansion of each new Emperor. On the death of a Sapa Inca (an Emperor), his land and buildings would be kept intact and entailed to a group of relatives and retainers to look after in perpetuity – his *panaca*, or estate, where his mummified body could reside. Meanwhile the incoming Emperor had to start from scratch and acquire his own lands – a powerful motive to wage war. As Huascar so volubly complained, each new Emperor even had to build a new palace in Cuzco.

So on Pachacuti's death, Machu Picchu would not necessarily have been Topa Inca's to use anyway, particularly if its function was more as a private residence than a state or religious one – it would have become part of the 'Pachacuti estate' and would have faded away as his *panaca* found it more and more difficult to maintain such an ostentatious place without the revenues of power. This could also explain why Machu Picchu was abandoned before the Spanish arrived, a fate which would surely never have befallen it if the site had had the religious significance that it is sometimes given.

To build Choquequirao as a replacement, Topa Inca might well have imported labourers from Chachapoyas to help him (just as Pachacuti had forcibly imported the Colla from Lake Titicaca to build Ollantaytambo): having conquered their province with some difficulty, Topa would have been only too aware of the Chachapoyans' astounding ability to construct sites in the remote mountains.

'What did you find at Choquequirao itself?' I asked Perci.

'Look, there are three things we discovered about Choquequirao,' he said, speaking in Spanish rapidly and lowly, almost as if we would be overheard by his colleagues at the other desks in the room, and leaning forward with great intensity. 'The first is that the site was burnt and seems to have been abandoned after a battle. The lower walls are discoloured by burning and there are carbon deposits at ground level. We found several unburied skeletons with axes in their skulls and many more bodies that were left unburied. This is so unusual that we must assume that the site was completely abandoned and burnt after being taken in an attack.'

Before I had time to digest this astonishing information, Perci rolled on.

'The second thing is that it was under construction at the time when it was abandoned, or at least they were expanding the *andenes*, the terraces. Because some terraces are half-built we can see how they made them – not least that they usually started with the bottom terrace and then built upwards. But there's a curious discrepancy. Not only was it still being built at the time that it was abandoned, but they were making some very odd alterations to the original structure.'

He showed me a photo. A doorway constructed in conventional classic Inca style had been filled in with the quicker rough *pirca* stonework usually associated with lower-grade buildings, to turn the ground above into a terrace as well. It was as if a desperate attempt was being made to turn every available inch of land into an agriculturally useful resource – even what had been a residence. In architectural terms it was quite clearly a bodged job, and I recalled being surprised by the blocked doorways seventeen years before.

Perci paused. By now it was getting late and most of his colleagues had left. From his high office window we could see the sodium lights of Cuzco flickering below.

'The third point is the pottery.' Perci was presenting his evidence in a very deliberate way and I could sense that we were close to a summing-up. I remembered the shards of ceramics Roddy and I had seen lying everywhere on the surface of the uncleared ruins. 'The design of the pottery is in the high aristocratic style of the Inca court at Cuzco, but manufactured using much coarser material – the clay which is only available locally in the Vilcabamba, with its *grano grueso*, coarse grain.'

Perci sat back and gave sentence. 'So what we have, as a proposal, is that this, just like Machu Picchu, was originally a classic Inca site, built perhaps by Topa Inca, designed for the pleasure of the nobility with only a few terraces for select cultivation of crops – possibly coca, as the terraces are so narrow – and with quick access to lower heights to provide the Inca and his court with more jungle produce. It had its own town of servants at a discreet distance.'

'But it does also look from our investigations as if the site was still being occupied in the last days of the rump Inca Empire as well, when they were on the run from the Spanish. This would explain why they were trying so hard to extend the terraces. What had once been luxury gardens for a court on holiday, used perhaps for a few months each year, had now to become subsistence terraces for a court permanently in exile – particularly a priesthood in exile, as my feeling is that this was used in the later stages as a religious centre.'

'The pottery suggests that the later Incas, while wanting to use the same designs they were accustomed to, were now forced to make them with the local coarser clay that was all that was now available, rather than the finer material from back in Cuzco.'

I thought about this. Choquequirao makes up a rough triangle with Cuzco and Vitcos, and it is equally difficult to get to from both. It was perfectly conceivable that Manco and his successors, while nervous about using Machu Picchu, as it was too close to the Spanish at Cuzco, could still have used this other remote site above the Apurímac during the years of retreat. It might well have been a central focus for the revival of Incaic religious customs that seems to have occurred in the reign of Titu Cusi between 1560 and 1570, when the Vilcabamba became an isolationist state. There was a theory that the young Tupac Amaru, the last Emperor of all, might even have been brought up there: we know that he was made a priest in his early years and Choquequirao would have been a more suitable place to raise a future Inca than the jungle city of Old Vilcabamba.

'What about the burning?' I asked.

Perci gave the Gallic shrug common to all honest archaeologists. There was no written evidence of such an event ever having taken place (indeed, there was no contemporary written evidence relating to Choquequirao at all). The burning might have happened in the chaotic dissolution of the Empire. Who knew?

I had my instinctive supposition for this: towards the end of the Vilcabamba rump state, as the Spanish closed in on Tupac's forces further north, the priests at Choquequirao must have become more and more isolated. The Chachapoyans in their service town of Pinchiyoq Unu could quite easily have revolted at having to service the Incas' ritual centre, just as we knew that their fellow displaced countrymen had tried to attack Manco on his retreat from Ollantaytambo. In the rioting that followed, the priests would have been killed, left unburied (a final desecration), and the site torched before the Chachapoyans presumably returned to their native homelands. It would have been a final reprisal for the enforced slave labour they had endured for generations. The Spanish would have known nothing about the whole affair, and indeed would have had no reason to go near Choquequirao, as their military campaign took them much further north, into the forests of the deep Vilcabamba where they pursued Tupac Amaru.

After many years of puzzling over the mystery of Choquequirao, I felt that at last I had, if not an answer, at least a working hypothesis.

*

The Cross Keys was a peculiar location, not only because it was an English pub in the middle of Cuzco (its upper rooms looking out directly over the square) but because, as the owner Barry Walker said, it seemed to be a meeting-place for just about everyone on the planet. It felt a bit like the bar in *Star Wars* where intergalactic species cohabit the same space without actually talking to each other. Greek tour parties collided with American slackers, hip Limeños and study groups led by earnest European academics, mashed together by the noise from a huge television above the bar, copious drinks and the noise floating up from the Plaza de Armas below.

Barry had many of the traditional qualities of a British publican (thickset, bluff manner, 'have another drink'), and many that weren't, not least a passion for tropical birds that had made him one of the foremost experts on the Manu wildlife parks, where he led study groups. He was also a passionate Manchester United supporter in a country where this aroused less antipathy than at home – indeed, I had already been asked to give detailed descriptions of the winning of the Triple Crown to several interested Peruvians. Now I had to repeat it all for Barry.

Barry had heard of my earlier trips and we talked a little of them; he wanted me to meet a legendary traveller who was in the bar that night, the writer Tobias Schneebaum, with whom he had been making a film in the jungle.

I knew Schneebaum's story, which was, to say the least, unusual. Tobias had travelled into the jungle in 1955. His experiences had been traumatic and it had taken him years to assimilate them, as so often with South

American travellers. Only in 1969 did he finally publish what became a classic of jungle literature, *Keep the River on your Right*. In it he described how he had lived with a Peruvian jungle tribe called the Akarama for eight years, participating in homosexual and cannibalistic rites.

The book caused a sensation. It blew away any last vestige of romantic mysticism about the life-style of such Amazonian tribes, and Tobias' delay in writing the book meant that he hit the 1969 *zeitgeist* spot on. A generation reared on the ethos of the sixties could immediately see both the appeal and the challenge: it was one thing to survive the tribal excesses of Woodstock or Monterey, but in the jungle the drugs were tougher, the nakedness perpetual and you could no longer spend weekends back with your parents to rest up. This was the logical extension of the hippy lifestyle and disillusioned travellers headed for the Amazon with Schneebaum's book in their pocket, along with Castaneda's books on Don Juan and plenty of Rizlas.

But Tobias himself had never returned to the Amazon – until now. Two enterprising New York film-makers, Laurie and David Shapiro, had persuaded him to go back, forty-five years after leaving. Barry had been their local guide (and enthusiastic fan – for Barry, as for so many, it had been Tobias' book that lured him to the Amazon in the first place) and they had all just returned to Cuzco together. Barry pointed Tobias out to me, a small shrunken figure sitting hunched up like a toad on one of the benches, almost lost in the crowd of travellers in their loud fleeces.

We went over to join him. It was disconcerting to hear him speak. Tobias had lived in New York most of his life and had the manners and accent of an old Manhattan homosexual who had never left the Upper West Side. Just as Warhol used to do in old documentaries (and although I didn't ask him if they had been friends, Tobias seemed to share much of the Warholian world-view and attitude), he would pronounce on things very slowly and without looking anyone in the eye. 'William Burroughs came to see me once. [Long pause.] He said my book was the only book by another writer he had wished he had written himself. [Long pause.] But he was so boring ... all he wanted to do was to talk about drugs.' Tobias pronounced 'drugs' as 'drergs' with a long, contemptuous exhalation. Barry brought him another drink. 'Lévi-Strauss's *Tristes Tropiques*? Of course it's a great book. But Lévi-Strauss was never honest about his homosexuality. I was always honest about the boys I slept with in the jungle.'

Tobias had found the experience of going back to the village in the Peruvian Amazon unnerving. He had expected (indeed hoped) that no one would recognise him. But some of the people who had known him as a young man did indeed remember him when they came face to face and –

the most mortifying detail of all for Tobias – told him that he had been a terrible hunter.

We talked of the Vilcabamba and of the Incas' last refuge there. A girl who'd joined our group knew nothing of this final drawn-out penumbral stage in Inca history, with a court in exile in the mountains. 'How sad,' she said. Tobias sniffed loudly to get attention, then paused to give judgement. 'Sad? Is it sad really? I don't think it's very sad.' He lapsed into silence and seemed to sink back into himself, his neck almost visibly withdrawing. Not long after, saying that he was still shaky after his visit to the jungle, he went to bed.

Two memorable conversations in one evening, and a prodigious amount of pisco sours on the house had fired me up. I stayed up late into the night talking with Barry. He had first arrived in Peru around the same time as me, in 1984, and had stayed in Cuzco all through the lean terrorist years when hardly anyone wanted to come. But now business was booming. The tourists would swing in, take the train to Machu Picchu and then quickly head on out for the next stage of their South American whistle-stop experience. There was talk of building a cable-car up to Machu Picchu from the railway station to make the process even faster. A helicopter service was already in place, so it was technically possible to fly to Cuzco in the morning, see the ruins and leave within twenty-four hours. And with the new landscape-format cameras, the tourists could take the same identical shots that much faster. Martín Chambi would have turned in his grave.

But the sheer accessibility of Machu Picchu meant that virtually no one went any deeper into the Inca heartland. The whole area further downriver – the Santa Teresa valley, the Vilcabamba region – that I had explored before was still associated with terrorism and (just as much a deterrent) required quite a bit of work to get to. The excellent local guide-book, *Exploring Cusco* by Peter Frost, said of the route from Yanama to Choquequirao which we had taken years before that 'The terrain is so rugged and the canyons are so infested with a vicious biting insect called *pumahuacachi* ('makes the puma cry') that it is not advisable to try.' This reluctance to penetrate beyond Machu Picchu had been exacerbated by a terrible landslide the previous year, which had been far more devastating for the area than all the attentions of the Sendero Luminoso.

The landslide had happened in a tributary valley of the Urubamba, the Aobamba, the very same valley we had descended on that hallucinatory day when we had discovered Llactapata. I had always been struck by its beauty. But the valley-floor had not only been swept away – it had deposited itself in the body of the main Urubamba valley below to disastrous effect, causing an unwanted dam and a resulting flood, obliterating the hydro-electric station, where we ourselves had once been suspected of being terrorists, and destroying the town of Santa Teresa, where we had begun so many journeys.

It had also swept away the railway below Machu Picchu, cutting the lifeline of the peoples of the lowland who could no longer travel up and down from the jungle with their produce. Ironically, the landslide had neatly managed to avoid the profitable tourist section of railway between Cuzco and Machu Picchu, and cynics maintained that this was why the lower section would never now be rebuilt.

I later heard a graphic account from a schoolteacher of what had happened to the very last train to be travelling up from Quillabamba before the landslide struck. Apparently the driver saw that the river was drying out as the train ascended. Realising with great prescience what must have happened to cause the sudden drought, he stopped the train and got the passengers to climb as high as they could above the bank of the river, some passengers apparently complaining vociferously about the inconvenience. They were just in time to hear the Urubamba surmount the dam caused by the landslide higher up the valley, and with a roar, it sent a solid sheet of water crashing down below. The little red-and-orange train which I had travelled on so regularly up and down the line was swept away. The railway track was left twisted like a hosepipe. Not a single passenger died. I only hoped they'd given the driver a medal.

Luckily the same instincts (an ancient Andean reading of the signs of a landslide) had saved the people of Santa Teresa, who had also fled their homes for higher ground and survived the flood. Their houses had been destroyed. The government had initially promised them a rebuilding programme for their village and the return of the railway. President Fujimori had personally promised that 'Peru would not be defeated by El Niño' (for it was assumed, like many disasters that year, that the changing climatic conditions in the South Pacific were at fault).

However, all these good intentions had quickly evaporated. As I drew into Ollantaytambo on the train the next day, I saw the evacuated Santa Teresa villagers living in tents by the side of the track. It looked as if their exile was becoming a permanent one. They were completely lost in the higher climate of the Ollantaytambo valley, where they could no longer grow the crops they were accustomed to. It would never have happened under the Incas, for their system of *mitamayo*, of transporting peoples to different parts of the Empire, however brutal it might be, was at least always careful to put the *mitimaes* into a similar climate and altitude – a fact which had deeply impressed the Spanish chronicler Cieza de León.

At Ollantaytambo I had a strange encounter on the station platform. I'd got in early that morning on the dawn train and was catching up with a late breakfast of *tamales*, boiled corn dumplings wrapped in leaves which came either *dulce* or *salado*, sour or sweet, in a way that was impossible to tell until you bit into them, like *dim sum*. With some coffee from a thermos, they made a great breakfast and the morning sun was warming me up after a frosty start from Cuzco.

A man loomed up over me as I squatted on the platform. He had heard from a friend that I was coming and wanted to talk to me. In an American accent, he introduced himself as Paolo Greer and handed me his card, which said 'Research and Exploration, Carabaya and Sandia provinces' and gave both a Peruvian address and one in Alaska.

Paolo had spent years of his life chasing after possible old mine-workings in Peru, endlessly criss-crossing the land and applying the same prospecting techniques to look for old maps in libraries. He was a tall man in a baseball cap, with a disconcertingly firm gaze. He looked about the same age as Harry Dean Stanton in *Paris, Texas* and reminded me a little of him, particularly the intense, very focused eyes and slightly wild presence.

Later he sent me an e-mail describing his wanderings: 'It is as if I have been a year or two away from Lima, and perhaps a decade south of Alaska. My wanderings sometimes make me feel that I have lived some lives already, in this same ragged body.'

He had to take the train downriver later that same morning on some urgent prospecting business and so we only had a short while to talk. Paolo spoke in a compressed, elated way, pouring out information in such a condensed rush that I sometimes needed to go back through it all with him, which added to the urgency of his tone as he told me what he knew. It was clear that he badly wanted to tell someone who would listen and appreciate what he had found.

Paolo had searched through countless Peruvian and American libraries looking for the maps that old prospectors and mining companies might have left behind. He did this on a commercial basis to see if modern mining techniques might re-open deposits. One of these searches had led by chance to a radical new discovery concerning Machu Picchu.

Current orthodoxy held that the first mention of the names Machu Picchu and Huayna Picchu had been by the Frenchman Charles Wiener in 1875, who put their names on the map without visiting them. Tantalisingly he wrote, 'They [the local Peruvians] also spoke to me of other towns, of Huaina Picchu and of Matcho Picchu [sic], and I resolved to make a final expedition towards the East,' but he never did and so has remained just a footnote in the history of exploration. Wiener's report had helped Hiram

Bingham make his 'scientific discovery' of the ruins of 1911. However, Paolo had come across evidence that the sites may have been known about earlier and that there had been considerable mining activity near them.

In 1872 an enterprising Cuzqueño from a good family, Baltasar de la Torre, had led an expedition through Paucartambo to try to find an easier passage from Cuzco to the Madre de Dios jungle. He died in the attempt, killed by thirty-five arrows in his body when he met with resistance from the local tribes. With him was a German engineer, Herman Göhring, who survived the expedition and published a book in 1874, *Informe Supremo de Paucartambo*, a book now so rare that even the descendants of the La Torre family had no copy.

Paolo had heard about the book from that same La Torre family, who still lived in Cuzco, and had immediately realised that it could contain interesting information about old mines. For many years he was unable to find it. Then one source led him to believe that the Biblioteca Nacional in Lima might have a copy. He went there: nothing was listed in the index. With typical persistence, he insisted on seeing the Director of the Library who, after lengthy consultation with his staff, denied that they had the book. Paolo went back to his original source, a bibliophile's reference guide published by G. K. Hall, a set of xeroxed library cards which he had painstakingly combed for a reference.

This stated that the Library had both the *Informe Supremo de Paucartambo* and a set of manuscript letters from Göhring about his work. After days of searching, the Library finally found both. With staff assistants to either side of him, and wearing plastic gloves, Paolo was allowed to go through letters looking for references to mines, Göhring's area of speciality. When he came to the book itself, he made an astonishing discovery.

At this point in his telling of the story, Paolo was almost hopping with excitement and he pulled out of a bag some copies of the maps in Göhring's book which he always carried around with him. I could see at once that the map covered not only the area around Paucartambo but also the Urubamba valley and there, clearly marked above the river, were both Machu Picchu and Huayna Picchu, the first known mapped reference to either.

In a further bibliographical twist that Borges would have enjoyed (it was remarkably like an episode in his classic story 'Tlön, Uqbar, Orbis Tertius' about an imaginary country which only appears in a single 1902 edition of the *Encyclopaedia Britannica*), Paolo later discovered that while a few other copies of the book were in existence, and while there had only been one edition, only a few copies actually contained the map.

It was no accident that Göhring had included the Urubamba area in his survey. For Paolo, fired up by this initial find, soon realised that the whole area around Machu Picchu had been much more heavily mined than had ever been imagined, and this was why it had attracted the interest of the German engineer.

Paolo discovered that the Torontoy hacienda estate which stretched almost from Ollantaytambo down to Machu Picchu had been owned for many years in the nineteenth century by one Augusto Berns. Berns had been convinced that there were possible mine-workings on his estate and in 1887 had formed an American company to try to exploit them, in the atmosphere favourable to foreign investment created after the War of the Pacific. Paolo had managed to track down the prospectus that Berns had issued to the company's shareholders, entitled *Prospecto de la Compañía Anónima Exploradora de las 'Huacas Del Inca' Limitada (Prospectus for the 'Inca Stone' Company Ltd)*. One of the stated aims of the company, in addition to exploiting old mine-workings, was to investigate old ruins as well (just as the Spanish after the Conquest had originally issued licences for the 'mining' of treasure from pre-Columbian sites).

On the map that Berns had issued to potential stockholders, a copy of which Paolo again showed me, the site of Machu Picchu was marked as 'Point *Huaca del Inca*', 'Point of the Inca Stone', possibly a reference to the stone now known as the Intihuatana at the centre of Machu Picchu site which is thought to have sacred significance: as such, long after the abandonment of the city itself, it could have continued to be a place of local veneration for the Indians of the valley, who rarely forgot a *huaca*. So important was it to Berns that he even named the company after it.

Even without the evidence of the map, it seems inconceivable that a local landowner, with the stated aim of excavating old ruins for treasure and who lived in the valley for many years, should not at some stage have been told about and found what it took Bingham a mere day to do – and while, for obvious reasons, Berns might not have wanted to publicise his exploitation of Machu Picchu to the Peruvian government (given that the melted-down proceeds were probably being exported back to the United States), he could easily have systematically stripped the ruins of their treasure.

This would certainly explain one striking fact noted by George Eaton in his description of the tombs he excavated in 1912 – that not a single object of gold or silver had been left, as might have been expected in a tomb, and that only objects which were of archaeological, not financial value were to be found – ceramics, plain *tupus* and of course the skeletons themselves, wrapped in cloth. It could also explain the occasional post-Columbian artefacts that were found in the caves – a fragment of bovine bone, a peach stone, a steel implement – which could have been left by Berns' organised teams of *huaqueros* as they worked through the caves. (Those same Western fragments have often since confused the issue of whether the Spanish did or did not know of Machu Picchu at the time of the Conquest – the persistent rumours of the ancient remains of a horse found at the site are another contributory, probably misleading, factor in this argument.)

Paolo and I had been talking so intensely that two trains had come and gone down the valley. Now the final and slowest train arrived, the *local*, which he had to take if he was to get downriver that day. He left me copies of his maps and a breakfast that had grown cold around me as I listened in fascination to his story – a story I later confirmed by going back to the original sources.

The idea that this section of the Urubamba was a heavily mined one well up to the end of the nineteenth century was quite at variance with the picture Bingham had always conjured up of a sleepy farming community of just a few homesteads, an area 'which the Spaniards never saw and which was inaccessible to explorers of the mid-nineteenth century'. When Bingham had arrived at the site that is now Aguas Calientes, directly below Machu Picchu, he noted the presence of some 'large iron wheels', which he presumed to be 'parts of a machine destined never to overcome the difficulties of being transported all the way to a sugar estate in the lower valley'. The machine had even given the site its local name – 'La Máquina'. However, judging from Berns' description, far from being for a distant sugar plantation, it was almost certainly part of the smelting equipment that Berns had installed for his mining works directly below Machu Picchu. It was only the recession at the very end of the nineteenth century that had caused such mining activities to fade away.

As so often in the story of the Vilcabamba, nothing was quite as it originally seemed.

*

Why is change so much more shocking for the traveller than for the inhabitant? Partly because for the inhabitant changes to a place can seem gradual and imperceptible, but also because the traveller is uniquely vulnerable to the foibles of his own memory. To see a place again after an interval of years is reassurance that part of your past survives. But having a fixed point of that memory whipped out from under you, like a rug, is for the same reason peculiarly disorientating. The experiences of that long-ago summer (I thought of it as summer although it was a Peruvian winter) became yet more dream-like now that so many familiar landmarks of the valley had been washed away by the flood.

Going into the Ollantaytambo hostel, the *albergue*, where I had once performed magicians' tricks, was equally disconcerting. Much had changed. Robert Randall had died in a terrible accident. He had been bitten by a neighbour's dog and contracted rabies, an endemic curse of the mountains. His widow Wendy had been forced by their landlords to move the hostel to different and smaller premises, almost on the station platform.

Adela, who had been a teenager then, was now married with kids. She instantly knew who I was when I jokingly checked in as 'El Mago'. Nathan, the five-year-old whose birthday-party it had been, and his younger brother Joaquin were now college students in the States, although as luck would have it, they had just come back to Cuzco for the vacation. They remembered the party well and brought out old photos to show me.

Indeed, the party had become something of a landmark for them all, perhaps because it harked back to a time when Randall was still alive. Wendy went through the photos with me: it was only seeing them that made me realise how much she herself had changed. Now she had short grey hair – in the photos she had black hair, worn loose and long in the style of the late seventies.

Nathan reminded me of some details about the party that, with a child's intense vision, he had remembered better than I had: I had taken sweets out of his ear; the dove that flew out of the bowler hat had been white with a black streak on its wing. Most of the photos were naturally of the kids, not of me, but my hands were extended into the frame, either extracting or delivering sweets. In the background was the clown, who Wendy told me had died of Aids. 'I've never known a community like the one we had around Ollantaytambo for so many deaths,' said Wendy sadly, 'or divorces and separations. Most of these couples are no longer together. But then I've never known such a community for births either.'

Ann Kendall had apparently also been in Ollantaytambo recently and her husband had also recently died. Over the years she had continued with the idea that had so impressed me at Cusichaca – the rebuilding of the Inca canal system. Now she had done the same in the hills above Ollantaytambo, but to a much more dramatic extent, re-irrigating some 160 hectares (around 400 acres) with restored pre-Columbian canals from the glacial melt-waters, and developing an extended scheme to help the local community – she had persuaded them, for instance, to use a simple form of plastic greenhouse, which at high altitudes could radically extend the growing season.

I learnt an astonishing statistic from this new project of hers: before the

Conquest, Ollantaytambo had cultivated 6000 hectares of land, enough to feed 106,000 people, far more than its actual population of 10,000. With the resultant surplus, Ollantaytambo was able to be a very successful exporter of its produce. Yet today, while the town still had about the same size of population, it struggled to grow enough even to feed itself.

In her writings, Ann lamented the way in which the Spanish had been so obsessed with mining and lucrative coca plantations down in the jungle that they had neglected the careful Inca infrastructure of repair and administration that had kept the canals and terraces of the High Andes maintained – a problem exacerbated when so many of the Quechua Indians had died in the epidemics of Western disease or in those self-same mines. Almost 500 years after the Conquest, communities were still struggling to restore productivity to anything near Inca levels.

While other explorers and archaeologists had been concerned with putting flags on maps, preferably with their own names flapping from them, Ann had quietly and patiently spent decades building up working relationships with small communities to help them. It was a genuinely heroic achievement.

*

They seemed like a perfectly normal tour group, a little older in profile maybe (but then Machu Picchu often tends to get older, wealthier tour groups), and an amiable enough bunch to share a dinner with that evening at the Ollantaytambo *albergue*. We were sitting around at the end of the meal and the older men started talking in a way it was clear they did each night, taking turns to describe the emotions they had experienced on that day of their journey – how they had felt as they went around Machu Picchu, how hard going up a bit of the trail was for them, what they thought they were gaining from the experience. So far, so reasonable.

Then it was the turn of the guy with the beard. 'I took an acid tab just as I went into the ruins,' he said, 'and immediately I realised that the entrance gate into the city is also a portal.' He paused to let this sink in. 'It's a portal to the crystal city which is *below* Machu Picchu.'

Everyone looked at him as if he was being completely serious.

The ascendancy of the New Age philosophies in the years since I had first been there has led to a huge growth in such thinking. This has been exacerbated, if unwittingly, by the notion of the Incas' own sense of 'sacred geography', on which much scholarly work had been done – particularly on the idea of the *ceques*, the imaginary lines that the Incas thought radiated out from Cuzco and which passed through a set of *huacas*, or shrines. Each *ceque* was the responsibility of one of the *panacas*, the royal lineages, who would maintain the *huacas* along its length.

However, this very specific idea has been wilfully distorted by some New Age advocates, who like to superimpose on the Incas a spirituality that they feel the modern world has lost. No one has yet taken ley-line directions from Glastonbury to Machu Picchu, but only because the string isn't long enough.

Machu Picchu is a deeply uplifting place and any personal spiritual fulfilment visitors find there is, of course, all to the good. The problem only arises when they assume that the Incas must have found Machu Picchu as purely spiritual a place as they do. It has become even more difficult to persuade such people that Machu Picchu was not principally a sacred place for the Incas, given that they have such a longing and hunger for it to be just that.

Yet in a conversation I had with Elva Torres Pino, an archaeologist who had been doing some limited excavations at Machu Picchu, she was at pains to describe the site both in terms of Pachacuti's estate (the 'winter quarters of the court') and as 'a political/administrative centre along a trade route down to the jungle'. She made no mention of religion.

Fernando de la Rosa and his wife Frances were also staying at the hostel. Fernando had helped mount one of the first exhibitions of Martín Chambi's photos, and was himself a distinguished photographer and novelist. We played the old Peruvian game of *sapo* in the hostel's back yard, where you try to throw coins from a decent distance into the mouth of a metal frog (the game was the subject of one of Chambi's best-loved photos). Like such equally nonsensical games as *pétanque* or shove-ha'penny, it was curiously addictive, particularly if one ever achieved the metallic slither of getting a coin down the frog's throat.

Fernando was a big, shaggy man, full of enthusiasm for everything, from where to find the most authentic sort of *aji*, Peruvian garlic sauce, to the more obscure works of Roland Barthes. I told him about the psychic voyagers and their crystal city underneath Machu Picchu, and he amused me at once by describing how he and Frances had also been to Machu Picchu that day and had heard some strange chanting and music coming from behind a rock. On closer examination, it had turned out to be a group from the States. Some were lying down on the Inca stones trying to hug them (with difficulty, as Inca stonework is angular and not designed to be hugged), while others circled around playing maracas. Fernando had dubbed them 'the Cult of the Maracas'.

Over trout from the local river that evening, he told another even better tale. It had begun when he was explaining a phenomenon I'd often wondered about in the High Andean villages – the preponderance of empty, abandoned houses. This was not due to depopulation. Rather it was because the Quechuans, on marriage, would always prefer to build a new house than occupy an old one, in the same way as the English dislike buying second-hand beds.

As a young man, Fernando had gone to live for three years in a remote village in the Valle Sagrado, not that far from where we were now. As an outsider, the same rules did not apply to him, and he was given his pick of the abandoned houses to live in.

One day, one of the village elders who spoke Spanish (Fernando had yet to learn Quechua) found Fernando by the stream doing his own washing. 'You can't do that,' he said, 'it's not our custom for men ever to do their own washing.' A young girl was deputised to do the washing for him. That night she was also at the house to cook for him and it was clear, although she couldn't speak Spanish, to sleep with him as well.

Fernando was embarrassed. He went back to the elder to explain that in his culture it was normal to be able to speak to a partner before developing a relationship. 'What do you need to speak to her for?' asked the village elder. 'Just throw her on the bed and get on with it.'

For a while Fernando and the girl co-existed uneasily in the house, in separate bedrooms. Apart from their complete inability to communicate, she unnerved him by coming into his room each morning and waking him by savagely pulling his hair. It was clear she wanted sex. In the life of the village, it was considered shameful not to be fecund. The sooner the girl could become pregnant, the happier she would be.

Finally Fernando succumbed to this irresistible pressure (this was the way he put it). They lived together for three years. But to her mortification she never became pregnant. Fernando thought then that this was due to him, but found out later that this was not the case. 'It was a terrible shame for her. I felt very sad about it.'

The time came when Fernando had to leave the village and return to Lima. For him, as for Tobias Schneebaum, the immersion in a completely different culture had been a crucial rite of passage – the moment, in Schneebaum's words, 'when my life began'. I asked Fernando if he, like Tobias, had ever been back.

'Once I drove in my car to a place where I could see the village. I stopped the car and looked at it for a long while. But I didn't want to set foot in it again.' It reminded me of the final passage at the end of the *Gormenghast* trilogy when Titus Groan returns to within sight of his ancestral castle after his wanderings, just to reassure himself it is still there – but then leaves.

Fernando had written a book called *El Camino del Mono* (*The Way of the Monkey*). It was a picaresque account of a young orphaned Limeño who, after living the low life in Peru as a salesman and frequenter of prostitutes, then lights out for Finland: there he proceeds to live the high life, courtesy of a rich wife and a compliant bourgeoisie unready for the street-fighting business tactics of a Peruvian *cholo*. What struck me most on reading it was the restlessness it displayed – the need of the Peruvian intellectual to escape imaginatively from Peru.

A recent literary periodical to which Fernando had contributed consisted of nothing but replies by leading Peruvian artists and writers to one simple question: 'Why have you left Peru?' (Fernando himself now lived most of the year in the United States). The answer was rarely a political one – repression of intellectuals had never occurred in Peru in the same way as it had in Argentina and Chile – but seemed more born of a febrile dissatisfaction, like the Finnish salmon Fernando talked about that needed to head out of the safe fjords and into the ocean.

ADENTRO (WITHIN)

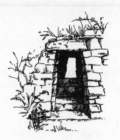

IN A WAY I WAS BEHAVING like Fernando or Titus Groan – returning to see a place that I had once known well. But I was also going further, for I was determined to press on down into the jungle and finally see the city of Old Vilcabamba at Espíritu Pampa, the last city of the Incas, a magnet for every explorer in this part of the Andes since Hiram Bingham himself. It rankled that it had eluded me before, and there was something about the descriptions of this huge city down in the rainforest that seemed incomplete or that I had found (perhaps wilfully, to force myself to travel there) impossible to visualise.

I was still as ambivalent about the Amazon as I had been when I first experienced it in Ecuador. I decided to go and see a man who knew about the jungle. It had taken me years to discover where Nicholas Asheshov lived (the last address I had had for him was at the *Lima Times*). I knew his name well from tales of explorers in the sixties. When I did finally manage to track him down, it came as a surprise to discover that he now lived just down the road from Ollantaytambo, where he was running a hotel.

'You'll see me at the bar,' Nicholas had said on the phone. 'I'm a white-haired old buffer doddering about.' In fact Asheshov, while about sixty and now partially sighted, was wearing a faded blue denim jacket and looked extremely fit. Later he told me that he deliberately dressed like a down-at-heel tourist in his own hotel so that no one would realise he was the manager and approach him with complaints about the service.

Nick had had a supremely adventurous life. As a young man in the fifties, he had come out to Peru ('for all those gorgeous girls – it sounded the nearest thing to a cowboy film') by working his passage on an oil-tanker and had then stayed to carve out a lively journalistic career with the *Lima*

Times. This had given him the means and the excuse to travel through much of what Paddington Bear would have called 'darkest Peru'. I knew that Asheshov had worked closely with such legendary explorers as Gene Savoy (indeed, he had often bailed Savoy out of jail) and had covered some of the small wars that occasionally erupted over the continent as a freelance for Fleet Street. He had also been responsible for the tabloid battle between the *Mail* and the *Express* that Ann Kendall had unwittingly found herself in (by his own admission, not perhaps his most glorious moment). Along the way, Asheshov had always made time for some supremely intrepid exploring.

It was a while before we circled around to talking about it, as we stood at the bar. Nick plied me with double whiskies (it was, after all, his bar) and told me he could still sail a thirty-foot yacht even though he had problems seeing which bottle of Scotch was which on the other side of the counter.

He noticed my clear curiosity about the hotel. 'I made a lot of money on the markets down in Chile during the boom years of the early 90s – enough to buy this place, which up until then had been a lumbering government-run white elephant. Now we want to turn it into a total experience for the traveller. We're going to call it Inca-Land.' Some disused railway-tracks (from a long-abandoned plan to connect the hotel to Machu Picchu direct by train) ran right up to the bungalow house to one side, a house which Asheshov had converted from the original railway station. Cattle now grazed on the grass covering the disused track.

He reminded me of a character out of Conrad: the same bullish determination to carve a way in a still surprisingly open part of the world, mitigated by long experience of the problems in doing so. Asheshov's father had been an émigré White Russian bacteriologist, his mother an English pathologist, and he had grown up in the West Country before getting the urge to travel himself. He had nine children, fathered over a thirty-year span – but he also had a nice line in self-deprecation which prevented any comparisons to Hemingway or the macho image which his record might suggest.

It was clear that Asheshov's heart was more in exploring than in the hotel business – he had spent much time in the little-known areas to the north-west of the Vilcabamba, along the Apurímac. 'The thing is, Peru's so littered with ruins that there's something seriously wrong if an area doesn't have any – either no one's looked hard enough or they're just incompetent.'

Asheshov was, like most explorers, slightly contemptuous of archaeologists. 'They're trained to keep their noses to the ground, preferably below ground.

So they rarely find the genuine lost cities out in the bush and frankly they don't even go looking for them. It wouldn't be *scientific*.'

'I used to think, perhaps naively, that if you found a lost city and so could provide work for needy archaeologists, they might respect you for it, or at least buy you a drink. Not a bit of it. They hated Bingham and disliked Gene Savoy intensely. Both of them were accused formally of being *huaqueros*, grave-robbers. It's unbelievable!'

In 1963 he had become involved in one of the strangest of all the expeditions to the Vilcabamba. Two Americans, Brooks Baekeland and Peter Gimbel, had decided that the only way to penetrate the higher interior plateau to the north-west was simply to parachute in. Using aeroplanes as a tool of exploration had already been extensively done – the Shippee-Johnson aerial expedition of 1931, for instance, had both mapped Chan-Chan by air and surveyed the Urubamba valley – but no one had ever parachuted into unknown territory before, at least not for a scientific and legitimate purpose. The area the Americans wanted to investigate through this radical plan was a large, intriguing plateau jutting right out into the Amazon basin like the prow of a ship, 9000 square miles of uninhabited land – a 'Lost World', as Asheshov described it.

Within seconds of arriving they realised why: 'I was just thinking that this [the parachute landing] was even better than we had dreamed,' wrote Baedeland later, 'when I felt cold water seeping in through the knees of my jump suit.' What looked like firm ground from the air was in fact a bog, and much of the plateau was similarly water-logged, making it totally unsuitable for human habitation, agriculture or indeed expeditions. In its exposed position, the plateau received the first drenching of water from the air flowing in over the Amazon basin.

The team were in real trouble. They had intended to make a bridge-head after their parachute drop and prepare an air-strip (Asheshov referred to it sarcastically as 'Vilcabamba International') so that further supplies could be brought and they themselves could at a later stage be flown out. To make the air-strip they had planned to drop a 700-pound bulldozer, which, even disassembled, was clearly not now a practical proposition. It looked as if they might have to walk out – a walk across completely uncharted territory, for hundreds of miles.

This was where Asheshov had come in. 'I could see from the word go that they were probably a bunch of assholes,' he said in his characteristically forthright way. 'And Brooks fulfilled that early promise by turning out to be a *total* asshole.' Not knowing the explorers myself, I refused to be drawn on this, although in the article they had subsequently written I had noticed a worrying tendency for them to say 'Holy Smoke' to each other, an expression I had otherwise only heard Batman use to Robin. There was also a terrific but equally worrying caption over a shot of the team wading through a mountain stream: 'A false step on these slippery rocks could be a man's last.'

Asheshov had been asked to find a way in to rescue them, although they themselves (and this was where Nick felt they had been such a liability) steadfastly refused to admit that they needed to be rescued. Nick went in with two local helpers ('Policarpio, a Campa chief, and a backwoodsman called Angel Soto') and tried to cut a way up the Pichari river, seemingly the only way through the high cliffs that surrounded the plateau from the Apurímac canyon. Initially he had with him a distinguished biologist, Hans Koepcke, but it was too much for the scientist and he turned back. (A few years later Koepcke's seventeen-year-old daughter Juliana was the only passenger to emerge out of the jungle after a plane crash in the Pucallpa region – because of Asheshov's connection with him, Koepcke allowed the journalist to get a front-page scoop on the story for the *Daily Mail*.)

The Pichari river proved a nightmarish mission from which Asheshov returned emaciated and exhausted – and without the American parachutists, who had refused to descend that way: he showed me a photo of himself hanging between the arms of his two Peruvian helpers, half his usual weight.

'I forget how Brooks and Gimbel, on one side, and me on the other quarrelled, but it was all done by letter on my side, and by walkie-talkie to the pilots on theirs. From the Drop Zone I sent Brooks and Gimbel some notes and suggestions. These were picked up by hooks trailing from the planes and Poli, Angel and I set up half a dozen pick-ups and rescued all their expensive parachutes. My notes, whatever they said – they were probably insufferably cocky – went down like lead balloons and we were told "not to come and rescue them and to get out of the Vilcabamba!" – the pilots were even told not to continue to supply us.'

'We headed off towards the Pongo, so as not to have to return down the Pichari, which actually had been pretty difficult, with dreadful thickets of cane, cliffs, waterfalls. We were wet, lost and hungry most of the time. Angel was at one point going along a very sharp ridge and almost fell off a precipice. He only saved himself by letting his baggage drop instead. I took it as a warning and decided to go back the way we'd come, which turned out to be as miserable as we thought it would be. I remember raiding our medicines for a few remaining cough drops because we were hungry. Poli managed to shoot some monkeys but they were so tough even after hours of smoking that I could only manage the heart, liver and kidneys.'

Meanwhile the American team above on the plateau were calmly doing the usual things expeditions like to put on their letterheads ('we studied the local topography and fauna'). Brooks Baedeland asked for new sneakers to be dropped down to him at regular intervals. After telling Asheshov to head back without them, they set off in the other direction, north-east towards the Urubamba, thinking that in the more open country they would have more chance of receiving regular air-drops (this had been one of their concerns about returning with Asheshov). However, although not as precipitous as the Apurímac territory, their route soon became heavily wooded and, good as the pilots were ('And they were very good,' said Asheshov), they couldn't make all the drops. 'What's more,' said Nick, with only an understandable hint of irritation from a man who'd offered them a quicker way out, 'instead of the fifteen days they thought this "shorter route" would take, it took sixty-one.'

By the time Baedeland and his team finally arrived at a Dominican mission on the Urubamba – 'Sod's law that you always emerge out of the jungle somewhere where you can't even get a decent drink,' commented Asheshov – they were nearly starved. They had also experienced close encounters with possibly hostile Indians ('Though we felt we had been observed, we couldn't be sure,' wrote Baedeland in what must be the most common of all jungle literature devices), snakes that never materialised and the usual literary incidents of travel in the Vilcabamba, including at one point a stoic – and, it must be said, absurd – line from Baedeland about how 'I thought I was going to die, but was not much concerned.' They had not discovered a single stone that could have been placed there by a human hand, pre-Columbian man clearly having realised early on that the whole area was best left well alone.

The experience with the American team had, if anything, just whetted Asheshov's appetite for more exploration. That was why he had been so interested when in 1970, now promoted to Features Editor at the *Lima Times*, he had been approached by one of his freelance writers, Robert Nichols, with a story about Paititi. Paititi was the name the Spanish conquistadors had given to a mythical *ciudad perdida*, a lost city of riches that was supposed to be as yet undiscovered in the jungle, an ancient legend that twentieth-century explorers had constantly ridiculed at the same time as they succumbed themselves to the same powerful myth.

'Now I'd always said that there was about as much chance of finding Paititi or El Dorado as of winning the New York State lottery. But Bob was a very tough guy,' said Nick, 'and a man who really knew what he was talking about. He wasn't a bullshitter. He'd spent years in the jungle on his own, writing stuff for me, and he'd travelled to some of the toughest places. If he said he'd come across something, then I believed him.'

Nichols showed Asheshov on the map where he was planning to go. 'To be honest, it was a busy day in the office, press day, and I didn't really concentrate too hard on precisely where he was heading. But later I remembered it was further down in the jungle from his old stomping ground of La Convención.' La Convención was the area of Peru that I had done most of my own exploring in and it was where I had first heard Nichols' name mentioned. 'I just gathered that he was heading into the Alto Madre de Dios jungles at the bottom of the Q'osñipata valley. It's still a tough place today but it was a really tough place back then in the sixties. I didn't like to press him too hard for the details of precisely where he was going – it was his story and, as you know, explorers can get cagey about that kind of stuff.'

Asheshov paused and a waiter came to take him over to the table which was reserved for him every evening. The waiter read the menu out to us but it was obviously a formality. 'I'll have the set meal as usual, Jorge,' said Asheshov before I could say anything, 'and so will Señor Hugo here.' Asheshov ate distractedly, hardly bothering about what was put in front of him. He was completely focusing on the events of thirty years before.

'To be honest, it was only when Bob didn't come back well over a month after he said he would that I started to get really concerned. Then more months passed. In the end, I headed down to the area myself.'

'Some priests from the Dominican mission at Shintuya told me that they had seen Bob and that he'd headed into the jungle with a pair of wild young French travellers. They were worried that none of them had returned. What's more, Bob had also set off with half a dozen Mashco Indians as guides. These guides had returned shortly afterwards. Apparently they had refused to go on past the Shinkikibeni petroglyphs. They said that Bob and the two Frenchmen had pressed on.'

More whiskies arrived at the table. 'I hired a plane to fly over the area in search of any traces, and at the same time I got a land expedition to go on their trail, led by Elvin Berg.' This was the same expert Peruvian guide who had explored with John Ridgway and who had later been savagely tortured and killed by the Sendero Luminoso in 1984. 'Even with Elvin leading the team, they had no luck at all.'

'This was 1970. We spent six more months looking with no success and no further indication of a Paititi. But two years later a quite young Japanese law student turned up out of nowhere and volunteered his help. He was very persistent. His name was Yoshiharu Sekino.'

Yoshiharu Sekino went into the jungle alone and eventually found what turned out to be the killers of Nichols and the two Frenchmen. It was an extraordinary achievement. From them and from other witnesses, Sekino pieced together the story of what must have happened to the explorers. This was the story as he had told it to Asheshov and as Asheshov now told it to me.

The two young Frenchmen (whom the missionaries had described to Asheshov as being volatile) had apparently made advances to the local Machiguenga women. 'Nichols would have been horrified,' said Asheshov. 'Years of living in the jungle had made him very careful.' Naturally this had not gone down well with the tribe. Relationships had quickly soured, leading to the murders of Nichols and his companions.

Yoshiharu Sekino had even been able to take a photo of the killers with Nichols' machete and some of his surviving possessions. Asheshov knew that one of the killers was still alive today, almost thirty years later.

As for Paititi, Sekino went back more than once trying to follow up Nichols' lead, armed with satellite photographs which did seem to show a curious series of 'dots', apparently in a neat triangular alignment. He found nothing. In the years that followed, Nichols' disappearance fuelled further interest in the Paititi legend.

By now we were on the fifth double whisky. Asheshov looked at me with his disconcertingly clear blue, almost sightless eyes: 'I still think a lot about Bob,' he said. 'The thing is, you see, he was stoned to death. It must have been a terrible way to die.'

*

At first the passengers in the bus out of Ollantaytambo were unsure about how to react when the young hustler in the Hawaiian shirt – a *cholo* of the streets if ever there was one – stood up and started to address them. These were mountain people, usually '*muy recto y callado*' ('very proper and reserved'), at least when sober, and they behaved much as a British train-carriage would when serenaded by a busker – by looking out of the window or exchanging amused glances of embarrassment. I was still nursing a vicious hangover from my evening with Nick Asheshov and had only slept for about four hours – but there was something about the hustler that commanded attention.

He was a good-looking young guy, with the darker skin and gold-capped teeth of the jungle towns and he brought a rush of vibrancy into the bus as we headed out of Ollantaytambo. His patter of ferocious and scatological Spanish came pouring out in a torrent as he began a series of magic tricks, standing in the aisle and swaying from the hips each time the bus took a corner on two wheels. 'Look at these cards – here's a Jack – you look a bit of a lad yourself, Sir' – this to a man who in Britain would have been wearing a grey suit. 'Now watch – I'm going to eat the card – and then this one too – and another – and now watch.' With elaborate pantomime he produced the missing cards from between his buttocks, digested and excreted intact. The fat lady travelling with her husband, kids and assorted agricultural produce gave a huge roar of laughter and nudged her husband so hard in the ribs she could have cracked them. *'Que cabrón!* What a stud!' she shouted.

Encouraged, the hustler began his own demographic survey of the passengers' bathing habits. 'Now, as we all know, the ladies are very particular about their soaps. Señora, what soap do you use?'

'Camay.'

'And you, Señora?'

'Lux' (pronounced 'looks').

'What about you, Sir, what soap do you use?' he asked a Señor in a battered straw hat who wasn't paying much attention. The man shrugged. *'¡Ya ven!* See what I mean!' screamed the Hawaiian-shirted one in triumph, 'that's the problem with men!'

By now he had the ladies in the palm of his hand, out of which he finessed some suspiciously sticky bars of nougat: 'I'm going to give one of these to each of you *sin compromiso* ['with no obligation']. You can always hand them back later if you don't want them. Otherwise they're yours for just two soles.'

Then he had a last trick for us. Whipping a tube of vivid red lipstick out from his bum-bag, he gave a dab to his lips and flounced the Hawaiian shirt around his waist. 'Do you think I'm a *marica* then, a *maricón*, a great big pansy?' The woman he was asking screamed with laughter and embarrassment. 'No, do you really?' The woman paused. Whatever she said was going to make her the centre of attention. 'No.' 'Then give me a kiss,' and he smacked her on the lips to a roar of approval from the rest of the coach.

He paused, as if a thought had just occurred to him: *'Momento.* Those delicious bars I gave you. The only problem is – now that you've handled the products, they may be too shop-soiled to sell again. Maybe you won't be able to give them back after all, so give me your money!' In the laughter that followed, he must have picked up about forty soles in profit – twice what a muleteer could hope to earn in a day.

Through a burst of static on the driver's radio came a fine Colombian rendition of *'La Cosita'*, 'The Little Thing', a salsa song about Wayne Bobbitt losing his penis (the said 'little thing'), with the singer trying to inspire Wayne with a philosophical attitude ('Why are you worrying, Wayne? . . .

What you've lost is only a little thing ... which can only lead to trouble for a man anyway'). The Bobbitt case had aroused considerable interest in South America, not least because his wife Lorena, who had done the Struwelpeter bit, was herself Ecuadorian.

We were beginning the long haul up the pass known as Málaga or Panticalla. Looming above us was the mountain of Verónica, or Wakay Willka, a perfect triangle of white above a patchwork of brown fields and thatched huts, each with its *chacra* or small-holding. It was still early morning (the bus had departed at dawn) and the early fires lit in some of the huts had left smoke seeping through every crack in the thatch, as if the whole building was smoking.

The very fact that there were alternative Spanish names here as well as Indian ones – the Málaga pass, Mt Verónica – in a mountain range of otherwise largely Quechuan peaks showed the importance of this area to the conquistadors. It marked the edge of their dominions: beyond lay the Inca rump kingdom of Vilcabamba that Manco Inca had established.

After Manco's death in 1544 at the hands of the treacherous Spanish he had taken in as refugees, the state of Vilcabamba had passed to his sons. Under first Sayri Tupac and then Titu Cusi the Incas had continued to hold the Spanish off by astute diplomacy. They had frequently pretended to be about to 'come out' from their hideaway and accept the lands that a succession of Spanish viceroys offered as bribes (Sayri Tupac did actually emerge towards the end of his life, in 1560, but disappointed the Spanish by promptly dying).

Titu Cusi, a tougher character altogether than Sayri Tupac, had flirted constantly with the Spanish, receiving envoys and allowing Christian missionaries into the Vilcabamba. He liked to give the impression that he was on the verge of giving way to Spanish importunities, while never quite doing so. In this he was helped by the turnover in Spanish viceroys: given potential assassination, disease and political intrigue, it was a job with a short life expectancy and none gathered quite enough momentum to really address 'the Inca problem'.

So by 1570 the state of Vilcabamba was still intact, some forty years after the Conquest. It had successfully preserved most of the Inca traditions, albeit in miniature and with limited resources.

My battered copy of Prescott's nineteenth-century classic, *History of the Conquest of Peru*, was no longer any good to me. He had ended his account of the Conquest shortly after the time of Manco's death and had shown little interest in the achievements of the very last Incas. However, one of John Hemming's great contributions in *The Conquest of the Incas*, his twentieth-century reworking of Prescott, had been to tell the story of the forgotten final years of the Empire as it survived after Manco.

John Hemming's reputation had grown enormously since I had first met him in the study of his house back in London. His book had been recognised as a towering work of scholarship which mined every available bit of source material to tell the detailed history. Back in Cuzco, Barry Walker's voice had grown positively hushed as he told me that John had once sat in his bar, having a quiet pint with him. 'Just over there,' he said, pointing out the precise chair he had sat on. The Peruvian government had awarded him the Ordén de Mérito. They hadn't yet got around to selling T-shirts in the Plaza de Armas saying 'John Hemming is God', but it was only a matter of time.

For his achievement in resurrecting the last days of the Vilcabamba Empire was two-fold: on the one hand it was simply a matter of putting the historical record straight – the broad outline of the story had always been known, but Hemming had filled out many details with contemporary sources and given it added legitimacy; perhaps more importantly, the book was also a resounding clarion call to a nation at times unsure of its own identity, for it was a reminder that the Incas did not go gently into that good night when the Spanish arrived (as the popular imagination supposed), but courageously fought a spirited rearguard action to preserve the essence of Quechuan culture – a culture which was now becoming increasingly viewed as Peru's natural patrimony.

Hemming had not only revisited the sources to tell the story of how protracted the end-game had been after Manco's death, but had also put forward an attractive picture of how Vilcabamba could possibly have continued indefinitely, 'a native enclave related to Spanish Peru in much the same way as Lesotho or Swaziland were related to modern South Africa'.

Unfortunately a viceroy arrived who was not content with this *status quo*: Francisco de Toledo, unlike most of his more aristocratic predecessors, was essentially a civil servant of great efficiency and he wanted tidy solutions to the problems that had beset Peru since the Conquest and caused endless civil wars. A principal problem was the continued existence of an Inca stronghold and Toledo determined to flush the Incas out of their lair. He was helped in this by the sudden death of Titu Cusi (probably from excess drinking, although his subjects suspected poison and brutally murdered a nearby Christian priest in retaliation). In the transitional period before the establishment of his successor, yet another son of Manco's called Tupac Amaru, the military commanders of Vilcabamba made misjudged decisions that Titu Cusi would never have done, needlessly killing some Spaniards and providing the sort of provocation that a legalist like Toledo could exploit to justify using force. So was to begin the agonising final invasion of Vilcabamba.

In April 1572, at the start of the dry season in the mountains, a party set off from Cuzco with a mission to destroy for ever the last vestiges of the Inca dynasty. Many of their old enemies joined the Spanish against them and took part in the expedition, including the Cañari tribe, one of the subject races the Inca Empire had treated with ferocity and who had been so ardent in their pursuit of Manco. There were also some members of Tupac Amaru's own family, who had defected to the Spanish – these last were to prove some of the most relentless in pursuit of their own kin, as much to prove to the Spanish that they had no residual rebellious tendencies themselves.

As we headed up to the pass that led to Vilcabamba, I was travelling on the route the Spaniards took on that final journey to get rid of the Incas. It was a spectacular and tough journey even by bus, as the road was bad and the pass was at around 14,000 feet. For the Spanish advancing into hostile territory, it must have been daunting. When the French traveller Charles Wiener came this way in the nineteenth century, he had been startled to come across 'un singulier monument': a pyramid of the skulls of horses that had died on the ascent.

The members of the punitive expedition were a pretty ragged bunch. These were no longer the tough conquistadors and battle-hardened fighters of the original Conquest. Three of the four Pizarro brothers had since died, all violently. The last brother, Hernando, had been held for twenty years in a Spanish prison and was a broken old man. Most of their original companions had died from disease or civil war. Instead Viceroy Toledo had assembled the best force he could from the riff-raff of Cuzco, including the dandies and merchants who wanted to go along for the ride. While only too happy to dress up in armour and live out some of the romantic legends of adventurous conquest they had been brought up on, many of them were far from being soldiers.

With the party were just three of the original *conquistadores*, now old men, who could advise on how to deal with an Inca attack. One of them, Alonso de Mesa, had been a bit of a lad in his youth, fathering six children by six different wives and a further child by a concubine. The early camp-fire talk as they set out from Cuzco would have tried to re-live the stories of derring-do and adventure from forty years before, doubtless much glossed over to ignore the slaughter of helpless Indians and exaggerate the chivalric prowess of the *conquistadores*.

The stories would have been of how Pizarro (or the Marquis, as he had latterly become) and his knights had been so few against so many, and yet prevailed. These tales – much embroidered – would have been part of the armoury that accompanied Toledo's expedition. Peru at that time was much like the American Old West in the way that history became mythologised almost as soon as it happened.

At the top of the pass was a tiny chapel where the driver and passengers got out to light a candle. From here one could see the wild lands of the Vilcabamba ahead, a great ridge of snow-lined peaks with savage indentations between. It was no wonder that the Spanish were said to have drawn back in horror from the region whenever they saw it. The sight would certainly have silenced the loose braggarts of the party who had set off from Cuzco on the assumption that this would be some sort of glorified hunting-party, a nostalgic recreation of the glory days of the Conquest. If the punishing climb of the 14,000-foot pass had not already given them an intimation of the hardship to come, this first view of the Vilcabamba would have brought home to them all that real blood was going to be spilt and that it would be a test of bravery and endurance to bring the last of the Incas out of a region grid-locked by canyons, jungle and mountain ranges.

Looking down, I remembered the magnificent opening lines of the Peruvian novelist Ciro Alegría's *La Serpiente de Oro* (*The Golden Serpent*):

> *Por donde el Marañón rompe las cordilleras en un voluntarioso afán de avance, la sierra peruana tiene una bravura de puma acosado. Con ella en torno, no es cosa de estar al descuido.* (Where the Marañón River breaks through the mountains in a headstrong surge of attack, the Peruvian sierra has the fierceness of a cornered puma. Just as with the river, it is wise to treat it with respect.)

La Serpiente de Oro is the first of a trilogy of novels Ciro Alegría wrote in the 1930s as a powerful meditation on the relationship between the people of the mountains and those of the jungle. The narrator of *La Serpiente* is a young *cholo*, a lad from the jungle, and he disdains the mountain people who come down to his village

> whimpering about mosquitoes. They would spend the whole night sensing snakes nearby, for all the world as if they'd laid their ponchos down on a nest of them ... They don't eat mangoes because they think it will give them fever. Even so, they still die shivering like wet dogs. This isn't the country for the Indians of the mountains and there are only a few who ever acclimatise. They find the valley-bottoms too febrile. Meanwhile, for those of us of the jungle, the solitude and silence of the mountains tightens our chests unbearably.

The Spanish plan was to encircle the Incas in their stronghold and force them down into the jungle. To this end they had sent other expeditions around the Apurímac from Cuzco, to close off all the mountain passes that led from the Vilcabamba. Only the northern exits to the Amazon would remain open to the Incas. The one problem with this strategy was that it might be successful – and then the Spanish would themselves have to go down into the jungle after them. For the Spanish, as for the Incas, this was the last place they wanted to wage a war.

Both sides shared a largely paranoid and irrational fear of the snakes, mosquitoes and wild animals waiting for them, although the threat of disease was very real. So too was the well-earned reputation of the Antis and the other jungle tribes for being some of the most effective fighters on the continent. The Antis' archers with their poisoned arrows were particularly lethal and were capable of defeating even the Spanish. When Manco had held Ollantaytambo against the conquistadors, these jungle archers had been one of his greatest assets.

Manco had been careful to forge alliances with the network of Amazon tribes behind his back when he arrived in Vilcabamba, and his successors continued those alliances after his death. During the time of the Inca Empire, the jungle had always been the least desirable posting and the site of some of the Empire's worst defeats. At one point the Emperor Topa Inca had become separated from his troops and managed to get lost in the jungle: he was found only after a frantic search party was sent by one of his generals. While the Incas expanded dramatically north and south along both the Andes and the coast from their base in Cuzco, their expansion into Antisuyo, as they called the eastern quarter of the Empire towards the Amazon, had always been a shallow one.

The Antis (Antisuyo was named after them) had a tradition of wholesale cannibalism that appalled the Incas as much as the Spanish. John Hemming told an amusing story of Titu Cusi wanting to impress a Spanish envoy called Rodriguez who had been sent to parley with him. The Inca summoned up a phalanx of jungle warriors who paraded in front of them and then offered to eat Rodriguez for the Inca if he so desired. The Inca, to Rodriguez's relief, turned down the offer, but the psychological effect this had when relayed back to the other Spanish in Cuzco can only be imagined. Certainly no one in the Spanish ranks can have relished the thought of heading into the jungle to meet them.

They would also have remembered the disastrous missions of men like Aguirre and Orellana into the jungle, missions in which most of the participants had died – and that Gonzalo Pizarro had, after all, succeeded in doing precisely what they were now doing thirty years before, when Manco was still alive and he had driven the Inca down into the Amazon. Yet Manco had survived, spirited away from tribe to tribe to re-emerge later and reclaim Vilcabamba when the Spanish had left it.

Something of the dangers of the Amazon area entered deep into the Peruvian psyche of the descendants of both the Spanish and the Incas and has remained to the present day. It is still *adentro*, the land within, hidden and dangerous. In Alegría's novel, the outsider who comes to live with the people of the jungle is at first seduced by the beauty of the river and the landscape, but is ultimately killed by it. Even now it is still remarkably unoccupied and communications remain abominable: there are many tribes who have only recently been contacted for the first time, and doubtless many more remain.

As we descended below the pass, a red-hawk flew by. This was wild, isolated country. Spanish moss hung over a landscape of pines. It was difficult to tell which trees were alive and which were dead. Great spills of red earth ended in abrupt cliff-faces. There was something Arthurian about it, a landscape of the Grail quest, the 'Sankgreal'.

We passed a truck that had gone off the road and down a canyon during the night. The skid marks were fresh in the mud. It must have happened only a few hours beforehand. The truck lay upturned, about a hundred feet below the road. We stopped to help, although there seemed to be no sign of any survivors. Oranges and apples were scattered pathetically down the side of the hill to where a local *campesino* was trying to hack his way across the steep bamboo to get to the upturned truck. '*Buenos Dias,*' he shouted up to us in a voice that was startlingly cheerful.

The landscape began to change lower down; small-holdings were growing coffee, some huts had papaya-trees outside, there were daktura lilies hanging overhead with their uniquely rotting, decadent smell, bromeliads in the trees, huge poinsettias and then, to my surprise, nestling in the verges as an odd touch of the suburban amongst this vegetal opulence, large clumps of busy lizzies, grown to a size that would win prizes at any village horticultural show in England.

On the other side of the valley I could see that the slash-and-burn methods of the *campesinos* had destroyed large sections of hillside. Apart from bamboo, very little grew back afterwards to replace the vegetation once the land was abandoned, as it invariably was. The slash-and-burn method was notoriously wasteful of top-soil and had been made illegal in Peru, although this was hard to enforce. '*Señor*, a fire starts, what can we do?'

It was ironic to think that when the first Europeans arrived they initially presumed that because the forests were so tremendously fertile, their agriculture would be as well. Much has been made of the subsequent destruction of the rainforest itself, but how cruel it must also have been for the first settlers, after laboriously clearing and sowing their first crops, to see the top-soils washed away by the rains once the retaining and protecting vegetation had been burnt. It must have been baffling to them that trees grew to hundreds of feet in height, yet the soil was too light to support more than a single crop of corn.

I was reminded of one theory about the decline of the early Mayan civilisations in Central America: having over-stripped the surrounding rainforest to maintain a growing population, they could not sustain the resulting imbalance and the cities imploded, aggravated by civil wars and a punitive theocratic system, leaving the rainforests to come back and take over. For an ecologist the story has a particular savour ('The rainforest will indeed come back and prevail!'), but as an example of the inability of man to maintain even the most advanced of civilisations in the face of hostile natural conditions, it has a certain sadness.

The technique of slash-and-burn, although the most short-term of solutions, would never quite go away in the Andes, for it did allow at least one brief crop to flourish before the land became useless. Transient farmers could move on after every crop. The effect was disastrous in the valleys, where it led to landslides like the one that had swept away the railway line.

The tendency of the Incas always to build high, on the sides or tops of valleys, could be attributed to a prudent aversion to such landslides – although the cynic could also point out that perhaps only the high ruins survive. There may have been many buildings on the valley floors which have been systematically destroyed over the centuries as landslides and floods occurred.

The bridge at Chuquichaca, which Roddy and I had crossed some two decades before, had been completely swept away by the flood. There were still some twisted remains of railway-line here and there, and a carriage on an old bit of siding.

It marked the point where the Vilcabamba river joined the Urubamba. Just as in Manco's day, this was one of the essential strategic points for the Spanish advance: again they managed to cross it and started to make headway along the banks of the Vilcabamba river towards Vitcos. However, not much further along, the track came to a narrow pass, crossing a spit of land with a drop either side. Red rice grass fringed the verge, so that we looked through a curtain of red at the ferociously steep gorge of the Vilcabamba river below.

It was here that the Incas ambushed the Spanish, attacking with courage and ferocity. An Inca captain leapt on Martín García de Loyola, one of the expedition's leading captains, and tried to topple with him over the ravine edge. Only the prompt action of García's servant, who slashed at the Inca warrior with a sword, prevented his death. Crude clubs and axes were as usual no match for Spanish firearms and although they killed a few of the enemy by rolling boulders down from above, the Incas retreated from this minor skirmish the losers.

When we reached the valley bottom, the sweat and smell began to rise inside the bus. We stopped to get a tyre fixed, to the indignation of many of the passengers. 'This was supposed to be an express service,' muttered the fat lady who had so enjoyed the Hawaiian-shirted magician's performance. She got up and started to berate the driver. 'This should all have been checked before the bus left. The *mantenimiento* just hasn't been done properly. You can see the whole bus is dirty.' She wiped a finger on the back of a seat-cover in the manner of an aunt from Blackpool and advanced menacingly. The driver maintained his equanimity impassively, given that he had 200 pounds of prime Andean womanhood bearing down on him. He gave a magnificent shrug. '*Lo arreglamos*, we'll fix it', he declared. But the other passengers had now taken up the cry: '*Vámanos, vámanos!* Let's go, let's go!'

'I tell you what,' said the driver, as if making a magnanimous gesture, 'we'll stop early for lunch.' Quite how this made any difference to our arrival time was unclear, but we were treated to a bowl of disgustingly awful stew with glops of potatoes and unidentifiable meat – from a place which clearly gave the driver both a commission and a free lunch.

It was nightfall before we reached Huancacalle.

*

Seeing it in the moonlight, with the tall eucalyptus groves surrounding it, made my arrival there some twenty years before, huddled in a truck and trying to evade the police checkpoints, seem even more phantasmagorical. Huancacalle now had a small hostel, set up by the Cobos family. It was spartan, but it had a shower and more importantly it had beer.

Leaning against the doorway was the tall, rangy figure of Gary Ziegler. Gary was an explorer who had worked in this area for thirty years. In his stetson and breeches, he looked as if he might just have stepped off a Colorado ranch – as indeed he had. Gary was a true *vaquero*, a cowboy. Part-owner of a hundred head of horses back in the States, he mixed his exploring with ranch management. In fact Gary mixed his exploring with just about everything else in the Tom Sawyer logbook of jobs for active boys: over sixty years of enjoyably hard living, he had worked as a photographer, mountain guide, geologist and yacht handler.

Once, after a trip exploring the Vilcabamba, Gary had arrived at a local train station, left his hired horse (he insisted on riding everywhere) and rolled wearily into the carriage with his companions. The Quechuan Indians on the train gave them a wide berth, but Gary and his crew were too tired to worry about what might be wrong. Finally one Indian sidled nervously up to Gary: 'Excuse me, *Señor*, but I've been talking with my friends and – are you Clint Eastwood?'

Over some vicious vodka martinis that Gary mixed up (I learnt later that he never travelled anywhere without a bottle of vodka and some green olives) we swapped stories.

Gary, like me, didn't like the Amazon much. 'I worked in intelligence in South-east Asia during the Vietnam war, and I tell you that was enough jungle for me. Used to go out on night patrols with infra-red vision to pick the enemy out with. Then we'd get those suckers. I tell you, being in the army is fun – at least in wartime. In peacetime it's kind of dull.'

He had climbed most of the major peaks in the area and many of the minor ones. 'I like those little suckers,' he said, 'the little insignificant peaks that no one else is ever going to bother with. Most have never been climbed before. Hell, most don't even have a name.'

I had originally got into contact with Gary via the Internet and discovered that he too had taken an expedition to Choquequirao. After swapping e-mails, we were now about to go together to one of the most remote and little-visited of Inca sites, that of Inca Wasi in the Puncuyoc hills. My interest in the place had been stimulated, as so often with exploring, by the discovery of a map.

*

I had first seen it at the apartment of the distinguished archaeologist Adriana von Hagen.

The map was in an old brown cardboard tube. Adriana had inherited it from her father, Victor von Hagen. She carefully extracted the two-foot-square piece of parchment paper, covered in the thin red lines of Inca trails which gleamed on the translucent paper. It was the only copy of an only copy of an only copy. The original map had been made in 1921 by Christian Bües, a pioneering German explorer of the Vilcabamba who had finally died of drink and poverty. His map (entitled '*El Señorío de Vilcabamba*', 'The Kingdom of Vilcabamba') had later come into the hands of a certain A. Palma, who in 1937 had copied what must have been the tattered original. This in its turn had come to the attention of Enrique Bernigau, a German doctor living in Urubamba, who had again painstakingly copied it and passed it on to Victor von Hagen when he came through Cuzco in 1952.

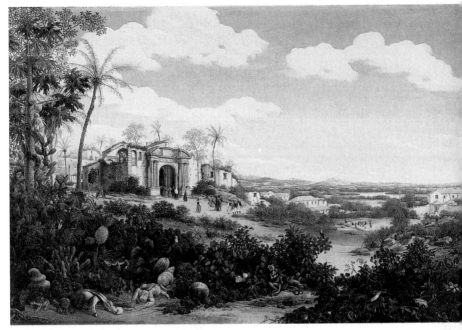

Frans Post, *View of Olinda, Brazil*, 1662. Painted eighteen years after the painter's return to Holland from South America. *'In South America, events of the distant past are often foreshortened and looked at with startling clarity.'*

John Everett Millais, *Pizarro Seizing the Inca of Peru*, 1846.

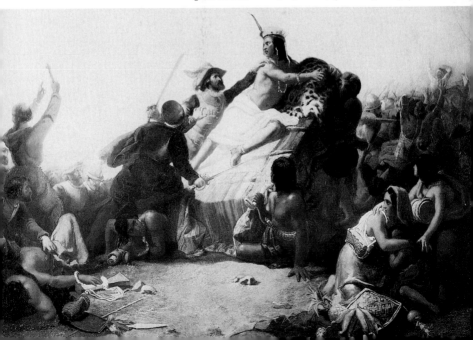

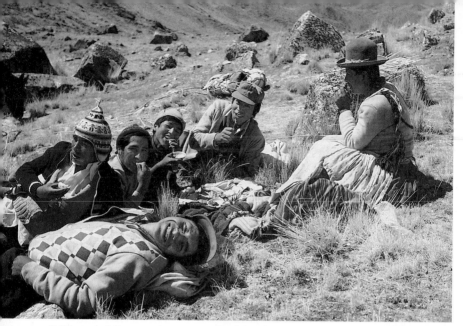

Bolivians picnicking near the start of the Takesi trail: *'¿Anda solito?* on your own?' *'Already twenty-one? You need a wife.'*

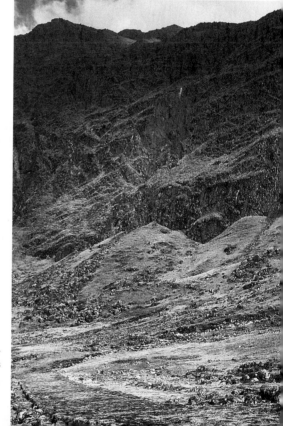

The Takesi trail in Bolivia, descending towards the Yungas lowlands.

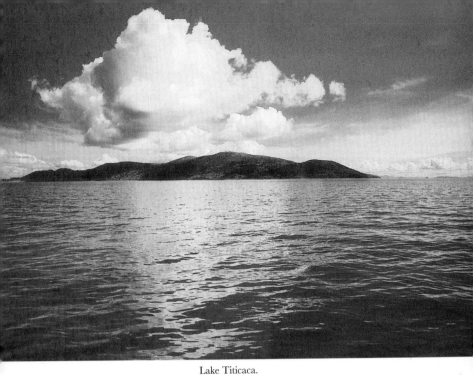

Lake Titicaca.

Ollantaytambo: *'These great upright monoliths of pink porphyry were almost all that remained of the sun temple. They were arranged so as to face the rising sun, and had some of the strange bosses and protuberances that so intrigued me.'*

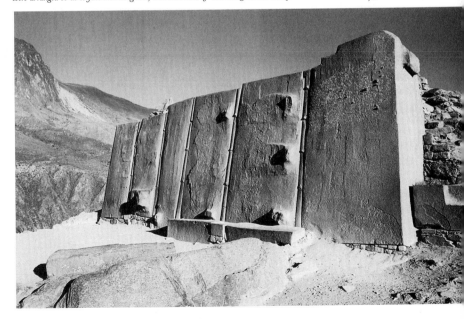

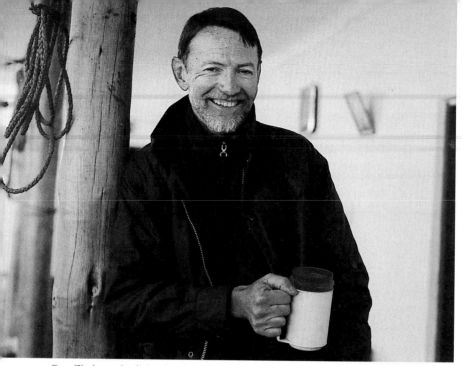

Gary Ziegler, at the Cobos family house in Huancacalle when I first met him: *'he looked as if he might just have stepped off a Colorado ranch – as indeed he had.'*

Camp near Inca Wasi at dawn, with Pumasillo massif beyond.

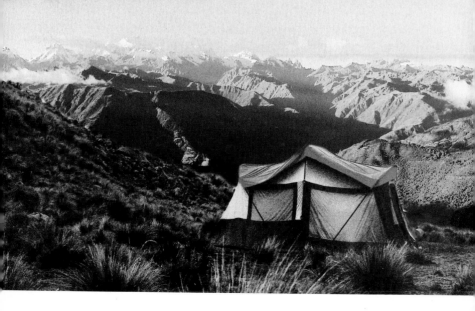

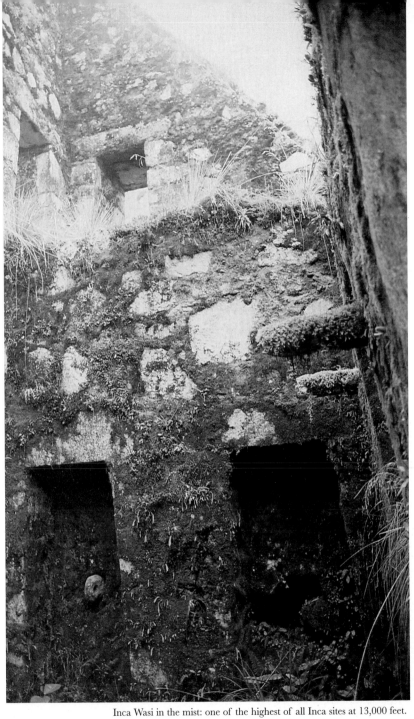

Inca Wasi in the mist: one of the highest of all Inca sites at 13,000 feet.

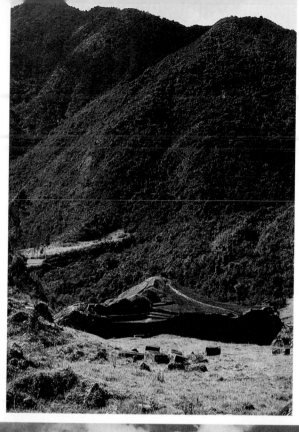

Chuquipalta, the White Rock.

Chuquipalta, the White
Rock: the northern side,
with projecting bosses.

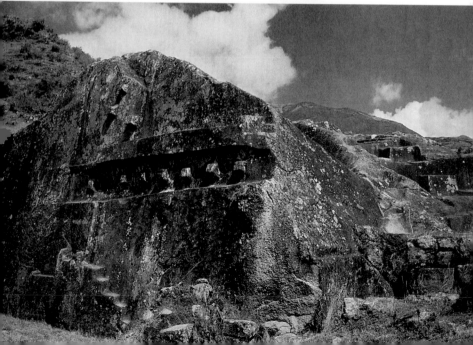

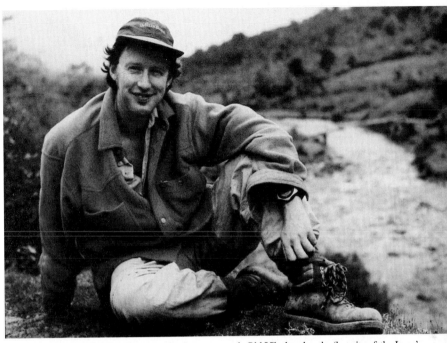

Just below the pass of Ccolpo Cosa, on the descent towards Old Vilcabamba, the 'last city of the Incas'.

Rónal with the horse that threw us both.

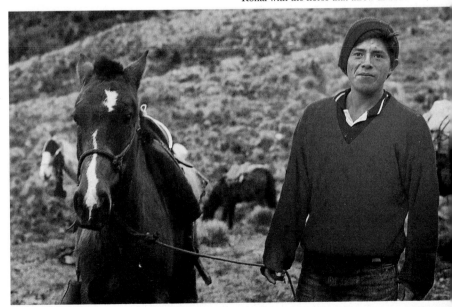

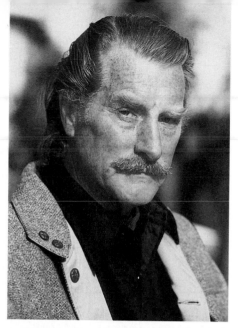

Gene Savoy, discoverer of Old Vilcabamba at Espíritu Pampa in 1964: *"'What you have to remember,' Nicholas Asheshov told me, 'is that Gene Savoy is a cult. A real this-man-is-the-centre-of-the-universe cult.'"*

Below The ruins of Old Vilcabamba at Espíritu Pampa, *'which Bingham liked to translate literally, as the "Pampa of Ghosts": the rain forest had taken over completely.'*

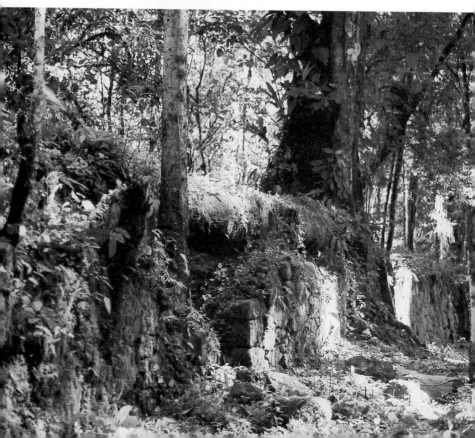

Von Hagen had not done much exploring himself in the Vilcabamba, but he had directed colleagues of his on the Inca Highway expedition to do so.

The reason that it had been so carefully preserved from one generation of explorers to the next was clear to me as soon as I saw it. Bües had obviously travelled far more extensively and thoughtfully than had ever been fully appreciated. His map was far more detailed than many I had seen from more recent years: he also appreciated fully the significance of the road network that linked Choquequirao and Vitcos.

Victor von Hagen must have seized on it. In his handwriting was a tiny cross he had added just off the map, to the north, in a range called the Puncuyoc hills. It was a place he had discovered but few had been to since, called Inca Wasi, one of the highest of all Inca sites at 13,000 feet. It was an irresistible temptation and I felt my blood rising as soon as I saw the map. I had to go there myself.

At least this time no one had painstakingly to sit down and spend what must have been a week's work tracing the map. Adriana took it down the road to a Lima photocopying house who specialised in large-format architectural drawings, and within five minutes I had my own copy.

*

The Coboses' house was almost the last house in the village of Huancacalle and had been the jumping-off point for most of the post-war expeditions into the Vilcabamba. They were a dynastic family of guides. Benjamín Cobos had travelled down to Espíritu Pampa with Gene Savoy in the sixties, José Cobos had worked with Vincent Lee in the eighties and now Juvenal Cobos and other younger members of the family were helping Gary and me on our expedition to the Puncuyoc hills and that little cross on the map.

We headed back to the small village of Yupanqa and started to load up the mules. As I knew from years of experience, this was not as straightforward as it might have seemed.

The procedure for loading mules is very similar to that which an elderly aunt of mine adopts when going on holiday. First the muleteers lay out all the bundles on the grass and move them around until they look deceptively ordered and graded. Then these bundles are packed into saddlebags and onto the mules (in my aunt's case, suitcases). Like her, the muleteers will invariably decide that everything is in the wrong place and must be taken out so that the process can be started all over again. The mule you most need to do this with has got bored and absconded over the horizon.

Experienced *arrieros* can spin this process out for hours. We were lucky and got off that same morning. In Bhutan, my film team were once compelled to spend the night on a Himalayan pass because the wranglers had managed a *tour-de-force* delay of four hours in loading the pack-animals.

Of course, one technique is to forget the mules and head on up a path in the hope that the muleteers will catch you later. But this, particularly on the first day of an expedition, can remain just a hope.

As we started up into the rugged, igneous peaks of the Puncuyoc hills and looked back, we could see why Vitcos was such a convenient centre for the Incas in their exile – it was the hub of a wheel, with spokes extending not only into the Puncuyoc, but away towards the jungle at Old Vilcabamba and up the Choquetecarpa pass towards Choquequirao: beyond were various areas around Pumasillo and Arma that remain under-explored. In the centre Vitcos rose up, a natural location for Manco's successor to use as Lords of the Vilcabamba.

As befitted a cowboy, Gary had made sure that we had riding horses for the trip. This was a novelty for me, and not a wholly welcome one: I was used to keeping two feet firmly on the ground. While the idea of occasionally mounting up and letting the horse do the work was agreeable, I suspected that the narrow overgrown paths wouldn't allow for much manoeuvring. Gary had a friend along with him on the trip called Joan Harrell, who looked equally fit – she alarmed me by saying that she'd trained for this by running marathons. The most exercise I had taken in recent months was to get the coffee and bring it back to the film cutting-room. It was going to be an unequal contest.

We set off up the hill at a ferocious rate, made harder by the fact that while the trail was initially surprisingly good, Gary suggested we lead rather than ride the horses. My own horse sensed that I was not a natural horseman so I had to pull it up most of the way. Just when I was regretting my lack of fitness, the others started to talk about 'running up the mountain, because walking's *so* boring'. They even had trainers packed for the eventuality. I put my best foot forward and thought of the vodka martini at the end of the day.

After a brisk 3000-foot ascent to a stopping-place for lunch, we saw a short, flat, open section extending ahead of us for a few hundred yards, before the trail re-entered the *selva*. 'This is where we get to ride,' said Gary. We duly rode for five minutes, before dismounting and leading the horses downhill for the rest of the day. Although mollified when Gary and Joan said that I was the first person who had ever managed to keep up with them, dragging a reluctant horse around the Andes in full sun was not my idea of fun. I asked a little petulantly what the point of having the horses was. 'Exercise,' replied Gary laconically.

By now anyway Joan was not feeling well – a combination of altitude and unfamiliar diet had taken its toll. She looked pale and had taken a full hit of 500 milligrams of Ciproxin. (There is a prevalent theory among expeditions in the Andes that it's better to have one huge dose of antibiotics rather than follow a course through to the end – an idea which runs satisfyingly against all medical orthodoxy.)

The diet was getting to us all. Gary was so flatulent that he could have been heard on the other side of the valley. 'Sorry about that,' he apologised. I couldn't resist. 'Don't worry, Gary. If you hadn't said anything, we'd have thought it was one of the mules.'

Below us down a ridge was the camp-site and our jumping-off point for the exploration proper. We were above the cloud-line and had a spectacular view of the Pumasillo mountain range rising up ahead. Mt Pumasillo has a curious characteristic: despite being 20,000 feet high, it is so shielded by a host of lesser mountains as to be completely invisible to the surrounding valleys and villages. Only when some distance away does it reveal itself: it was not even accurately put on the map until 1956.

Our cook's name was Aurelio (what with our chief guide Juvenal, we seemed to be in the middle of some classicists' convention) and he had gone ahead to prepare a *dieta de pollo*, steaming chicken broth with a large hunk of bird in the middle. Aurelio, like most camp cooks, had a few quirks (in his case cooking delicious food hours before it was needed, so that it had grown cold by the time we ate), but he was a dab hand with the machete, whether for cutting up chickens or undergrowth. On a memorable later occasion he slaughtered a sheep he'd brought with us over the mountains. After hanging it for a day in a nearby tree, he roasted the carcass in hot stones and *ichu* grass for the Andean dish known as *pachamanga*.

I sat up late with Gary and Joan, talking about previous expeditions. Gary had enormous energy for archaeological exploration and an instinct for finding the spoors of long-forgotten Inca roads and buildings that came from years of hunting them down. He also brought an immense range of knowledge to his exploring, from geology to obscure forms of cattle disease, fuelled by an obsessive drive that had kept him coming back again long after most men would have hung up their boots. 'The thing is, guys like us are all a little off-centre,' he told me. 'Explorers have to be. Otherwise we just wouldn't do it.'

That night I tried to keep quiet about the fact that I had a self-inflating sleeping-mat (sleeping on the ground had been fine twenty years before, but now I needed a little comfort) and after a couple more of Gary's vodka martinis I sank into a strange dream that was a badly shot melange of cinematic clichés: for some reason, I met Tobias Schneebaum at the airport, who showed me a photo of himself years earlier, alone in the jungle. 'Naturally it's in black and white,' he said in his New York drawl. Then I was on the plane without a ticket, knowing that I had no ticket and waiting to be discovered. In a hammy moment, my dream-vision pulled focus past the approaching stewardess, who looked Hitchcockian, blonde and reproving, to an envelope with my name on it tucked into the bulkhead beyond. Inside, I felt suddenly sure, was my ticket. I woke up just as the plane started to spiral down towards the jungle.

Mist swirled around the tents. The cloud had risen around us during the night. Even though we had Juvenal and José Cobos with us, who had worked with those few explorers who had come here before, it was tricky finding the way. To help us there were some sections of Inca stone-laid path and an unusual amount of *miradores*, stone platforms built out from the contouring path from which (on a clear day at least) one could view the valley. These were good signs of an Inca presence, but nothing prepared us for what lay ahead.

As we came through two *miradores* flanking the path on a shoulder, the path widened dramatically and there were traces of an Inca bridge crossing a stream. We looked up. The wind was blowing the mist and in one clear gap we saw a glimpse of what was unmistakably Inca Wasi high above us, a single dramatically gabled building right on the ridge with (just as at Machu Picchu) a summit rearing up behind it. Then the mist closed in again.

I remembered the words of Stuart White: 'The site has no particular strategic advantage but it is awesome for the size of the mountain at its back and the depth of the valley falling away below it.'

Stuart White was the first explorer to have seen Inca Wasi before he wrote about it. Others, such as Victor von Hagen, had relied on reports and this had led to their making substantial errors (von Hagen had even claimed it might be the lost city of Old Vilcabamba, a wild guess from a man who hadn't been there). Nor had the archaeologists been much better: White noted sharply in his subsequent report that while two prominent Peruvian archaeologists, Victor Angles Vargas and Edmundo Guillén Guillén, had discussed Inca Wasi (Vargas hypothesising that it must have been a communications post), 'unfortunately neither of these investigators have actually reached the site'. White had written his report as recently as 1983. I was continually surprised at how young such real knowledge about the Incas was.

One dramatic feature about Inca Wasi is its elevation. It stood at 13,000 feet. By way of comparison, Machu Picchu, which most visitors feel to be up in the clouds, is at a mere 8000 feet.

White had made a convincing case for this being the site of the oracle that the Emperor Sayri Tupac, Manco's son, was known to have consulted in 1557, before leaving the Vilcabamba. By then, the Inca guerrillas had been holed up in the province for twenty years. After Manco's death, Sayri – made of less stern stuff than his father – began to find the continuing rigours of existence in the highlands not to his taste. He finally succumbed to Spanish blandishments and the offer of a comfortable existence back in Cuzco (with lands, a title and protection) – but not before going with all his advisers to consult this oracle on a high mountain near Vitcos.

We began the climb up to it along an extraordinarily well-built path, which showed Inca Wasi to have been a destination of some ceremonial importance: it was a finely laid Inca causeway some ten feet wide in places, which negotiated the marshy side-valley before entering a tangle of trees that over the centuries had uprooted some of the thick stone blocks. The forest was so overgrown that I needed my machete to hack a way through. At times the road faded, but then emerged clearly again, cut into the side of the slope and contouring around, with views of the small side-valley below. As we got higher, the vegetation became gradually more stunted, shrouded in mosses, lichens and epiphytes.

I thought of Sayri Tupac being carried up here on his litter to consult the oracle, with the sound of his trumpets filling the valley and the priests and attendants ahead of him. The writer of the contemporary *Relación Francesca* had witnessed just such a procession: 'There were in front of him [the Inca] many Indians who cleared the road in spite of the fact that it was rather clean and there was nothing to pick up.' The Incas would have fasted all that day, and by tradition no fires could be lit along the way for warmth. By the time the stone path climbed above the tree-line, they would have been bitterly cold. Even with several layers of polar fleeces and a thermos of coca tea, I was still shivering.

I climbed the last stairway alone, as Gary and Joan had stayed below for a while to look at a small site on the approaches. The stairway mounted in a sharp and slightly uncharacteristic zig-zag, perhaps determined by the unusually steep slopes. As I came up the final rise, the building was in front of me, a terrace with nine trapezoidal niches rising up to a two-storeyed building, steeply gabled, positioned on a knife-edged ridge that spread the cloud to either side.

It was remarkable for being so well preserved, partly because at this altitude it was above the tree-line; trees can be more destructive to old Inca stone than erosion or even the attentions of *huaqueros*, the treasure-hunters. The local granite stonework had probably been originally covered with a red plaster and there were still residues of it in some of the niches. With its two storeys and high gables, it reminded me of the great buildings at Choquequirao, and like Choquequirao it had stone eye-bonders set into the wall. These curious and finely worked rings of stone had exercised the imaginations of many investigators in the past. The Comte de Sartiges, the early French traveller to Choquequirao, had wondered fancifully if they were used to tether pumas – although the more likely and mundane use may have been to secure hanging doors and textiles.

The American explorer Vincent Lee had described this as being 'one of the most elaborate, best preserved examples of Inca architecture in existence'. But as fine as the building was, it was what you could see from it that made for a memorable experience. As the mists cleared again, I witnessed a remarkable phenomenon. On the other face of the valley was a monumental rock, which had a striking white spot on its summit. From Inca Wasi, this spot was perfectly reflected in the lake directly below, with an odd ghostly effect of white on water. 'Jesus,' whispered Gary softly as he joined me. It seemed as if the building was placed to be precisely on the sight-line for this reflection – and we later saw that Inca stonework had been used to dam the lake below, thereby creating the effect artificially. If you moved just a few feet away from the centre of the terrace the reflection was lost.

The building of Inca Wasi had a clear spiritual axis: to one side lay the valley of Vitcos and the Inca's temporal domain; to the other, in this hidden valley, lay what must have been the oracle, for the striking reflection in the waters of the lake cried out for divination.

The Inca captains were in great difficulties as to whether Sayri Tupac should depart from the Vilcabamba. They held many meetings and conferences on the matter until the day of Our Lady in September 1557, when all agreed to make sacrifices according to their custom and to ask for a response from the Sun, the Earth and the other *huacas* that they had. And so, on the morning of that day, having ordered that all should fast and that no fire should be lit, all the captains climbed a high mountain and the Inca went with them, with his trumpets, taking with him and in front of him the priests, who are greatly respected and strictly obeyed. The priests then asked the Sun, the Earth and the *huacas* to declare if the departure would turn out well. When that was done and the omens had been read, the priests said that they had received from the Sun, the Earth and the *huacas* the reply that the departure would be successful and fortunate. All their questions had been answered with 'yes', in contrast to the requests that they had made at other times, when other governors had tried to arrange a departure.

(Diego Fernández, *Historia del Perú*, 1571)

So Sayri Tupac left Vilcabamba and was rapturously received by the Spanish. As it turned out, the oracle was wrong, at least for Sayri personally. After his conversion to Christianity, he was allowed to live on the old royal estates of his grandfather Huayna Capac, at Yucay in the Sacred Valley, which contained many contemplative lakes of the sort we had seen below Inca Wasi. However, the estates had been severely reduced by both Spanish colonists and the predations of a local Cañari chieftain called Francisco Chilche (originally moved there under the Incas' *mitamayo* policy) who, like most of his tribe, hated the Incas with a vengeance – a vengeance which in his case he may have taken personally, as when Sayri Tupac died suddenly three years after his surrender, Chilche was arrested on suspicion of poisoning.

It must have been a miserable last few years for the displaced Inca – walking in the ravaged remains of what were once great pleasure gardens, humiliated by the meanest conquistador who chose to insult him and surrounded by former subject-races who were naturally hostile. Even surveying his gardens in the fertile Yucay valley can have given him little enjoyment. The exotic fruits and plants his ancestors had grown there – the cucurbitae, the coca, the sweet potatoes, the peanuts – were once imperial symbols of Inca victory over the far-flung provinces where such rare produce originated. Now they would have been reminders of all that they had lost.

Yet for the Inca State (and the increasingly powerful priesthood who had interpreted the oracle for Sayri Tupac), the decision that he should leave may have been the right one. It completely wrong-footed the enemy. When Sayri left the Vilcabamba and his subjects, he also – unbeknown to the Spanish – left behind the *borla*, the 'royal fringe' and insignia of the Emperor which was worn around the head: Sayri told the Spanish he wasn't wearing it because he didn't want to offend them by claiming imperial jurisdiction, a ruse the legalistic Spanish accepted hook, line and sinker. The Spanish naturally assumed that they now had control of the Inca and therefore of any further rebellion. It was some time before they realised that his much tougher brother Titu Cusi (who had narrowly escaped being assassinated with his father Manco when he was just a boy) was not only wearing the *borla* in his place, but firmly intended to maintain the independent rump-state of the Vilcabamba.

With Sayri's premature death in 1560, Titu Cusi came out into the open as the new and extremely competent Emperor. Unlike Sayri, he showed no signs of weakening towards the Spanish, although he was very capable of pretending to accede to their demands whenever it suited him. The Spanish still had a problem in Vilcabamba, and it was to be a further ten years before they regained enough political momentum and Viceroy Toledo sent his final expedition to try to capture Titu's own successor, Tupac Amaru. On the expedition, heading his troop of Cañari Indians, was that same Francisco Chilche who had been accused of murdering Sayri Tupac.

By now it was getting late and we stumbled down in the gloom. In the dark, the trees that had ripped up the old Inca causeway took on a malevolent Arthur Rackham aspect. Lower down we came to an area where fire had cleared away the thick shrub, always a boon to the explorer if not to the ecology: Gary spotted some Inca stonework off to one side. 'It's mine, it's mine,' he shouted excitedly as we rushed over to examine the perfectly formed stone bath built up over the stream bed. Below, by a path we had not previously taken, there was more − a small complex of waterways and buildings near a waterfall and a large chunk of phosphorescently white granite, at about 11,000 feet. The baths here had a beautifully channelled water system, with overflows and complex drainage. It was clear that Inca Wasi was only the very apex of a whole set of buildings and that many of those were in the 'pleasure building' category I was familiar with from Machu Picchu and Choquequirao. Had Manco (and perhaps later his various sons) built this site up not only as an oracle but as a *moya*, 'a place of leisure' for his own personal retreat in the manner that his great antecedents had done in more liberated days? Even in exile (perhaps particularly in exile), the Inca would have wanted to continue the lifestyle to which an Emperor was accustomed.

We passed a small pile of roofing-pegs by the lake that had been prepared for insertion but never used. There were abandoned hammer-stones nearby. These seemed to testify to the mournful idea that work on the complex was abandoned before it could be completed, just as at Ollantaytambo and Choquequirao.

It was getting dark and we still had some distance to travel, but with the euphoria of these findings it was difficult to drag ourselves away. As we crashed down through the jungle following a trail that José Cobos had cut for us, trying not to trip over roots in the approaching gloom, we saw building after building loom up out of the dense greenery. 'This is *exciting*,' said Gary. 'It's like Chachapoyas. These are ruins all around us.' It would take a later expedition (and some serious clearing) to see what was there.

It was another few days before we returned to the valley and the road-head. We had camped by a lake called Llana Cocha (the Dark Lake), with

Andean gulls and black loons flying overhead, near some simple pre-Inca circular stone foundations. The field nearby had been freshly hand-ploughed, almost like archaeological test-trenches (if a little less carefully than archaeologists themselves would have liked) and shards of crude, simple pottery lay everywhere.

On the last day, Gary and Joan decided they were going to 'run off the mountain' and were wearing little running shorts and extremely technical trainers to do so. 'We'll wait for you and Aurelio at the bottom.' Originally this had not seemed such a bad idea – Aurelio was terrific company and had some good Quechuan jokes if we were to make up the slower rear party – but as the two runners set off, something in me bucked at the thought of being last, perhaps spurred by Aurelio's gentle jibe about being the tortoise to Gary's hare. I took off down the mountain myself and, despite heavy boots and a full pack (and laughing too hard), found I could not only keep up with Gary and Joan but easily outdistance the Americans – mainly by the technique of using boots to scrunch down the scree while they jogged more genteelly on the path itself. With some elation, if breathlessly, I found myself the first to run across the bridge at Yupanqa, 3000 feet below.

It is an image that is anyway a staple of Andean exploration: emerging out of the *selva* at midday after a long trip – the wide brown streets, with brown houses, everything brown and stark from the overhead sun – the gringo lumbering down the main street, silhouetted with his backpack, walking loose, already punch-drunk from his discoveries before he's even had a beer. It felt delirious and wonderful.

*

Back at Huancacalle, it was time to revisit the White Rock itself. The walk from the village up towards Chuquipalta was as lovely as ever. Opposite the Coboses' house were little pools for breeding trout, and the river came down with a freshness that sang out against the silvery grey of the eucalyptus groves. As I climbed, I could look back on the village – it seemed virtually unchanged after almost twenty years. Indeed, the whole valley was still remarkably unspoilt and must have looked much the same to the Incas. The one exception to this, the groves of eucalyptus trees (a later import brought over from Australia for their resilience and good timber), now looked as natural to the valley as chestnuts in an English landscape.

A small boy came down the hill with his sister and some friends, on their way to the village school. They asked if I had any money or biros. I didn't, but I had a bright blue glass button in my pocket, a good luck charm. I squatted down with the kids on the ground, took the button out and told them that it was *mágico* and that if one of them closed his eyes and made a wish, it would come true. The kids' eyes opened wide and I told the boy to shut his tight as he touched the button. He gripped it hard. Then I whispered to him close, so that none of the others could hear, '*Lo que quieres más en el mundo, vas a conseguir*' ('Listen, whatever you want most in life, you can achieve'). Then they went on their way.

I crossed over the meadows. An electric-green *rocotillo* snake threaded its way elegantly across the grass. The White Rock still loomed up like a battleship out of the meadow, with its extraordinary carvings and coursed waterway leading to an Inca fountain nearby. It seemed as little visited as ever. I had borrowed the key from the curator down in the village, whose log-book showed only a handful of travellers coming through. The key was for a gate in the cursory fence that had been put up around the rock to keep the cattle out (most of them seemed to be inside the fence anyway), but the site itself was exactly as I had remembered it.

If there had been any changes, it was in the sensibility with which I now looked at it. Twenty years before there had been a reluctance to consider such stonework aesthetically. Archaeologists were still so concerned with function (which was often difficult to ascribe to the carved free-standing stones of the Incas) that the accomplished sculptural quality of the work had received hardly more than a passing nod. The feeling that these carved stones were exclusively religious in purpose had also side-tracked any aesthetic assessment. While Western critics could quite happily ignore the religious connotations of a Renaissance Maestà when discussing an Italian artist, they seemed to be inhibited by the far less specific religious con- notations of pre-Columbian work.

Perhaps because I was trying to secularise what had always seemed to me an excessive tendency to attribute spiritual values to every Inca monument, I found it easier to see the stones for what they were: quite extraordinary sculptures. And of all the many examples I had seen, the White Rock was still the most extraordinary of them all, each side a developed yet unexpected part of the whole. On one side a glissade of rock, with a water channel carved into it; on another, a symmetrical descent of huge sloping steps cut into the granite; and on the highest wall, the series of asymmetric bosses projecting spectacularly from the sheer granite. By any standards it had to rank as one of the world's finest sculptures, even if it had been parked in some white-walled gallery. Here, in a small side-valley of the Vilcabamba, with the flow of surrounding mountains behind, it was luminous. The original whiteness of the stone had long since turned to dark grey with the growth of lichen, but the shape shone through.

Nor was the White Rock alone. Scattered over the meadows for some way below, in amongst the arum lilies and the grazing cattle, were many other carved stones in what was a veritable sculpture park. One, a carved chair, was similar to a Henry Moore: others followed the usual tactful Inca convention of allowing the stone still to speak for itself, while adorning and shaping edges. In any other part of the world UNESCO would have declared it a world heritage site. Yet in the days I spent there, the only visitors were two English girls who surveyed the site from on top of the rock like conquerors and departed within five minutes.

However, the feeling that these stones had validity as sculptures was slowly spreading. An Argentinian artist called César Paternosto had written a book, *The Stone and the Thread: Andean Roots of Abstract Art*, challenging the archaeologists' hegemony over the carved stones, and trying to reclaim them as art. Although he hadn't written about this particular site, César had some interesting comments on the strange bosses or protuberances the Incas often used, which had made such a strong impression on me the first time I had come to the White Rock.

Archaeologists in the past had performed intellectual contortions to try to explain why these bosses protruded so dramatically from otherwise flat walls of carefully hewn granite. Were they unfinished work, or props to lean the stones up with before they were dropped into place? Or were they used for some unspecified religious purpose (as when they occurred at religious sites like the Coricancha, the Sun Temple, in Cuzco, or at Ollantaytambo), such as to hang sacred weavings? I had seen similar curious bosses at Machu Picchu, on the so-called 'House of the Princess'. Some commentators had speculated that they might be weathered corbels supporting some form of shutter. To me they seemed purely decorative, and decorative in a flamboyant way. The bosses called attention to the sheer virtuosity of the granite carving which could leave such vivid protuberances coming back out from the rock, like faces through a sheet.

They were sublime stone-working which served to demonstrate a supreme mastery of the material – to leave such bosses in place is to work completely against the grain of the stone. César suggested another parallel idea. Much has always been made of the fact that the Incas had no formal system of writing, but relied on a system of knotted cords, the *quipu*, to pass on information. The *quipu* was an old Andean tradition which the Incas had inherited from the Huari. Knotted cords in different colours were hung from a central cord, and these knots could then be 'read' by skilled interpreters, the *quipucamayos*. (César had quoted the Taoist master Chuang Tzu, who said that 'keeping records on knots was the sign of a happier, earlier age'.)

The conquistadors had frequently lamented this system (and evidenced their own system of writing as one of the benefits that a more advanced society could bring). It is only recently that scholars have shown the *quipu* to be a more inventive and flexible means of recording information than a mere mnemonic device to inventory the Inca holdings. It may, for instance, also have been used as an aid for story-telling, a historical prompt.

César had compared the logic of the *quipu* system with its random system of knots, which remain indecipherable today, to the similarly indecipherable protuberances, or stone knots as he described them, across the face of the carved stone. It was an exciting idea. Rather than functional work whose function we did not understand, the bosses could be considered as being expressive and significant, writing with stone.

It was hardly surprising that the conquistadors themselves had failed to recognise the stones as sculptures, although the more acute writers of the time, like Cieza de Léon, had at least commented on their unusual nature. What was more peculiar was that the twentieth century had equally failed to do so. Henry Moore and his modernist contemporaries had fallen on the more figurative art of the Aztecs in Mexico with relish. (The figure of the *chac-mool*, the upturned body on which sacrificial offerings were placed, managed to combine solidity with unease in a way completely at one with their own sensibility.) Yet the more abstract work of the Incas had been ignored, despite the fact that they had a functionalist's love of simple structural surfaces that would not have been out of place in the Bauhaus.

We would desperately like the Incas to have been different from us, to be part of that Other we crave and feel we have lost. But if anything, the Incas are often remarkable for having anticipated – in their mountain aesthetic, in their sculptural aesthetic – twentieth-century sensibility.

The Incas were one of the last cultures that had grown autonomously to an advanced level before being discovered by Europeans. In our enclosed monoculture, they fulfil a need for the unfathomable and incomprehensible. However, in our desire to discover their difference, we are blinded to those elements we may have in common with them, particularly as any Enlightenment ideals about the universality of mankind have been eroded by our own contemporary belief in the primacy of cultural difference.

Sitting on the perfectly weighted steps of the rock itself, I remembered my feelings of mortality and fear of death when I'd first come here. In a curious way that had now passed from me. Something, I am not sure what, had lifted off me in the intervening years, some anxiety. It felt a place of deep spiritual rest.

There were some women gathering firewood near the White Rock. It turned out that, like just about everybody else in the village, they were related to the Coboses, and I talked to them about my forthcoming trip down into the jungle, to the last city of the Incas, Old Vilcabamba, near the modern settlement of Espíritu Pampa. 'You don't want to go down into the jungle, Señor,' one exclaimed. 'They have enormous *serpientes* down there.' She held up a hefty forearm and wiggled her leg, to the amusement of her friends. 'Long as my arm and thick as my thigh!'

I laughed with them, if a little hollowly. But no amount of stories about snakes were going to stop me – I'd failed twenty years before to get to Old Vilcabamba and this time I was going to get there.

THE LAST CITY OF
THE INCAS

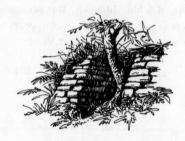

BEFORE MY RESOLUTION FAILED ME, I planned to set off for Espíritu Pampa the next day, taking Rónal Cobos with me: at a mere eighteen, Rónal was the latest in the Cobos dynasty of guides. He came highly vouched for by his uncles Juvenal and Benjamín and was the son of José Cobos, who had cut a way for Gary and me through the wilder bits of Puncuyoc. Rónal had been on that same trip and we had got on well, not least because we had both been thrown by the same horse, much to Gary's amusement. (I later managed to crack a rib in a fall. Andean horses are sure-footed but stubborn as mules – indeed, sometimes are mules – and they like to assert themselves occasionally.)

Any academic wanting to illustrate the principle of 'verticality' in the Andes would have been delighted by the Cobos family, who farmed here in Huancacalle at around 10,000 feet and also grew tropical fruits in Espíritu Pampa, way down below on the edges of the jungle. As a result, Rónal knew our route well, as they were forever bringing produce up from their jungle small-holdings.

To my surprise and delight, Adrian Gallop arrived to accompany me on the trip. He was a good friend of a good friend and I had only met him the once in England, but had immediately taken to him as having precisely the *mentalidad latina* I valued: in a hopeful way I had suggested we might link up for this trip. But that had been months ago, and aside from a few e-mail messages I had not been able to get in contact since. For months he had been travelling in Peru on his own.

I was pleased to see him. Half-Peruvian, tall, amiable and an experienced trekker, Adrian was the perfect travelling companion. He also had the foresight to bring some basic supplies from Cuzco for the trip, which was more than I had, including enough sugar to keep even a 'four spoonfuls a cup' muleteer happy.

This was lucky, as while Gary had assured me I could get any supplies I wanted in Huancacalle, in practice there was nothing at all. We couldn't even get the Andean staple of *qucker* (Quaker Oats). Señora Cobos took pity on us and slaughtered a turkey, which gave us all the cold meat we needed. We also managed to find chillies, black pepper and garlic which, together with Adrian's food, would make bearable an endless succession of tomatoes, rice and tuna-fish.

I enviously remembered Hiram Bingham's account of how he had equipped his teams as if for an Edwardian picnic. Each food box had contained sliced bacon, tinned corned beef, roast beef, chicken, crushed oats, milk, cheese, salmon, coffee, sausages and kippers.

He had commented that 'many people seem to think it is one of the duties of an explorer to rough it and trust to luck for his food. I had found on earlier expeditions that the result of being obliged to subsist on irregular and haphazard rations was most unsatisfactory ... Some of the younger men on our parties sometimes feel that their reputation as explorers is likely to be damaged if it was known that strawberry jam, sweet chocolate, cheese and pickles are frequently found on their bill of fare!' (I'd found this in an early report of the expedition that he had written in 1916. He seems to have suppressed such details in later books, like *Lost City of the Incas* of 1948, when he himself was more concerned about his reputation as a tough explorer.)

Rónal spent a long time packing the food, particularly the eggs, in an elaborate arrangement of cardboard and string, helped by Benito, our lone muleteer. Then they turned to me in distress. 'Señor, we have the rice, the eggs, the tomatoes, but where are the *prenglees*?' I had never heard of '*prenglees*' and puzzled on what essential basic supplies I could possibly have forgotten, until Rónal went off and returned with five large cartons of Pringles crisps.

This was going to be a lean team, with just the two mules and a horse in case anyone got sick and we needed to get them back out. I tried unsuccessfully to argue for at least a minimal supply of beer (surely if we had Pringles we needed beer), but got vetoed by Benito on the grounds that it would be too heavy for his mules – and you can never argue with muleteers about how large a load his animals can or can't take.

I was victorious on one issue, though. Rónal didn't own or want to take a machete (on the grounds, I later discovered, that he'd rather be carrying his radio). Unfairly, I mentioned the matter to his uncle Benjamín, who still had the black piercing eyes Gene Savoy had commented on thirty-five years before when he had guided Savoy down to Espíritu Pampa. Don Benjamín was taking a familial pride in outfitting our little expedition. 'Is it really wise,' I asked, trying to look suitably serious, as if I was a bank-manager enquiring after a reckless loan, 'for us not to have a machete with us?'

A worried Benjamín went off to confer with Rónal, and Rónal shortly emerged with a red-handled machete that looked old enough for Benjamín to have used with Savoy back in the sixties – and which proved invaluable later, as well as a soothing implement for Rónal to swing at passing vegetation with whenever he got bored on the long journey. Unfortunately, he still found a way of carrying a radio strapped to his shoulder.

The Cobos house was both hostel and local store, and I couldn't help noticing a charming note which had been sent by one of their relatives from an outlying farmstead. It read like a Beatrix Potter letter: '*Hermano Benjamín, te suplico enviarme dos leche de magnesia purgantes por la digestión, urgentemente*' ('Brother Benjamín, would you be so good as to send me two tins of milk of magnesia urgently, for my digestion').

The family waved us goodbye as we left in the early dawn, climbing up from the back of Huancacalle towards the pass of Ccolpo Cosa which lay high above us. After a few hours we came to the Spanish colonial silver-mining town of San Francisco de la Vitoria de Vilcabamba, often called *Vilcabamba la Nueva* ('Vilcabamba the New'), to distinguish it from our final destination, Old Vilcabamba, which the Incas had built in the jungles below.

New Vilcabamba was a soulless place. It felt like one of those towns where Clint Eastwood is about to ride in and chide the local inhabitants for some long-concealed crime. At an altitude of over 11,000 feet and in an exposed position, the church had been ravaged by wind and storms. At some stage in what must have been endless rebuilding, the original entrance chapel had got detached from the main body of the church and now stood as a ruined hulk in front of the new entrance.

We hitched the mules and the horse up to a post and went into the one grocery store, recognisable only from the tin placard tucked into the window. A sour-faced Señora sold me a *refresco* as if her teeth were being drawn.

The Spanish had tried to settle this part of the world after their final destruction of the Incas, but it had never worked. It was too high and remote to grow coca or to attract Spanish settlers when there were easier pickings elsewhere – particularly as they were always worried, rightly or wrongly, that the high altitude might affect their sperm count, and nothing was more off-putting for a Spaniard than any risk to his fertility. The leader of the expedition sent to capture Tupac Amaru, Hurtado de Arbieto, later became governor of the province and quickly exhausted the land with the usual mixture of rapacity and neglect.

The only thing that could bring the settlers in was mining. During the period when Manco and his sons had ruled the Vilcabamba, they had tried strenuously to prevent any silver mines being opened, for they knew that the lure of silver deposits would precipitate a Spanish invasion. However, in 1586, many years after the fall of Vilcabamba, the widow of Sayri Tupac revealed to the then Viceroy the existence of silver mines high up on the pass above us. This town of San Francisco de la Vitoria de Vilcabamba had been built expressly to service these mines, which explained its inhospitable, exposed setting.

Indeed, for many years the only travellers to this part of the world were those brought by the lure of finding veins of silver. In 1710, one of these, a mineral prospector called Juan Arias Diaz Topete, travelled right into the interior of the Vilcabamba. He left a fascinating letter behind describing his journey, a document which was only recently discovered. In it, Diaz Topete listed the four principal Inca sites he had come across as he combed the hills. Three of these sites correspond remarkably accurately to what are now called Choquequirao, Vitcos and Old Vilcabamba, although he gives some of them different names, and it was not until this century that they were again found, by explorers unaware of Diaz Topete's letter. Tantalisingly, the fourth site he describes, apparently equally large, has yet to be rediscovered: Diaz Topete described it as 'Chuquitira, which means "Gold poured out"'.

By the end of the eighteenth century, the silver deposits were almost completely exhausted and even the prospectors stopped coming. The area reverted to a backwater and New Vilcabamba, intended to be a symbol of Spanish conquest, became a ghost-town. We rode out of it with some relief and headed up on to the pass.

Tupac Amaru and his followers would have come up here at considerable speed. He knew that if he kept ahead of the Spanish and used defensive positions down the long Pampaconas valley on the other side of the pass, there was a good chance of either defeating the enemy or at least disappearing into the jungle, just as his father Manco had done a generation before.

Because Tupac Amaru was the very last of the Inca Emperors, he has been subject to even more over-romanticisation than the others. He is often described as a teenage youth who was thrust into the limelight by the premature death of his brothers. But in truth he was at least twenty-seven at the time of his accession, ten years older than his father Manco when he had become Emperor, and had served a long apprenticeship in the religious centres of Vilcabamba: Gary Ziegler had hypothesised that he might have been brought up at Choquequirao, easily accessible from Vitcos by a route over the Choquetecarpa pass (a route I later took with Gary): this was based partly on the assertion that while Titu Cusi was alive and Emperor, he had deputised his brother and the priests to look after the body of their dead father Manco, and Choquequirao would fit the bill as a religious retreat in which to do so far better than any other. It is a dangerously seductive idea and one which some of the romantic nineteenth-century travellers to the area, like Angrand, had also liked to picture – the young last Emperor growing up in a lost city which the Spanish never discovered – but it is certainly possible.

Wherever his upbringing, one can imagine Tupac as a tough leader, brought up by priests on the traditions of his ancestors and indisposed to pander to Spanish demands – it was the precipitate actions of his military commanders in killing a Spanish envoy and an Augustinian friar which had brought on this final assault by the Spanish. Around him he had a group of Inca captains battle-hardened by years of guerrilla activity.

As I headed up to the pass at 12,500 feet, I was again impressed by the determination of the Spanish. If I had pursued my enemy this far, I would not have felt like following him over yet another tough pass and down into the sodden jungle, with my local troops warning me that there were poisoned arrows and disease ahead. By now the more feckless of the motley army that had set off from Cuzco would have fallen away and returned home, leaving a core of the professional soldiers, who saw this as a way of gaining both a reputation and a coat of arms to their name.

This was one of the few stretches where riding was both feasible and enjoyable, and Adrian and I took it in turns to mount the white horse. Apart from the (immediately suppressed) illusion of being a conquistador oneself, riding allowed one to look around and ahead more than when trudging away on foot, and coming over the pass was even more exhilarating than usual as we left the Vilcabamba massif behind and crossed the watershed towards the Amazon.

An unexpectedly finished stretch of Inca stairway gave us the beginnings of a grand descent down towards the jungle. With the sun behind us, the distant falling green hills were bathed in a soft light that seemed strangely benign, despite the rain clouds that were sweeping up towards us. Hiram Bingham had described the view when he first came over this pass as 'a great wilderness of deep green valleys and forest-clad slopes'.

Below us we could see lonely thatched small-holdings dotted over the mountainside. There were farmers ploughing by hand, which seemed an archaic throwback (even in the remotest Himalayas, I had seen the

Bhutanese use oxen). A school of thought held that hand-ploughing was in fact better than the Mediterranean style of drawing by beasts of burden, as it dug less deeply into the top-soil.

The large amount of arable land up here reminded me of one of Peru's most peculiar and perverse paradoxes – that the country has significantly greater areas of farmland at very high altitudes than it does at the more normal lower ones, but only certain subsistence crops – like potatoes or quinoa – can be grown there.

One of our pack-mules began having problems. We had brought a tiny Primus stove with us to supplement the firewood if it started to rain (which it already had), and the noise of liquid rolling around inside the stove so alarmed the mule that he was continually bolting and shying. A mule of Benito's had once broken a leg in the boggy ground near the top of the pass, and so Benito was being particularly careful about this one. (Bingham had also experienced problems here with pack-animals – one had wandered off in search of some particularly 'succulent grasses' and got 'thoroughly mired in the bog'.)

We came down to the little settlement of Pampaconas in a drizzle. The Primus was by now such a problem that we simply abandoned it and camped near a hut by the river, so that we could cook on the owners' stove under cover.

The clouds started to lift and there was a wonderful sight of flocks of parrots wheeling in and out of the mist, almost disappearing completely into the haze and the forest before wheeling back again, shrieking as they came. Patches of mist blew towards us over the grass and there was a white horse wandering by the river. It felt wild and lost and Celtic. Around us was the sort of grey drizzle on moorland with light breaking through that I associated with the Scottish Highlands.

'Fucking parrots,' said a voice beside me. Leonidas Tapia, the owner of the hut, gazed at them with some irritation. 'They eat the maize, the bastards.' He grimaced, not entirely because of the birds. It seemed he had some sort of *cólico*, a stomach pain that wouldn't go away. I went through his symptoms carefully, resisting the temptation to give antibiotics, despite his requests. There were travellers who passed through the hills dishing them out like sweets, unaware that the people of the hills were not used to such strong medicine. In my role as lay pharmacist, I kept to simple paracetamol for pain relief and a careful look at diet (I discovered that Leonidas was drinking nothing but black coffee, which can't have done his stomach pains much good). But he was grateful for the help and the *pastillas*, the pills.

We talked in the awning of his house, as Rónal brewed up coca tea and Adrian smoked roll-ups. Leonidas could remember when '*El Saboyo*', as he called Gene Savoy, had come through in the sixties. The thing that had most struck him was that Savoy spoke almost no Spanish and had to work through an interpreter. '*No encontró nada sin un nativo*, he never found anything without a local guide,' he added, as true for Savoy as any explorer. There had been a local uproar when a *denuncio*, an indictment, was broadcast over the radio, claiming that Savoy was a *huaquero*, a treasure-hunter, and was absconding with forty mule-loads of gold from the valley.

'He never paid anyone properly either,' grumbled Leonidas, gazing into the smoking embers of the fire. 'Gave us all half-pay. Still, *El Saboyo* ... he was really quite something. Quite a man.'

*

Gene Savoy was a deeply controversial figure. Nicholas Asheshov had told me much about him back in Ollantaytambo: 'The extraordinary thing about Gene is that he manages to produce the real thing while being such a complete con-artist as well!'

I had been intrigued to find out more from Nick. Savoy, like the unfortunate Robert Nichols who had died looking for Paititi, had also worked for Asheshov as a stringer on the *Lima Times* when he first came down from the States ('a hack about town', as Asheshov put it). Somehow he had managed to get enough finance together to mount the first of his expeditions – some said from marrying a rich Peruvian woman, others that he had set up a travel agency to find lost cities and sold tickets to those who wanted to accompany him. Asheshov's explanation had been much simpler: 'He was just a brilliant bull-shitter.'

Whatever the means, the result was spectacular – the discovery of Old Vilcabamba at Espíritu Pampa in 1964, the biggest discovery since Hiram Bingham's day, indeed a discovery that built directly on Bingham's own work. For, ironically, Bingham had found a small Inca settlement in almost precisely the same place fifty years earlier and had dismissed it as being too insubstantial to be the lost city of Old Vilcabamba that he was searching for – and so he had not looked any further.

If ever there was an example of how explorers can never overcome their own preconceptions, this was it. The site Bingham found didn't fit with his romantic vision of what such a lost city should look like. Machu Picchu, on the other hand, could have been designed by a Hollywood art director, albeit one with exceptional talent. So Bingham twisted himself into intellectual contortions to try to prove, against all the evidence, that Machu Picchu itself must have been Old Vilcabamba, the 'Last City of the Incas', simply because it looked better.

Savoy pressed further into the surrounding jungle beyond Bingham's initial discovery and found out quite how extensive the site really was. On the evidence of his discoveries, John Hemming had then shown with a scholarly study of all available source material that Savoy was right and Bingham wrong: the great lost city of the Incas, the so-called Old Vilcabamba where they retreated in their final days, was not Machu Picchu but the far lower site at Espíritu Pampa, to which we were now descending.

The Peruvian government had not particularly thanked Savoy for his achievement. 'You see, Savoy always looked more like Buffalo Bill than Harrison Ford,' Asheshov had said. 'He didn't naturally inspire confidence in authority, let alone in the archaeologists. And even though he made a lot of play about having checked up old records to find out where he should look for ruins, most of it was just gut instinct. Left to himself, Gene wouldn't get round to reading a paperback, let alone an old manuscript. But he had an uncanny ability to bring home the bacon.'

For Espíritu Pampa was just the first of Savoy's extraordinary finds. He went on to explore further in the Chachapoyas area to the north, the area that Topa Inca had subdued. Here he found first Gran Pajatén in 1965 and then, much later, Gran Vilaya in 1985, two equally remarkable sites. Gran Pajatén was an impressive citadel, while Gran Vilaya was a complex of thousands of buildings which Savoy could claim with some justification as being the capital of the Chachapoyan empire.

'For an ignorant son-of-a-bitch,' Asheshov had said affectionately, 'it was some achievement. And I've told him so to his face.' Asheshov and Savoy had remained friends since their early days together.

Savoy had also inspired a host of followers. 'What you have to remember,' Asheshov had said mischievously, 'is that Gene Savoy is a cult. A real this-man-is-the-centre-of-the-universe cult.'

Savoy had apparently founded a church in Reno, Nevada where he lived. The church was explicitly centred around him and his discoveries. A man who could find so many lost cities in the jungle, went the line, could undoubtedly find true religion as well. He had attracted many followers to the International Community of Christ, as he called the movement. Savoy taught his members that the secret to immortality lay in staring directly at the sun and thereby absorbing God as raw energy. He claimed that this secret had been revealed to him in the jungles of Peru.

Asheshov, like other explorers I talked to, had become a bit obsessive about the number of young female devotees that Savoy's cult had attracted. It was something he mentioned several times during the course of that long night's whisky-fuelled conversation. 'Gene has all these beautiful girls around him, and he's in his seventies now. His current companion, Belinda, who's interested in spiritual values, is a very beautiful, young, very intelligent woman. And then he keeps building these boats ...'

As if being both the most successful Andean explorer since the war and the leader of his own cult was not enough for one man, Savoy had evolved a parallel career as a high-profile yachtsman. His first exploit had been to try to sail reed-boats across Lake Titicaca in the sixties and he had recently set out on another sea-faring adventure around the world, this time in a seventy-foot mahogany catamaran with two carved Mochica dragons as prows. On the stern of the boat were a pair of Cadillac fins. The only surprise was that Savoy had never tried to become a rock-and-roll star, although perhaps he thought that would have been too dull.

'Seventy foot is one hell of a big yacht,' Asheshov had said. 'That's a foot for every year of his life. He just won't stop. At his age he should be restricting his energy output to a weekly visit to the urologist.'

There was a reason for these ocean voyages. Savoy had decided, like Thor Heyerdahl before him (and Heyerdahl had also lived in northern Peru), that the answer to questions of cultural origin lay in possible transoceanic crossings between civilisations and that the only way to really prove this was to do it yourself.

Archaeologists like to tar Savoy with the diffusionist brush (the idea that the advanced ancient cultures of each continent must have influence each other, or at least evolved from some lost meta-culture, Atlantis being the usual contender). Most diffusionist ideas are eccentric and patronising to South Americans, implying that they could not possibly have built pyramids, learnt astronomy or worshipped the sun if somebody else hadn't taught them to do so. Diffusionists try to point out specific similarities (the building of pyramids on both sides of the Atlantic, for instance), but again these were achievements that could have been reached independently given the same criteria: how to achieve impressive, stable buildings of large volume. The enormous appetite for diffusionist theories seems to come from some hunger for a common ancestor. There are currently over 2000 books registered and filed on Atlantis alone.

But Savoy's main point was not about trans-Atlantic crossings – rather, he thought it inconceivable that there had been no connection between the pre-Columbian civilisations of the South, around present-day Peru, and those of Central America such as the Nahuatl (the Aztecs) and the Maya. Archaeologists liked to draw neat containment circles around each of these civilisations, but Savoy felt that there were too many points of similarity for there not to have been some contact, particularly between such highly consumerist civilisations who continually sent merchants on long journeys to acquire prized goods. There is considerable evidence that the Maya and the coastal civilisations of Northern Peru set out on such journeys. Bartholomé Ruiz, Pizarro's pilot, reported large sailing rafts plying the Ecuadorian coast equipped with masts and cotton sails, rigged as effectively as any Spanish ship. Smallpox travelled down from the Caribbean area to Peru long before the Spanish arrived themselves: there must have been a human chain of contact to allow it to do so.

Savoy had once tried to demonstrate the contact between the two areas of civilisation by setting off from the coast of Peru in a historically accurate tortora-reed raft he called *The Feathered Serpent* and heading north towards Mexico. Asheshov had laughed about it. 'Unfortunately Gene ended up doing nothing of the kind, though he may be right anyway about ancient Peruvians and Mexicans being in contact. He raft-wrecked himself in stormy circles up off Panama. His main achievement was not becoming lunch for sharks.'

Asheshov's final words on Savoy had been admiring: 'What a hell of a man. Did you know he has six lawyers working full time just to fight the US tax system?'

Sitting in the hut, I thought of Savoy in earlier days when he had passed through this way, a buccaneering adventurer out to make his first discovery. He was already thirty-five. He'd had a roving, tough life: the first words of his long-out-of-print autobiography, *Antisuyo*, set the tone: 'Men dream of adventure and I am no exception. I cannot remember not wanting to be an explorer. I hated school when I was a boy.'

If Bingham had portrayed himself as an Arthur Conan Doyle hero, then Savoy's model was Hemingway. Like Hemingway, Savoy was a *mythomane* determined to ignore the more banal details of his life story and instead create a heroic curve.

He briskly sketched out the preliminary details of his life – both his first wife and the American company he had built up are lost in a single line. When he went to Peru, it was to re-invent himself after what he perceived as the failure of his earlier self ('the beginning of my re-birth'). In 1962 he moved with a new wife to Yungay, a town in northern Peru's Cordillera Blanca. Tragedy struck. It was an area prone to landslides and a bad one engulfed the town: Savoy and his family survived the earthquake but his young son, Jamil, died in the epidemic that followed.

By now Savoy had fallen under the influence of the Peruvian archaeologist, Julio Tello, who had promoted a site called Chavín de Huántar as the centre of the earliest Peruvian culture then known, that of the Chavín (800–200 BC). What intrigued Savoy about Tello's theories was the idea that the Chavín (and by implication all the later Andean cultures) had their origins in the east, in the jungle. Tello had based this idea on the images of jaguars and serpents he saw carved on a great stela at Chavín. The assumption of most archaeologists, swayed perhaps by the Incas' own creation myths, had always been to assume a mountain origin for both them and their Andean predecessors.

The central driving idea behind all Savoy's exploring in the succeeding years was to show that the jungle was not on the fringes of Peruvian culture but at its very centre. It was what led him later to his obsessive search into the Chachapoyas, which he saw as essentially another jungle culture overlooked by academics more concerned with the mountains (the area of Chachapoyas lies between the two). When he travelled down towards Espíritu Pampa from the Andes it was not, as Bingham had done, with a sense of mild regret at what the Incas might finally have come to – instead he saw Manco Inca as having proudly led his troops down to Old Vilcabamba as a 'symbolic' return to the ancestral homeland. Savoy postulated: 'Was his [Manco's] cry, "back to the place of origin from whence we will re-build and re-conquer"?' Savoy, unlike Bingham, actually wanted to find the 'last city of the Incas' in the jungle.

This superficially attractive idea defies the clear indication that the Incas themselves (if not all their antecedents) had a mountain origin, either from near Titicaca or, more obviously, from around Cuzco itself. It also ignores the obvious. Manco was a leader on the run, with a Spanish army at his heels. He led his men into the Vilcabamba because it was militarily expedient and because he had little choice – after his last stand at Ollantaytambo, there was nowhere else to go. It was not a symbolic return to the Homelands. Indeed, all the available evidence suggests that Manco – and, for that matter, Tupac Amaru a generation later – hated the jungle as much as the Spanish did and regarded it as a retreat of last resort.

The iconic use of feline shapes and serpents by mountain peoples may have been just as much because they were talismans of the unknown and mysterious (a role the jungle has always been able to play) rather than of the familiar and ancestral.

I had rung Savoy from England before coming out and told him I was heading down to Espíritu Pampa. 'Ah yes,' he said, 'you'll feel the sadness there.' As befitted a cult leader, Savoy spoke deliberately and let his words hang in the mid-Atlantic air. I recognised the way he was talking. Savoy, like many of the rock-and-roll stars I had interviewed, was a man surfing on his own myth.

He had never been to Choquequirao (the guerrillas had prevented him from getting there in the 1960s) and I told him of my journey over to the city in the 1980s. I asked why he had kept on exploring (he had just got back from yet another trip to Chachapoyas, after thirty-five years of expeditions there).

'Why explore? ... Some people climb mountains. Why do they climb mountains? ... Because they need to.'

I asked him about the controversy some of his views had caused. 'I'm not a maverick, not a rebel,' he told me a little unconvincingly. But his views on archaeologists were trenchant: 'You've got to be a member of their club, like a golf-club or something ...' He warmed to his theme. 'What's an archaeologist? Someone who puts their head down a hole for forty years – but doesn't have much of an idea of what's outside the hole. They're so specialist they lose the plot. And they presume that anyone who doesn't have a bit of paper stuck on the wall as a diploma can't be intelligent. Look what they've said about us, about people like our wonderful Bingham, about Schliemann who's been criticised by pygmies who wouldn't even reach up to his boots.'

An unfortunate episode in 1984 had doubtless spurred Savoy's antagonism towards archaeologists. In that year, the archaeological department of Colorado University had sent a team to look for sites in the Chachapoyas area.

The press release they issued on their return in early 1985 had newspapers salivating and losing all sense of balance. According to the front page of the *Washington Post*, 'One of the fabled "lost cities" of the Andes has been found ... the region is so remote, the peaks and rivers have no names. "When you walk in," Dr Thomas Lennon [of Colorado University] said, "you walk off the map." '

American papers competed in a feeding frenzy over the story. The new discovery was so momentous it would, according to the *Post*, 'explain the cause of the Inca Empire's collapse'. Fertility symbols were found at the site with what the *Denver Post*, a family newspaper, coyly described as 'assertively male attributes' (i.e. erect penises). The archaeologist, Thomas Lennon, had made the tantalising suggestion that 'There's a good chance we'll find mummies in the tomb,' a line *Time* fell on with breathless anticipation. The story had sex, mummies and Americans discovering something. Sub-editors all over the country made allusions to 'the real Indiana Jones' who had done it. Colorado University positioned itself in the press release as now being at the forefront of pre-Columbian studies, with all the assurances of future funding that this would bring.

All would have been well had Gene Savoy himself not already discovered precisely the same city some twenty years beforehand and named it Gran Pajatén. The ruin was by now so well known that it was listed in *The South American Handbook*, with instructions on how to get there. When this was pointed out to the newspapers who had trumpeted this 'new discovery', there was much embarrassment all round. Both the *Washington Post* and the *New York Times* ran full retractions.

Colorado's University's response to this disclosure revealed every arch-aeological prejudice. The public relations department admitted that Gene Savoy had been first to find the ruin, but said of Savoy's expedition, 'They are adventurers, explorers. They go charging through the jungle finding wonderful things.' The implication was clear. No ruin was properly 'dis-covered' until a qualified archaeologist had been there.

It was not surprising that Savoy now spoke of archaeologists as 'hyenas' coming in to scavenge the scraps that explorers left behind: 'They are professional thieves, scientific thieves, grave robbers.' He was clear about why he himself had never excavated: 'One, because I'm not qualified. And two, because I just don't like doing it.' But he emphasised that he continually returned to historical sources in order to find clues for his searches. 'No sensible man goes down into the jungle unless he's got something to fol-low.'

This was born out by his record. Re-reading his account of searching for Espíritu Pampa showed an attention for detail that belied Asheshov's rather unkind comment that 'Gene would never get around even to reading a paperback.' It was his scrupulous concern to go back to those sources that had led him to question Bingham (a man whose writ had still run large through all questions of Inca exploration) and return to see if he had been wrong.

Nor had he always been as indiscriminately diffusionist as his academic critics liked to make out. In an early piece for the *Explorers Journal*, he had written of the Chachapoyans and their famously fair skin, blue eyes and tall build, a quality for which their women had been much prized by the Incas before the arrival of the Spanish. The conquistadors were to be equally admiring: Cieza de León had commented, 'The Inca took many of their [the Chachapoyans'] women because they are handsome and comely and very white.' The twentieth-century suggestion that this whiteness was due to an Aryan super-race finding their way across the Atlantic in the distant past (Vikings were always being mentioned) was a sensitive issue for many Peruvians.

In this early article, Savoy rejected such an idea and made a plea for the notion of racial diversity within the Americas, explicitly repudiating diffusionism: 'Only the superficial-minded speculate on [pre-Columbian] contact between the New World and Europe across the Atlantic.' Instead he pointed out that many of the original Caribbean peoples (mostly now extinct from disease) were lighter-skinned than the Portuguese explorers who first saw them. Some indigenous inhabitants of Bolivia sported better beards than their conquerors. Savoy argued that the Americas were already, without any outside contact, as much a racial tapestry of different colours as Europe and Asia, and that the truly demeaning approach was to assume that they were a 'mono-race' – 'as absurd as talking of a typical Caucasian'.

Re-reading some of Savoy's early pieces showed a subtlety of approach that academic archaeologists had often misinterpreted. 'I see explorers as people with open minds who can scan many different sources for information, unconfined by an academic discipline, just like computers scan the Internet,' he told me. It was an attractive idea and he left it hanging between us. 'We've all learnt that the great thing is to follow the roads, Hugh. Roads lead to ruins.'

*

That first night we had a superb *sopa peruana* – everything in it with a hunk of turkey that only just fitted the bowl – a bachelor dinner, washed down with the water we'd boiled from the stream. I loved not only the taste but the smell of that water – it seemed to carry the wood-smoke still coiled within it as you drank it from the bottle. Benito and Rónal, huddled over the stove in the wooden hut, looked like figures from a Van Gogh print.

As we slept, the mosquitoes came at me in waves and I awoke with a solid band of bites around my wrist and neck. Like junkies, mosquitoes always seem to know instinctively how to find a fresh vein. Some of the bites looked a little different and were ones I'd acquired sitting and half-dozing in Leonidas' hut. I suspected not for the first time on this trip that they were from the little biting insects called *vinchucas*, that are often found in adobe huts and can cause the particularly nasty Chagas disease, an infection that causes much mortality in the Andes. (A blood test later back in England showed that I had been exposed to infection but did not have serious levels in my blood, which for a life-threatening condition I found only partly reassuring.)

We descended and the vegetation of the high cloud-forest, what the Peruvians call evocatively *la ceja de selva*, 'the eyebrow of the jungle', gave way to the beginnings of the thicker rain-forest cover that had washed up the sides of the Andes from the Amazon.

The nineteenth-century French traveller Charles Wiener had a strange and arresting phrase for this area – *'belle d'une beauté superflu'*. There was convolvulus everywhere, threading its twines through the matted trunks of trees, bromeliads, wild papaya trees and large ferns. I realised the scale of the vegetation when I noticed that the gunnera plant, a dominating giant when it appears in an English garden, was here one of the smallest.

Rónal killed a small but nasty *culebra*, a viper, flicking it away from the path with his machete. 'Looks small, but if that had bitten you, you would have died an agonising death,' he said, with a mild air of relish. I believed him.

However, I still gave him a hard time over the radio. Rónal was an ardent *huaynero* and we seemed to be permanently tuned to a *huayno* radio station. The years had not improved my tolerance of *huayno* – it still sounded like a cheese-wire being sharpened. I pleaded for a radio station that played anything else: *salsa*, *criolla*, even the bastardised version of rap that had started to creep into Peru. But Rónal was addicted to his *huayno*. The compromise was that he held it to his ear with the volume down. It was like travelling with a leaky Walkman.

The sun came out and began to burn us up. The path would contour into a hill and there would be a moment's relief with soft green and shadow and sometimes a small stream, before you were swung back out into the exposed sun again, like being turned on a spit-roast over a fire.

Rónal had noticed the pharmaceutical help I had given to Leonidas and now fell back to join me. '*Señor, ¿no tiene algo para el piel?* Do you have anything for my skin?' I hadn't noticed before, but he had bad acne. Although there was no medicine for it, we fell to talking anyway. Rónal was a keen football player and was devastated that Solano had gone to play for Newcastle United. '*Bueno, supongo que El Shearer, ¿si que es uno de los mejores jugadores del mundo?* I suppose El Shearer is one of the best players in the world, isn't he?' he said, as if consoling himself for this loss to Peru.

We were passing one of the most emotive stretches of the Inca retreat before the conquistadors. Retreat is perhaps too fine a word – it must have been a rout, with Tupac Amaru's men in headlong flight down the narrow valley, chased by the Cañari, the native auxiliary troops of the Spanish. But they had a last chance to resist.

We could see the narrow ridge of Huayna Pucará rising to our left, dominating the path below. The friar Martín de Murúa had described it as 'a knife edge which two men could not walk along side by side'. It was here that the Incas prepared a potentially devastating ambush, as the Spanish did not know of the fortifications that had been built on the hill. Hiding on the heights, the Incas planned to roll boulders down onto the horses and the conquistadors as they passed. The captains who ringed Tupac Amaru (and who ran what was a necessarily militaristic state) had realised that one of the few ways to destroy an armoured horseman was with such an ambush. They had had a generation since the days of Manco to prepare Huayna Pucará as the fort to launch it from.

All would have been well had not one of those same Inca captains, a certain Puma Inca, defected to the Spanish, apparently because he had fallen out with Curi Paucar, the most militaristic of the Inca commanders.

Puma Inca betrayed the position of Huayna Pucará and revealed the ambush plan, which included a contingent of the Inca's jungle Indians, the Chunchos, waiting on the other side of the bank with their poisoned arrows to kill any Spanish who escaped the boulders.

After what, according to Martín de Murúa, was a considerable amount of debate, the Spanish decided to outflank the fort and come on it from above. Looking at the terrain, this must have been quite an achievement, as it was covered in the densest of trees and with *cedrala*, the thick jungle thorn, through which the Spanish had to crawl on all fours. Martín García de Loyola, one of the young blades of the Cuzco party, went ahead with some of the Cañari and managed, after seven hours of crawling through this stuff, to appear above the ambushers to their surprise and demoralisation. At the same time, the other Spanish attacked from below. The Incas fled the hill. They had lost their last effective chance to defeat the Spanish. All they could do now was bolt into the jungle basin below and hope the Spanish didn't follow. What eventually happened to the Inca traitor Puma Inca is not recorded.

There was a fly-infested patch of open grass at the bottom of the ridge by an abandoned hut – Bingham wrote that in this part of the world 'any little natural breathing space at the bottom of a canyon is a *pampa*' – and we rested for a while looking at the lie of the land. We were just approaching a narrowing of the path under the ridge, the spot at which the Spanish would have had boulders rolled on them from above.

It was only as recently as 1984 that Vincent Lee first discovered the ruins on top of the hill and identified the site as Huayna Pucará. Vince was an explorer after my own heart. He was an architect who had spent time mountain-guiding and he brought a draughtsman's eye to his meticulously thorough exploration of this valley, together with a happy-go-lucky temperament – a good combination. His maps of the sites were superb, with a technical thoroughness which had also produced immaculate GPS readings: no ruin got lost again once Vince had found it.

I liked his approach. He had named his exploring team the 'Sixpac Manco Crew' on the grounds that Tupac's problem was that he didn't have enough beer to do the job properly. Huayna Pucará was probably his most significant new identification of a site ('From my days as a Marine Officer, I knew something of the defensive use of terrain'), but I also enjoyed the moment when one of his team had stumbled across another Inca building when wandering off into the brush 'to take a dump' – probably a moment when many explorers have accidentally come across interesting finds, given the need for an 'off the beaten track' moment, although few have the candour to admit it.

Other explorers were always horrified at Vince's determinedly lean-burn approach to the field. 'He won't use horses,' Gary had told me in the mystified tones of one for whom the horse was sacrosanct: 'he carries everything himself, eighty-pound packs. He must be crazy.' Vince's reasoning was that 'A strong backpack outfit can out-run a string of pack animals easily and enjoy much greater freedom.' The phrase 'out-run' is telling: Vince had apparently prepared his team for one trip by getting them to sprint up and down from Cuzco to Sacsahuaman with full kit-loads. Gene Savoy, a man who liked to live well however arduous his expeditions, had been even more apoplectic at Vince's approach: 'He carries dehydrated food! No wonder he comes back a stone lighter than he went in.'

But Vince's approach was not simply a masochistic one. He had told me that 'I find the way you find things is to sit around with the locals drinking and sharing in their miseries of trail life – you need to cut a trail yourself and kick it with your foot ...' It was a view I shared.'

We had not gone far from Huayna Pucará when I realised I'd left a stick behind that Rónal had cut for me – it would be useful on the increasingly steep descent. After collecting it and hurrying back to catch up with the others, I stopped up short: there on the path in front of me, looking as if it had been deliberately placed to frighten, was an extremely large green-and-yellow snake. I immediately assumed that Rónal and Adrian had put a dead one there as a joke (it was precisely what I would have done), particularly as I could see them in the little clearing beyond, presumably waiting for my reaction. But I also wasn't going to take any chances.

'Uh, guys,' I shouted, feeling stupid, 'you didn't happen to leave a snake on the path by any chance, did you?'

'What snake?'

'You have thirty seconds to tell me it's a joke. Either that or get back here with the machete right now!' It was almost my worst nightmare – confronted by a snake with just a wooden stick in my hand. In the true nightmare, I would have been naked, without the stick.

After a few moments Adrian and Rónal appeared around a corner, advancing with a natural caution. Adrian lobbed a cautious stone at the snake. It reared up and we all went very still. 'Shit!' said Rónal, panicking completely, '¡Mátalo, mátalo! – Kill it, kill it!'

To my amazement, Adrian started to get even closer to the snake while Rónal and I hung back. Adrian seemed to be moving with preter-natural calm. With a careful thwack, he hit the snake cleanly across the head with the machete and flipped the decapitated body into the bushes. Although Rónal and I tried not to show it too much, we were deeply impressed.

On leaving a peaceful settlement called Vista Alegre (where we had camped on our second night), we had to walk the mules over the river-bed to by-pass steep cliffs. The red flash of a cock-of-the-rock went by, identifiable even by a non-ornithologist like me, and Adrian (a closet twitcher) told me a little about its habits. The male cock-of-the-rock has the very masculine trait – potentially endearing, depending on your sexual politics – of trying to attract the female of the species by congregating on the same branch as other males: when an audience of expectant females has duly arrived, they then try to push each other down to impress them – 'knocking each other off to knock off a female', as Adrian put it poetically. The resulting victor would indubitably be the 'cock-of-the-rock'. With no hint of irony, the Peruvians had adopted the bird as their national emblem, and anyone who has ever witnessed the locals' attempts to chat up European tourists in the bars of the Plaza de Armas could see the appropriateness.

A small stream emerged near the camp, with an overpowering smell of the fresh spearmint that grew around it. I was washing there early in the morning when I looked up suddenly to see two inquisitive faces staring down at us from the top of the *barranca*. These hills were sparsely populated and it was a tough life, as of necessity the inhabitants were continually moving from lowland to highland and back again with their produce, with all the health problems this caused. Political elections were to be held soon for this area of Convención and it was disconcerting to pass boulders in the middle of nowhere daubed with slogans and instructions on whom to vote for (according to Rónal, the leading candidate was standing on a *Convenciónista* ticket, which could be more or less summarised as meaning 'Convención for the *Convenciónistas* who live there' – as good a slogan as any).

It had rained lower down, and being Saturday, there was a constant stream of mules taking goods up to the market at Huancacalle; quite soon we found the narrow path turning to mud up to our knees. Wading through it was slow and painful. Vincent Lee had once described similar conditions as being 'like a vertical swamp' and Savoy's mules had gone up to their bellies in the sticky ooze. The real problem was that the thick vegetation to either side prevented the slightest *desviación* (deviation) to get around the mud. As Savoy had said, 'I can quite agree with whoever it was that first called the jungle "a green hell".' Within the hour we had mud coming out of our boots, then out of our trousers and increasingly, as we kept slipping in what had become a barrel-ride of a path, oozing from every pore of our bodies as well.

The mud was not the only demoralising factor. Day after day we had been descending and my altimeter had already dropped 9000 feet since we had crossed the pass: it was a punishing long descent, made longer by the constant switchbacks over the Concevidayoc's tributaries and by the knowledge that later we would be returning back up the same way. The heat, the sweat and the flies were getting to me. There are people who like the jungle, it's true, but there are people who like root beer and Swedish pickled herring. Each to his own. For my part, every mile we descended from the mountains was a steady deterioration in the quality of life.

By the time we got to a little hut for lunch, we were exhausted. Rónal cheered us up with the story of how this hut had been the site of a shoot-out between the Sendero Luminoso and the local constabulary in the previous decade. It sounded pure Bonnie-and-Clyde, at least the way Rónal told it. The police had surrounded the hut in the early morning and (for some curious reason, not explained) let off a warning shot. Two of the *terroristas* rushed out, '*metiendo los pantalones*, still putting on their trousers', and were mown down just where we were, at the front of the hut. Rónal paused to let this sink in and then added, unnecessarily: '*Esas piedras estaban manchadas de sangre*, these rocks were stained with blood.' Benito's face had become round-eyed and absorbed. Rónal knew how to tell a story.

'What happened to the others?' we all chorused.

'*Se escaparon por atrás*, they escaped out the back,' said Rónal, giving a vague wave of the hand to include the whole of the *montaña* beyond. '*Se escaparon como los incas y se escondieron*, they escaped like the Incas, and hid.' He settled back and gave a thoughtful munch on his Sublime chocolate bar. '*Ay, así fue*, that's how it was.'

By the time we came to our fourth long day of forced marches, we were more than ready to arrive at Old Vilcabamba, which for Tupac Amaru and his forces had been their last real place of refuge on the run from the Spanish. The supplies had dwindled to nothing and the night before I had attempted to make a tomato sauce Italian-style, with garlic, sugar and salt and the over-ripe squashed tomatoes that had been on the mule's back in the sun since we left. Rónal and Benito had grudgingly granted that it compared favourably with the Peruvian version. Now we were down to cans of tuna-fish and some raw sugar-cane we took from the fields. Martín de Murúa tells the story of how one of the conquistadors' party, a *mestizo* soldier called Alonso Hernandez de la Torre, broke open some sugar-cane to eat near here, and was soundly beaten for this indiscipline (for leaving his station, not for eating Indian cane).

From the *mirador*, the Inca viewpoint at the head of the great stairs descending to Espíritu Pampa, we could see the lie of the jungle valley – broad, fertile and completely covered in vegetation. Without prior knowledge, it would have been impossible to guess that there was a city hidden in its middle.

The stairway itself was the most impressive stretch of Inca stonework we had come upon since leaving Huancacalle, descending in a long swathe towards Old Vilcabamba. The Incas always knew how to make an entrance and they had forty years to ensure that this hidden city was built up into something that was worthwhile for a court in exile.

We arrived first at the modern hamlet of Espíritu Pampa, where Rónal had some relatives: the ruins themselves were a little beyond. Despite all Rónal's entreaties, there was nothing to eat. This was a bad moment. Rónal had for days been painting a picture of the jungle delicacies we would be feeding on once we arrived: bananas, chickens and even, when he felt we were flagging, *chicharrones*, the delicious roast pork that is Peru's finest dish (guinea pigs being strictly for the tourists).

We spotted a tree obscenely laden with grapefruit. Surely a few wouldn't go missing? Rónal was annoyed anyway with his relatives for their stinginess. '¡*Este no lo puedo creer!* This is just unbelievable! They're cousins of my wife's brother-in-law. How can they not give us food?' While one of us stood guard, the others attacked the tree with a long pointed stick and, feeling like urchins in an orchard, we gorged ourselves on the juicy yellow fruit. It was time for the ruins.

*

Nothing anyone had told me had quite prepared me for the difficulties in actually seeing Old Vilcabamba, the last city of the Incas. The rainforest had taken over completely. Giant trees, towering hundreds of feet above us, had split much of the surviving masonry apart. It was an extraordinary achievement for first Hiram Bingham and then Gene Savoy to have found anything at all. I could immediately understand something which had always puzzled me: why such a determined explorer as Bingham had only discovered a tiny fragment of the site (which he called 'Eromboni Pampa'), when the rest of what was a considerable city lay only a hundred yards away. Now I saw that you could pass within feet of a wall without knowing it, so dense was the covering. Only by using a machete could we cut away enough to examine the stonework.

Ironically, it was Bingham himself who commented that 'nothing gives a better idea of the density of the jungle than the fact that the savages themselves have often been within five feet of these fine walls [those of Eromboni] without being aware of their existence'. If he had followed this thought through to its logical conclusion, he might well have done more work himself in the nearby trees.

In fact Bingham stayed for a very short space of time – a few days, unlike Savoy, who, fifty years later, came for a full four months – and it's clear that this was partly because Bingham simply didn't like the Espíritu Pampa area. One reason he refused to credit that this was Old Vilcabamba and hence the last city of the Incas, an identification which would have displaced Machu Picchu as such, was that he felt the priests and Virgins of the Sun 'would not have cared to live in this hot valley'. An irresistible image is conjured up of Virgins of the Sun looking like Delores del Rio and languishing in the heat as they asked the Inca to pour them out another sherbet.

Bingham also made the mistake of relying on Machiguenga Indians as guides. The Machiguenga, in their intensely practical way, have always been supremely indifferent to ruins and only notice any if they lie directly on one of their hunting-trails – trails which they venture off with extreme reluctance for fear of the 'spirit-infested woods'. As a result Bingham found little with them. Savoy, however, had the Cobos family with him instead, mountain men who had no such inhibitions. The old dictum still held true – an explorer was only as good as his guides. As a result, Savoy was able to uncover the full extent of the complex, with some 400 stone structures still evident – enough to make it a city, given that there would have been many more ancillary wooden outbuildings which have not survived.

It was midday and the sun was strong, sending occasional shafts of light through the rainforest canopy, sometimes picking out a bit of wall or a sunken doorway collapsed into the jungle debris. The sheer quantity of detritus and rubbish always surprises those who go to the jungle for the first time – the experience is like walking over and through a compost heap. *Matapalos* were everywhere, the carnivorous jungle trees that, once their seeds have been spread by birds to a branch, send shoots downwards to the ground and then back up the main trunk, effectively strangulating their hosts. We came across a colony of jungle ants, marching their cut leaves across the trial – it was oddly cheering to come across some creatures here who at least had a purpose in life.

There were butterflies all around, of a bewildering variety. Used to the fifty-eight native British varieties that I had studied as a boy, the sheer cornucopia of species was overwhelming.

The Victorian naturalist Henry Walter Bates had been the first to notice a strange phenomenon in his classic account of 1863, *The Naturalist on the River Amazon*. He was obsessed by butterflies. As he travelled up the Amazon from Brazil towards Peru, he began to realise that the number of butterfly species was increasing dramatically as he approached the Brazilian–Peruvian border. Bates theorised from this that the greatest concentration of all must be found in the region I was now in, just below the Andes where the

Amazon tributaries emerge. To his intense regret, he was beaten back by malaria and so was unable to get here himself, and so never saw that his theory was correct, as I could see with my own eyes: there was a quite astonishing number of butterfly species, thought to be greater here than anywhere else in the world. A study had been made of a 4000-hectare plot nearby: over 1300 species had been counted in that one small area, three times as many as in the whole of Europe.

There were butterflies with vivid pink upper wings and blue lower ones, like a two-tone handbag: others in clouds feasting on the secretions of sap and some so perfectly camouflaged against the bark of trees that they would rise up from beneath your feet like dust when you brushed past them.

As I sat with flights of butterflies around me, my eyes adjusted to the penumbra and began to make out the shape of what must once have been a fine city. The great plaza found by Savoy was as impressive as any in Inca civic planning, even if one could not now see from one end of it to the other. There was a long *kallanka* to one side and terraces surrounding it. Somehow one doorway had managed to survive intact enough to allow us to enter and go up to a terraced set of buildings a little above the plaza. In one of them an enormous *ceiba* tree had split a niched wall apart. There was even a *huaca*, positioned to dominate the plaza, although it was a far cry from the glories of the White Rock in the mountains above: this was uncarved, leaning on its side 'like a great egg', as Savoy had reported, and with a tree wrapped around the top.

Bingham liked to translate Espíritu Pampa literally, as the 'Pampa of Ghosts'. Gene Savoy and others had also reported a melancholy descending on them at this site. I could see why even the normally ebullient Savoy had felt that way, given the 'atmosphere of deadly silence' that played around the light, the ruins and the trees. It felt like an odd cosmic joke, a reminder of the temporality of man's achievements: here was the last great Inca city, built with all the craftsmanship that they had evolved over the lifetime of an Empire, now completely covered and reclaimed by the rainforest in a way that would have delighted an ecologist but left me feeling apocalyptic.

Rónal was looking melancholy too, staring ahead into the greenery with unfocused eyes.

'¿*Que te pasa?* What's wrong?' I asked.

He gave a great sigh. '*Lamentablemente, todos los árbitros en Perú son comprometidos. Eso es la verdad. Pero, ¿que vamos a hacer?* Unfortunately all the referees in Peru are crooked. It's as simple as that. But what can one do?'

Above us, the forest canopy seemed to descend in endless, weighted layers of heavy green.

*

We would know little of the last days of the last Inca were it not for the remarkable discovery of a document left by the friar Martín de Murúa, a chronicler of the Conquest who was sympathetic to the Indians (the only other accounts of this campaign are the often self-serving military reports by the conquistador leaders themselves).

Murúa's chronicle lay neglected and unread in a Spanish library (like many other historical records of the Conquest) until 1813, when Napoleon's brother Joseph Bonaparte, temporarily installed on the Spanish throne, was forced to flee by the approach of Wellington's armies. He grabbed this document as part of the booty he wanted to take back to France in his coach, together with a job-lot of looted Italian paintings. A squadron of British dragoons gave chase and Joseph Bonaparte was finally forced to abandon the coach and jump on a fast horse, escaping only by minutes. The recovered booty from the coach found its way back to the Duke of Wellington.

The Duke was more interested in the Italian paintings than a dusty old manuscript, however well bound, but he took it with him back to London. Only later did he begin to suspect that Martín de Murúa's account might be valuable, and he sent it to Sir Walter Scott for possible translation or adaptation, but Scott returned it unread. The document then remained hidden in the library at Apsley House right up until 1945, when it was found again by the Duke's descendant. Murúa's manuscript was first published (in Spanish – it remains untranslated) in 1962, almost 400 years after the events it describes.

Martín de Murúa told the story, which he had personally gathered from eyewitnesses, of how, when the Spanish troops finally entered Old Vilcabamba, they found it deserted. The Incas had fled into the surrounding jungle, '*pegando fuego a todo lo que no pudieron llevar*' ('having set fire to all they couldn't take with them'). The temple of the sun was still smoking, as were the *depósitos*, the storehouses. The Incas clearly hoped that this scorched-earth policy would force the Spanish back to the mountains, just as it had a generation before when Gonzalo Pizarro had chased Manco Inca down here and he had similarly 'disappeared' into the jungle.

But this time the Spanish were determined to press on to the bitter end. Despite their fear of the many '*viboras de cascabel*' (rattle-snakes), they relentlessly pursued the last of the Inca nobility to their jungle hiding-places. They managed to capture not only the nobles, but Manco's mummy, which had been held in the Vilcabamba as a symbol of resistance. They also found the golden image of the sun, the Punchao, and much other treasure, which they divided up between them. Martín de Murúa's censorious comment here is telling:

Some [of this treasure] had escaped the hunger of the Pizarros in Cuzco and some had been hidden and then retrieved and some had even been made here [in Old Vilcabamba] as a substitute for the great quantity that the Spanish had already taken from them without fear of God or of order. For the Spanish acted as if the Incas were not the Lords of their own dominions and this treasure could belong to whosoever could take it by force.

The Inca himself, Tupac Amaru, was the last to be captured. He had gone very deep into the jungle, and a party of Spanish (led by Martín García de Loyola, the same dashing young blade who had outflanked the Incas at the fort of Huayna Pucará) had to travel some 250 miles further downriver to follow him – a formidable challenge for the Spanish, although they were aided by the fact that Tupac Amaru's wife was pregnant and so travelling slowly, '*temorosa y triste*' ('fearful and sad').

The Spanish followed on rafts, which kept breaking. They would have lost the Inca completely, had his wife not refused to cross a river by canoe because she was too scared, an episode that Martín de Murúa lamented. Tupac, devoted to his wife, decided to retreat into the rainforest, confident that the Spanish would never come that far anyway. So it was that Loyola's men were able finally to track the last Inca Emperor down to a small camp-fire (the light of which the Spanish had seen from afar), where Tupac was huddling miserably with his wife, both of them terrified of the jungle around them.

Their pursuers promised that they would be well treated, with assurances that the Inca's nephew, Quispe Titu, had already been captured and was being safely looked after (in fact he had been stripped naked and thrown in a cell). They told the Inca that he would have a safe passage back to Cuzco and that his lands would be restored.

Martín de Murúa has a sad phrase about Tupac, whom he clearly admired for his affability and steadfastness: apparently the Inca 'never resented his losses, however much had been taken from him, even when they stripped him of his fine coloured cloak, which seemed like the purest *raso* [silk] of Granada.'

When Tupac Amaru returned to Cuzco, Viceroy Toledo arranged for him to be quickly condemned to death by a show trial: his execution was to be in the main square, on a scaffold covered in black, on 24 September 1572. Martín de Murúa wrote:

On that day there was such an infinity of Indians that one could not pass through the streets and the balconies were filled with women who were so moved by pity that they started to cry. What was extraordinary was that despite the enormous multitude of Indians who had gathered to watch their lord die, and their great noise that filled the sky with cries and lamentations, as soon as the Inca himself raised his hand, all fell silent, so that it seemed as if there were not a living soul in the plaza.

Tupac Amaru had never been in Cuzco before and had never seen the great square of his ancestors, lined with their palaces. His first view of it was his last. The executioner (a Cañari Indian) bound his eyes and cut off his head with one stroke of the sword. So died the last Inca Emperor.

The Viceroy made sure that the captured mummy of Manco Inca was also brought back to Cuzco and burnt, in a high fortress above the city that he had once almost succeeded in taking from the conquistadors. It seemed as if the Spanish had finally extinguished the last embers of Inca resistance.

*

Julia Flores spread out the *manta*, the weaving, carefully on the bench next to her loom. She was a Quechuan woman of about fifty and she knew as much as anyone I had ever met about the textile traditions of the high Andean villages.

'*¿Tupac Amaru? Esta manta le cuenta la historia*, this weaving will tell you his story.'

It was about two feet by three feet, worked in the faded blacks and cochineal reds of the traditional style of weaving found above Lares and in Chincheros. There were narrow geometric bands representing *las flores salvajes*, the wild flowers, and stylised representations of condors, eagles and (since this was a *manta matrimonial*, a double blanket) a pair of hummingbirds sipping from the same flower. These symbols I already knew. But there were curious ones that were less familiar, and these Julia started to explain.

'*Eso es el símbolo de Tahuantinsuyo*, this is the symbol of Tahuantinsuyo, with the four quarters of the old Empire. And here is Tupac Amaru, being pulled apart.'

The small panel showed a hominoid figure being literally ripped in four directions, as if hung, drawn and quartered. It took me a moment to realise what the symbols of the executioners reminded me of – they were like the Pacmen of early video games, all mouth and no body.

'But look here,' said Julia, and she showed me a central panel. In this, the same symbols showed Tupac Amaru's death. But the motif had been extended to show condors themselves attacking those who were pulling Tupac Amaru apart. '*La verganza*, the revenge,' said Julia.

'Why do the weavings show this? Because after Tupac Amaru's capture in Vilcabamba, the royal weavers who were with him remained – and they told their story, and that story has been retold in all the weavings since.

'Do you like Elvis Presley?' added Julia unexpectedly. 'When I was *muy niña*, very young, I loved Elvis. I cried when I saw the auctioning of his possessions on TV the other day. I loved him so much that I called my son Elvis. Elvis Richard Flores. Elvis for Elvis Presley and Richard for Richard Nixon. You never forget the death of someone you love.'

I spread the weaving out and studied it carefully. It is in these weavings that much of the oral history of the Andes has found its promptings, along with the *quipus*, the knotted cords. This was perhaps one reason why cloth was so obsessively valued by the Incas, far more than if it were just for clothing. There are numerous stories of retreating Inca armies burning the cloth in their warehouses, a gesture understandable to rival pre-Columbian peoples but completely incomprehensible to the *conquistadores* who pursued them.

I remembered the *orejón* at Sacsahuaman who, 'perceiving that they had conquered him and had taken his stronghold at two or three points, threw down his arms, covered his head and face with his *manta* [his woven cloth]', and then 'threw himself down from the level to a spot more than one hundred *estados* below, where he was shattered'. I thought of Tupac Amaru, stripped even of his cloak.

The Spanish never understood the secret messages contained within the *mantas*, the weavings, just as they never understood the system of the *quipu*. And so for centuries after Tupac Amaru's death the legend of the Incas, with accompanying talk of the resurrection of their Empire, was kept alive in the high villages and valleys of the old Inca strongholds near Cuzco. The Spanish *encomendero*, as he despatched his seemingly passive *nativos* to do increasingly back-breaking duties, can never have realised that around their shoulders were often wrapped symbols of revenge and of uprising.

The idea of an Inca who would return and set his people free became a cult called the Incario, which kept a rebellious fervour going for long after Tupac Amaru's execution in 1572. In the eighteenth century, this burst dramatically out into the open with an uprising led by a direct descendant of Tupac Amaru, who in 1781 laid siege to Cuzco. While ultimately unsuccessful, Tupac Amaru II, as he came to be called, became an inspiration for the independence movements that finally liberated South America in the nineteenth century.

In the twentieth century this same fervour was tragically misappropriated first by the Sendero Luminoso with their Cambodian-style Year Zero, and then by the Movimiento Revolucionario Tupac Amaru (the MRTA), who drew even more explicitly on the legend before being effectively wiped out in the Japanese Embassy siege of 1996–7.

But the strong current that the Incario represents – the idea that what best remains of the Inca legacy, their collaborative community projects, their superb agriculture and husbanding of shared resources, a spirituality rooted in stone and maize and the mountains, can once again be res-urrected – this current will surely one day re-emerge in full flood to wash away the centuries of exploitation by the *encomenderos*, the *hacendados* and, more recently, the dictates of a Lima government remote from the concerns of the mountains.

Julia wrapped the manta around my shoulders as she gave it to me. '*Siga caminando, Señor Hugo, ya tiene que ir lejos todavía.* Keep walking. You still have a long way to go.'

*

Why is it that Peru, or the idea of Peru, carries such allure? Nicholas Asheshov had summed it up for me: 'As far as exploration goes, Peru is still part of the nineteenth century.' It is one of the few places left in the world where new ruins continue to be discovered.

It is intriguing to compare this with the world-view of the *conquistadores*, who lived in one of the most heady times for exploration that the world has ever known. In just one century the boundaries of the known world were trebled, as the Americas were revealed and Vasco da Gama rounded the Cape of Good Hope, bound for India. It is difficult for us, as we pace the cage of an ever-contracting planet and renounce our space programme, to imagine quite how exhilarating (and at times disorientating) this must have been psychologically. Keats' later lines about 'stout Cortez' as the first man to view the Pacific, doing so 'with a wild surmise', may have been technically wrong (Cortés was by no means the first conquistador to stand on a peak in Darien), but capture perfectly the adrenaline rush that accompanied exploration and to which so many of the conquistadors (and later explorers) became fatally addicted, so often ploughing on for that one expedition too many that ended in disaster – what Gene Savoy has called 'an excitement that takes over, an excitement that only discovery produces, an intoxicating feeling'.

John Hemming would argue, and he may well be right, that we have now moved into a different age of exploration, in which the scientist rather than the adventurer is dominant and is beginning the study of the most inaccessible of the world's habitats – the rainforest canopies or ocean depths – and doing so with real rigour, unlike the old death-or-glory merchants.

But this is discovery at a new and more sophisticated level. Peru is one of the last places left where man can satisfy the primitive and elemental need to find the unknown, to confront the 'other'. In Peru's case, importantly in the monoculture that the world is becoming, this is also an unknown with a culture and a set of values resiliently independent of the West.

How has Peru (or, to be more accurate, eastern Peru) managed to preserve the exclusivity of the unknown when others of the world's caskets have been prised open long ago? It is largely due to what my Peruvian friend Fernando la Rosa described to me as 'the wonderful but impossible geography of the country', the compacted nature of the terrain, in which the desert rises up to meet the Andes which, in their turn, herring-bone down into the dense jungle vegetation of the Amazon. Communications are still almost non-existent: whereas in the Himalayas one can send a fax from the tiniest of hilltop villages, once *adentro* in Peru, in the true interior, it is impossible to contact anyone with anything but short-wave radio. Add a legacy of political violence, a ferocious rainy season, a few snakes and one of the worst records in the world for off-road driving and you have a cocktail for a tough trip.

But the real appeal is that there are clearly still ruins waiting to be found out there: the cloud-forest and the Amazon have by no means given up all their secrets. Whether in Chachapoyas, where new finds are being made on a regular basis, in the more remote areas of the jungle Antisuyo or, just as importantly, in the forgotten recesses of libraries and archives, one thing is almost certain: the twenty-first century will see new discoveries being made, and with those new discoveries will come more knowledge of the Incas and their extraordinary Empire.

Inca Genealogy

(Pre-Conquest dates are estimates)

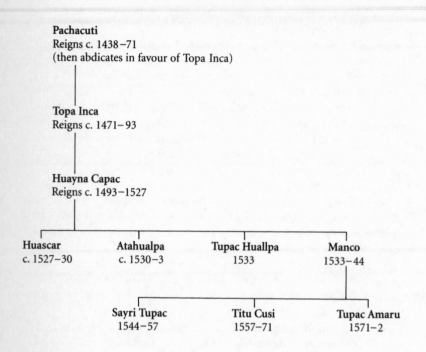

Pachacuti
Reigns c. 1438–71
(then abdicates in favour of Topa Inca)

Topa Inca
Reigns c. 1471–93

Huayna Capac
Reigns c. 1493–1527

Huascar	**Atahualpa**	**Tupac Huallpa**	**Manco**
c. 1527–30	c. 1530–3	1533	1533–44

Sayri Tupac
1544–57

Titu Cusi
1557–71

Tupac Amaru
1571–2

(Tupac Huallpa was briefly appointed Sapa Inca after the death of Atahualpa, but died shortly afterwards. His role was insignificant and he is not mentioned in the text.)

CHRONOLOGY OF THE INCA
EMPIRE AND SPANISH CONQUEST

(All dates of pre-Conquest events in the Inca Empire are estimates and are often disputed among scholars.)

c. 1438. Pachacuti defeats the Chanca when they attack Cuzco. He becomes Sapa Inca (Emperor) as a result.

c. 1438–71. Reign of Pachacuti (then abdicates in favour of his son, Topa Inca). During his long period as Sapa Inca, he expands the Inca domains down the Vilcanota/Urubamba river, past Ollantaytambo and into the Vilcabamba.

c. 1450s. Inca conquest of Tiahuanaco area.

c. 1460s. Inca victory over the Chimú in northern Peru.

c. 1471–93. Reign of Topa Inca. Both while serving under Pachacuti and during his own reign, he expands the Empire northward, conquering Chachapoyas and moving into modern-day Ecuador. He also advances south along the Chilean coast.

1492. Columbus lands in America.

c. 1493–1527. Reign of Huayna Capac.

c. 1490s. Huayna Capac campaigns in Chachapoyas.

1508. Probable first publication date of *Amadis de Gaul*.

c. 1516. Huayna Capac campaigns in the Ecuador area.

1526. Preliminary expedition by Francisco Pizarro makes 'first contact' with Inca civilisation when they encounter an ocean-going boat on the northernmost fringes of the Inca Empire.

c. 1527. Huayna Capac's sudden death in the middle of what was probably a smallpox epidemic precipitates a civil war between his sons Huascar, the legitimate claimant in Cuzco, and Atahualpa, the illegitimate pretender based in Quito. After a savage struggle which decimates an Empire already weakened by disease, Atahualpa wins.

1529. Francisco Pizarro is given royal blessing in Spain to attempt the conquest of Peru. While at court, Pizarro meets Cortés, the conqueror of Mexico. He recruits a band of conquistadors from his homeland around Extremadura and sails south from Panama at the very end of 1530. The expedition is led by Pizarro and his partner, Diego de Almagro, with Pizarro's three brothers as important members of the 180-strong party. They have 37 horses.

1532. The conquistadors' journey inland from Tumbes marks the start of the actual Conquest. In November they capture Atahualpa at Cajamarca. Francisco's cousin Pedro Pizarro is his page and leaves a detailed account of the early campaign.

1533. Atahualpa is executed. The Spanish take Cuzco. Manca Inca is installed as a 'puppet Inca'.

1534. Hernando Pizarro docks in Seville with treasure from Peru. Pedro de Cieza de León sees it as an impressionable 17-year-old and soon sails for the New World himself.

1536. Manco rebels against the Spanish and takes Sacsahuaman. Juan Pizarro is killed. Manco is narrowly prevented from regaining Cuzco and retreats to Ollantaytambo.

1537. Manco is chased into the Vilcabamba by the Spanish, but is able to escape.

1539. Gonzalo Pizarro leads a second punitive expedition against Manco in the Vilcabamba and pursues him down into the jungle. Manco again just manages to escape capture, and is reported to shout defiance at his persecutors as he is borne off into the jungle by his allies in the Amazon.

1540. Gonzalo Pizarro's Amazon expedition sets off from Quito. While Pizarro himself returns, his lieutenant, Francisco de Orellana, continues downriver and emerges on the Atlantic coast two years later.

1541. Francisco Pizarro is murdered by a civil war faction.

1544. Manco Inca, having given refuge to Pizarro's assassins, is himself murdered by them at Vitcos, in the heart of the Vilcabamba. His son Titu Cusi narrowly escapes. Another son, Sayri Tupac, becomes the Sapa Inca and builds up the Vilcabamba as a miniature Inca state.

1547. Gonzalo Pizarro's rebellion is defeated outside Cuzco by forces of the Spanish crown and he is beheaded. Pedro de Cieza de León is part of the Spanish Royal Army which defeats him and he continues on from Cuzco to

Lake Titicaca, describing all that is left of the Inca Empire.

1553. Cieza de León publishes his *First Chronicle* in Seville, but is prevented from publishing more due to political problems with the Inquisition. He dies shortly afterwards.

1557. After consulting oracles, Sayri Tupac leaves the Vilcabamba for a 'retirement' under Spanish control at Yucay near Cuzco. He dies shortly afterwards, in 1560, possibly poisoned.

1557–71. Titu Cusi rules Vilcabamba as the Sapa Inca. In 1570 he dictates his own account of the events of the years during and after the Conquest.

1569. Viceroy Toledo arrives in Peru. In 1572 he sends an expedition against Tupac Amaru, another son of Manco's, who has succeeded Titu Cusi. Toledo's expedition chases Tupac Amaru down to Old Vilcabamba and captures him in the jungle beyond.

1572. Tupac Amaru is executed in the main square of Cuzco.

CHRONOLOGY OF THE EXPLORATION

OF THE VILCABAMBA

1710. Juan Arias Diaz Topete, a mineral prospector, travels into the interior of the Vilcabamba and leaves a document (only recently discovered) listing the four principal Inca sites he comes across. Three of the sites correspond to the modern names of Espíritu Pampa, Vitcos and Choquequirao. However, the fourth site he describes, apparently equally large, has, at the time of writing, yet to be found.

1768. Cosmé Bueno, travelling through the area, writes that all mining activity has effectively ceased and that 'there has remained only the memory of the retreat of the Incas'.

1781. Tupac Amaru II, a descendant of the last Incas, leads a rebellion against the Spanish, ending in the siege of Cuzco. He is captured, then hung, drawn and quartered.

1814. Alexander von Humboldt publishes *Vues de Cordillères et Monuments des Peuples Indigènes de l'Amérique*, which helps focus attention on pre-Columbian civilisations such as the Incas and suggests that they are a legitimate area of study.

1833–4. The Comte de Sartiges, an enterprising young French diplomat based in Lima, leads an expedition around Mt Salcantay to reach the Santa Teresa valley, from where he cuts his way through to Choquequirao. A humane observer of Andean life, he criticises the priests for extorting money from the faithful villagers and the *hacendados* for holding their workers in perpetual credit bondage to 'the company store'.

1847. Léonce Angrand visits Choquequirao by the same route and makes drawings of the site. Both he and Sartiges report that this must be Old Vilcabamba, the last city of the Incas.

1847. William Prescott, a half-blind American lawyer, publishes his *History of the Conquest of Peru*, using source material from the Spanish archives. This precipitates a search for further source material in those archives.

1865. Raimondi, the great Italian geographer, visits the Vilcabamba area, although not the section of the Urubamba near Machu Picchu.

1872. Baltasar de la Torre leads an expedition from Cuzco beyond Paucartambo and into the jungle. He is killed, but the German engineer who accompanies him, Herman Göhring, survives and in 1874 publishes an account and map which mentions both Machu Picchu and Huayna Picchu.

1875. Charles Wiener visits Ollantaytambo. Told of possible ruins at Machu Picchu, and mentions these names in his book of 1880, but does not visit them.

1877. George Ephraim Squier publishes *Peru: Incidents of Travel and Exploration in the Land of the Incas* and draws attention to the Tiahuanaco ruins.

1879–83. The War of the Pacific between Chile, on the one hand, and Peru and Bolivia, on the other, over a valuable region in the northern Atacama Desert. Peru and Bolivia are defeated, with a considerable loss of territory: Bolivia loses its vital access to the Pacific.

1891. Raimondi's map is published, featuring 'Mt Machu Picchu', but not indicating that there are ruins there.

1892. Alphons Stubel and Max Uhle publish *Die Ruinenstatten von Tiahuanaco im Hochlande des Alten Peru*, a detailed assessment of the Tiahuanaco culture.

1895. A road is blasted down the Urubamba valley to aid the rubber plantations downstream.

1896–7. Max Uhle excavates at Pachacamac. Along with earlier work at Tiahuanaco, this confirms his idea that there had been many civilisations predating the Incas who had also expanded to influence large areas of territory.

1908. Guaman Poma's magnificent manuscript, *Nueva Corónica y Buen Gobierno*, a description of the Inca realm originally written as a letter to the King of Spain and never published, is discovered in the Royal Library of Copenhagen. Written in a Joycean mixture of exuberant Spanish and Quechua, it is copiously illustrated with the writer's own drawings and gives a particularly sympathetic picture of Inca customs.

1909. Hiram Bingham visits Choquequirao in February, the rainy season, approaching along the shorter route from the Apurímac.

1911. The next Bingham expedition finds Machu Picchu (on 24 July), using this same road. Subsequently he travels on down the Urubamba to discover Vitcos (on the hill at Rosaspata), the White Rock (Chuquipalta or Ñusta España) and the site of Espíritu Pampa, although he only finds a small outlying section of these last ruins. On the basis of these discoveries, he claims that Machu Picchu is Old Vilcabamba, the 'last city of the Incas'.

1912. Bingham returns to clear and excavate the site of Machu Picchu. His colleague George Eaton analyses skeletons and concludes (erroneously) that there were more females than males at Machu Picchu. Bingham explores the Aobamba valley and finds Llactapata and Pallcay.

1914–15. The fourth and final Bingham expedition. He discovers a large section of the Inca road leading up to Machu Picchu from Cusichaca, now referred to as 'the Inca Trail'.

1919. Julio Tello excavates at Chavín de Huantar, the cradle of one of the most ancient of Peruvian cultures, the Chavín (800–200 BC).

1925. Julio Tello excavates on the Paracas peninsula and finds mummies wrapped in fine textiles, with gold masks.

1920s–30s. Cuzco photographer Martín Chambi goes on private visits to Machu Picchu and photographs the ruins, which have largely become covered again by vegetation.

1931. The Shippee-Johnson aerial expedition maps much of Peru, including the Urubamba valley, from the air, revealing many new archaeological details. (They produce a film in 1931, *Wings Over the Andes.*)

1934. Peruvian archaeologist Luis Valcárcel clears Machu Picchu.

1937. After many years of wandering in the Vilcabamba hills, the prospector Christian Bües draws a detailed map of the area. He dies afterwards of drink and poverty.

1940–41. The Paul Fejos expedition from the United States discovers the Wiñay Wayna and Inti Pata sites close to Machu Picchu, and the remaining section of the modern 'Inca Trail'.

1945. The crucial first part of Martín de Murúa's *Historia General del Perú* is discovered in the Duke of Wellington's library (having been taken from Spain in the Peninsular Wars). It contains specific details about the last city of the Incas, Old Vilcabamba, which help a later identification of Espíritu Pampa as that site: that it lay at a low altitude, that it was burnt at the time of the final Spanish taking of it and (most importantly of all) that the Incas used Spanish roofing tiles on the buildings. The manuscript is published in 1962.

1948. Hiram Bingham publishes *The Lost City of the Incas*, in which he still asserts that Machu Picchu was the site of Old Vilcabamba.

1950. Earthquake in Cuzco. The homes of thirty-five thousand people are destroyed. Some colonial buildings collapse, revealing Inca structures beneath.

1952. Victor von Hagen leads an expedition from Lake Titicaca to Quito

following the Inca Royal Road. In Cuzco he comes across the Christian Bües map. His associates revisit the Puncuyoc hills north of Yupanqa and see the Inca Wasi site.

Che Guevara arrives in Cuzco.

1953. Julian Tennant and Sebastian Snow go on an expedition to the lower Urubamba, which Tennant describes in *Quest for Paititi*.

1961. The Richard Mason and John Hemming expedition to the Iriri river in the Amazon. Mason is killed.

1963. G. Brooks Baedeland and Peter Gimbel parachute into the plateau of north-western Vilcabamba, as this is the only way of gaining access. They are aided by Nicholas Asheshov. The team cover the whole plateau, but find nothing and have difficulty in leaving.

1964–5. Gene Savoy penetrates further into the jungle at Espíritu Pampa and reveals that the site there is far more extensive than Bingham had realised. Further Savoy expeditions are curtailed by the growth of the guerrilla movement led by Hugo Blanco. Savoy switches focus to the Chachapoyan ruins in the north, discovering Gran Pajatén in 1965 and Gran Vilaya in 1985.

1970. Robert Nichols dies in mysterious circumstances looking for Paititi in the Peruvian jungle. Nicholas Asheshov goes in search of him. The circumstances of his death are finally revealed by Yoshiharu Sekino.

The publication of John Hemming's *Conquest of the Incas* establishes beyond doubt that the ruins at Espíritu Pampa are the remains of Old Vilcabamba and therefore 'the last city of the Incas'. One key piece of evidence is supplied by the recently discovered source material of Martín de Murúa.

1972. Death of Martín Chambi.

1977–83. The Cusichaca Project led by Ann Kendall excavates sites around the bottom of the Cusichaca valley and works with the local community to restore Incaic irrigation canals.

1979. The Cusichaca Project, working with John Beauclerk, locate the neo-Inca site of Acobamba near Arma, the possible residence of Titu Cusi.

1982. David Drew of the Cusichaca Project, working with an expedition led by Hugh Thomson, re-find the site of Llactapata between Santa Teresa and the Aobamba valley, within sight of Machu Picchu.

Hugh Thomson expedition goes on to follow the route of the Comte de Sartiges from the Santa Teresa valley towards Choquequirao and finds the nearby Espa Unuyoc site (later renamed Pinchiyoq Unu), which has Chachapoyan elements.

1983. A document of 1568 is discovered in a Cuzco archive: compiled by Augustinian monks, it lists properties in the Urubamba valley and makes clear that Machu Picchu was part of 'the royal estate of Pachacuti', as John H. Rowe describes in an article published in 1987.

1984. Vincent Lee, with his 'Sixpac Manco' expedition, identifies the site of Huayna Pucará, the fort used by the Incas in their defensive withdrawal from the Spanish. This is further confirmation of the identification of Espíritu Pampa as Old Vilcabamba.

1987. The discovery of the intact tomb of Sipán, a Moche burial site in the north of Peru, with a rich panoply of turquoise armour and gold jewellery. The finds are excavated and preserved by Walter Alva.

1984–90. Increased activity by the Sendero Luminoso in the Apurímac region, and the consequent Peruvian military response, make working in the Vilcabamba area difficult. John Ridgway describes the difficulties when travelling through the area in 1984 in search of the explorer and guide Elvin Berg (he discovers that Berg has been murdered by the Sendero).

1990. Robert Randall dies of rabies when on an expedition with the Cuzco Ramblers.

Sonia Guillén publishes a re-evaluation of George Eaton's analysis of the skeletons at Machu Picchu.

1983–99. Ann Kendall continues with a series of community-based archaeological projects near Ayacucho and Ollantaytambo.

1993–6. Perci Paz and fellow archaeologists from COPESCO excavate at Choquequirao.

1994–9. Elva Torres of the INC begins small-scale excavation works around the buildings and tombs of Machu Picchu.

1998. A landslide destroys the lower Aobamba valley and sweeps away the railway below Machu Picchu.

GLOSSARY

Abra. Mountain pass.

Adobe. Bricks of dried mud bound with straw, widely used in the Andes for construction.

Aclla. A 'chosen woman' of the Inca.

Ají. Hot pepper grown on the slopes of the mountains, from which a sauce is made.

Alpaca. Domesticated camelid highly valued for its wool.

Altiplano. High plateau.

Andén. Terrace.

Antisuyo. North-eastern quarter of the Inca Empire, extending into the jungle (hence *Antis*, the people who lived there).

Apacheta. Cairn.

Arriero. Muleteer.

Arroba. Weight-measurement for selling produce like potatoes – strictly speaking about 25 pounds, but often applied loosely in the mountains to any large bag.

Aymara. Ethnic group and language of the peoples living to the south and east of Lake Titicaca.

Ayllu. Kinship group.

Baño. When used archaeologically, a ceremonial bath (when used in everyday speech, the bathroom or toilet).

Barranca. Ravine.

Borges. Jorge Luis Borges, the master Argentinian story-teller whose world of labyrinthine fictions has been deeply influential in South American literature – hence 'Borgesian'.

Borla. The 'royal fringe', the insignia of the Emperor which he wore on his head (the Quechua term for it was *llauto*). Pedro Pizarro describes it as 'made in the manner of a crown, but round and not having points, being a hand's breadth wide and encircling the head. At the front was a fringe ... made of very fine scarlet wool, evenly cut, and adorned with small golden tubes.'

Cacique. Spanish colonial term for local native leader.

Cambio. As in *casa de cambio*, exchange-rate for money.

Cancha. Small plot of land, football pitch.

Capac-nan. The 'Royal Road' of the Incas from Quito to Cuzco.

Cañoso. Strong alcoholic spirit distilled from sugar-cane.

Campesino. Worker of the land.

Cedrala. Jungle thorn.

Ceiba. The large silk-cotton tree found in the Amazon and other American rainforests.

Ceque. Imaginary line radiating out from Cuzco and passing through a set of *huacas,* shrines. Each *ceque* was the responsibility of one of the *panacas,* the royal lineages.

Cerveza. Beer.

Coca. Plant (*Erythroxylon*) used by Indians for stamina and health and by the drugs trade for the extraction of cocaine.

Cocal. Coca plantation.

Collasuyo. South-eastern quarter of the Inca Empire (from the Colla ethnic group near Lake Titicaca).

Comedor. Dining-room.

Condesuyo. South-western quarter of the Inca Empire.

Cordillera. Mountain range.

Coya. Consort of the Sapa Inca (the Emperor), and sometimes his sister, on the basis, in Pedro Pizarro's phrase, that 'no one was worthy of them save themselves'.

Creole. Peruvian-born person of European descent. Discriminated against by Spanish colonial laws, they were the prime movers in the later Wars of Independence. *Criolla* cooking and music are predominantly styles of the coast in Peru.

Cumbia. Colombian version of *salsa,* popular across South America. *Techno-cumbia* is a modern hybrid form.

Cusichaca. Complex of archaeological sites at the confluence of the Urubamba and Cusichaca rivers, excavated by Ann Kendall in the late 1970s and early 1980s as part of the Cusichaca Project that she initiated.

Cuzco. Capital of the Inca Empire.

Cura. Priest.

Cuy. Guinea pig. In a nice phrase of the Comte de Sartiges in 1834, they are the 'paying guests' of huts in the mountains, being kept as pets, hoovers and finally food.

Chacra. Cultivated field, small-holding.

Chan Chan. Capital of the Chimú, near the modern city of Trujillo on Peru's north coast.

Chasqui. State runner, courier.

Chavín de Huantar. Lying in the mountains on an important trade route between the jungle and the coast, this ancient site (800–200 BC) is an early example of the importance of cross-fertilisation between Peru's different zones, as its builders, the Chavín, mixed elements of coastal architecture with jungle images of jaguars and snakes on their stelae and friezes.

Chicha. Fermented maize drink, traditionally made using saliva.

Chicharrones. Deep-fried pork, a great Andean delicacy.

Chimú. The great contemporary rivals of the Incas, who expanded their empire along 800 miles of the northern Peruvian coast and were conquered by the Incas before the arrival of the Spanish.

Chinchaysuyo. The northern quarter of the Inca Empire, extending into Ecuador and modern Colombia.

Choclo. Corn. *Choclo y queso*, corn on the cob with a slab of cheese, is a popular combination sold by market vendors.

Cholo. Indigenous man of the people, a 'lad'.

Choquequirao. Inca site near the Apurímac. The name means 'cradle of gold' in Quechua.

Chullpa. Tomb, burial chamber.

Chuño. A form of dried potato.

El Dorado. The legend of *El Dorado* told of a tribe in the north of South America where gold was so common that the native king covered himself in gold dust at an annual ceremony. Successive Spanish expeditions (and Sir Walter Raleigh) went in fruitless search of the truth behind the legend.

Encomienda. Area of land under the Spanish colonial system, whose native inhabitants paid tribute to an *encomendero*. The edict that forbade *encomenderos* from living on their own tribute-land caused problems: intended so that there would always be a group of conquistadors centred in the main towns for militia purposes, the result was to create a class of absentee landlords, with consequent abuses of the Indian population.

Espíritu Pampa. Modern-day settlement in the rainforest of the Andean lowlands (around 3000 feet) near which the Inca city of Old Vilcabamba was found by Gene Savoy in 1964.

Estado. The rough height of a man (5–6 feet), used for measuring vertical distances ('the wall was 4 *estados* high').

Eye bonder. Architectural term for the pierced stones often found in Inca buildings, usually round and protruding from a wall or gable. Sensible suggestions for their use include the securing of thatched roofs and hanging doors; less sensible ones include the securing of prisoners and wild animals.

Fuerza. Strength.

Gringo. Irritating and mildly pejorative term for white foreigners, supposedly originating in Mexico from the song 'Green grow the rushes oh' sung by American soldiers.

GPS. Global Positioning System, a boon to explorers for its ability accurately to pin-point the location of ruins using satellites. Lightweight instruments became widely available in the 1990s.

Guanaco. Fast-running camelid related to the llama and the alpaca. Exceptionally curious creatures, large groups of them will sometimes congregate near hunters to see where the shots are coming from. As a result, their numbers are in decline.

Hacienda. The building, usually substantial, at the centre of an estate of land. Also used to refer to the estate itself, the successor to the colonial *encomienda* system. The owner was the *hacendado*. The system was reformed in the late 1960s by the Velasco government.

Huaca. Carved stone or feature of the landscape, thought to have sacred significance.

Huaqueros. Tomb-robbers, treasure-hunters.

Huari. A civilisation that flourished in the highlands around Ayacucho from c. 650–800 AD and whose influence spread to the coast. Its precise relationship with the contemporary *Tiahuanaco* culture is a contentious issue among archaeologists. The Incas appropriated some Huari legacies such as their use of the *quipu* and of a road system to connect distant colonies.

Huayno. A particular music of the Peruvian Andes, with high-pitched vocals: an acquired taste. Fans are known as *huayneros*.

Huayna Picchu. The ruins of Machu Picchu lie on a saddle between two mountains, Mt Machu Picchu and the much-photographed Mt Huayna Picchu. *Huayna* in this context means 'lesser', to distinguish it from *Machu*, meaning 'greater', as Huayna Picchu is the lower of the two mountains. There is a small Inca ruin on its summit. On the far side of the mountain there is a cave with some beautifully fitted Inca masonry, known (for no good reason whatsoever) as 'The Temple of the Moon', and Inca paths have recently been discovered leading to the valley below.

INC. '*Instituto Nacional de Cultura*', National Cultural Institute, the Peruvian government department responsible for archaeological sites.

Ichu. Multi-purpose mountain grass, used for cooking, roofs, llama fodder and occasional auguries.

Inca Wasi. Extremely high Inca site in the Puncuyoc hills (13,000 feet), probably first discovered by Christian Bües in the 1930s.

Inti. Sun.

Intihuatana. 'Hitching post of the sun'. Term used for some Inca sculptures, such as the one at the centre of the Sacred Plaza in Machu Picchu.

Intipunku. The Sun Gate. Site on the approach to Machu Picchu from the Inca Trail.

Kallanka. Inca meeting-hall.

League. A distance of about three miles, or how far a person could walk in an hour.

Limeño. Inhabitant of Lima.

Llactapata. Site discovered by Bingham in 1912 on a mountain ridge between the Aobamba and Santa Teresa valleys, and then lost again. The name means 'high town' in Quechua.

Llauto. Cf. *borla.*

Llipta. An alkaline substance used in order to break down the coca leaf when chewing.

Machu Picchu. The best-known of Inca sites, lying on a ridge at almost 8000 feet between Mt Machu Picchu and Mt Huayna Picchu. It is thought to have belonged to the estate of the Inca Emperor Pachacuti and seems not to have been 'discovered' by the Spanish at the time of the Conquest, although this concept needs care: while no Spanish chronicle of the time mentions Machu Picchu, they likewise mentioned few other Inca sites unless they had military or financial cause to do so; they were not studying Inca archaeology.

Mamacona. A woman dedicated to serve the state religion and, by extension, the Sapa Inca.

Manta. Weaving, cloak.

Matapalo. The strangler fig, a parasitical jungle plant that grows down from the branches of the host tree and ends by enveloping and killing it.

Mestizo. Phrase used after the Spanish Conquest to refer to those of mixed Indian and European blood.

Mirador. Viewpoint platform. A common feature of some Inca paths (like the approach to Inca Wasi in the Puncuyoc hills).

Mita. Inca system of compulsory community labour.

Mitamayo. The practice of transplanting populations from one part of the country to perform *mita* in another, with those transplanted known as *mitimaes.*

Moche. Small but exuberant civilisation which flourished on the northern coast of Peru in the first millennium, to around 600 AD. They left superbly expressive ceramics depicting the human face and finely worked jewellery such as that recently found at Sipán. The ceramics give a vivid picture of the various warlike and sexual activities practised by the Moche.

Moraya. Freeze-dried potato.

Montaña. Literally 'mountain', but also generic for forested hillside.

Moya. A garden or orchard, but used more widely to refer to 'a place of leisure' for enjoyment and relaxation, often with ornamental baths or lakes.

Nazca. Coastal culture which was at its peak from around 100 BC–700 AD. While adopting some customs from the preceding Paracas civilisation nearby, it is most famed for the great line-markings on the plain of Nazca. Some of these geoglyphs are geometric, some figurative – like the figure of an enormous 300-foot humming-bird. The lines have attracted much speculation, most of it extremely loose.

Orejón. Spanish term for the Inca nobility, literally meaning 'big ear' on account of the distinguishing ear-plugs they wore.

Paititi. 'Lost city in the jungle', probably mythical, frequently searched for and never found.

Pallcay. Small classical Inca site at the head of the Aobamba valley, sometimes also known as Llactapampa ('flat town').

Pampa. Literally 'a plain', as in Argentina, but often used in the Andes for any small enclosed flat area.

Panaca. Royal descent group and estate perpetuated after the death of an individual Sapa Inca (Emperor). There were twelve in Cuzco at the time of the Conquest.

Paracas. Peninsula on the coast which has given its name to an ancient culture that flourished there from 300 BC–200 AD. Celebrated for its elaborate funerary textiles, it may have influenced the nearby Nazca culture which emerged later.

Paseo. The charming Spanish custom, transported to Latin America, of taking an evening turn around the square or the principal drag of a town.

Pirca. Technical term for a lower-grade form of Inca construction using field stones and rubble.

Pisco Sour. Drink made from Pisco (Peruvian brandy), lemon and egg white.

P'olqo. Cloth used for protecting llamas' feet.

Poporo. Ceremonial coca-dipper used in order to break down the leaf with an alkaline substance, *llipta*, for chewing: often elaborately worked items.

Pumahuacachi. A gnat so savage in its biting that it 'makes the puma cry'. The only insects comparable in their viciousness are those found in San Blas in Mexico and certain areas of Scotland in August.

Puna. High-altitude Andean grassland, above the tree-line. Hence: *puna* hawk.

Puncuyoc. Range of hills to the north of the Vilcabamba valley, where the site of Inca Wasi is located.

Punchao. The golden image of the sun, at the heart of Inca religious practice. While there were several such images, designed to reflect light and dazzle the onlooker, it is thought that the principal one was captured at the time of the Spaniards' last engagement with Tupac Amaru and subsequently sent to Europe.

Qollqa. Warehouse, often built as a symbol of the Inca revenue being stored inside.

Quechua. Dialect adopted by the Incas to be the *lingua franca* of the Empire and still widely spoken. Also used to refer generically to their descendants.

Quinoa. A grain that is one of the few crops that can be grown at extreme altitudes in the Andes. Now popular in Western health food shops.

Quinta. Neighbourhood restaurant.

Quipu. Inca mnemonic device for recording information on knotted cords. The knots could then be 'read' by skilled interpreters (the *quipucamayos*).

Refresco. Soft drink.

Retama. Bright yellow Andean broom.

Rocotillo. Snake that whips itself around the legs or arms of a supposed attacker (also known as a *látigo*, a whip, for that reason). While it is not poisonous, the shock is not recommended for those of a nervous disposition.

Sabor. Taste.

Salsa. Loose musical term first used in New York to market Latin music with an Afro-Cuban beat for a North American audience.

Salteña. Spiced Bolivian pastie, filled with hot vegetables, cheese or meat. Elaborate versions can contain egg or olives.

Selva. Jungle. The phrase *ceja de selva*, 'the eyebrow of the jungle', is often used to refer to the cloud forest on the descent to the Amazon basin.

Sol(es). The Peruvian unit of currency (or, as Bingham put it excitedly, 'a silver dollar').

Soroche. Altitude sickness.

Sucre. The Bolivian unit of currency.

Tahuantinsuyo. The Inca Empire, which was divided into four quarters.

Tío/Tía. Uncle/Aunt, used often in an affectionate rather than a literal way: '*Tío Guillo*, Old William'.

Tiahuanaco. Ruins near Lake Titicaca, the centre of a culture which flourished between c. 250–1000 AD and extended over highland Bolivia and the south of Peru. The Incas were much influenced by Tiahuanacuan architecture and appropriated the shrines on the Islands of the Sun and of the Moon as their own.

Tambo. Lodging-house along Inca highways; also used for storage.

Trago. Shot of a drink, as in a *trago* of rum.

Tumi. Ceremonial knife.

Tupu. Pin used by Inca women to hold a shawl in place.

Valle Sagrado. The so-called 'Sacred Valley of the Incas' lies along the Vilcanota river to the north of Cuzco, where substantial Inca sites were built at Pisac, Yucay and Ollantaytambo. The climate is suitable for growing maize, essential for the ritual drinking of *chicha* which the Inca practised. It was an important area for them, for agricultural as well as possible religious reasons. However, the actual term 'Sacred Valley' was not used by the Incas themselves, as is often assumed, but was a marketing invention of 1950, designed to promote a driving rally held in the valley that year.

Vicuña. Camelid with exceptionally fine wool – smaller than the llama or alpaca, it has never been successfully domesticated, and was hunted by the Incas.

Vilcabamba. An area north-west of Cuzco, centring on the River Vilcabamba, to which the Incas retreated after the Conquest. Also used to refer to the Inca city of Vilcabamba (now identified as being near the present site of Espíritu Pampa), which is referred to in this book as 'Old Vilcabamba' to avoid confusion. A 'New Vilcabamba', the mining town of San Francisco de la

Vitoria de Vilcabamba, was built in a different location by the Spanish after the Conquest.

Vilcanota. Alternative name for the upper Urubamba river where it runs through the Valle Sagrado near Cuzco.

Waru waru. Raised field, as used by the Tiahuanaco civilisation around the shores of Lake Titicaca.

Wiñay Wayna. Attractive site close to Machu Picchu, discovered by the Paul Fejos expedition of 1940–41.

Yanacona. Servant of the Inca.

(For almost all the terms above that are Quechuan, there are possible spelling variants: *-suyu* for *-suyo* etc.)

SELECT BIBLIOGRAPHY

For many years, knowledge of the Incas was warped by Garcilaso de la Vega's exuberant but inaccurate and highly partisan account of his ancestors, *The Royal Commentaries of the Incas*.

Recently more of the original chroniclers have become available in English, with new scholarly translations of Juan de Betanzos, Bernabé Cobo and Pedro de Cieza de León. No translations of the important accounts by Pedro Pizarro, Martín de Murúa or Titu Cusi are currently available.

Modern Inca archaeological studies began in 1944 with the publication of John H. Rowe's *An Introduction to the Archaeology of Cuzco*, which revealed the sketchiness of previous work. Over a long life, Rowe has continued to contribute to the growth of studies in this area, including an important paper in 1987 on the ownership of Machu Picchu. At the time of writing, his work remains un-anthologised.

John Hemming's *Conquest of the Incas* of 1970 together with Gasparini's and Margolies' *Inca Architecture* of 1980 provided the essential scholarly foundations for further work in this area. John V. Murra made an influential study of the dynamism of Inca trading patterns while Tom Zuidema has written on the system of *ceques* around Cuzco.

Younger scholars such as Brian Bauer and Gary Urton have usefully challenged some of the preconceptions about the growth of the Inca Empire under Pachacuti. Craig Morris and John Hyslop have added substantially to knowledge of Inca town planning and road-systems. The Peruvian ethno-historian María Rostworowski has represented the events of the Inca Empire from a more Andean perspective, with a particular stress on the importance of the *panaca* system of inheritance and how dominated it often was by a line of female influence. Recent contributions by writers like Susan Niles (her excellent *The Shape of Inca History*) point the way forward to the growth in Inca studies that is surely still to come.

The only book by Hiram Bingham still in print is his *Lost Cities of the Incas*, first published in 1948. It is also worth reading the earlier books and magazine articles he wrote at the time of his discoveries, although these, like many accounts by other explorers, can be difficult to obtain.

EXPLORERS
(in chronological order)

Comte de Sartiges, *Voyage dans les Républiques de l'Amérique du Sud,* written under pseudonym of M. E. de Lavandais, in *Revue de Deux Mondes* (Paris, 1850). Also translated as *Dos Viajeros Franceses en el Perú Republicano: De Sartiges-Botmiliau,* trans. Emilio Romero (Lima, 1947).

Léonce Angrand, in Ernest Desjardins, *Le Pérou Avant La Conquête Espagnole* (Paris, 1858).

Herman Göhring, *Informe Supremo de Paucartambo* (Lima, 1874).

George Squier, *Peru: Incidents of Travel and Exploration in the Land of the Incas* (New York, 1877) (republished by Harvard University Peabody Museum, 1972).

Charles Wiener, *Pérou et Bolivie: Récit de Voyage* (Paris, 1880).

Augusto R. Berns, *Prospecto de la Compañía Anónima Exploradora de las 'Huacas del Inca' Limitada* (Lima, 1887).

Edward Whymper, *Travels Amongst the Great Andes of the Equator* (London, 1892).

Hiram Bingham, *Across South America* (New York, 1911).
Inca Land (Boston, 1922).
Machu Picchu, a Citadel of the Incas (New Haven, 1930).
Lost City of the Incas (New York, 1948).
'The Ruins of Choqquequirrau' (*American Anthropologist,* 12, 1911).
'Vitcos the Lost Inca Capital' (*Proceedings of American Antiquarian Society,* April 1912).
'A Search for the Lost Inca Capital' (*Harper's Magazine,* 1912).
'In the Wonderland of Peru' (*National Geographic,* April 1913).
'The Ruins of Espíritu Pampa' (*American Anthropologist,* 16, 1914).
'Along the Uncharted Pampaconas' (*Harper's Magazine,* Aug. 1914).
'The Story of Machu Picchu' (*National Geographic,* Feb. 1915).
'Further Explorations in the Land of the Incas' (*National Geographic,* May 1916).

Alfred Bingham, *Portrait of an Explorer: Hiram Bingham, Discover of Machu Picchu* (Iowa State University Press, 1989).

George F. Eaton, *The Collection of Osteological Material from Machu Picchu* (Memoirs of the Connecticut Academy of Arts and Sciences, Boston, 1916, translated into Spanish with Introduction by **Sonia Guillén,** Lima, 1990).

Paul Fejos, *Archaeological Explorations in the Cordillera Vilcabamba, Southeastern Peru* (Viking Fund Publications in Anthropology, No. 3, New York, 1944).

Victor von Hagen, *Highway of the Sun* (New York, 1957).

Julian Tennant, *Quest for Paititi* (London, 1958).

G. Brooks Baedeland and Peter Gimbel, 'By Parachute into Peru's Lost World' (*National Geographic,* 126, Aug. 1964).

Gene Savoy, *Antisuyo* (New York, 1970) (published as *Vilcabamba, Last City of the Incas,* in UK, 1971).

'The Feathered Serpent' *(Explorers Journal,* Jun. 1977).

'The Discovery of Vilcabamba' *(Explorers Journal,* Mar. 1978).

'Return to Vilcabamba' *(Explorers Journal,* Dec. 1978).

John Beauclerk, 'La Cordillera Vilcabamba, Ultimo Refugio de los Incas' *(Boletin de Lima,* Nos. 4 & 5, Lima, Mar. 1980).

Stuart White, *Preliminary Site Survey of the Puncuyoc Range, Southern Peru* (Papers of the Institute of Andean Studies, 22–3, Berkeley, 1984–5).

Vincent R. Lee, *Sixpac Manco: Travels among the Incas* (self-published, Wilson, 1985).

Chanasuyu: The Ruins of Inca Vilcabamba (self-published, Wilson, 1989).

Inca Choqek'iraw (self-published, Wilson, 1997).

Forgotten Vilcabamba (Sixpac Manco Publications, 2000).

Gary Ziegler, *Machu Picchu Abandoned* (self-published, Crestone Press, 1996).

The Empire Strikes Back! Choquequirao, The Inca's Last Secret (self-published, Crestone Press, 1998).

Royal Geographical Society, reports Nos. 492, 1010, 1068, 1081, 1089, 1143, 1604, 1085 and 1297 contain useful material on the area, as does the quarterly magazine of the South American Explorers' Club.

An update on recent discoveries may be viewed at www.thewhiterock.co.uk

CHRONICLES

Juan de Betanzos, *Suma y Narracion de los Incas* (1551), translated by Roland Hamilton and Dana Buchanan as *Narrative of the Incas* (University of Texas Press, 1996).

Pedro de Cieza de León, *Crónica del Perú* (1550–53).

The Incas of Pedro de Cieza de León, introduction by Victor von Hagen (University of Oklahoma, 1959).

Bernabé Cobo, *Historia del Nuevo Mundo* (1653), translated and edited by Roland Hamilton as *History of the Inca Empire* (University of Texas Press, 1979) and *Inca Religion and Customs* (University of Texas, 1990).

Titu Cusi, *Relación de la Conquista del Perú* (1570), (Lima, 1973).

Also in *En el encuentro de dos Mundos: los Incas de Vilcabamba,* ed. María del Carmen Martín Rubio (Madrid, 1988).

Felipe Guaman Poma, *Nueva Corónica y Buen Gobierno* (c. 1580–1620) (published in 3 vols., Lima, 1956–66).

Martín de Murúa, *Historia General del Perú, Origen y Descendencia de los Incas* (1590–1611) (Madrid, 1962–4).

Pedro Pizarro, *Relación del Descubrimiento y Conquista de los Reinos del Perú* (1571).

Relation of the Discovery and Conquest of the Kingdoms of Peru (New York, Cortes Society, folio edition, 1921).

Garcilaso de la Vega, *Los Comentarios Reales de los Incas* (1609–17), translated as *The Royal Commentaries of the Incas* (University of Texas Press, 1966).

Several contemporary chronicles (*La Relación Francesa,* Cristobal de Mena etc.) are collected in *Las Relaciones Primitivas de la Conquista de Perú (Early Accounts of the Conquest of Peru),* ed. Raúl Porras Barrenechea (Lima, 1967).

HISTORY AND ARCHAEOLOGY

Marcia and Robert Ascher, *Code of the Quipu: a Study in Media, Mathematics and Culture* (Michigan, 1981).

Brian S. Bauer, *The Development of the Inca State* (University of Texas Press, 1982).

Brian S. Bauer and David Dearborn, *Astronomy and Empire in the Ancient Andes: The Cultural Origins of Inca Skywatching* (University of Texas Press, 1995).

Richard L. Burger, *Chavín and the Origins of the Andean Civilization* (Thames and Hudson, New York, 1995).

David Drew, *The Cusichaca Project: the Lucumayo and Santa Teresa Valleys* (British Archaeological Reports, International Series 210, Oxford, 1984).

J. H. Elliott, *The Old World and the New 1492–1650* (Cambridge University Press, 1970).

Joseph A. Gagliano, *Coca Prohibition in Peru: The Historical Debates* (University of Arizona Press, 1994).

Graziano Gasparini and Luisa Margolies, *Arquitectura Inka* (Venezuela, 1977), translated by Patricia J. Lyon as *Inca Architecture* (Indiana University Press, 1980).

Edward Goodman, *The Explorers of South America* (Macmillan, New York, 1972).

Edmundo Guillén Guillén, *'El Enigma de los Momias Incas'* (*Boletín de Lima* 5, No. 28, 29–42, July 1983).

Victor von Hagen, *The Realm of the Incas* (New York, 1957).

John Hemming, *The Conquest of the Incas* (Harcourt Brace, 1970).
The Search for El Dorado (Michael Joseph, 1978).
The Golden Age of Discovery (Pavilion, London, 1998).

John Hemming and Edward Ranney, *Monuments of the Incas* (Boston, 1982).

Lorenzo Huertas Vallejos, *'Memorial Acerca de las Cuatro Ciudades Inkas Situadas entre los rios Urubamba y Apurímac'* (*Historia y cultura* 6, Lima, 1973) (contains details of the report written by the prospector Juan Arias Diaz Topete in 1710).

John Hyslop, *The Inca Road System* (Academic Press, New York, 1984).
Inca Settlement Planning (1990).

Ann Kendall, *Current Archaeological projects in Central Andes: some approaches and* *results* (British Archaeological Reports [BAR], International Series 210, Oxford, 1984).

Aspects of Inca Architecture: Design, Function and Use (BAR 242, Oxford, 1985).

Inca Planning north of Cuzco between Anta and Machu Picchu and along the Urubamba valley, in Nicholas J. Saunders and Olivier de Montmollin, eds, *Recent Studies in Pre-Columbian Archaeology* (BAR 421, Oxford, 1988).

Restauración de Sistemas Agricolas Prehispánicos en la Sierra Sur, Peru, ed. Ann Kendall (Cusichaca Trust, 1997).

Irving A. Leonard, *Books of the Brave: Being an Account of Books and of Men in the Spanish Conquest and Settlement of the 16th Century New World* (University of California, 1949).

James Lockhart, *Spanish Peru, 1532–1560* (Wisconsin, 1968).

Michael A. Malpass, *Daily Life in the Inca Empire* (Greenwood Press, 1996).

Lynn Meisch, ed., *Traditional Textiles of the Andes* (Thames and Hudson, 1997).

Craig Morris and Donald E. Thompson, *Huánuco Pampa. An Inca City and its Hinterland* (Thames and Hudson, 1985).

Craig Morris and Adriana von Hagen, *The Inka Empire and its Andean Origins* (Abbeville Press, 1993).

The Cities of the Ancient Andes (Thames and Hudson, 1998).

Michael Moseley, *The Incas and their Ancestors* (Thames and Hudson, 1992).

John V. Murra, 'Cloth and its Functions in the Inca State' (*American Anthropologist* 64, no 4, 1962).

The Economic Organisation of the Inca State (JAI Press, 1980).

Keith Muscutt, *Warriors of the Clouds* (University of New Mexico Press, 1998).

Susan A. Niles, *The Shape of Inca History: Narrative and Architecture in an Andean Empire* (University of Iowa Press, 1999).

César Paternosto, *The Stone and the Thread: Andean Roots of Abstract Art*, translated by Esther Allen (University of Texas Press, 1996).

William H. Prescott, *History of the Conquest of Peru* (New York, 1847).

Jean-Pierre Protzen, *Inca Architecture and Construction at Ollantaytambo* (Oxford University Press, 1993).

Johan Reinhart, *Machu Picchu – The Sacred Center* (Lima, 1991).

María Rostworowski de Diez Canseco, *Historia del Tahuantinsuyu*, translated as *History of the Inca Realm* (Cambridge, CUP, 1999).

J. H. Rowe, 'An Introduction to the Archaeology of Cuzco' (Papers of Peabody Museum of American Archaeology, Vol. xxvii, No. 2, Cambridge, Mass., 1944).

'Inca Culture at the Time of the Spanish Conquest' in *Handbook of South American Indians* (Bureau of American Ethnology, Bulletin 143, Vol. 2, Washington, 1946).

'Machu Pijchu a la Luz de Documentos del Siglo XVI' (*Kultur* 4, Lima, March–April 1987) (also *Historica* 14 (1), Lima, 1990).

Inge R. Schjellerup, *Incas and Spaniards in the Conquest of the Chachapoyans* (Gotarc Series B Gothenburg Archaeological Theses No 7).

Karen S. Stothert, *Pre-Colonial Highways of Bolivia* (Publicación de la Academia Nacional de Ciencia de Bolivia, No. 7, La Paz).

Gary Urton, *At the Crossroads of the Earth and the Sky* (University of Texas Press, 1981).

The History of a Myth: Pacariqtambo and the origin of the Inkas (University of Texas Press, 1990).

Valencia and Gibaja, *Machu Picchu: La Investigación y Conservación del Monumento Arqueológico después de Hiram Bingham* (Lima, 1992).

Horacio Villanueva Urteaga, *'Documentos sobre Yucay en el siglo XVI'* (Revista del Archivo Historico del Cuzco 13 (1970), 1–148).

R. Tom Zuidema, *Inca Civilization in Cuzco* (University of Texas Press, 1991).

RELATED TEXTS

Ciro Alegría, *La Serpiente de Oro* (1935).

Jorge Casteñada, *Compañero, the Life and Death of Che Guevara* (London, 1997).

Martín Chambi, *Photographs, 1920–1950* (Smithsonian Institution Press, 1993).

Adrian Forsythe and Ken Miyata, *Tropical Nature* (New York, 1984).

Peter Frost, *Exploring Cusco* (Lima, 5th edition, 1999).

Eduardo Galeano, *Open Veins of Latin America: Five Centuries of the Pillage of a Continent* (New York, 1973).

Ernesto Che Guevara, 'Machu Picchu: Enigma de Piedra en América', December 1953, reprinted in *Revista de la Casa de las Américas* (Havana), Vol. 28, No. 163, July–August 1987.

The Motorcycle Diaries, A Journey Around South America (London, 1995).

Hergé, *The Adventures of Tintin: Prisoners of the Sun* (1949).

Alan L. Kolata, *Valley of the Spirits: A Journey into the Lost Realm of the Aymara* (John Wiley & Sons, 1996).

Erik Larsen, *Frans Post* (Amsterdam/Rio de Janeiro, 1962).

Matthew Parris, *Inca Cola* (London, 1993).

Claude Lévi-Strauss, *Tristes Tropiques* (Paris, 1955).

Stephen Minta, *Aguirre* (Jonathan Cape, 1993).

Pablo Neruda, *'Confieso que he Vivido'* (Seix Barral, 1974).

'Las Alturas de Macchu Picchu' in *Canto General* (Mexico, 1950).

John Ridgway, *Amazon Journey* (London, 1972).

Road to Elizabeth (London, 1986).

Tobias Schneebaum, *Keep the River on your Right* (1969).

Charles Waterton, *Wanderings in South America* (London, 1826).

NOTES AND REFERENCES

xvii *'I don't know who you are. I wish I did.'*
Vincent Lee, *Sixpac Manco*,
Introduction.

7 *naming any new geographical features they came across after their girlfriends.* Or in Kit Lambert's case, presumably boyfriends. He was flamboyantly gay.

7 *Theodore Roosevelt, when he led an American expedition to the Amazon in 1913.* Roosevelt went on the expedition with Colonel Rondón. His son Kermit nearly drowned. By the time Roosevelt got to Manaus, the ex-president was reported to be 'a shadow of his former self' and this may have contributed to his death five years later. See Edward Goodman, *The Explorers of South America.*

7 *Mason was the first person to walk along it.* Characteristically, John's response to the killing was to leave some machetes for the hostile Indians (the Panar) to find, as a sign of peaceful intent.

11 *Various expeditions (like the Fejos one) had tried and failed over the following seventy years to re-find it.* It is of course possible that it had been relocated without any record being left.

11 *Bingham's seductive account of the ruin.* Hiram Bingham, *Lost City of the Incas,* 135.

14 *'I am inserting some of these things just as they come to my memory.'* Pedro Pizarro, I, 244.

14 *Atahualpa dropped a bit of food on his clothing.* Pedro Pizarro, I, 224f.

15 *an insulting present of ducks gutted and filled with straw.* María Rostworowski de Diez Canseco, *History of the Inca Realm,* 126.

15 *'to everything which he had ever touched.'* Pedro Pizarro, I, 225.

16 *he could at the very least have been sent into exile, either to Panama or Spain.* Pedro Pizarro, I, 218f. Pizarro argues that he could have been sent to Spain (partly on the grounds that he would probably die there quickly anyway, 'out of humiliation').

16 *'the treatment of Atahualpa was one of the darkest.'* William H. Prescott, *History of the Conquest of Peru,* 341.

16 *Tahuantinsuyo, as the Inca Empire was known.* Rostworowski points out that this term may not have been used by the Incas themselves, Rostworowski, 223.

16 *'it looked as if a black cloth had been spread over the ground for half a league.'* Pedro Pizarro, I, 301.

17 *the overwhelming superiority of the Incas.* Manco Inca was too honourable in his attack, summoning all his forces and only then beginning when the enemy knew what they were up against. To win, he needed to kill the Spaniards in their beds and the horses in their stables, something they themselves would have had no compunction in doing. See both Prescott and Hemming for full accounts of the siege.

18 *the fabulous reports of the treasures being discovered in the New World and of the men who found them.* See Irving A. Leonard, *Books of the Brave,* where he comments that 'to be young in the Hispanic Peninsula during this period of human experience was to have faith in the impossible'.

19 *'as the walls are high, and as all those who*

first fell died.' Titu Cusi, *La Relación*, 83.

19 *eleven bodies had been found, apparently of Inca warriors who it was presumed had died in the siege.* As so often, care has always to be taken with such identification, as later post-Conquest Quechuans often had their corpses moved by relatives from churches and secretly buried at Sacsahuaman as a symbol of revolt.

24 *'if the expedition had had anyone with archaeological training on its staff.'* John H. Rowe, *An Introduction to the Archaeology of Cuzco*, 12.

24 *a zealousness that had done little for archaeological preservation.* As in 1934, when it was cleared by Chavez, a follower of Julio C. Tello, for the 400th anniversary of the foundation of Cuzco as a colonial city.

24 *It was apparently in use before the Inca occupation.* See *Restauración de Sistemas Agrícolas Prehispánicos en la Sierra Sur, Peru*, ed. Ann Kendall, 4.

25 *'which it is death to try to cross?'* Bingham, *Lost City*, 106.

25 *a quite astonishing statistic of waste.* Ann Kendall, ibid., 4.

29 *'The mystery of the deep valleys.'* Bingham, *Lost City*, opening of Chapter XI.

30 *Sayac Marka (the 'inaccessible town').* This was the name given to it by Paul Fejos in 1940: Hiram Bingham had called it Cedrobamba.

30 *One explorer had quoted Frank Lloyd Wright to describe them.* Victor von Hagen on Pisac, *Highway of the Sun* (New York, 1957), 92.

30 *This was where we left the Inca Trail.* There is a much clearer trail striking off for Pallcay earlier, before Runcu Raccay and Sayac Marka, which Hiram Bingham noted when he found the Inca Trail in 1915. *Lost City*, Chapter XI, 197.

32 *he dedicates it 'In all Humility – to Myself.'* This was in later editions of the book. The original dedication was to his wife's grandfather, who had helped fund the expedition. However, when he later re-issued *Highway of the Sun*, after separating from his wife, he not only removed all references to her but changed the dedication – to himself.

34 *It must have been some honeymoon.* Dorothy Menzel went on to have a long and distinguished academic career in pre-Columbian studies.

34 *'There is always a certain uneasiness.'* Von Hagen, 31.

34 *sending a telegram.* Von Hagen, 252.

35 *for thinking, by helping to conceive the relationship of one place to another.'* John Hyslop, *The Inca Road System* (New York, 1984), 340.

35 *stone and tiles brought from Cuzco to Quito [a distance of 3400 miles], where they are still to be seen.* Pedro de Cieza de León (University of Oklahoma, 1959), 77.

35 *three roads seemed to point to precisely the same destination.* Cieza de León, 137.

38 *'the ruins of a small Inca country-house.'* Bingham, *Lost City*, 197. See also David Drew, *The Cusichaca Project: the Lucumayo and Santa Teresa Valleys* (BAR 210, Oxford, 1984), 355.

43 *'We could only scratch at a tiny proportion.'* cf National Geographic 1913, 521, where Bingham says that he wanted to return to Llactapata as 'it would be interesting to excavate for three or four weeks and get sufficient evidence in the way of shreds and artefacts to show just what connection the people who built and occupied this mountain stronghold had to the other occupants of the valley.'

44 *David described these buildings as being of classical Inca proportions and detail.* See also Drew, BAR 210, 357.

44 *a reminder that one could be yards from a site and never realise it.* Some years later, Gary Zigler went to the Llactapata site with GPS equipment, and gave the UGS co-ordinates of the site as '18L 07 62 15, U 85 41 00 at about 2700 meters, using the MAPI topo sheet' (personal communication from Gary Ziegler).

46 *Message from a village headman to the Comte de Sartiges in 1834.* See *Dos Viajeros Franceses en el Peru Republicano: De Sartiges-Botmiliau*, trans. Emilio Romero (Lima, 1947), 87.

52 *'some of the most magnificent scenery in the Americas.'* De Sartiges, ibid., 79f.

54 *this was, as the counsellors say, ground for conflict.* J.B. recently put his own revisionist view of this to me in a letter: 'Porridge. I recall Roddy and I getting exceedingly cross with you. On a number of mornings on the way to Choquequirao, Roddy and I rose early and typically went off to forage for wood or collect water – whilst you remained in your sleeping bag, reading, sleeping or writing up your blessed diary. We would then return – horrified to discover that you "had had a go" at cooking the porridge. After several attempts at chipping into what looked like nearly set concrete, we forbade you from touching the box of Quaker Oats again.'

55 *there was a useful source of water and there might be none below.* A wise decision as there indeed turned out not to be any until the Río Blanco was reached far below.

56 *a nameless small river.* Later identified as the Río Blanco.

58 *This was not a site that the Comte de Sartiges had come across.* The precise route Sartiges took is unclear from his description. Having left Yanama, he may have descended to the Apurímac and avoided the San Juan pass, coming back up the river now known as the Río Blanco. He certainly seems to have ascended the slopes above Pincha Unuyoc, as he refers to plateaux ascending one above the other up mountainous slopes, which would correspond with this route, as does his late night spent below a precipice before arriving at the ruins the next morning.

58 *at least six or seven layers of terraces.* I returned to this site in 1999 with Gary Ziegler shortly after a forest fire had cleared the upper slopes and revealed how extensive the terracing was: the presence of many simple circular foundations at the top of the site and relatively few better-built buildings at its centre tend towards the idea that this was an agricultural supply centre for Choquequirao, lived in by workers.

58 *we were the first to do so.* See our report lodged with Royal Geographical Society (RGS No. 1143).

58 *Gary Ziegler in 1994.* See Gary Ziegler, *The Empire Strikes Back! Choquequirao, The Inca's Last Secret* (self-published Crestone Press, 1998).

58 *the architect Vincent Lee in 1995.* See Vincent Lee, *Inca Choqek'iraw* (self-published, Wilson, 1997).

58 *later renamed Pincha Unuyoc.* By Ziegler, or Pinchiyoq Unu by the Peruvian archaeologist Perci Paz.

59 *Donne's lines 'and that this place may thoroughly be thought / True Paradise, I have the serpent brought.'* In 'Twickenham Garden', *The Songs and Sonnets*, ed. Theo Redpath (London, 1956).

61 *a small two-roomed building with an outer rampart.* Known as the Outlier Group.

61 *a spectacular view down both sides of the ridge to the river.* I have since noticed that the Outlier Group has a clear sight-line to a site called 'Huaca Mayo' ('the River Shrine') recently found by Gary Ziegler on a spur in the next valley high above Pincha Unuyoc, and so could have been used as a signalling station back towards Cuzco.

64 *Even the local shop had nothing for us.* Nothing had changed in this respect since the days of the Comte de Sartiges: he was also refused eggs by the inhabitants of one village, who claimed they had none. This blatant lie so annoyed his *mestizo* manservant that he stole some and almost caused a riot.

65 *'those are pearls that were his eyes.' The Tempest,* I ii 396.

67 *built by either Pachacuti or his son Topa Inca.* Later indications are that it was built by Pachacuti. See Rowe, 1987.

73 *the Incas had used llama grease to slide them together.* See Kendall, *Restauración,* 19.

73 *the final run-off took the water down to the terraces below.* The American hydrologist Ken Wright has done much work to investigate the Machu Picchu water supply system. See South American Explorers Club (SAEC) magazine #46.

74 *coca was certainly grown in the valley below Machu Picchu.* Cf. Rowe, 1987: coca was delivered in tribute from this section of the valley and the Pijchu Indians had

to submit 105 baskets (*cestos*) of coca leaves a year.

74 *many of them aligned on some of the peaks the Incas held sacred.* Cf. Johan Reinhard, *Machu Picchu – The Sacred Center.*

75 *fortifications were light compared to others in the Inca Empire.* The conclusion of the Fejos expedition. See Paul Fejos, Bibliography.

75 *the little signal station on its top.* The Fejos expedition thought that this was a signalling station, but this has been disputed since.

76 *'a deep sense of religious mystery.'* John Hemming in *Monuments of the Incas* (Boston, 1982), Machu Picchu chapter.

77 *He remembered later that in 1943 at Machu Picchu.* Pablo Neruda, *'Confieso Que He Vivido'* (Seix Barral, 1974), 235.

77 *He speculated that one set of buildings.* John Hemming in *Monuments of the Incas* (Boston, 1982), 156.

78 *Hemming had noticed.* Ibid., 145.

78 *'no one now disputes.'* Hiram Bingham, *Lost City of the Incas,* opening of Chapter IX.

79 *'For centuries travellers could not visit it.'* Bingham, *Lost City.* Preface.

80 *Bingham elsewhere reveals he had with him.* Ibid., Chapter VI.

80 *As one Peruvian commentator wryly put it.* Rafael Aguilar Páez in 1961.

82 *'we were discovered by a huge condor.'* Bingham, *Lost City,* Chapter IV.

85 *'a mountainous country, with imposing geography.'* Irving A. Leonard, *Books of the Brave,* 4.

88 *the street where her father had always had his studio, the Calle Marqués.* The Chambis moved a few houses along the street after the earthquake of 1950 wrecked the original studio.

88 *'there are some areas of Perú.'* Raimondi, *El Perú* (1874–1913).

88 *Sadly the camera proved to be not quite so portable as he had hoped.* The invention of the first truly hand-held camera (the Leica) in 1926 meant that every explorer could easily take his own stills.

88 *'in my archive I have more than two hundred photographs.'* Martín Chambi in *Hoy* (Santiago), 4 March 1936.

91 *'an autochthonous exemplar of the race.'* In José García Uriel, 'Martín Chambi, Artista Neoindigena'. *Excelsior,* Aug–Oct. 1948.

91 *the picture of the Wiñay Wayna complex he took soon after their discovery and clearance.* See cover.

95 *'like a dismembered animal on the hillside.'* Motorbike Diaries, 99.

95 *'Cuzco invites you to turn warrior.'* Ibid., 88.

96 *'It doesn't really matter what the origin.'* Ibid., 95.

97 *Bingham was forced to return any new finds.* Cf. *Lost City of the Incas,* end of Chapter X: 'The archaeological material is mostly in the Yale University Museum, except that which was excavated in 1914–1915, which was all returned to the Peruvian government.'

97 *the bones were and still are the principal find of interest.* At the time of writing there are persistent and unsubstantiated claims that a horse's bones have also been found buried on the site: if so, this would not necessarily indicate a Spanish discovery at the time of the Conquest or that the last Incas might have used it on their retreat from Cuzco: it could equally well have been left by nineteenth-century *huaqueros,* although it is, to say the least, a curious place to take a horse at any time.

98 *The distinguished Peruvian archaeologist Sonia Guillén recently made a search.* See her Introduction to the Spanish edition of George F. Eaton, *The Collection of Osteological Material from Machu Picchu,* 1916 (translated by Sonia Guillén, Lima, 1990).

103 *'for wherever the Spaniards have passed.'* Cieza de León, 62.

104 *'these lands will soon be ours.'* Ibid., 158.

104 *'these natives were stupid and brutish beyond belief.'* Ibid., 25.

105 *'I hate to think of those who have governed.'* Ibid., 155.

106 *'the excessive cold of this region.'* Ibid., 265.

109 *it looked like a Mediterranean idyll.* I revisited Taquile in 2000: the co-operative system of tourism was still being used and the islanders have been successful enough to introduce solar

power to many of the houses. While men and women still knit continually, they now tend to use more synthetic fibres.

112 *The name Copacabana was precisely right.* The Bolivian resort was in fact the original, from which its more famous Brazilian counterpart took its name.

121 '*the first thing we see as we travel around the world*' and the following quote are from Claude Lévi-Strauss, *Tristes Tropiques* (Paris, 1955), Chapter 4, 'The Quest for Power'.

125 '*coca is a plant that the devil invented.*' John Hemming, *The Conquest of the Incas*, 354.

126 '*Into the wine of which they were drinking.*' From *The Odyssey*, Canto 4, 220–26, Lattimore translation.

127 *The Inca stone path branched up from the road.* See Karen S. Stothert in the Bibliography for the Incaic nature of the path.

128 *the principle of 'verticality'.* See Michael Moseley, *The Incas and their Ancestors*, 43f., and John V. Murra, *The Economic Organisation of the Inca State*.

130 '*murmuring something in the Gaelic tongue.*' Squier, 273.

133 *it may have been the Incas themselves who moved many of the stones at Tiahuanaco.* See Moseley, 230.

133 *thought them the work of giants.* Cf. Bernabé Cobo, *Inca Religion and Customs*, 104.

134 *At Nazca, they brutally built a 24-foot wide road.* See Victor von Hagen, *Realm of the Incas*, 27.

137 *the distinguished Andean scholar John Rowe once suggested.* In *An Introduction to the Archaeology of Cuzco*.

139 '*The gloss, splendour and sheen of this feather cloth.*' From Cobo, *Inca Religion and Customs*, 226.

140 '*would often be given to childless women.*' Von Hagen, *Realm of the Incas*, 48.

142 *Topa Inca and his descendant Atahualpa led fleets of such reed rafts.* Cf. Rostworowski, 114.

144 *The historian J. H. Elliott has described these first reactions to America.* In some lectures on *The Old World and the New.* He also noted: 'The sheer immensity of this challenge goes a long way

towards explaining one of the most striking features of sixteenth-century intellectual history – the apparent slowness of Europe in making the mental adjustments required to incorporate America within its field of vision.'

149 *He chose to stay for many years in his birthplace of Tumipampa.* See Rostworowski, 86.

149 '*he drank for the poor, of whom he supported many.*' Pedro Pizarro, I, 199.

154 *Gonzalo Pizarro had been the first to hear rumours both of El Dorado and cinnamon.* The first in the southern territories of Ecuador and Peru. Expeditions had already tried to find it from Venezuela in the north. See John Hemming, *The Search for El Dorado*.

155 *who now remembers Francisco de Orellana, the discoverer of the Amazon?* The river was in fact called the Rio Orellana briefly, against his wishes, before receiving its current name.

156 '*if a hundred thousand men came here.*' In a letter of 1561 quoted in John Hemming, *The Search for El Dorado*, 144.

157 *would have made his son illegitimate by the Inca rules of succession.* Legitimacy in the line of Inca succession is a complicated issue. Cf. Rostworowski, 97f. Also Titu Cusi, 17, where he claims (for his own dynastic reasons) that both Huascar and Atahualpa were illegitimate.

157 *Atahualpa has always been inextricably associated with the North.* The chief chronicler supporting the Ecuadorian princess idea was Garcilaso, an unreliable witness at the best of times and one who was biased against Atahualpa for reasons of his own lineage. The *Garcilasista* version of events dominated Inca history until comparatively recently; more credence is now given to the rival account by Juan de Betanzos. See Rostworowski, 106f.

157 *The endless campaigns that Huayna waged in Ecuador left a permanent standing army in the North.* This also became an extended abuse of the *mitamayo* system, with consequent social unrest.

157 *Huayna Capac's sudden and disastrous death in around 1527.* For the date of the epidemic and Huayna's death, see Susan A. Niles, *The Shape of Inca History*, 120.

157 *The resulting civil war between the Ecuadorian and Peruvian sides of the Empire.* See Rostworowski, 33, and elsewhere for discussion of how the dispute over the succession was also between the rival *panacas* of Pachacuti and Topa Inca.

158 *Spanish contemporaries such as Lope de Vega were indeed producing.* Lope de Vega, *El Nuevo Mundo descubierto por Cristóbal Colón* (1614).

159 *'the bodies formed mounds and suffocated one another.'* Ruiz de Arce, quoted by John Hemming, 43.

160 *'the Indians surrounded them [the conquistadors] in such a manner.'* Pedro Pizarro, I, 237f.

164 *An early traveller in the nineteenth century.* The Comte de Sartiges in 1834, describing a funeral in Lares, op. cit., 95.

164 *'the evil genius' of the Conquest.* Prescott, 461.

166 *'he felt compelled to give satisfaction to the Antis.'* Titu Cusi, *La Relación*, 93.

172 *'he pushed on down the Urubamba asking for ruins.'* Bingham, *Lost City*, Chapter V.

173 *'an obscure fastness in the depths of the Andes.'* Prescott, 463.

180 *It must have seemed extraordinarily providential.* See Schjellerup, 73.

180 *'Because the barbudos, the bearded ones.'* Schjellerup, 78.

183 *It is probable that much of it had been already built by Pachacuti.* See Bernabé Cobo and also Rowe (1987): Pachacuti used it as a base to launch attacks on the Chanca; Titu Cusi reported that on Manco's arrival in Vitcos 'he had a house built for himself, as the ones already there were those of my ancestors Pachacuti, Topa Inca and Huayna Capac'. Titu Cusi, 100.

184 *Manco managed to escape and was reported to have shouted defiance.* Titu Cusi records him as shouting 'I am Manco Inca! I am Manco Inca!' at the pursuing Spanish, like a playground taunt. In their frustration at losing him, the Spanish took savage reprisals against those of Manco's family they were able to capture. Titu Cusi, *La Relación*, 111f.

184 *'Manco did not trust the promises of the white man.'* Prescott, 546.

185 *'a mass of rough potsherds, a few Inca whirl-bobs.'* Hiram Bingham, *Lost City*, Chapter V.

186 *'Here before us was a great white rock.'* Ibid. Bingham is quoting the eyewitness account of Captain Balthasar de Ocampo in the seventeenth century, one of the few Spanish to penetrate into the Inca heartland after the fall of Vilcabamba.

187 *the ornamental niches they probably once had.* Some of the foundation work was impressive, with classic stone-working, but there was also evidence of later low-quality *pirca* in-fill, possibly by the Incas in their period of exile.

187 *Although Titu Cusi's captains wanted to kill the Christians.* One of the friars, Diego Ortiz, was martyred after Titu's death in the following year, an incident that precipitated the very final invasion of the Vilcabamba by the Spanish. Cf. Hemming, 402f.

192 *'the mummy's attendants drinking on behalf of the corpse.'* Bernabé Cobo, *Inca Religion and Customs*, 40.

192 *'so many nobles were involved in serving these dead bodies.'* Ibid., 41, cf. also Pedro Pizarro, I, 205.

193 *he had been forced, to his fury, to build a new palace on the hill above.* Pedro Pizarro, I, 75.

193 *how savage the civil war between the brothers had sunk.* Rostworowski, 32, 125. The mummy was burnt after Huascar's main army had been defeated and Atahualpa had taken Cuzco.

193 *they seem to have passed back into native hands.* For discussion of what happened to the mummies of past Incas, see Edmundo Guillén Guillén, *El Enigma de los Momias Incas* (1983).

193 *'the beastly act of venerating the bodies of the dead.'* Bernabé Cobo, *Inca Religion and Customs*, 39.

196 *It was ironic that Sendero should have grown*

out of *Ayacucho*. The city was also the
scene of a decisive battle in 1824 in the
Wars of Independence.

197 *there were a few intrepid archaeologists who
were still able to get permission to go there.*
Like the American Vincent Lee.

202 *Cuzco really meant 'placenta of the world'.*
See article by Claudette Kemper
Columbus in *SAEC Journal*, Autumn
1999.

203 *Perci Paz, the archaeologist who had been
working at Choquequirao.* Perci Paz
worked at the site from 1993 to 1996;
other groups from COPESCO have
since done further excavation there.

206 *a theory that the young Tupac Amaru, the
last emperor of all, might even have been
brought up there.* Originally mentioned by
Angrand in the nineteenth century. See
Desjardins. More recently repeated by
Gary Ziegler in his article on
Choquequirao.

207 *After twenty years of puzzling over the
mystery of Choquequirao.* I learnt some
interesting and possibly related
evidence for this when I met Elva
Torres, the archaeologist in charge of
some limited excavation at Machu
Picchu from 1994 onwards. She was
unaware of Perci Paz's work at
Choquequirao, but she did tell me that
her recent excavations showed there
may well have been a fire at Machu
Picchu as well (again from the traces
of carbon deposits) and that it also may
have been abandoned while building
work was still proceeding.

209 *'the terrain is so rugged and the canyons are
so infested.'* Peter Frost, *Exploring Cusco*,
4th edition 1989, 188 (a new edition has
since been published).

210 *the lower section [of the Machu Picchu
railway] would never now be re-built.* At the
time of writing there are still no plans
to do so.

210 *I later heard a graphic account from a
schoolteacher.* Personal communication
via Gary Ziegler.

210 *a fact which had deeply impressed the Spanish
chronicler Cieza de León.* Cieza de León,
60.

212 *the first known mapped reference to either.*
On Göhring's map, Mts Machu Picchu

and Huayna Picchu are reversed.

213 *possibly a reference to the stone now known
as the Intihuatana.* There is another *huaca*
in the valley below as well, slightly
downriver, also known as the
Intihuatana. Cf. Hemming, *Monuments*,
176.

214 *'large iron wheels', which he presumed to be
'parts of a machine'.* Bingham, *Lost City*,
Chapter V.

215 *re-irrigating some 160 hectares (around 400
acres).* Kendall, *Restauración*, 4.

217 *Yet in a conversation I had with Elva Torres
Pino.* Elva Torres also told me that the
first limited analysis of pollen and seeds
on some of the terraces indicated the
presence of types of zucchini and other
'luxury' cucurbital plants – additional
support for the idea that the terraces at
Machu Picchu were designed for
courtly pleasure rather than subsistence
agriculture.

219 *A recent literary periodical.* Margenes
(Lima).

222 *the Shippee-Johnson aerial expedition of
1931.* See *SAEC Journal*, Summer 1998,
Daniel Buck, 36.

222 *wrote Baedeland later.* National Geographic,
August 1964, 278.

223 *Koepcke's seventeen-year-old daughter
Juliana was the only passenger to emerge.*
After the Electra turboprop she was
flying in crashed, with 60–70 dead, it
took Juliana several nightmarish weeks
to travel out of the jungle and reach
help. Werner Herzog made the
documentary *Wings of Hope* (1999) about
her experiences, his first return to the
Peruvian jungle after making *Aguirre:
The Wrath of God*.

226 *He found nothing.* Yoshiharu Sekino
went on later to explore many other
parts of Peru.

229 *his [John Hemming's] achievement in
resurrecting the last days of the Vilceabamba
empire.* Sir Clements Markham had
already begun this process in his 1910
book, *The Incas of Peru*.

229 *'a native enclave related to Spanish Peru.'*
Hemming, *Conquest*, 324.

230 *'un singulier monument': a pyramid of the
skulls of horses.'* Wiener, 346.

232 *he was found only after a frantic search*

party was sent by one of his generals. Cf.
Rostworowski, 80 for a description of
Topa Inca's defeat when fighting in the
Antisuyo.

232 *John Hemming told an amusing story.*
Hemming, *Conquest*, 315.

240 *von Hagen had even claimed.* Von Hagen,
Realm, 103.

240 *White noted sharply in his subsequent report.*
See Bibliography, Stuart White.

241 *'There were in front of him [the Inca].'*
Relación Francesa, quoted by Hyslop,
34.

243 *he was allowed to live on the old royal
estates of his grandfather Huayna Capac.*
Niles, 142f., for discussion of royal
estates and *moyas*.

243 *Chilche was arrested on suspicion of
poisoning.* The case was never proved
and he was released after just a year.
Cf. Villanueva Urteaga, 5f., Niles, 131;
also Hemming, *Conquest*, footnote 290.

244 *The baths here had a beautifully channelled
water system.* As mapped by Vincent
Lee. See *Chanasuyu*.

247 *to hang sacred weavings ... Some
commentators had speculated.* See
Hemming in *Monuments*, Machu Picchu
chapter.

247 *faces through a sheet.* Of all the
commentators, Hiram Bingham is one
of the most interesting in his original
speculation about the White Rock, put
at length in *A search for the lost Inca capital*,
Harpers magazine 1912, in which he
suggests that the projections were
essentially *intihuatanas* and that there
are many on the north side of the rock
so as always to get the sun.

248 *It is only recently scholars have shown that
the quipu.* See Marcia and Robert
Ascher, *Code of the Quipu*.

251 *'many people seem to think it is one of the
duties of an explorer.'* Hiram Bingham,
National Geographic, May 1916, 431.

253 *a document which was only recently
discovered.* See Lorenzo Huertas Vallejos
in the Bibliography.

253 *he gives some of them different names.*
Choquequirao he does call by its
current name, which he translates as
'gold cradle'.

254 *romantic nineteenth-century travellers to the*

area, like Angrand, had also liked to picture.
Desjardins, 145.

258 *There was a reason for these ocean voyages.*
For an account of the more recent and
equally disastrous shipwreck of *Feathered
Serpent III*, see 'Crazy for Adventure',
Brad Wetzler, *NY Times*, 6 June 1999.

259 *'the beginning of my re-birth.'* This and
some other later biographical details
are from Savoy's interview with Alvaro
Rocha in Peru, *El Dorado*, 1995.

260 *Savoy postulated: 'Was his [Manco's] cry.'*
Savoy, *Antisuyo*, 60.

261 *the archaeological department of Colorado
University had sent a team.* The
archaeologist Dr Thomas Lennon went
with a plastic surgeon from Boulder,
Colorado, called Alan Stormo, who had
an interest in the subject, and two of
his friends.

262 *there was much embarrassment all round.*
An excellent and full account of this
story was given by Doug Vaughan in
the *SAEC Journal* at the time.

262 *'the Inca took many of their [the
Chachapoyans'] women.'* Cieza de León,
98.

262 *'Only the superficial-minded speculate.'*
Explorers' Journal, Dec. 1978, 82.

263 *'belle d'une beauté superflu.'* Wiener,
347.

264 *'a knife edge which two men could not walk.'*
Martín de Murúa, 256.

265 *'any little natural breathing space.'*
Bingham, *Lost City*, Chapter V.

265 *'from my days as a Marine Officer.'* Lee,
Sixpac Manco, 40.

267 *Savoy's mules had gone up to their bellies.*
Savoy, *Antisuyo*, 106.

268 *Martín de Murúa tells the story.* Martín
de Murúa, 258.

270 *The Machiguenga, in their intensely practical
way.* Cf. Savoy, *Explorers' Journal*, Dec.
1978.

271 *Bingham liked to translate Espíritu Pampa
literally.* Bingham, *Lost City*, Chapter VI.

272 *the often self-serving military reports by the
conquistador leaders.* See Loyola's account
and Arbieto's letters.

273 *Martín de Murúa's censorious comment.*
Martín de Murúa, 261.

274 *'On that day,' wrote Martín de Murúa.*
Martín de Murúa, 271.

274 *the captured mummy of Manco Inca was also brought back to Cuzco.* Shortly after Tupac's execution in 1572, his native persecutors, the Cañari and the Chachapoyans, were both granted exemption from paying tribute as reward for their services to the Spanish crown in finally defeating the Incas. Their only duty was to guard the same fort where Manco's mummy had been burnt. Cf. Niles, 303.

275 *'that story has been re-told in all the weavings since.'* In the telling of this story, Julia interestingly conflates two events, the death of the first Tupac Amaru in 1572 and the death of Tupac Amaru II two centuries later. Tupac Amaru was beheaded, while Tupac Amaru II was hung, drawn and quartered.

275 *why cloth was so obsessively valued by the*

Incas. See John V. Murra, *Cloth and its Functions in the Inca State.*

279 *All dates of pre-Conquest events … are estimates.* As recently as the Second World War, scholars such as Philip Ainsworth Means were estimating the chronology by simply taking an average of the wildly divergent dates given by different chroniclers. Rowe established a more stable framework in 1944. For a thorough discussion of the vexed issue of dates, see Niles, 114f.

287 *Borla* description, P. Pizarro, I, 222.

288 *'no one was worthy of them save themselves.'* P. Pizarro, I, 194.

293 *a marketing invention of 1950, designed to promote a driving rally.* Cf. Demetrio Roca Wallparimachi, *Mito y Maiz en Yucay-Urubamba*, Revista del Instituto Americana de Arte, 14, 1994, footnote 2.

If not given above, full details of works referred to are in the Bibliography. References to John Hemming's *The Conquest of the Incas* are from the revised paperback edition of 1993 and references to Prescott's *History of the Conquest of Peru* are from the Random House edition of 1998.

INDEX